REFLECTIONS ON JUDGING

REFLECTIONS ON JUDGING

❧❧

RICHARD A. POSNER

HARVARD UNIVERSITY PRESS

Cambridge, Massachusetts
London, England
2013

Library of Congress Cataloging-in-Publication Data

Posner, Richard A.

Reflections on judging / Richard A. Posner.

pages cm

Includes bibliographical references and index.

ISBN 978-0-674-72508-9 (alk. paper)

1. Judicial process—United States.

2. Appellate procedure—United States.   I. Title.

KF9050.P55 2013

347.73'24092—dc23

2013007344

For Charlene

Contents

CONTENTS

CONTENTS

REFLECTIONS ON JUDGING

INTRODUCTION

A Judge on the Challenges to Judges

Everything should be made as simple as possible, but not simpler.

Attributed to Albert Einstein

My subject is the challenges that the federal courts face today, with particular emphasis on rising complexity. My approach is personal, in the sense of drawing heavily on my own experience as a judge. It is also realistic, in the sense of rejecting formalist approaches to law. Those are approaches premised on a belief that all legal issues can be resolved by logic, text, or precedent, without a judge's personality, values, ideological leanings, background and culture, or real-world experience playing any role. The realist tradition in judging is the tradition shaped by such outstanding judges as John Marshall, Oliver Wendell Holmes, Louis Brandeis, Benjamin Cardozo, Robert Jackson, Learned Hand, Roger Traynor, and Henry Friendly. It is distinct from, though it overlaps, the "legal realist" movement of the 1920s and 1930s, which petered out, though not without leaving a mark.[1] I need to say more about formalism and realism, which provide a contrast fundamental to this book, and will do so shortly.

I was sworn in as a judge of the United States Court of Appeals for the Seventh Circuit (the federal judicial circuit embracing Illinois, Indiana, and Wisconsin) on December 4, 1981, and so I have been a federal court of appeals judge for more than thirty-one years. I have heard oral argument in more than six thousand cases; I have read (not every word of) many more than fifteen thousand briefs[2] (many cases are not orally argued but all are briefed); I have written more than 2,800 published judicial opinions. I have sat with the twenty-two different judges whose service on the court has overlapped with mine (a number of them are now deceased), not to mention visiting judges. I have conducted trials, and sometimes pretrial proceedings and settlement negotiations, in a number of cases, mainly civil jury cases, as a volunteer in the district courts of my circuit, mainly the Eastern Division of the Northern District of Illinois (the division that includes Chicago). I have also participated in three-judge district court decisions, and briefly sat in another court of appeals (the U.S. Court of Appeals for the Federal Circuit) as a visiting judge. I was chief judge of my court for seven years (1993–2000)[3] and so during that time I was an *ex officio* member of the Judicial Conference of the United States. (If the federal judiciary were a republic, the Judicial Conference would be its legislative branch.) I may be a good judge, a bad judge, or an indifferent judge, but I am undeniably an experienced judge, though my judicial experience is limited to the federal judiciary.[4]

1. A useful compendium is *American Legal Realism* (William W. Fisher III, Morton J. Horwitz, and Thomas A. Reed eds. 1993). An authoritative modern assessment is Brian Leiter, "Rethinking Legal Realism: Toward a Naturalized Jurisprudence," 76 *Texas Law Review* 267 (1997).

2. The figure fifteen thousand is based on a guess that in about five-sixths of the six thousand orally argued cases (that is, in five thousand cases) the appellant filed a reply brief; hence five thousand × three total briefs in argued cases.

3. The chief judgeship (a seven-year, nonrenewable term) devolves automatically on whichever judge of the court has the most seniority, but has not reached the age of sixty-five, when the position becomes vacant.

4. I had, of course, a legal career before becoming a judge. I was a Supreme Court law clerk the year after graduating from law school, then spent five years as a

Naturally over this long span of time and wide span of experience I have formed judgments about a variety of issues that face federal judges and the lawyers who appear before them. The issues include how appellate judges should go about deciding cases, what their judicial opinions should be like (and hence how judges should manage their staff, consisting mainly of law clerks), how lawyers should brief and argue cases, how the trial process can be made more accurate, more expeditious, and cheaper, how federal judges should be selected and trained, and, of urgent concern today, how the federal judiciary can cope with the increasing complexity of federal cases, an issue entwined with the other issues that I've listed. We judges are failing to keep up with the dizzying advances in technology (broadly understood), and in other fields of knowledge (such as knowledge about foreign cultures), that are making federal cases ever more complex, and ever more challenging therefore to judges and lawyers alike. Yet rarely when judges voice their concerns is the challenge of complexity among them.[5]

Two Kinds of Complexity

I must explain what I mean by "complexity." (I give a fuller explanation in Chapter 3.) A question can be difficult without being complex—for example it can be an ethical or other values question, or simply a question to which no answer can be given, for want of data. A question is complex in the sense in which I shall be using the word when it is difficult by virtue of involving complicated interactions, or, in other words, involving a system rather than a monad. The system can be economic—a market, for example, which involves interactions between sellers and buyers and frequently tacit interactions among competing sellers. It can be political—the international balance of power, for example. It can be ecological—a population of ani-

---

federal government lawyer, then thirteen years as a law professor. I have continued to teach, and do academic writing part time, since becoming a judge.

    5. See, for example, Randall T. Shepard, "Elements of Modern Court Reform," 45 *Indiana Law Review* 897 (2012). Some judges would be embarrassed to acknowledge being flummoxed by complexity.

mals that compete to maximize (unconsciously of course) their genetic fitness. It can be technological—a cell phone or other complex machine. Indeed, it can be almost anything—a business firm, a college, the cells of a living body, the combination of subatomic particles that form an atom, the solar system.

All these are examples of complexity that are external to the legal system, that are part of the environment that generates cases. But like other professions, the judicial profession generates its own complexity, which I call internal, and which makes it more rather than less difficult for judges to cope with external complexity. "Professionals are rated by the presumed complexity of what they know and do. So to retain or raise an occupation's status, tasks are made more mysterious, usually by taking what's really simple and adding obfuscating layers."[6] Abetted by lawyers, law professors, law clerks, and legislators, judges "complexify" the legal process needlessly—and do so in part to avoid the struggle to understand the complex real-world environment that generates much of the business of a modern court. The formalist wants to use a complex style of legal analysis (involving, for example, as we'll see in Chapter 7, numerous "canons of construction"—principles of statutory interpretation) to resolve cases without having to understand factual complexities. The realist, in contrast, wants to impose a simple style of legal analysis on a sure understanding of the scientific or commercial complexities, factual rather than legal, out of which cases arise.[7] The realist thinks that law is or can be made simple but that the subject matter of many legal cases is irreducibly complex.

The character of legal formalism can be captured in such slogans as "the law made me do it" or "the law is its own thing." The law as seen from the formalist perspective is a compendium of texts, like the Bible, and the task of the judge or other legal analyst is to discern and apply the internal

6. Andrew Hacker, "How He Got It Right," *New York Review of Books*, Jan. 10, 2013, pp. 16, 18.

7. I use "simple" in the apolitical sense of analytically simple, which should be distinguished from wanting to shrink government, the sense in which "simple rules" is used in Richard A. Epstein, *Simple Rules for a Complex World* (1995). The word "complex" in the title of Epstein's book means detailed or complicated, rather than complex in the sense I emphasize, which stresses the interactive character of systems.

logic of the compendium. He is an interpreter, indifferent or nearly so to the consequences of his interpretations in the real world. He is not responsible for those consequences; if they are untoward, the responsibility for altering them through a change in law falls to the "political branches" (as judges like to call the legislative and executive branches of government, thus distancing themselves from the taint of politics). On this view, judges who take into account the consequences of alternative interpretations are stepping outside law. Only the orthodox materials of legal analysis—statutes, constitutions, regulations, precedents, other legal documents—are law; all the rest is policy, or politics (or economics!). As one notable formalist has put it, impressively but opaquely, "formalism treats the law's concepts as pathways into an internal intelligibility."[8]

Legal realism is harder to describe than legal formalism, because it is everything in legal thought and practice that is not formalism, and it is also, as I noted at the beginning of this Introduction, the name of a specific movement in American legal thinking that flourished in the 1920s and 1930s. Legal realism in a sense distinct from the movement called legal realism is, to begin with, deeply skeptical of formalism, regarding it as more rhetoric than analysis—a rhetoric that conceals the actual springs of decision. The realist places emphasis on the consequences of judicial rulings, and in that regard is pragmatic but only if the realist considers systemic as well as case-specific consequences and thus avoids shortsighted justice —justice responsive only to the "equities" of the particular case—and is analytical and empirical rather than merely intuitive and political. Systemic consequences include the effect of a doctrine or decision on the predictability of law, on caseloads, on administrability, on the work of other branches of government (such as the legislative branch, which would be thrown into disarray if judges paid no heed to statutory language), and on reasonable expectations both private and public.

I am a pragmatic judge[9] and years before I started worrying about the growing complexity (largely technological) of the cases that the federal

8. Ernest J. Weinrib, *The Idea of Private Law* 146 (1995).

9. See Robert F. Blomquist, "Judge Posner's Pragmatism in Action 1981–2011" (Valparaiso University Legal Studies Research Paper No. 12-10), http://papers.ssrn.com/sol3/papers.cfm?abstract_id=2151503 (visited Feb. 13, 2013).

courts were being asked to decide I noted the affinity between legal pragmatism and science, saying that "the brand of pragmatism that I like emphasizes the scientific virtues (open-minded, no-nonsense inquiry)."[10] But I don't need to limit legal realism to pragmatism to make the points I want to make in this book. The core of a defensible legal realism is the idea that in many cases, and those the most important, the judge will have to settle for a reasonable, a sensible, result, rather than being able to come up with a result that is demonstrably, irrefutably, "logically" correct. Law is not logic but experience, as Holmes famously put it. And experience is the domain of fact, and so the realist has a much greater interest in fact than the formalist, and in "fact" in a richer sense than what a judge can glean from a trial transcript. And today that richer sense encompasses the findings of science, along with statistical and other systematic data. But science and data will no more resolve every case than orthodox legal texts will. What is reasonable or sensible will often depend on moral feelings, common sense, sympathies, and other ingredients of thought and feeling that can't readily be translated into a weighing of measurable consequences.

But openness to facts not limited to those found in judicial records is what I want to stress. I will illustrate with a discussion of an article by the distinguished legal realist Grant Gilmore (with whom I overlapped on the faculty of the University of Chicago Law School in my early years there). His subject was the famous (or notorious) seventeenth-century English case of *Chandelor v. Lopus*,[11] in which the plaintiff had paid the defendant £100 for what the defendant "affirmed" but did not "warrant" was a bezoar (or "bezar") stone. In fact it wasn't a bezoar stone, but the court held that the plaintiff could not obtain relief on the basis of a mere affirmation. The court's holding was understood to make implied warranties unenforceable. Although the plaintiff's lawyer conceded that the defendant may not have known whether it was or wasn't a bezoar stone, the court said that the plaintiff would lose even if the defendant knew it wasn't; and from this dictum the doctrine of *caveat emptor* derives. Both the nonenforceability of implied warranties and the doctrine of *caveat emptor* were eventually discredited.

10. Richard A. Posner, *The Problems of Jurisprudence* 28 (1990).
11. 3 Cr. Jaq. 4, 79 Eng. Rep. 3 (Exch. 1603).

About this much-criticized case Gilmore remarked that "the report of the case does not bother to explain what a bezoar was—presumably everybody knew what a bezoar was, just as we all know what a diamond is. It occurred to me one day, in thinking about the case, that I for one had no idea what a bezoar might be."[12] So he did some research and quickly discovered that a bezoar stone was a mass in the stomach of an animal, like a goat, that doesn't pass into the intestine—and that it was believed to be of great medicinal value (£100 was a large sum of money in the seventeenth century), especially as an antidote to any poison. This discovery led Gilmore to rethink the received wisdom about the case: "It was generally known that there were true, or magic, bezoars. It must also have been a matter of common knowledge that it was extremely difficult, if not impossible, to tell a true bezoar from a false one. And no doubt the attitude of the user counted for something: if I believed in my bezoar it might indeed preserve me from the plague while the same stone in the hands of a skeptical rationalist would be worthless. Under such circumstances a court might hesitate to impose liability on a seller who had merely said that, to the best of his knowledge, he believed (or affirmed) the stone to be a bezoar, but did not warrant it. It may be that the seventeenth-century concept of liability was not as narrow as we have supposed it to be."[13] And now the punch line: "This digression, at all events, goes to the point that law cases—and rules of law—are really not abstract propositions, although we like to phrase them, and talk about them, as if they were. The cases and the rules—and indeed the codifying statutes—are merely particular responses to particular states of fact (assumed to be true whether or not they are). The law is, and I dare say always will be, *ad hoc* and *ad hominem* to a fault."[14] Yes, and that is an essential insight of legal realism. As a positive theory, it teaches that legal decisions and doctrine are fact-driven, not theory-driven. As a normative theory, it teaches that that's how law should work.

The age-old conflict between realism and formalism has a new sharp-

12. Grant Gilmore, "Products Liability: A Commentary," 38 *University of Chicago Law Review* 103, 107 (1970).

13. Id. at 108.

14. Id.

ness. Formalism has, surprisingly and perversely, a renewed appeal to judges and lawyers in our technological era, even though it retards the profession's ability to solve the novel legal problems that arise in such an era. Legal realists are bound to find technology more congenial than legal formalists do—especially since technology is gaining on law. This is shown in the following graph, which uses Google's Ngram Viewer program. The program counts the relative number of appearances of a word or phrase in the literally millions of books that Google has scanned to create its database. We see that in 1920 "law" was a word much more likely to be encountered than "science," "technology," or "complexity"—or for that matter all three combined—whereas by 2008 (when the database ends), the sum of the relative frequencies of the three words exceeded that of "law." The relative frequency of "science" has not increased, but then science was already an important part of the social environment in 1920. The relative frequency of "complexity" and especially of "technology" *has* increased—manyfold in the case of "technology."

If complexity grows slowly in the next thirty years, future judges, who are lawyers in their twenties today and on average much more comfortable with modern technology than the current crop of federal judges (the average age of district judges is sixty, of court of appeals judges sixty-two, and of Supreme Court Justices sixty-six), will be better equipped to handle technologically complex cases. But if as seems much more likely technology continues its rapid advances, future judges will be as strongly challenged by technology as current judges are, or even more so, unless they make peace with technology or until technology, which has done so much for legal research already, becomes a component of legal analysis and not just legal research, perhaps by merging computer software into the human brain.

But I need to remind the reader that even if "technology" is broadly defined, as it should be, to take in for example "financial engineering," it is not the only source of the complexity of modern society. Globalization, changing social mores, and innovations in financing political campaigns are other examples, along with law itself, including legal institutions such as the federal judiciary, which are growing more complex from within. But

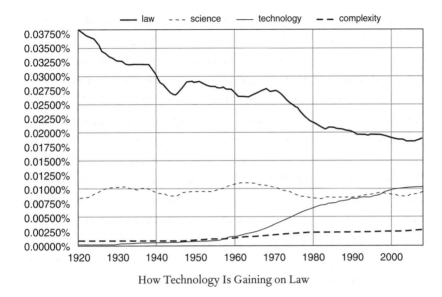

How Technology Is Gaining on Law

the biggest challenge is that of the growing complexity of many of the activities that give rise to litigation.

I am not myself a techie. I was an English major in college, and my only postgraduate education was law school. I have used differential calculus and multiple regression analysis in some of my academic work, but at very modest levels of sophistication. In recent years, however, I have become increasingly worried about the gap between law on the one hand and math, science, and technology on the other hand. In 2004 I published a book on catastrophic risks, and in it I noted the resistance of the legal culture to science and technology.[15] In recent years I have been conducting patent trials as a volunteer in district court, and increasingly I find myself writing judicial opinions in cases that involve technological issues. Recently I stumbled on an interview that I had given almost twenty years ago, in which I find in embryonic form a number of points that I elaborate in this book.[16] But my concern with complexity is new.

15. Richard A. Posner, *Catastrophe: Risk and Response* 200–213 (2004).

16. Jeffrey Cole, "Economics of Law: An Interview with Judge Posner," *Litigation,* Fall 1995, p. 23. The title is misleading; economics is touched on but is not a dominant theme of the interview.

Extrajudicial Writing by Judges

This book belongs to the genre of extrajudicial writing by judges. American judges have done a lot of such writing,[17] in part because of the lateral-entry character of an American judicial career; the judicial opinion is not the only vehicle in which judges who had another legal career before they became judges know how to express their thoughts.

Much extracurricular judicial writing, however, is propagandistic: judges assuring the small public that takes an interest in such matters that they are hardworking, conscientious, and, above all, apolitical—they apply law, they don't ever make it. A more rewarding segment of the genre consists of judges' candid reflections on their judicial philosophy. The outstanding examples are still Cardozo's *Nature of the Judicial Process*[18] and Holmes's essays, notably but not only "The Path of the Law,"[19] and his letters. But some contemporary judges, such as Michael Boudin, Frank Easterbrook, and J. Harvie Wilkinson III have also written illuminatingly about their judicial philosophy.[20] Some current Supreme Court Justices have contributed as well.[21] And a few judges have written nuts-and-bolts

17. For serviceable anthologies, see *Judges on Judging: Views from the Bench* (David M. O'Brien ed., 3d ed. 2009); *Views from the Bench: The Judiciary and Constitutional Politics* (Mark W. Cannon and David M. O'Brien eds. 1985).

18. Benjamin N. Cardozo, *The Nature of the Judicial Process* (1921).

19. O. W. Holmes, "The Path of the Law," 10 *Harvard Law Review* 457 (1897).

20. See, for example, Michael Boudin, "Friendly, J., Dissenting," 61 *Duke Law Journal* 881 (2012); Boudin, "Judge Henry Friendly and the Craft of Judging," 159 *University of Pennsylvania Law Review* 1 (2010); Frank H. Easterbrook, "Textualism and the Dead Hand," 66 *George Washington Law Review* 1119 (1998); J. Harvie Wilkinson III, "Of Guns, Abortions, and the Unraveling Rule of Law," 95 *Virginia Law Review* 253 (2009). I am one of the judges who have written about the judicial process. See, for example, Lee Epstein, William M. Landes, and Richard A. Posner, *The Behavior of Federal Judges: A Theoretical and Empirical Analysis of Rational Choice* (2013), and Richard A. Posner, *How Judges Think* (2008).

21. See, for example, Antonin Scalia, *A Matter of Interpretation: Federal Courts and the Law* (1997); Scalia, "The Rule of Law as a Law of Rules," 56 *University of Chicago Law Review* 1175 (1989); Stephen Breyer, *Active Liberty: Interpreting Our Demo-*

descriptions of their approaches to judging, notable examples being *Ways of a Judge*[22] by Frank Coffin, who was a member of the U.S. Court of Appeals for the First Circuit, and a very recent memoir by a federal district judge, Frederic Block.[23] These works are useful too.

This book mixes the academic with the personal; it is a study of the judicial process mixed with personal recollections, references to a number of my own judicial opinions, and recommendations to judges and judicial administrators. Rarely do the extracurricular writings of judges offer pointers to other judges, and I hope this aspect of the book doesn't strike my judge readers as an impertinence. I am aware that judicial methods that may work in some courts may not work in others, depending on workload, traditions, the personalities of judges, and, related to the last point, the degree to which judges (in an appellate court, where decision is by committee) tolerate differences in methodology and judicial philosophy. I am not talking about substantive disagreement but about the willingness of a judge to join an opinion that, were he the assigned authoring judge, would read very differently. In some courts a culture of "live and let live" prevails, and judges join each others' opinions when they agree with the result and the basic analysis and find nothing that augurs trouble in future cases, even though they may not like the way in which the author has articulated his analysis. In other courts a majority opinion is regarded as a genuine joint product rather than an individual's product to which his colleagues broadly assent, and in such courts the author's judicial colleagues may undertake to edit his draft.

---

cratic Constitution (2005); Breyer, "On the Uses of Legislative History in Interpreting Statutes," 65 *Southern California Law Review* 845 (1992).

22. Frank M. Coffin, *The Ways of a Judge: Reflections from the Federal Appellate Bench* (1980). Among article–length treatments, Robert A. Leflar, "Honest Judicial Opinions," 74 *Northwestern University Law Review* 721 (1979), is outstanding. Also very good is Harold R. Medina, "Some Reflections on the Judicial Function at the Appellate Level," 1961 *Washington University Law Review* 148 (1961).

23. *Disrobed: An Inside Look at the Life and Work of a Federal Trial Judge*, pts. 2–3 (2012).

The academic as distinct from judicial extracurricular literature on the judicial process is vast,[24] but a judge's reflections on the process can, if the judge is both candid and self-aware, valuably supplement the academic literature. Judges can be hard to study from the outside. They tend to be secretive, and most limit their law clerks' access to the judge's thinking—and the law clerks tend to be secretive too and often protective of their judge long after the clerkship has ended. Also. people who are not judges have difficulty imagining what it is like to be a judge; in Chapter 8 I'll note that failure of imagination in appellate advocates. For all these reasons much that is written about the judicial process from the outside is unrealistic, with the major exception of empirical studies that use the methods of the social sciences.

Among other sources of information about the judicial process, judicial biographies deserve emphasis. An important recent example is David Dorsen's biography of Judge Henry Friendly,[25] which draws on an unparalleled wealth of material concerning Friendly's career. The biographer has the advantage over the judge of not being the judge. But the judge has the advantage over the biographer of being the judge. Their roles as expositors of the judge's approach are complementary. There is also good journalistic writing on the judicial process, especially as that process operates in the Supreme Court.[26]

Plan of the Book

The first chapter of this book describes how I became a judge, and the second how the job of a federal appellate judge, and how the federal judiciary more broadly, has changed since my first encounter with the judiciary, as a law clerk for a Supreme Court Justice in the Court's 1962 term. I point out

24. For an exhaustive listing, see Epstein et al., *The Behavior of Federal Judges* 89–99.

25. David M. Dorsen, *Henry Friendly: Greatest Judge of His Era* (2012).

26. A recent example is Jeffrey Toobin, *The Oath: The Obama White House and the Supreme Court* (2012). Besides Toobin, legal journalists of note include Emily Bazelon, Linda Greenhouse, Adam Liptak, Dahlia Lithwick, and Stuart Taylor.

that while much of the change has been a response to increased caseload (though an increase for which the courts themselves are responsible to a significant extent), there has also been an internally generated change related to but not entirely the product of caseload—rather a change reflecting organizational or bureaucratic imperatives (see Chapters 2 and 3). Bureaucratization, or "managerialism," is a general feature of the modern American legal system, and it conduces to hypertrophy, or metastasis, colorfully illustrated by the mindless growth of the *Bluebook* citation manual (see Chapter 3).

The year I became a judge, 1981, proved fortuitously to be a watershed year. It was the tail end of twenty years of torrid growth of federal court caseloads. That it was ending was not apparent; judicial reformers remained for a time preoccupied with how to manage the swollen caseload and curb further growth. The growth did slow, and the swollen caseload was somehow managed. But something else, what I am calling complexity, was beginning to grow rapidly. Its growth is continuing and in fact accelerating, but it has yet to be widely recognized as an important and threatening trend. Technological advances, along with a variety of social changes that also provide grist for the federal judicial mill, are making cases more difficult for judges to understand and by doing so are challenging our ability to cope effectively with modernity.

I begin my systematic discussion of that challenge in Chapter 3, but also discuss there the self-generated complexity, mentioned above, that I call internal, a phenomenon of the organizational incentives and constraints that condition the behavior of the personnel of an organization rather than a phenomenon of technology. Like other professionals, judges don't want to be transparent to the laity. They want their calling to be a mystery, and one way to make it so is to complexify what they do.

The remaining chapters deal with how appellate judges (Chapters 4 through 8), appellate lawyers (Chapter 8), trial judges (Chapter 9), and law schools and other nonjudicial institutions (Chapter 10) are coping with the conditions (not limited to complexity external or internal) of litigation in the modern federal judiciary. Some judges and lawyers are retreating to judicial philosophies that enable them to forgo acquiring a rich understanding of the activities out of which cases arise—philosophies such as legal formalism, judicial self-restraint, and (an aspect of formalism) theories of constitutional and statutory interpretation. The strategies that judges employ to avoid grappling with complexity actually, as we'll see, mainly just replace one type of complexity with another (though judicial self-restraint is an exception). They escape from complexity into complexity.

I place particular emphasis on legal formalism as a resurgent attitude that draws judges away from confronting the technological and other complexities of the environment that generates legal disputes. I urge throughout the book, but particularly in Chapters 4 and 7, a renewal of legal realism.[27]

Because of the emphasis that I place on the challenge of complexity, and the distinction I draw between internal and external complexity, the reader may find the following table a helpful overview. It lists sources of external complexity and the fields of law affected by them, the sources of internal complexity, and (overlapping those sources) the escape routes that judges follow in an effort to avoid rather than meet and overcome the challenge of complexity. I am sure the table is incomplete.

APPENDIX

EXTERNAL VERSUS INTERNAL COMPLEXITY IN FEDERAL ADJUDICATION

Sources of Complexity That Are External to the Judicial System:

Biochemistry
Bite-Mark Evidence
Catastrophic Risk
College and University Hiring and Promotion
Corporate Governance and Compensation

27. For additional discussion of the formalism-realism face-off, see Epstein et al., *The Behavior of Federal Judges*, ch. 1.

DNA Evidence

Economics

Electronic Surveillance

Energy

Engineering

Environmental Evidence

Estimation of Economic Damages

Eyewitness Testimony; Line Ups; Photo Arrays

Fertility and Pregnancy

Financial Engineering

Fingerprint Evidence

Firearms-Identification Evidence

Foreign Customs and Conditions

Genetics, including Genomics

Gun Violence

Human Resources

Immigration

Judicial Psychology

Jury Psychology

Lie Detectors

Marketing

Medical Evidence and Epidemiology

Mental Illness

Microscopic Hair Evidence

National Security

Neuroscience

Online Services

Penology

Pension Systems

Pharmaceutical Drugs

Physics

Pollution and Toxicology; Environmental Science

Psychology

Recidivism

Sociology

Software Engineering; Electrical Engineering More Broadly; Engineering More Broadly

Statistics, including Multiple Regression Analysis

Surveillance Technology

Survey Research

Telecommunications

Fields of Law Affected by External Complexity:

Antitrust

Asylum

Bankruptcy

Computer Crimes

Contracts

Copyrights

Corporations

Criminal Law

Education

Election Law

Environmental Protection

Evidence

Food and Drug Regulation

Foreign and International Law

Insanity Defense

Patents

Pension Benefits

Property

Search and Seizure

Second Amendment

Sentencing

Social Security Disability

Taxation

Telecommunications Regulation

Torts

Trademarks

Zoning

Sources of Complexity That Are Internal to the Federal Judicial System:

Delegation of Opinion Drafting to Law Clerks

Expansion in Size of Judiciary

Expansion of Judges' Staffs

Formalism, including Canons of Construction

Obsession with Citation Form

Verbose, Overly Complex, Vague, Poorly Written Judicial Opinions

Judicial Escape Routes from Having to Meet the Challenge of External Complexity:

Delegation of Decision Making to Trial-Court Judges, Jurors, and
    Administrative Agencies

Formalism

Jargon

Judicial Self-Restraint

Multifactor Tests

Theories of Constitutional and Statutory Interpretation

Umpireal (versus Managerial) Conception of Judging

THE ROAD TO 219 SOUTH
DEARBORN STREET

My chapter title is not as dramatic as *The Road to Wigan Pier* by George Orwell or *To the Finland Station* by Edmund Wilson; 219 South Dearborn Street in Chicago, the address of the federal courthouse that houses the United States Court of Appeals for the Seventh Circuit, simply turned out unexpectedly to be my career destination. The "road" I took offers some insight into the complexification of the federal judiciary, however, which is a major theme of the book.

Education and Early Career

I entered Yale College in 1959 at sixteen, having skipped my last year of high school.[1] I went to Yale for no better reason than that my father had

1. I would have been seventeen had I not entered first grade earlier than most kids, in part because I had started in nursery school (the well-known Walden School,

read in the *New York Times* that Harvard and Yale were admitting kids after three years of high school (the University of Chicago had long been admitting them after only two years of high school,[2] but, ironically in light of where I've ended up, nothing west of the Hudson River existed for me at the time). I applied to Harvard and Yale, was rejected by Harvard and accepted by Yale, so I went to Yale. I would have preferred (mistakenly, as I'm about to note) to go to Harvard, and if I had remained in high school for the fourth year and reapplied then I would have been admitted; but I wanted to get on with my career. I am surprised at how little haste the modern young feel in establishing themselves in their chosen career, or indeed in deciding on a career.

I majored in English at Yale—literature having long been my favorite subject, which I attribute in part to my mother, a high school English teacher, who started reading Homer and Shakespeare to me when I was three years old (maybe earlier). The New Criticism—which, downplaying biographical and historical approaches to literature, treated the literary work as an autonomous aesthetic object, accessible to understanding and appreciation without the reader's having to know much at all about the author or the author's times—was in its heyday when I was in college, and Yale was its center. Cleanth Brooks, a famous New Critic, was my senior thesis advisor. (My thesis was a book-length study of W. B. Yeats's late poetry.) I was and remain enthusiastic about the New Critical approach. I mention this because it has influenced my judicial approach; it has made me a better close reader than I otherwise would have been, able to interpret complicated texts. A related point is that the New Critical approach liberated me from excessive dependence on history as a guide to understanding a text.

I don't think the New Criticism had much purchase at Harvard, which along with the fact that Yale was more focused on undergraduate education makes me grateful for having been turned down by Harvard.

---

in Manhattan) at two years, eight months. I must take this opportunity to thank my parents (now long deceased), especially my mother, for having pushed me, from my earliest youth, to excel academically, much as Asian American parents push their kids.

2. Hugh Hawkins, "The Higher Learning at Chicago," 20 *Reviews in American History* 378 (1992).

I entered Harvard Law School directly after Yale. I had no burning interest in law. But my father was a lawyer (and businessman) and law was, as it still is to a considerable extent, a default career choice. And while I loved literature, I was not attracted to the idea of earning a living from writing about it and was not attracted to teaching. I had applied to Yale Law School as well and been accepted, but decided that Harvard would be the greater challenge; it didn't baby the students, as Yale Law School did and does. I think I made the right choice.

I loved my first year at the Harvard Law School, in all its brutishness. Harvard stacked its best teachers in the first year and they were superb, though cold, demanding, and at times nasty. At the end of the year I had the strange feeling that I was markedly more intelligent than I had been a year earlier. I had also developed a respect for law and lawyers (at least lawyers personified by the members of the Harvard Law School faculty), and specifically for the common law, which dominated the first-year curriculum. The second- and third-year curricula I found much less interesting. (Several of the courses were taught quite badly—that's when I discovered that the law school stacked its best teachers in the first-year courses.) I cut many classes the second year (so my grades fell, and as a consequence I was a more conscientious student in my third year), and spent most of my time during my last two years working as a member of the Harvard Law Review—a truly meritocratic institution, by the way. Membership was based entirely on grades (that is no longer the case), and although the president of the law review was elected by the members, there was no politicking (also no longer the case). There was a slight tendency to elect the best student provided he had taken his duties as a member of the review very seriously.

I assumed that I would practice law in New York (I had been born in New York, and grew up there and in Scarsdale), though I had not worked at a law firm in the summer after either my first or second year—summer law firm jobs were unusual in those days, and I did not apply for one. I had no interest in law teaching and no thought of becoming a judge, though I recall dimly having thought that being a federal district judge might be fun. I had no idea how one became a judge if one wanted to be one.

Paul Freund, a well-known Harvard Law School professor to whom Justice Brennan (himself a Harvard Law School alumnus) had delegated the selection of his two law clerks each year (such delegations were common in those days), asked me to clerk for Brennan, and I agreed. I have to say at the risk of blasphemy that I found the Supreme Court an unimpressive institution. I was stunned to discover that Supreme Court Justices didn't write all their own judicial opinions (Douglas did—and his were the weakest, though not because he was dumb—rather because he was bored); the Harvard law professors, although extremely critical of the liberal Justices, had not let on that law clerks played such a large role. In preparation for the Brennan clerkship I read a number of his opinions and was impressed by them; only later did I learn that the best of them had been written by a former clerk of his, a brilliant Harvard Law School graduate named Dennis Lyons.

Brennan had been a very successful lawyer and later a distinguished member of the Supreme Court of New Jersey. I'm sure he could have written good judicial opinions, and indeed I'm told that there were years during his long service on the U.S. Supreme Court when he had a law clerk whose opinion drafts didn't satisfy him, and so he wrote those opinions himself and they were good. I think most federal appellate judges could write at least okay opinions. But it's also true that law clerks, being selected by judges rather than, as the judges are, by politicians, are often abler legal analysts and writers than their judge. Most judges don't much like to write and prefer therefore to review and edit law clerks' opinion drafts. The editing is sometimes very light.

The Supreme Court's work tempo my year (the 1962 term) was slow; I worked less hard that year than any year since. I read a great deal of literature in the evenings and on weekends, particularly classic English and American novels, from Dickens to Faulkner, because I had concentrated on poetry and drama at Yale, the preferred subjects of the New Critics. I discovered that I didn't (yet) really have much interest in law, and I even toyed with the idea (though I quickly abandoned it) of quitting law and getting a graduate degree in English. But quite by chance, shortly before the clerkship ended and I was to start as an associate at a large New York law firm

(Paul Weiss), I was offered a job as an assistant to an outstandingly able Federal Trade Commissioner named Philip Elman (a former law clerk of Frankfurter's and a longtime member of the Solicitor General's staff). I worked for him for two years and learned a great deal; he was a terrific lawyer.

I had developed an interest in antitrust law working on a major bank merger case as a Brennan clerk,[3] and my interest deepened at the FTC, which has an antitrust as well as a consumer-protection jurisdiction—and I found consumer protection interesting too. Under Elman's guidance and with considerable staff assistance I wrote the commission's statement promulgating and justifying a rule requiring health warnings in cigarette labeling and advertising.[4] Although quickly preempted by Congress, the rule was the beginning of the eventually very successful regulatory efforts to curb smoking.

In my time at the commission I became friendly with its chief economist, Willard Mueller, and developed a nascent interest in economics. Oddly, the seed of this interest had been planted in my first month or so on the Harvard Law Review, when I was quite by chance assigned to cite check a chunk of an antitrust article by Derek Bok (then a law professor at Harvard, later dean of the law school, and after that president of Harvard)—the chunk in which he discussed the economic theory of oligopoly. I had never heard of the theory of oligopoly, but I found it intriguing and drew on it in the bank-merger opinion that I wrote for Justice Brennan.

From Elman I went to the Solicitor General's office,[5] where I stayed for

3. *United States v. Philadelphia National Bank*, 374 U.S. 321 (1963).

4. Trade Regulation Rule on Cigarette Labeling and Advertising, 29 Fed. Reg. 8324 (FTC July 2, 1964).

5. At Elman's suggestion and largely arranged by him. A curious feature of my career, rare today because job markets are far more competitive, is that, except when applying for law firm jobs when I was a law student and Supreme Court law clerk (jobs I never took), I've never really sought a job. I did not campaign to be president of the Harvard Law Review—there was, as I said, no campaigning for the job in those days. I did not apply for a Supreme Court clerkship. I did not apply to work for Elman but was asked to interview with him by one of his assistants, a former president of the Harvard Law Review whom I knew. I formally applied to the Solicitor General's of-

a little more than two years, writing many briefs and arguing six cases in the Supreme Court. My particular focus was antitrust and regulation, and I became really interested in these fields. But I didn't think that the government's briefs or oral arguments swayed decision—whatever drove Supreme Court decisions, it wasn't lawyers' advocacy. So as my second year in the Solicitor General's office drew toward an end, and I began to receive invitations to interview for teaching jobs, I decided to try teaching. (Practice held no appeal for me. I don't remember why, but my guess is that it was a combination of not wanting to continue working for others and not wanting to have to defend positions not my own, but a boss's or a client's). I accepted an offer from Stanford but before starting there spent my last year in the government working (again by invitation, not application) on the staff of a presidential task force on telecommunications policy. This was a fascinating assignment and cemented my interest in antitrust and regulation—and also in the use of economic analysis, in which, however, I was very much a tyro, to inform the law in those fields. The research director of the task force, a very able RAND economist named Leland Johnson, greatly stimulated my interest in economics.

It is worth mentioning, in light of my discussion in Chapter 10 of the relation between the judiciary and the academy, the conversation that persuaded me to take a whack at law teaching. The dean of the Stanford Law School was a brilliant and charismatic corporate lawyer named Bayless Manning. In the spring of 1967, my second year in the Solicitor General's office, Manning (whom I'd never met or indeed heard of) called or wrote me and said he'd be in Washington and would I have lunch with him. I said

---

fice, but Elman, an alumnus of the office, had urged me to do so and I believe urged the Solicitor General (Archibald Cox) to hire me. I did not apply for a law school job but was solicited by several law schools, and accepted Stanford, and later the University of Chicago—to which I also did not apply. During the latter portion of my academic career, I was president of a consulting firm, Lexecon Inc., but I was the senior member of the founding group rather than an applicant for the position. And, as explained in the text below, I did not apply for a judgeship. Finally, the chief judgeship of my court, another of my (former) jobs, is, as I mentioned in the introduction, an appointment based purely on seniority.

sure, and we had lunch. It was very shortly after the Arab-Israeli Six-Day War, and that was virtually all we talked about. I was fascinated by the breadth of his interests and knowledge and began to think that maybe law professors were more interesting people than other lawyers. (I didn't realize that Manning had an especially deep interest in foreign affairs; he later became president of the Council on Foreign Relations.) But when he tried to interest me in law teaching, I said that I didn't see myself writing academic articles. He said that didn't matter—law professors could contribute to the law in other ways. Anyone who said that to a law school faculty recruiter today would be instantly dismissed from consideration. Academic law, which in the 1960s was more closely identified with the legal profession than with the academic culture of the universities, is today quite as much "academified" as the core university departments, resulting in a division between law professors and legal practitioners—including judges—that has deprived the judiciary of much-needed assistance in meeting the challenge of rising complexity.

After a year at Stanford, during which I had the good fortune to get to know Aaron Director and George Stigler, two outstanding University of Chicago economists (Director had retired to the Bay area and had an office at the Stanford Law School, and Stigler happened to be a visiting professor at Stanford during part of my time there), I accepted an offer from the University of Chicago Law School because of its unique concentration of economists accessible to law professors and interested in law. And from then on I taught, and published academic work, in the emerging field of economic analysis of law. I also did a good deal of consulting, particularly in antitrust law but also in public utility and common carrier regulation, for example in the airline and railroad industries. I also did consulting on environmental regulation and on the Ford Administration's ill-fated price controls.

The Federal Judicial Appointment Process in 1981

I never thought about becoming a judge. But one day in June 1981, when I was in my office at the consulting firm (Lexecon Inc.) that I had started in 1977 with William Landes and Andrew Rosenfield, a friend and former

Stanford colleague of mine named William Baxter, who had had been appointed by President Reagan to head the Justice Department's antitrust division, called me out of the blue and asked whether I'd be interested in being appointed to the Seventh Circuit. I said no, and he said that's what he'd thought I would say. But as he was about to hang up I said, Well let me think about it for twenty-four hours, and he said fine. So I thought about it and talked to my wife (who was willing to accept a substantial reduction in our income—I had both a generous academic salary and a larger income from consulting), and to my father and Phil Elman, both of whom urged me to accept the judgeship; and within the twenty-four-hour deadline I told Baxter I'd like to think about the prospect some more. About a week later I said I'd do it. I had decided that the reduction in my income would be tolerable, since I would be able to teach part-time while being a judge and so have a teaching income, albeit a much lower one than when I had been full-time, to supplement my judicial income. And I was bored with consulting, in part because much of my time was taken up not with analysis but with pitching our services to clients, since I was the senior member of the firm.

I also thought a federal appellate judgeship would be an interesting and challenging job because of the variety and importance of many federal cases, that I would have an opportunity both to apply economic analysis in a real-world setting and to employ rhetorical methods that would be out of place in academic writing, and that it would be fun to test myself against the great judges of the past. And all this has turned out to be true. But I should mention a final, quite petty consideration that played a role in my decision to accept the appointment. The day before my first visit to the Justice Department to discuss the possibility of my accepting the appointment, I happened to testify before an administrative law judge of the (now defunct) Interstate Commerce Commission. I was subjected to very effective cross-examination by a young lawyer from Covington & Burling—William Livingston—and my client, the general counsel of a western railroad, was very annoyed with me for letting myself be yanked around by Livingston. My reaction was, Who needs this? I want to be on the other side of the bench. I want to be the torturer rather than the victim.

I wanted to keep doing academic work, and I guessed (correctly as it turned out) that with no more consulting, only part-time teaching, and none of the administrative responsibilities of a regular member of a law faculty, I would have enough time left over from judging to do about as much academic writing as I had been doing as a full-time academic. I also felt a sense of public duty pushing me to accept the judicial appointment. I was very conservative in the 1970s (after having been a liberal until the late 1960s), in part as a reaction to the disorder of the 1960s and in part under the influence of Chicago-style free-market economics. I had voted enthusiastically for Reagan and I felt that if his government wanted me as an official I shouldn't refuse. I would have refused had it meant a real financial sacrifice or the job had been uninteresting, but reluctance to refuse a summons to public service had some weight in my decision.

I have continued to do academic writing, mainly though not only academic writing that applies economic analysis (and sometimes related fields of social science) to law, throughout my judicial career. I have applied such analysis to various substantive and procedural areas of law,[6] but also to judicial behavior itself.[7] And I have used economic analysis in a number of my judicial opinions. Economics is basically about how people respond to incentives and constraints, and how those responses shape (or undermine) rules, practices, and institutions, including the rules, practices, and institutions of the legal system. Legal realism is thus far more congenial to economics than legal formalism is. My interest in economics both reflected and reinforced reservations that I felt early on about legal formalism, which turned me toward realism.

I need to say something about the judicial appointment and confirmation process in 1981, because it was so different from what it is today, and although rather slapdash and almost comical it was superior to what it has become. The changes in the process exemplify the growth of what I am calling internal complexity.

6. See, for example, my book *Economic Analysis of Law* (8th ed. 2011), now more than one thousand pages long.

7. Beginning with "What Do Judges and Justices Maximize? (The Same Thing Everybody Else Does)," 3 *Supreme Court Economic Review* 1 (1994), and continued most recently in *The Behavior of Federal Judges: A Theoretical and Empirical Study of Rational Choice* (2013), coauthored with Lee Epstein and William M. Landes.

After I told Baxter that I was interested in the job, I underwent the usual screening, which involved filling out forms that required me, as I recall, to list all my addresses since birth; an FBI investigation in which the bureau searched its files for anything about me and asked neighbors and professional associates about me; a screening of some sort by White House staff; a further screening by the staff of the Senate Judiciary Committee, which was given a summary of the results of the FBI's investigation; and interviews by the Deputy Attorney General and by a committee of the American Bar Association. The ABA committee, unimpressed by my academic accomplishments, and negatively impressed by my lack of trial experience (at the time, and maybe today as far as I know, the ABA, a trade association of practicing lawyers, thought that federal judgeships should with very rare exceptions be given only to trial lawyers), rated me "qualified" but not "well qualified." All this took about four months. But all that I had to do, besides sit for the interviews, was fill out the forms, and that was only a minor bother. Finally the President nominated me and a hearing on my nomination was scheduled before the Senate Judiciary Committee.

There were two hitches in the process. One, which turned out to be trivial, was my mother's checkered past. My parents, but especially my mother, were very left wing, and indeed admirers of Joseph Stalin—the day he died was a day of mourning in my home. In the late 1950s and early 1960s my mother had become a principal figure in an organization called "Women Strike for Peace," which advocated nuclear disarmament.[8] Many of the leaders of the organization were ex-Communists. In 1962 the House Un-American Activities Committee decided to investigate this sinister cabal of middle-aged upper-middle-class suburban women, and my mother was among those summoned to testify. She was asked whether she had been a member of the Communist Party USA for a period ending in 1951, and took the Fifth Amendment.

This turned out to be the last investigation by the House Un-American Activities Committee. The investigation of these harmless women was rid-

8. See Amy Swerdlow, *Women Strike for Peace: Traditional Motherhood and Radical Politics in the 1960s*, 110–111 (1993).

iculed in the press,[9] and the committee was abolished shortly afterward. But when I was offered a job in the Solicitor General's office, a job for which an FBI screening was required, I mentioned my mother having been a Communist (in all likelihood—she never admitted having been a member of the Communist Party, and I believe that the FBI had no actual list of its members but relied on informants, who are not always reliable). But by this time (1965) no one cared. And in 1981 when I agreed to be considered for the judgeship, I told the Justice Department about my mother, and it was indifferent also.

Still, the FBI must have included the information in its report to the Senate Judiciary Committee, because shortly before the hearing I was called by the committee's chief investigator, who said that Senator Thurmond, the committee chairman, had requested that he ask me two questions about my mother. The first was whether I agreed with her political views, to which I truthfully answered "no." The second was whether I thought the Communist Party was an ordinary political party like the Democratic and Republican Parties. To that question I also truthfully answered "no," adding that it was actually an arm of the Soviet government. The chief investigator said that my answers were fine and that Senator Thurmond had told him to assure me that, provided my answers were satisfactory, as they were, I would not be asked at my confirmation hearing about my eighty-one-year-old mother, in order to spare her embarrassment. That was very considerate of Senator Thurmond. But I smile when I think about his wishing to spare the feelings of someone he must have regarded as little better than a traitor.

The only potential obstacle to my appointment was Senator Percy, a very prominent Republican senator from Illinois who was chairman of the Senate Foreign Relations Committee. Percy had his own choice for the vacancy on the Seventh Circuit and it wasn't me. He had never met me and I had never had anything to do with politics; I wasn't even a native of Illinois, having lived there for only twelve years—a carpetbagger. He could have invoked senatorial courtesy to block my confirmation. But the White

9. Id. at 117–118.

House, I later learned, had its own problems with Percy. First of all, it didn't much like him, because it didn't consider him a real conservative. Second, it thought him weak (a kinder assessment would have been moderate, good natured), and thus unlikely to oppose a strong push by the White House. And third, it wanted (I believe this was Edwin Meese's idea—he was the White House Counsel at this time) to change the political complexion of the federal courts of appeals by appointing conservatives (traditionally, appointments to these courts had largely been patronage appointments by senators). To that end it wanted to appoint conservative law professors, believing they'd be more ideological than practicing lawyers.

So the White House struck a deal with Senator Percy: if he would support my appointment, the next vacancy on the Seventh Circuit would be filled by his candidate. He agreed (they honored the deal they'd struck with him, by the way), and he graciously offered to introduce me to the Judiciary Committee at my hearing.

Senator Percy's offer came in a phone call to me in which he explained that he had initially opposed my nomination because he believed that only lawyers who had been district judges should be appointed to the court of appeals. He explained that he had made one exception, namely for John Paul Stevens (who was a Seventh Circuit judge before his appointment to the Supreme Court but had not been a district judge previously), because Stevens had been his college roommate, but that after talking to Edward Levi (the president of the University of Chicago) he had decided to make a second exception, for me. It did strike me, in my naïveté , as odd that being one's college roommate was considered a substitute for being a federal district judge as a qualification for an appointment to a court of appeals. But in fairness to Senator Percy, he may have meant simply that he knew Stevens really well and could be confident of his ability to be an able appellate judge despite lacking prior judicial experience; and Stevens, unlike me, had trial experience, though I don't know how much.

The day of my Senate hearing arrived in November 1981. The nominees (there were several of us, mainly nominated to district courts) met with Justice Department officials at the department shortly before the hearing—where we were told what questions we would be asked by the Republican members of the Judiciary Committee! I was taken aback; this was like being given the answers to the questions on an exam before one takes the exam.

We were trundled off to the Hill and there led into the audience section of a hearing room. Shortly after we arrived, a man entered the room who vaguely resembled what I thought Senator Percy looked like, only much older (the only picture I recalled having seen of him must have been taken many years earlier). What struck me was that he entered with his right hand thrust forward and immediately people rose and started shaking it, from which I inferred that he was a politician. Thinking slowly, I decided that a politician who looked like Senator Percy and was where Senator Percy was supposed to be, since he'd agreed to introduce me at my hearing, probably *was* Senator Percy rather than his father, so I went up and introduced myself.

Shortly before the hearing began, Senator Thurmond beckoned the two of us to the front of the hearing room and asked Senator Percy whether he supported Professor Posner's appointment. Percy began by saying that actually he had supported someone else, but that—whereupon Thurmond interrupted impatiently and said: Do you support Professor Posner *now*? And Percy said yes, and Thurmond turned to me and said that if the chairman of the Foreign Relations Committee supported me, that was good enough for him.

The hearing started. Thurmond was the only member of the committee in attendance, and when my turn came Percy introduced me and began by saying that "he [Posner] has written so many articles on so many subjects that he could be hanged for almost any of his views."[10] This sally was greeted with laughter. He continued: "They [the articles] are controversial, without any question. But even those who might oppose those views look upon them as creative, imaginative, bold, and scholarly in every respect."[11] Such praise would today be more than enough to disqualify a judicial candidate.

10. "Confirmation of Federal Judges," Hearings before the Senate Committee on the Judiciary, U.S. Senate, 97th Cong., 1st Sess., pt. 2, p. 70 (Nov. 20, 1981).
11. Id.

Thurmond's first question to me was whether I had brought any members of my family with me to introduce to the committee. I had noticed that the nominee who had preceded me had been asked that question and had responded by introducing his wife and I think another relative as well, but it had never occurred to me to invite members of my family to the hearing; apparently it was customary but the Justice Department had neglected to tell me this (for which I am thankful). I answered Thurmond's question by saying, "I am afraid they were not able to come with me." (I confess I wasn't being honest, as I had never asked them to come, and my wife, at least, could have come.) Thurmond frowned at me and said, a little suspiciously I thought, "I believe you have two children, Mr. Posner," which I confirmed.[12]

My answer satisfied him and the questioning proceeded. It occupies just two pages in the printed transcript of the hearing[13]—it can't have lasted more than five minutes. There were no trick or follow-up questions, just such predictable and easily answered questions as, "You would be willing to subjugate your personal views to the statute or the law?"[14] I was excused, shortly afterward reported favorably by the committee to the full Senate, and confirmed without any floor debate. I took the judicial oath of office and began my duties as a judge on December 4, 1981. The entire process from start to finish had taken six months.

So that was the process for an appointment to a federal court of appeals thirty-one years ago of a law professor who had published extensively, who was controversial, who had no political backing, and who received only a "qualified" rating from the ABA committee. It is unlikely that I would have been confirmed after the Republicans lost control of the Senate in 1986.

The process was casual. The presumption was that the President could appoint whom he wanted, especially if his party controlled the Senate, unless there was a serious issue of ethics or competence concerning a nominee, or the nominee was a political extremist. The political polarization of the Senate lay in the future. Candidates for a federal judgeship receive

12. Id. at 90.
13. Id. at 90–92.
14. Id. at 91.

much closer scrutiny nowadays. The process is protracted and highly invasive of privacy,[15] and controversial candidates have little chance of being nominated or if nominated confirmed. As a result there has been a reduction in the variance of court of appeals judges (also of federal district judges and Supreme Court Justices); there are fewer duds, but also fewer stars.

So much for the appointment. The transition to a judicial career is abrupt. I heard my first oral arguments a week after taking the oath of office. Some months later there was a seminar for newly appointed court of appeals judges at the Federal Judicial Center (an agency of the federal judiciary) in Washington. It lasted one or two days and had little content, as near as I can recall. In fact all I can recall is an argument over how to designate sections and subsections of opinions, with Judge Ruggero Aldisert, who was giving a talk to the group, very insistent that they should be designated as statutory sections and subsections generally are (that is, 1(a)(1)(A)(i)—I don't know what comes next). I have avoided having to grapple with this profound issue by never dividing my opinions into sections.

Transition, and the Question of Initial Judicial Training

When I was appointed, I didn't know any judges, whether of my court or any other court, except of course Justice Brennan, and also Carl McGowan of the D.C. Circuit, with whom I had once taught at a summer program sponsored by the Salzburg Seminar in America Studies. My "training" as a court of appeals judge consisted largely of my asking questions from time to time of our circuit executive (the senior judicial civil servant in the circuit—Collins Fitzpatrick, who had been appointed to the position before there was such a position and who remains in it today as the dean of circuit executives, serving in a challenging position with great distinction). But in the six months between my agreeing to be considered for appointment and

15. Grotesquely so in the case of Supreme Court candidates. See Elie Mystal, "So You Want to Be a Supreme Court Justice? Don't Sniff Glue," in *Above the Law,* July 23, 2012, http://abovethelaw.com/2012/07/so-you-want-to-be-a-supreme-court-justice-dont-sniff-glue/#more-176665 (visited Jan. 5, 2013).

my taking my seat on the court I had done a considerable amount of reading, mainly of judicial opinions by outstanding judges such as Holmes and Learned Hand and Robert Jackson but also of books and articles on federal jurisdiction and procedure. My academic career had focused on economic analysis of law, and though I had taught a variety of law school classes and done extensive consulting my knowledge of constitutional law, for example, had not progressed since my leaving the Solicitor General's office in 1967, so I had a good deal of catching up to do. I was surprised to learn how many goofy constitutional decisions had been rendered in the intervening fourteen years.

New judges would benefit from a better-designed and more extensive (and intensive) training program. At a minimum, it should last a week, and the focus should be on management, with particular emphasis on the selection and use of law clerks.

I take up issues involving both initial and continuing judicial education in the last chapter of this book. But since the present chapter has been about becoming a federal court of appeals judge, let me end it with a brief summary of the things that such a newly appointed judge needs to be thinking about:

1. The decision whether to write one's own judicial opinions or work from law clerks' opinion drafts. There are several alternative models for allocating work among law clerks and between the judge and the law clerks, and the training program should expose the judge to the alternatives.

2. How to pick law clerks. The judge who writes his own opinions will place less, and maybe no, emphasis on writing skills in selecting law clerks, and more emphasis on knowledge, intelligence, and research skills. I think it important to impress on judges that law clerks are not personal servants but civil servants, paid for by the taxpayer rather than by the judge. To select law clerks on personal grounds, such as friendship with an applicant's parents or the fact that the applicant is an alumnus or alumna of the judge's law school or is charming, personable, or good looking, is therefore inappropriate. Political criteria are also unsound and improper grounds for selecting law clerks. Selecting political allies to be law clerks reflects and reinforces the tendency of some judges to allow their political views to exercise

undue influence on their judicial votes, and, worse (because a judge prone to using political criteria in selecting law clerks is already predisposed to see his judicial role as political), it deprives the judge of the stimulation of diverse views within his office.

I think it *very* wrong for judges to make exploding offers (that is, setting a deadline, often no more than an hour or two and sometimes much less, for the applicant's response to the judge's offer of a clerkship). Such offers unduly constrain an applicant's choices, as well as harm judges who do not make such offers. New judges also need to be warned against placing excessive weight on interviews in selecting among applicants.[16] The information conveyed by an interview is meager in relation to information obtainable from an applicant's academic and job record and from assessments by teachers or supervisors who have had extensive contact with the applicant.

I'm assuming that the judge is hiring law clerks to serve for just one year. That is the norm for appellate judges (many district judges hire clerks for two years). Many judges, however, have a career law clerk. New judges can have only one career clerk, but that is a recent rule and judges who had more than one permanent clerk when the rule took effect can retain them. Except for very weak judges, having a career clerk is a mistake, as it tempts the judge to delegate excessively to that clerk because of his or her experience. Sometimes the career clerk becomes, in effect, a deputy judge.

3. There are different styles (in the broad sense) of opinion writing, and the judge must choose among them, whether he writes the first draft or the law clerk does. There are also different styles of preparing for oral argument, dealing with nonargued cases, doing research (for example, deciding what role Internet research should play), and moving an opinion from initial draft to final product.

4. New judges need to be instructed on the importance of collegiality in an appellate court; breakdowns in collegiality give rise to delay, unnecessary dissents, and animosities that can influence judicial votes. New judges

16. A common cognitive fallacy. See R. Bryan Kennedy, "The Employment Interview," 31 *Journal of Employment Counseling* 110 (1994).

should be warned against dissenting at the drop of a hat, and against bluster, exaggeration, anger, and snideness directed toward their colleagues whether in person or in opinions.

5. Newly appointed appellate judges who have no prior courtroom experience should be encouraged to conduct trials as a volunteer in one or more of the district courts of their circuit. The experience obtained in conducting trials, especially jury trials, enables an appellate judge to review rulings made in a trial with insights that are difficult to obtain from reading trial transcripts or reading about the trial process. I try to conduct a trial every year, though I am sometimes thwarted by the parties' decision to settle. I have been conducting trials since I was first appointed to the court of appeals, despite my lack of trial experience before I became a judge.

❦ 2 ❦

THE FEDERAL
JUDICIARY EVOLVES

A Half-Century of Change

My firsthand acquaintance with the federal judiciary began in 1962 with my clerkship for Justice Brennan. That's more than half a century ago. The federal judiciary has changed quite a bit since then, and even quite a bit just since 1981, when I became a judge. I touched briefly in the preceding chapter on the increase in the length and rigor of the screening of judicial candidates, and questioned the value of the increase from the standpoint of the quality of the judiciary. I don't deny that it serves senators' political goals, or that it may be the inevitable product of the decline of personal privacy as a result of advances in the scope and penetration of electronic surveillance. Recently a candidate for a federal judgeship was directed by the Justice Department to order the candidate's children to "friend" a government investigator so that the investigator could read the children's Facebook pages for material that might reflect unfavorably on the candidate.

Two other changes over the past half-century were inevitable, and one has been both uncontroversial and an unalloyed benefit to the judicial process (and is another product of the electronic revolution): electronic legal research (enabled mainly though not only by Westlaw and Lexis) has enormously increased the accuracy of legal research and at the same time enormously reduced the amount of time required to complete a given research task, enabling more, as well as more accurate, research to be done by a judge or his law clerks. Also an unalloyed benefit to the judicial process, I think (a minority view among judges, however), is online factual research enabled by Google and other search engines (see Chapter 5).

The second inevitable change has been the growth in the number of judges and the size of their staffs, both their personal staffs (mainly law clerks, externs, and interns—the ratio of secretaries to judges has shrunk as a consequence of the computer revolution) and their shared staffs. Every court of appeals and some district courts have a pool of law clerks, called staff clerks or staff attorneys, who are not assigned to individual judges but instead are shared among the judges and assist with motions and with many appeals, especially appeals that are not orally argued (many of these are pro se appeals; that is, appeals in which the appellant does not have a lawyer).

The increase in the number of judges and the size of judicial staffs has been driven by the steep increase in case filings in the courts of appeals since 1960. Fewer than four thousand cases were filed that year; in 1990 more than forty thousand cases were filed and since then the number of filings has risen by another 10 percent. So the caseload of these courts has increased elevenfold in half a century. There has been a parallel increase in the number of cases in the district courts, but the increase in the courts of appeals has been larger in percentage terms because the appeal rate has risen.

Such a big increase was bound to trigger a major expansion in staff. It also gave rise to economizing efforts, such as a big reduction in the percentage of orally argued cases and of decisions citable as precedents and a shortening of the permitted length of briefs and especially of oral argument.

The number of judges has increased too in response to the growth in caseload, though not elevenfold. There were 68 authorized court of appeals judgeships in 1960; there are now 179, an increase of 163 percent.[1] The corresponding figures for the district courts are 241, 667, and thus 177 percent.[2] So the increase in the number of judgeships has fallen far short of the increase in caseload. (This does not explain the increase in the number of law clerks for Supreme Court Justices, however; I shall return to that anomaly.) But that is unavoidable because of the difficulty of coordination that would be created were there a much greater number of judges, especially with the Supreme Court having only nine Justices—a number Congress could increase, but there is no pressure for such a move. The Court is to the entire judiciary as the brontosaurus's brain is to its entire body. The increase in staff relative to judges has created a management challenge for judges, as we'll see.

The fastest growth in caseload preceded my appointment. In 1960 only 329 cases had been filed in the Court of Appeals for the Seventh Circuit, and that number had jumped to 2,165 in 1982 (my first full year on the court)—an almost sevenfold increase in twenty-two years. In the thirty years since, the number has increased by only 40 percent. The number peaked at 3,926 in 2005 and has dropped sharply, to slightly more than 3,000 per year, in the last seven years. For the entire period since 1960, the increase in my court's caseload has been slightly below average.

Since 1982 the number of judgeships on my court has increased from

1. United States Courts, "Judges and Judgeships: U.S. Courts of Appeals: Additional Authorized Judgeships—Since 1960," www.uscourts.gov/JudgesAndJudgeships/Viewer.aspx?doc=/uscourts/JudgesJudgeships/docs/authAppealsJudgeships.pdf (visited July 24, 2012).

2. United States Courts, "Judges and Judgeships: U.S. District Courts: Additional Authorized Judgeships—Since 1960," www.uscourts.gov/JudgesAndJudgeships/Viewer.aspx?doc=/uscourts/JudgesJudgeships/docs/authDistrictJudgeships.pdf (visited July 24, 2012).

9 to 11 and the number of cases per judgeship per year from 241 to 273. But these are not meaningful comparisons. They ignore sittings by senior judges (judges who having reached retirement age have decided to sit on a part-time basis rather than either continue as full-time judges or retire) and by visiting judges. The comparisons also ignore vacancies: there were three until the end of 1982 and there is one today. Calculating a meaningful number of full-time judge equivalents in my court would for these reasons be difficult, and I have not attempted it. But I am confident that the number of cases per judge (including all judges, not just judges in active service) is little changed over this long period, although the average complexity of the cases has increased.

When I started, each judge was entitled to three clerks, but for many years I hired only two. Several years ago I experimented with hiring a third clerk, and, the experiment proving successful, I have continued hiring three law clerks each year and now regret not having done so from the beginning. It has enabled me to obtain deeper research in every case and more help in preparing for oral argument, while also enabling me to obtain a broader range of skills in my staff and to complete and circulate my opinions sooner after oral argument. Many court of appeals judges now have four law clerks (each judge is allotted five slots, which he can fill with any combination of law clerks and secretaries—and no judge needs two secretaries anymore). Some have five, dispensing with a secretary altogether and sharing out the secretary's work among the law clerks. District judges are allotted four slots, and so have three or four law clerks; I discuss the reason for their having fewer slots than court of appeals judges at the end of this chapter.

The ratio of staff attorneys to judges has also increased—I am guessing that it's doubled since I was appointed. In addition more judges have interns (generally, law students working part-time) or externs (generally, law students working full-time during summers) or both (I have neither). What is more, the average quality of law students, and hence of law clerks, staff attorneys, externs, and interns, has increased since the early 1960s with the growth in demand for lawyers and, until the economic crash that began in 2008, in lawyers' incomes. As law became a more lucrative profession, law schools attracted abler students. This will change if the current weakness in the market for lawyers persists. But as of now, the quality-adjusted increase in judicial staff since the early 1960s has been significantly greater than the raw increase in numbers.

Input-Output, with Special Reference to the Supreme Court

The staffing changes that I have just described have, together with more careful screening of candidates, increased the average quality of the output of the courts of appeals despite caseload pressures, and were a rational response to the steep growth in caseload since the early 1960s. That growth is often attributed to decisions by the Supreme Court in the Earl Warren era that expanded legal rights and access to courts, though a similar increase in state court caseloads suggests that the Warren Court wasn't entirely responsible for the increase in the federal caseload. Whatever the cause, the heavier caseload increased the demand for federal judicial services and by doing so induced a corresponding increase in supply. Yet the Supreme Court has experienced significant growth in staff while reducing its output. Both Supreme Court Justices and most court of appeals judges now have four law clerks. But because of the much higher caseload of the courts of appeals, the average court of appeals judge writes fifty opinions a year and the average Supreme Court Justice only twenty (both figures include concurring and dissenting opinions as well as majority opinions), making the ratio of opinions to law clerks 12.5 to 1 in the courts of appeals compared to only 5 to 1 in the Supreme Court.

The increased ratio over time of quality-adjusted staff to output in the Supreme Court might be expected to lead to an increase in the quality of that output, though such an expectation would depend on an assumption that the quality of the Justices had either remained constant (despite aging and replacements) or had not declined enough to offset the increase in the ratio of staff to work. My impression, for what it's worth, is that Supreme Court opinions are on average better written, in the sense that they would receive higher grades in a freshman composition course (I taught such a course at Harvard College when I was a third-year law student), than they were in the 1960s, but that there has been no increase in the average quality of Supreme Court *decisions*. For that depends on more than on how well written its opinions are. Indeed, the Warren Court of the 1950s and 1960s, despite its mistakes and excesses, remains unmatched in the scope and durability of its impact on American law and society since the Chief Justiceship of John Marshall—an unfair comparison, though, since the Marshall Court was writing on a clean slate. The Roberts Court seems to some observers a comedown even from the Burger and Rehnquist Courts.[3] The average quality of the Justices, however, doesn't seem to have changed a great deal since the 1950s. It probably was higher in the 1940s than at any time since, when the Justices included Frankfurter, Jackson, Stone, Douglas (before he soured on judging), Black (also in his prime as a Justice, like Douglas), and Rutledge, though they got along badly with each other and as a result the whole was less than the sum of its parts.

The paradox of increased inputs, decreased output, yet no discernible overall increase in quality deserves attention, though I acknowledge the difficulty not only of assessing the Court's overall quality at any particular time but also of apportioning responsibility for any change in quality between changes in staff and changes in Justices, including changes in the personal "chemistry" among the Justices, which can affect the quality of the Court's output.

I will focus on staff changes. The Justices were first authorized "legal secretaries" late in the nineteenth century, and they really were secretaries. Their evolution into law clerks was gradual. But by the 1930s all the Justices had a law clerk in approximately the modern sense, except that they were mainly research assistants and sounding boards (though they might also summarize petitions for certiorari for their Justices); almost all opinion

---

3. For sharp criticisms of the Roberts Court by a conservative Republican former Justice of the Supreme Judicial Court of Massachusetts and U.S. Solicitor General, see Charles Fried, "The June Surprises: Balls, Strikes and the Fog of War" (forthcoming in an Oxford University Press volume on *National Federation of Independent Business v. Sebelius*, 132 S. Ct. 2566 (2012), as well as in an upcoming issue of *Journal of Health Politics, Policy, and Law*); Fried, "On Judgment," 15 *Lewis & Clark Law Review* 1026 (2011).

writing continued to be done by the Justices themselves. Most of the clerks were fresh out of law school, and generally there were only a few applicants for each clerkship. Justices didn't encourage applications, and often delegated the picking of their clerks to friends or law-professor acquaintances, as Justice Brennan had done with Professor Freund. And many qualified law school graduates had no interest in clerking for a judge or Justice;[4] the position was less prestigious and less coveted than it has become—for example, there were no law-firm signing bonuses for law clerks.

Today each Supreme Court law clerk has had at least a year of clerking on a lower court under his belt, and almost two-thirds have had more extensive professional experience. Each Justice receives many more applications than in the old days, and screens them more carefully, often with the aid of his or her former law clerks. No one is hired without an interview, in advance of which the applicant studies the Justice's opinions and seeks tips from the Justice's former law clerks on how to make a good impression.

Supreme Court law clerks work longer hours today than they did forty years ago even though the caseload per clerk is smaller. Although 2.5 times more petitions for certiorari are filed per term nowadays than in 1960, all the clerks have been formed into a pool (except Alito's clerks) for preparing memos recommending for or against the Court's hearing cases it is asked to hear. A member of the pool writes a cert memo for all the Justices and as a result the number of cert memos per clerk is lower than it was when I was a law clerk, despite the overall increase in petitions. Moreover, the majority of the cert petitions are filed by indigents (mainly prison inmates) and are frivolous. The "paid" docket (the indigents are excused the filing fee) has not quite doubled since 1960—an increase that the institution of the cert pool alone could have enabled the law clerks to handle with no increase in their number; but in fact their number doubled.

Although the cert memos written by the law clerks in the pool tend to be longer and more careful because written for a larger audience, the average time that law clerks spend on their memos must have fallen because of

4. I did not apply for a clerkship, although, as mentioned in the previous chapter, I received one. I have long regretted not having applied for a clerkship with Judge Friendly, as I think I would have learned more than from a Supreme Court clerkship.

the reduction in the number of memos written by each clerk relative to the modest increase in the number of nonfrivolous petitions.[5] It's true that the number of petitions for certiorari is approaching eight thousand a year, but if that number is divided by thirty-three—the number of clerks of Justices who belong to the cert pool (that is, excluding Alito's clerks)—the number of cert memos per clerk per year is only 242, or fewer than five per week, and many of them are short because many of the petitions are frivolous— indeed most of the petitions on the indigent docket are, and the number of paid petitions is only about 1,600 (and many of them are frivolous too). Sixteen hundred divided by thirty-three is only 48.5, which is less than one per week.

And whereas when I was a law clerk the Justices decided about 150 cases a year with the assistance of only two law clerks, today they decide roughly half that number with the assistance of twice as many clerks. The ratio of law clerks to cases has thus quadrupled at the same time that the average quality of the law clerks has increased.

Besides drafting cert memos, most law clerks write bench memoranda, which can run to fifty pages or more, for their Justice in advance of oral argument of the cases the Court has decided to hear. For the most part law clerks also write the first drafts of their Justices' opinions, which the Justices edit, some heavily, some not. In a striking inversion of what one might have thought the relation between Justice and law clerk, Justice Blackmun, a genuine eccentric, after his first few years on the Court left the opinion writing to his law clerks and concentrated on cite checking their drafts. He was by all accounts a cite checker *nonpareil.*

How to explain the remarkable fact—an apparent contradiction of basic economic theory—that despite the large quality-adjusted increase in the Court's staff, the Court's output has decreased. The number of plenary decisions (that is, decisions in cases the Supreme Court has ordered to be fully briefed and orally argued), which is the Court's major output, has declined from an average of 183 decisions a term in the 1930s, and as I said

5. Artemus Ward and David L. Weiden, *Sorcerers' Apprentices: 100 Years of Law Clerks at the United States Supreme Court* 142 (2006).

about 150 in the early 1960s, to 64 in the Court's most recent complete term at this writing (the 2011 term), excluding per curiam opinions, which usually are perfunctory, issued mainly in cases that the Court does not bother ordering fully briefed and argued. The average opinion is longer today and there are more dissenting and concurring opinions, and the Court's total word output is actually greater despite the drop in the number of opinions. But no one thinks that the length of Supreme Court opinions is positively correlated with their quality.

But aren't the Supreme Court's cases more difficult today? I don't think so, if one confines attention to the cases that the Court agrees to hear, as distinct from the much larger number of cases that it is asked to hear, but refuses. Although American law is more complex than it was in the 1930s or for that matter the 1960s or even the 1990s, this is primarily because of developments in areas of law—such as securities regulation, antitrust, taxation, federal pension law, and intellectual property that involve either complex technology such as computer software and pharmaceutical drugs or complex financial and other commercial instruments, systems, and transactions—that the Justices tend to shy away from in favor of constitutional, criminal, and procedural and jurisdictional cases. (Yet the law of criminal sentencing has also become more complex; see Chapter 3.) In part this reflects the Justices' tastes and aptitudes, but it may also reflect the tastes and aptitudes of the law clerks, whose cert memos influence the Justices' decisions to grant or deny petitions for certiorari. Constitutional cases are often "difficult" in the sense of eluding satisfactory resolution, but frequently this is not because they are complex but because they are indeterminate as a consequence of the vagueness and antiquity of the constitutional text, the limitations of historical, philosophical, and social scientific approaches to the analysis and resolution of difficult constitutional questions, and the emotionality and political sensitivity of many constitutional cases.

To measure output just in quantitative terms is seriously incomplete; one must adjust for quality. This is extremely difficult to do in the case of Supreme Court decisions—maybe impossible. To ask whether the fraction of "correct" decisions is greater today than in the 1930s would be fatuous, because there is no benchmark for determining the correctness of a Supreme Court decision. Comparison over time is especially difficult because issues are in constant flux. One can apply to the opinions from both eras quality-related criteria, such as clarity, brevity, guidance provided to the lower courts, and candor in explaining the true grounds of decision. But if one does that, one isn't likely to find a quality difference except that, as I said, the opinions today are on average somewhat better written than was true before (I am guessing) the 1970s, but no better written than they were in the 1930s and 1940s. There has been a huge upsurge in concurring and dissenting opinions since the late 1940s, most of them ephemeral.[6] Today's opinions are more "scholarly," and more carefully cite checked than those of yore, but these are modest virtues—even scholarliness is. Neither judges nor their law clerks are scholars (this is obvious in the opinions' misguided explorations of eighteenth-century history in vain quest of answers to questions of constitutional meaning—see Chapter 7). The scholarly apparatus of judicial opinions belongs to the rhetoric rather than the substance of judicial decision making.

Could it be that the Justices were abler in the 1930s than they are today and so needed less staff? There were some very distinguished Justices then, notably Brandeis, Cardozo, Hughes (the Chief Justice), and to a slightly lesser degree Stone. (Holmes and Frankfurter served only briefly during that decade.) No current or recent Supreme Court Justice has achieved the stature of such Justices, but comparisons over time are treacherous, especially when the comparison is between long-dead Justices and Justices who have not completed, and in some cases have only recently begun, their service on the Court. Many of today's Justices have impressive academic and professional backgrounds. But quality is never the sole, and often not the primary, consideration in the appointment of a Supreme Court Justice, any more than it is in other high-profile presidential appointments.

Although Supreme Court opinions are not worse written on average than they were when all or at least most Justices wrote their own opinions

6. Lee Epstein, William M. Landes, and Richard A. Posner, *The Behavior of Federal Judges: A Theoretical and Empirical Study of Rational Choice* 266 (2013) (fig. 6.1).

from scratch, and indeed the opinions have as I suggested become better written since the 1960s as the number and quality of the Justices' law clerks has increased, there is a loss when opinions are ghostwritten. (That is a recurrent theme of this book.) The Supreme Court law clerks are very bright but also inexperienced; and judges often fool themselves when they think that by careful editing they can make a judicial opinion their own. Some can and do (Justice Stewart and the second Justice Harlan are examples); some can and don't; some can't. If an editor changes thirty words on a page that contains three hundred words, the page will look heavily edited because handwritten changes are larger than type, but only 10 percent of the words will have been changed and many of the changes will have been inconsequential.

Moreover, a judicial opinion, especially one would think at the Supreme Court level, is ideally a product not only of analysis but also of experience, which is why brilliant twenty-five-year-olds are not judges. The twenty-five-year-old can do the analysis, but he cannot articulate the judge's experience. The clerk-written judicial opinion lacks color, depth, and authenticity. The Justice who does not write his own opinions may not understand them very well, moreover, or may forget them quickly, and in either event have difficulty assessing their bearing on subsequent cases.

A striking change in the Supreme Court in recent decades has been the enormous increase in the number and variety of the Justices' extrajudicial activities—presiding at mock trials of fictional or historical characters (like Hamlet, Richard III, and George Custer) or of historical issues (such as whether Shakespeare's plays were actually written not by him but by Francis Bacon or Edward de Vere), writing books and promoting them on book tours, debating each other on television talk shows, lecturing abroad.[7] I don't think the lightening of the Court's caseload is the only reason for the Justices' increased immersion in the modern celebrity culture, but it is a reason. "Today's Justices have a lot of time for extrajudicial matters. From an historical perspective, their workload is extremely light."[8]

7. See id. at 37–40; also my article "Mock Trials and Real Judges" (forthcoming in *Cardozo Law Review*).

8. Craig S. Lerner and Nelson Lund, "Judicial Duty and the Supreme Court's Cult of Celebrity," 78 *George Washington Law Review* 1255, 1267 (2010).

And so, as far as I can determine, a large quality-adjusted increase in inputs, having mainly to do with the increased quantity, quality, and computer-enabled efficiency of the law clerks, seems not to have yielded a quality-adjusted increase in output. I suggested that such a result contradicted fundamental laws of economics, but I was thinking of business firms, which if they discover they're adding costs without generating commensurate increases in profits will cut back. Government agencies are not subject to market discipline. And though Congress controls the Supreme Court's budget, that budget—currently only about $75 million a year—is so small a fraction of the overall federal budget that respect for the Court as a coequal branch of government (with Congress and the President) has assured generous funding. If the Justices want more law clerks or more up-to-date computer software, Congress will not begrudge them these things. It will not insist that the Justices "manage by the numbers" and thus demonstrate that an additional expense will add greater value to the Justices' work product.

The question remains why the Court's inputs have grown. It's been argued plausibly that the increased number and quality of the law clerks are mainly the unintended consequences of administrative measures beginning with Chief Justice Hughes's innovation of the "dead list."[9] Until then, all petitions for certiorari had been discussed at the Court's weekly conference. The Chief Justice would first summarize the petition and give his view on whether it should be granted, and the other Justices would respond and would vote to grant or deny cert. When the Chief Justice decided to circulate a list of cases that he thought should be denied without discussion at the conference, the other Justices, deprived of his summary, had to evaluate the dead-listed cases on their own, and they turned to their clerks. The clerks thus ceased to be merely research assistants.

Clerk "networking," which enhanced the clerks' individual and collective influence, was unknown before the Justices moved into their new building, completed in 1935, in which each Justice and his law clerk (each Justice had only one law clerk at that time) had offices. Until then the Justices had worked out of their homes and provided space there for the clerk

9. Ward and Weiden, *Sorcerers' Apprentices*, 113–114.

to work. (The Court heard oral argument in a courtroom in the basement of the Capitol.) The clerks had little contact with each other, being dispersed, before the move to the new building, and even for a time afterward.

Next, and very important to the enlargement of the clerks' role, in 1947 Chief Justice Vinson decided that each Justice should be assigned the same number of majority opinions to write; until then, faster Justices had been given more assignments. The slower Justices, now more heavily burdened with writing assignments, began delegating opinion drafting to their law clerks. The Justices also wanted an additional clerk, and Congress obliged —of course by giving *all* the Justices another clerk, not just the slowpokes. The staff expansion spurred clerk networking. Finally, with the advent of the cert pool in 1970, the law clerks began spending less time on petitions for certiorari, and this freed up their time to write opinion drafts. As the number and experience of law clerks rose (increased competition for clerkships is one of the things that has made previous clerkship experience a prerequisite—Justices can be pickier when they are fishing from a larger pool, and can thus insist on more experienced applicants), clerks' ability to write good opinions increased and the Justices began reconceiving their own role as that of editors. Even experienced writers often find writing a first draft burdensome. And so with a competent ghostwriter at hand, the temptation to delegate that drafting can become irresistible.

The more clerks a judge has, the more time he must devote to recruitment, orientation, supervision, reading memos and other materials produced by the law clerks, and talking to clerks, and therefore the less time he has for writing opinions. Another consequence of the Justices' burgeoning staffs has been an increased concern, amounting to an obsession, with maintaining secrecy, since the larger a staff, the likelier are leaks. Not only are there more potential leakers, but the more potential leakers there are, the more difficult it is to discover, if there is a leak, who the leaker was. I don't recall from my time as a law clerk anyone saying *anything* about confidentiality, though we clerks assumed that we weren't to gossip about the Justices or discuss pending cases with outsiders. Now there is an elaborate code of conduct for clerks, enjoining them to utmost confidentiality as if they were handling national-security secrets. But being a function of the number of secret bearers, leaks can't be prevented by rules. The effect of the rules is merely to delay the leaks. Clerks delayed blabbing about the internal machinations in *Bush v. Gore*[10] for several years; but blab they eventually did.[11] More recently, with virtually no delay they blabbed about the internal machinations attending the decision in the Affordable Care Act case.[12]

The Justices' official papers, moreover, are increasingly voluminous (elaborate documentation is one of the defining characteristics of bureaucracy) and, in tension with the efforts to seal the law clerks' lips, are increasingly available to scholars. Justice Blackmun's papers are a veritable mine of gossip. And from Justice Lewis Powell's extensive papers we learn that Powell modeled his judicial role on that of the senior partner of a small law firm; it seems that rather than write judicial opinions he wrote memoranda instructing, complimenting, and in short "mentoring" his law clerks. Chief Justice Rehnquist was candid in publicly acknowledging the large role played by his law clerks in the opinion-writing process.[13]

The hypertrophy of staff is a general characteristic of modern American government. It has an arms race aspect. If one Justice has a large and able staff, other Justices are placed on the defensive and want to catch up even though the principal effect of the larger staffs may merely be longer and superficially more erudite opinions. Not that that's the only effect; for clerk networking is far more extensive than it was, for example, when I was a clerk a half century ago. At times, it seems, clerks have formed cabals to influence Justices, not only in voting but also in selecting new clerks.

It has been suggested that the Supreme Court publish the cert memos written by the law clerks who are in the cert pool.[14] There is no published

---

10. 531 U.S. 98 (2000).

11. David Margolick, Evgenia Peretz, and Michael Shnayerson, "The Path to Florida," *Vanity Fair*, Oct. 2004, p. 310.

12. See Jeffrey Toobin, *The Oath: The Obama White House and the Supreme Court* 288 (2012); Orin Kerr, "Who Leaked," *The Volokh Conspiracy*, July 1, 2012, www.volokh.com/2012/07/01/who-leaked/ (visited July 26, 2012).

13. William H. Rehnquist, *The Supreme Court* 261–263 (new ed. 2001).

14. Ward and Weiden, *Sorcerers' Apprentices*, 247.

statement of the reasons for denials of certiorari, and this deprives the bar of valuable information. The reasons given by a law clerk for wanting to deny cert in a case will sometimes differ from the reasons that persuade six Justices to vote to deny (six because only four votes are required to grant), but there would be fewer futile petitions (the Court grants only a little more than 1 percent of the petitions for certiorari that it receives) if the bar had a better sense of the reasons that the Court's key staffers give for turning petitions down. There might also be fewer denials.

The Court's preoccupation with the confidentiality of its internal workings makes an illuminating contrast with the English judicial tradition (now in rapid decline because of caseload pressures) of "orality." Everything English judges did was to be done in public so that their performance could be monitored. They did not deliberate. A judge had no staff, no office, no library, and there were no briefs. The judges would read cases, statutes, etc., handed up to them in the courtroom by the lawyers arguing the case. So appeals might take days to argue, which is why the tradition has eroded as caseload has increased.

Our Supreme Court has gone to the opposite extreme, imposing—or rather attempting with mixed success to impose—a regime of secrecy on the judicial decision-making process. The argument is that secrecy is necessary for candid communications among the Justices and between the Justices and their clerks. But judicial decisions, unlike business and political decisions and decisions relating to national security, are supposed to be, and rightly so, based on reasons that can be stated publicly without embarrassment. The aptly named book *Sorcerers' Apprentices* quotes some disreputably partisan clerks' memos in "hot" cases, for example involving abortion.[15] If publicity deterred clerks from writing such memos, the nation would not be the loser. Of course clerks must not leak information about cases not yet decided; but that seems to be the only secret-keeping that should be required of them. (It is the only secret-keeping that I require of my law clerks.) As for deliberations among the Justices, they are by all accounts stilted and brief. The only embarrassment, were transcripts of their deliberations published, would be that the public would realize that

15. Id. at 130.

the Supreme Court of the United States is *au fond* a committee of lawyers. A bit more of the mystique of judging would be chipped away.

Staff and Specialization in Relation to Rank

I have been discoursing at such length about the Supreme Court because the evidence that expanding staff may not be the answer to the problems of the federal judiciary is most dramatic there. Staff *had* to expand in the lower federal courts, because of the enormous increase in caseload, which had no parallel in the Supreme Court. But the Court's experience reveals three things that judges of lower courts as well should bear in mind: expanding staff is not necessarily a panacea for workload pressures; staff can expand in response to internal pressures—the desire of judges for more help, whether or not they need it; and more staff need not result in an increase in the quality of a court's output.

I mentioned that court of appeals judges are given five staff slots and district judges only four. Since most judges want to have a secretary, most court of appeals judges have four law clerks and most district judges only three, so most court of appeals judges have a third more law clerk assistance than most district judges. And because a court of appeals clerkship is more prestigious (there are fewer than a third as many court of appeals judges as district judges and appellate opinions are more influential than trial court opinions), the average quality of court of appeals clerks is somewhat higher. Yet district judges have a considerably heavier workload. Why then isn't the staff allocation reversed? Were staff proportional to caseload, district judges would have the largest staffs and Supreme Court Justices the smallest, with court of appeals judges in between.

Against this it can be argued that the Justices need more law clerks because their cases are more important. But the average quality of their law clerks is highest, and they have the benefit of an appellate opinion from a lower court (usually a state supreme court or federal court of appeals) in every case, better advocacy, more and better amicus curiae briefs, much more time to spend on each case, and more colleagues to discuss each case with. The same is true of court of appeals judges relative to district judges.

Thus staff allocation in the judiciary is proportional not to need but to rank. Higher judges get more staff because they are higher judges. This may simply be the consequence of the hierarchical nature of the human animal, in this respect much like the other social species. But it is unfortunate not only because it leaves the district judges understaffed but also because management of staff is a bigger challenge for judges the larger their staffs. An unnecessary increase in staff not only is a waste of money but also may cause a fall in quality, not of the clerks but of the judge's output. Three law clerks is probably the right number for court of appeals judges, but district judges could use four, and Supreme Court Justices might be better off with just two unless and until the Court decides to hear many more cases than it has been hearing in recent years.

There is another anomaly in the structure of the federal judiciary. One finds in the usual hierarchical organization specialists at the bottom rung and generalists at the top rung—specialization is inverse to rank.[16] Specialists develop their own jargon and therefore have trouble communicating with people in different specialties. And they tend to be immersed in their specialty and thus lack time to develop an understanding of the other specialties in their organization. The federal judiciary used to approximate this management model. The district judges were (and are) specialized to the conduct of trials, and related tasks such as sentencing criminals and supervising settlement negotiations. Rarely were lawyers without substantial trial experience appointed as district judges, and this remains largely true. Court of appeals judges traditionally have been less specialized, since they have to range across a wide set of fields but without having to manage actual litigation.

Supreme Court Justices used to be even less specialized. All were lawyers, but many had also been high government officials—senators, governors, solicitors general, attorneys general, other cabinet officers, and even a President (William Howard Taft) and a presidential contender (Charles Evans Hughes). No more. The Court has I think suffered from the narrowness of the pre-appointment careers of the current and recent Justices.

16. See Daniel Ferreira and Raaj K. Sah, "Who Gets to the Top? Generalists versus Specialists in Managerial Organizations," 43 *Rand Journal of Economics* 577 (2012).

One sees that in the Court's unanimous refusal in *Jones v. Clinton* to give President Clinton the modest extension of immunity from Paula Jones's suit that he sought (a refusal that precipitated the gratuitous impeachment and Senate trial of Clinton); in the political naïveté of the Supreme Court's campaign-donations jurisprudence as typified by the *Citizens United* case; and in the clumsy handling of the 2000 election crisis in *Bush v. Gore* and of the challenge to the Affordable Care Act in *National Federation of Independent Business v. Sebelius* during the 2012 election campaign.

Something is askew in the management of the federal judiciary. The need for managerial improvement is one of the themes of this book.

Here's a final paradox: staff quality can degrade judge quality, with especially serious consequences if staff quality is positively correlated with judge rank. The politicians who influence the appointment of federal judges, notably the President himself, are not interested in appointing the most qualified person in a conventional sense of "qualified," which is to say without regard to race, sex, services to the party, friendship with the President or other influential politicians, or political inclinations, as distinct from professional competence and relevant experience. Judicial appointments are political appointments. But the appointing authorities are not indifferent to professional competence. They don't want to appoint a judge or Justice who will embarrass them. The abler a judge's staff, the less emphasis the appointing authorities need place on the judge's ability, because, especially if he is an appellate judge, he can hide behind the staff, delegating opinion writing to staff and relying heavily on staff for advice on how to vote. The potential effect on the quality of Supreme Court appointments is disturbing to contemplate.

❧ 3 ❧

THE CHALLENGE
OF COMPLEXITY

Law must apply itself to the life of a society driven more and more by technology and technological improvements. Judges and lawyers do not have the luxury of functional illiteracy in either of these two cultures [science and the humanities].

Judge David Hamilton

Complexity Further Explained

I need to explain at somewhat greater length than I did in the Introduction what I mean by "complex" and "complexity." I do not mean "difficult" and "difficulty." A question can be difficult without being complex. Many issues are difficult for judges to resolve—even insolubly difficult, because they require value choices that can't be shown to be correct or incorrect or because the facts that would be needed to resolve issues in a case satisfactorily are unobtainable. That has always been a problem in our legal system, and the only solution, though incomplete, is to have a diverse judiciary imbued with a spirit of professionalism.

A question is complex when it is difficult by virtue of involving complicated interconnections or interactions—in other words when it is a question about a system rather than a monad.[1] The study of systems with many moving parts is the domain of "complexity theory" and "systems analysis,"[2] though these and related terms such as "complexity," "system theory," and "theory of complex systems" bear additional senses in science and math.[3] The problems in the domain of complexity theory that I'll be discussing are ones that specialists understand and often can solve but that generalists have difficulty understanding. Most judges are generalists, and increasingly we are confronted by complexities that most of us have difficulty understanding.

The obvious barrier to understanding technical materials is the technical vocabulary. But that is superficial, for it's easy enough to look up words. Technical *processes*, especially when they require math to de-

---

1. "A complex system consists of *diverse* entities that interact in a *network* or *contact* structure—a geographic space, a computer network, or a market. These entities' actions are *interdependent*—what one protein, ant, person or nation does materially affects others." Scott E. Page, *Diversity and Complexity* 25 (2011). Alternatively, "complex systems consist of diverse, interdependent, interacting entities whose aggregate behavior can often transcend the characteristics of the parts." Andrea Jones-Rooy and Scott E. Page, "The Complexity of System Effects," 24 *Critical Review* 313 (2013). There is no single, canonical definition. See Dominique Chu, "Criteria for Conceptual Notions of Complexity," 14 *Artificial Life* 313 (2008).

2. For a classic study, see Robert Jervis, *System Effects: Complexity in Political and Social Life* (1997), especially chapters 1 and 2; and the review of the book by Scott E. Page, *Journal of Artificial Societies and Social Simulation*, vol. 2, no. 1 (1998), http://jasss.soc.surrey.ac.uk/2/1/review4.html (visited Oct. 28, 2012). Jervis's book is a notably lucid introduction to systems analysis. More difficult, though still intelligible to a layperson, is John H. Miller and Scott E. Page, *Complex Adaptive Systems: An Introduction to Computational Models of Social Life* (2007), part of a series called Princeton Studies in Complexity. Both the Jervis book and the Miller-Page book deal with social rather than technical systems. Crime and its control exemplify a complex social system that has a ubiquitous presence in litigation.

3. See, for example, "Complexity Theory," *Wikipedia*, http://en.wikipedia.org/wiki/Complexity_theory; "Systems Theory," *Wikipedia*, http://en.wikipedia.org/wiki/Systems_theory (both visited Oct. 23, 2012).

scribe, are what are difficult to understand, usually because they're complex.[4]

I gave some examples of complexity in the Introduction, and let me give a few more. A company experiences a cost increase. It must decide whether to raise its price in order to pass on a portion of the cost increase to its customers. Its decision will depend in part on an assessment of how its competitors will react and in part on an assessment of how its customers will react, while its competitors' reactions will depend in part on their assessment of how the company if it does raise price will react to their responses to the price rise, and so on in a circle. Or consider a decision to allow more drilling for oil on federal land. The increased drilling will affect wildlife. Suppose a species will be rendered extinct that is the principal predator of some other species and the principal prey of still another species. Its extinction will affect the populations of these other species, and changes in those populations will in turn affect the populations of still other species, and eventually there may be significant effects on human welfare as well. Competition among species is replicated within the individual animal. The cells in our bodies "want" to grow, necessarily at the expense of each other. When the genes that limit that growth are damaged, and cancer ensues, cellular competition is unleashed that is apt to kill the host body.

And since this is a book about judges, let me give an example of complexity in the interactions among them. When I was a law clerk at the Supreme Court in the early 1960s, and a few years later when I was an assistant to the Solicitor General, Supreme Court Justices didn't ask many questions at oral argument. In contrast, the current Justices are so voluble (all but Justice Thomas, who hasn't asked a question in years) that the law-

4. And so an article like Jean Decety and Margarita Svetlova, "Putting Together Phylogenetic and Ontogenetic Perspectives on Empathy," 2 *Developmental Cognitive Neuroscience* 1 (2011), though written in a highly technical idiom, is readily intelligible to a lay reader who just wants to decode the basic message of the article and not worry about the details. Cognitive neuroscience is plenty complex in my sense, but not every article on neuroscience is focused on its complexities.

yers can barely get a word in edgewise.[5] What explains the change? One possibility is what students of complexity call a "phase transition," illustrated by the effect of temperature on H_2O. At 32°F and colder, it is a solid; at 212°F and hotter it is a gas; and in between it's a liquid. Each state is an equilibrium, that is, a state that will persist unchanged unless and until disturbed by some outside force, such as application of heat or cold. But the equilibrium can be destroyed quite suddenly by a seemingly minor change in the environment. So consider a Supreme Court in which all but one or two Justices ask very few questions; and now there is a change of membership and as a result two very talkative Justices replace two silent ones. The remaining silent Justices may begin to feel uncomfortable, to feel like wallflowers, worrying that the media will raise questions about their competence—will suggest that maybe they aren't quick enough or sufficiently well prepared to be able to participate actively in the give and take of oral argument. There hadn't been a former law professor on the Supreme Court for a number of years before Antonin Scalia was appointed in 1986. A few years later former law professors Ruth Ginsburg and Stephen Breyer joined him. All three are voluble at oral argument. Now there is one more former law professor, Elena Kagan, but four of the other five (all but Thomas), that is, of the five Justices who are not former professors, are about as voluble as those Justices who are former professors.[6]

Both economists and biologists deal with living systems, but of course many mechanical systems are highly complex too. And the law itself is a complex system, and also a system of such systems. Consider what happens when a legislature decrees a substantial increase in the maximum sentence for some crime. The incidence of that crime may fall; but as an unanticipated and undesired byproduct, the incidence of a similar crime may rise. For it is now relatively cheaper to commit (expected punishment cost being a cost of committing crime), inducing criminals to substitute that

5. See Lee Epstein, William M. Landes, and Richard A. Posner, *The Behavior of Federal Judges: A Theoretical and Empirical Analysis of Rational Choice*, ch. 7 (2013).

6. For statistics (omitting Kagan, because of the recency of her appointment), see id. at 329–330.

crime for the now more heavily punished one. At the same time, the ratio of convictions after trial to guilty pleas by persons charged with the more heavily punished crime may shrink, because the prospect of a heavier punishment creates a wider plea-bargaining range. The defendant will consent in a bargained guilty plea to a stiff sentence in order to avoid the imposition of a much stiffer one if he's convicted after a trial. The defendant's offer to accept the sentence will be an attractive alternative to a trial, with its uncertain outcome, from the prosecutor's standpoint as well. So there will be more plea bargains and thus fewer trials.

Even a manual on citation form—the infamous *Bluebook*[7] discussed at the end of this chapter—engenders complexity in the interactive sense in which I'm using the word. Like the many "canons of construction" (a pompous term for principles of interpretation), the extreme length of the *Bluebook*, a consequence of the number of rules and examples in it, creates a demand for clarifying supplements, such as the Harvard Law Review's *Blackbook*. The supplements make cite checking even more time-consuming, and cite checking (for conformity to citation format, as distinct from ensuring substantive accuracy) distracts law students and lawyers from legal analysis and breeds a culture of formalism, nitpicking, and manual gazing (for example at the thousand-page *Chicago Manual of Style*, another bible of law review cite checkers).

I treat the complexities over which the legal profession has no control as givens; obviously judges are not going to improve the understanding of biological organisms or computer software. The complexities of these systems are external to the legal system, though as a major part of the environment that generates cases they affect the operation of the system profoundly. Other complexities are internal to the legal system. Nothing outside law requires the Supreme Court to be overstaffed and produce increasingly complicated opinions, or requires a manual on legal-citation form to balloon to more than five hundred pages. Nothing outside law requires Justice Scalia to enumerate seventy canons of construction, fifty-

---

7. *The Bluebook: A Uniform System of Citation* (19th ed. 2010).

seven of which he endorses and thirteen of which he rejects (see Chapter 7).

I don't need to explain the growth of external complexity, which is not a judicial responsibility. But I do need to explain the growth of internal complexity, something for which we judges, along with law professors, practicing lawyers, legislators, and regulators, *are* responsible. One can get little help with the explanatory task either from the academic literature on complexity in the sense in which I am using the word, or from academic legal literature. The latter literature, with just a few exceptions of which I'm aware,[8] does not recognize complexity as a characteristic of systems, that is of sets of interacting components. Instead it "define[s] a legal system as complex to the extent that its rules, processes, institutions, and supporting culture possess four features: density, technicality, differentiation, and indeterminacy or uncertainty."[9] Alternatively, "the complexity of legal rules refers to the number and difficulty of distinctions the rules make."[10] The literature is thus concerned with how detailed and complicated the law is or should be and why it is becoming more detailed and complicated.[11] It is

---

8. Such as Lon Fuller, "The Forms and Limits of Adjudication," 92 *Harvard Law Review* 353 (1978); Eric Kades, "The Laws of Complexity and the Complexity of Laws: The Implications of Computational Complexity Theory for the Law," 49 *Rutgers Law Review* 403 (1997), and J. B. Ruhl and Harold J. Ruhl, Jr., "The Arrow of the Law in Modern Administrative States: Using Complexity Theory to Reveal the Diminishing Returns and Increasing Risk the Burgeoning of Law Poses to Society," 30 *UC Davis Law Review* 405 (1997). Fuller's article, apparently largely written in the 1950s but not published until after his death, was remarkably prescient.

9. Peter H. Schuck, "Legal Complexity: Some Causes, Consequences, and Cures," 42 *Duke Law Journal* 1 (1992). Shuck's is the fullest definition that I've found of "legal complexity" as the term is used in most legal literature.

10. Louis Kaplow, "A Model of the Optimal Complexity of Legal Rules," 11 *Journal of Law, Economics, and Organization* 150 (1995) (footnote omitted).

11. See, besides Schuck, "Legal Complexity," and Kaplow, "Optimal Complexity," David Frisch, "Commercial Law's Complexity," 18 *George Mason Law Review* 245 (2011); R. George Wright, "The Illusion of Simplicity: An Explanation of Why the Law Can't Just Be Less Complex," 27 *Florida State University Law Review* 715 (2000);

not concerned with judicial encounters with technological and other external complexity.

Examples, Primarily from Criminal Law and Sentencing

The sentencing of convicted criminals illustrates both sorts of complexity. The Sentencing Reform Act of 1984 created within the federal judicial branch the U.S. Sentencing Commission, which promulgates guidelines for federal sentences. A minimum of three of the seven members of the commission, including the chairman, must be federal judges. The guidelines, which thus are internal products of the legal system and indeed to a large extent of the judiciary, make sentencing far more complex than it had been —previously, federal district judges in fixing sentences had roamed at will between the minimum and maximum sentences set by Congress for the crime in question, with neither the judges nor the legislators having anything but seat-of-the-pants intuitions to guide them and with appellate review of sentence length so light as to be almost nonexistent. The result had been an anarchic system of arbitrary, and often very large, differences across judges in sentencing severity. The guidelines establish sentencing ranges inside the statutory minimum to maximum sentencing ranges, thus narrowing judicial sentencing discretion.

One might have expected the Sentencing Commission, in designing guidelines, to have regrounded federal sentencing in the latest social scientific understanding of crime and punishment. But the social science of penology is not very advanced. Although it might seem obvious that punishing crime more severely reduces crime rates, even that is uncertain.[12] Nor did the commission think it had the necessary political support for a radical overhaul of sentencing. Essentially it based its sentencing ranges on aver-

---

Eric W. Orts, "The Complexity and Legitimacy of Corporate Law," 50 *Washington and Lee Law Review* 1565 (1993).

12. Justin McCrary and Sarath Sanga, "General Equilibrium Effects of Prison on Crime: Evidence from International Comparisons," 2 *Cato Papers on Public Policy* 165 (2012).

age federal sentences across the United States, thus reducing regional and idiosyncratic sentencing variance.

That was a step in the right direction. But then the Supreme Court pulled a constitutional rabbit out of its hat in the *Booker* decision,[13] demoting the sentencing guidelines to advisory status and thereby restoring the judges' pre-guidelines sentencing discretion. The Court tried to make the exercise of that discretion more disciplined by nudging the judges to articulate and apply thoughtful theories of punishment and by continuing to require the sentencing judge to calculate the guidelines range—the range, within the broader range between the statutory minimum and maximum sentences, that the Sentencing Commission considers appropriate for the particular crime and criminal. The judge can sentence outside the range or within it, but in either case must justify the sentence by reference to sentencing factors listed in the Sentencing Reform Act,[14] such as the need for deterrence or incapacitation, though the factors are multiple, open-ended, and so only minimally constraining.

The result of the restoration by the *Booker* decision of broad sentencing discretion has been a partial return to the arbitrary disparities in sentence length for the same crime (and for the same or a similar criminal, measuring sameness and similarity by criminal record and other individual factors affecting the appropriate sentence) that preceded and gave rise to the Sentencing Reform Act. For example, sentence length varies with the region of the country in which a defendant is prosecuted—federal judges in the former states of the Confederacy impose on average substantially heavier sentences than federal judges elsewhere in the country.[15] Indeed, when federal criminal sentences deviate, as the *Booker* decision permits, from the guidelines created by the Sentencing Commission, they seem largely random.[16]

13. *United States v. Booker*, 543 U.S. 220 (2005).

14. See 18 U.S.C. § 3553(a).

15. Epstein et al., *The Behavior of Federal Judges*, 251 (tab. 5.19).

16. Amy Farrell and Geoff Ward, "Examining District Variation in Sentencing in the Post-Booker Period," 23 *Federal Sentencing Reporter* 318, 322–323 (2011) (tabs. 2 and 3).

It is not just sentencing law that has become more complex; crime itself has become more complex as Congress in an effort to respond to technological developments (such as the Internet), and to stop up loopholes, has criminalized more and more conduct (mainly related to sexual activities, financial practices, drug trafficking, public corruption, and immigration offenses). Criminals have in response turned to novel methods of evading detection, some involving technology (such as disposable cell phones). So there is an arms race. Congress has also made sentences stiffer, producing the substitution effects that I discussed earlier. Further complications are that the social costs of crime (especially victimless crime like the sale of illegal drugs) are not well understood, nor the deterrent effects of punishment on crimes committed because of compulsion, rage, or mental disease or defect rather than because of hope of monetary or other tangible gain. No one is clear on the incremental deterrent effect of capital punishment or for that matter of life imprisonment, or the feasibility of rehabilitating criminals.

For years the courts have struggled to determine what should count as a "crime of violence," which if part of a defendant's criminal record requires a stiffer sentence for the crime for which he has currently been convicted.[17] An attempt, successful or not, to break out of a jail or prison is pretty clearly a crime of violence. But what about a "walkaway" escape, from an unlocked place of detention, or a failure to show up on time at the jail or prison to begin serving one's sentence? Whether these more placid forms of eluding custody create a risk of violence comparable to that of crimes that would be widely agreed to be violent crimes ought to be resolved by data rather than by judges' guesses. We need evidence-based law across the board, just as we need evidence-based medicine across the board, and not a combination of scientific and folk medicine.

There is less arbitrariness in federal sentencing than in the pre-guidelines era, but more than when the guidelines were mandatory. The result of relaxing the guidelines has been not only greater variance in sentences, but also, on average, more lenient sentences, which is probably a

17. See, for example, *Chambers v. United States,* 555 U.S. 122 (2009); *Begay v. United States,* 553 U.S. 137 (2008).

good thing; federal sentences are extraordinarily severe by international standards, and parole has been abolished. The costs of imprisonment are high, and higher still when the labor income that prisoners would earn if they were not in prison is taken into account; that forgone income is a social cost. And remember that the effect of increased severity of punishment, which usually takes the form of longer prison terms, on crime rates remains uncertain.

The rise and decline in the authority of the sentencing guidelines have been accompanied by a proliferation of federal sentencing statutes more limited in scope than the Sentencing Reform Act, such as the Armed Career Criminal Act, which increases the sentences of repeat offenders in vaguely defined crime categories. There are complex interactions between these statutes and the sentencing guidelines (which contain, for example, a career-offender guideline parallel to the Armed Career Criminal Act). There has also been an explosion in the number of federal criminal statutes—there are now more than four thousand separate federal criminal prohibitions. Again complex interactions have resulted. An example is the multiplicity of overlapping statutes punishing sexual abuse of minors.[18] Inducing a minor to engage in "sexual activity for which any person can be charged with a criminal offense" under either federal or state law is made —if certain jurisdictional conditions are satisfied, for example that the inducement involved the mails—a federal crime punishable by a minimum of ten years in prison and a maximum of life.[19] The question has arisen whether the term "sexual activity" includes masturbating in a child's physical or online presence or soliciting a child to masturbate.[20] Nowhere does the federal criminal code define "sexual activity." It does define "sexual act"—and defines it as involving an actual touching of the victim: "the intentional touching, not through the clothing, of the genitalia of another person who has not attained the age of 16 years with an intent to abuse, humiliate, harass, degrade, or arouse or gratify the sexual desire of any

18. See Virginia M. Kendall and T. Markus Funk, *Child Sexual Exploitation and Trafficking: Examining the Global Challenges and U.S. Responses*, ch. 7 (2012).

19. 18 U.S.C. § 2422(b).

20. See *United States v. Taylor*, 640 F.3d 255 (7th Cir. 2011).

person."[21] My court concluded that "sexual activity" should be equated to "sexual act" as defined in the code, as otherwise a person could be sentenced to life imprisonment for "flashing," since it is a sexual crime, though usually just a misdemeanor even if the flasher intends to be seen nude by a child. Congress's confused terminology is a typical consequence of a complex verbal system.

Complex statutes have also been enacted dealing with post-conviction remedies and prison inmates' civil rights, and these statutes have given rise to a sprawling case law interpreting both them and the constitutional provisions that bear on prisoners' rights.

Some of the complexity of federal criminal law is the gratuitous product of the belief of lawyers and legislators (the latter not all lawyers of course, but the actual drafting of legislation is dominated by lawyers) that more words are always better than fewer—a recurrent problem and a good example of what I am calling internal complexity. Consider the statute that makes it a federal crime to commit an assault on federal property, such as a federal prison. The crime of "assault resulting in serious bodily injury" carries a maximum sentence of ten years.[22] Until 1993 the term "serious bodily injury" was not defined. That year Congress defined it as a "bodily injury which involves . . . a substantial risk of death," "extreme physical pain," "protracted and obvious disfigurement," or "protracted loss or impairment of the function of a bodily member, organ, or mental faculty."[23] So now a defendant can pick through the definition of "serious bodily injury," denying, as in a recent case,[24] that his assault actually created "a *substantial* risk of death," inflicted "*extreme* physical pain," caused "protracted and obvious *disfigurement*," or caused a "*protracted* loss or impairment of the *function* of a bodily member, organ, or mental faculty." No longer is a holistic or aggregative assessment of the gravity of the injury permitted in a case in which, for example, the assault creates a risk of death, inflicts considerable physical pain, causes visible scarring, and may have inflicted sig-

21. 18 U.S.C. § 2246(2)(D).
22. 18 U.S.C. § 113(a)(6).
23. 18 U.S.C. §§ 1365(b)(2), 1365(h)(3).
24. *United States v. Wilson*, 698 F.3d 969 (7th Cir. 2012).

nificant psychological injury. Left undefined, the term "serious bodily injury" is intuitive—a concept jurors can understand and apply. Before the 1994 amendment my court said "there is no mystery to the words 'serious bodily injury'" and approved a jury instruction that simply told the jury that, to convict, "the injury [of the victim of the assault] would have to be more than slight and of a grave and serious nature."[25] That is all the instruction a jury needs—and "more than slight" could be omitted too, along with "and serious," without loss of clarity or definiteness. The statutory definition added gratuitous complexity.

Refusing, as most judges do, to elaborate to a jury the meaning of "reasonable doubt" is a rare example of a wise acknowledgment of the limitations of definition (which is not to say that "beyond a reasonable doubt" is the clearest possible formulation of the burden of proof in criminal cases; "firmly convinced" of the defendant's guilt might be clearer[26]). Congress would have been wise to exercise similar verbal self-restraint with regard to "serious bodily injury."

The attempt to elaborate a simple, intuitive definition is one way of gratuitously creating internal complexity but another—its opposite—is to attempt to reduce a heterogeneous body of phenomena to a single term. Take the well-known legal term, used mainly though not exclusively in tort cases, "proximate cause." It seems to have been around forever.[27] The conventional definition is "one which in a natural and continuous sequence, unbroken by any efficient intervening cause, produces the injury, and without which the result would not have occurred."[28] What "natural" and "continuous" and "unbroken" and "efficient" and "intervening" mean in the context of determining causal responsibility remains, after centuries, unclear. Yet the conventional definition remains orthodox, though the current edition of *Black's Law Dictionary* attempts a clarification. It defines proxi-

---

25. *United States v. Webster*, 620 F.2d 640, 642 (9th Cir. 1980).

26. See Dennis J. Devine et al., "Jury Decision Making: 45 Years of Empirical Research on Deliberating Groups," 7 *Psychology, Public Policy, and Law* 622, 710 (2001);

27. See, for example, *Peters v. Warren Ins. Co.*, 39 U.S. 99 (1840).

28. See, for example, *Spicer v. Osunkoya*, 32 A.3d 347, 351 (Del. 2011).

mate cause as "1. A cause that is legally sufficient to result in liability; an act or omission that is considered in law to result in a consequence, so that liability can be imposed on the actor," or "2. A cause that directly produces an event and without which the event would not have occurred."[29] The effort at clarification is a flop. Definition 1 begs the question ("legally sufficient to result in liability"), and definition 2 founders on the uncertain meaning of "directly."

Judges actually use the concept of proximate cause, sensibly enough, to require a reason for picking out one antecedent condition—namely the defendant's act—of a specified consequence—the plaintiff's injury—and making that antecedent condition a basis for legal liability. The doctrine of "proximate cause" rules out the causes that should not give rise to liability because doing so would not have socially desirable effects, such as deterrence. (So the thinking behind "proximate cause" would be easier to understand if the doctrine were instead called "remote causation.") The doctrine's sundry different applications include protecting the ability of primary victims of wrongful conduct to obtain compensation; simplifying litigation; bowing to the limitations of deterrence (unforeseeable consequences of a person's acts will not influence his decision on how scrupulously to comply with the law's prohibition of those acts); eliminating some actual or possible but probably minor causes of injury as grounds of legal liability; and preventing over-deterrence (the issue in suits against gun manufacturers for gunshot wounds). In other words, there are multiple reasons for deciding what causal factors in what circumstances should not give rise to legal liability. The reasons are heterogeneous as well as multiple and judges and lawyers are not helped by subsuming them under a term, "proximate cause," that cannot even be defined and should therefore be avoided.

I gave criminal law as an example of intertwined internal and external complexity. Another example is immigration law. Frequent amendments to that law have made it immensely complex—a system with many moving parts spawning complicated interactions—at the same time that increased

29. *Black's Law Dictionary* 250 (Bryan A. Garner, editor in chief, 9th ed. 2009).

international mobility has brought immigrants to the United States from all over the world, seeking asylum from oppressive regimes and thus challenging our immigration judges to learn about the political, religious, and legal cultures of foreign countries. These judges have found it very difficult to meet that challenge.[30]

A disturbing paradox is that post-conviction procedure and immigration law, though now among the most complex areas of federal law, are areas in which, because there is no entitlement to counsel in post-conviction proceedings and because the immigration bar is weak, private litigants—criminal defendants, prison inmates, and aliens—confront the mighty U.S. government with limited effective assistance (sometimes no assistance) from lawyers.

In both areas, efforts to deal with complexity are frustrated by an absence of consensus, both normative and empirical. In criminal law it is an absence primarily of consensus on what conduct should be criminal, which crimes are most and which least serious, the proper balance among deterrence, incapacitation, retribution, and rehabilitation as goals of criminal sentencing, and the effects of alternative sentencing regimes. An absence of normative consensus implies a presence of soft variables, well illustrated in criminal sentencing by retribution—the desire to impose a punishment somehow commensurate with the gravity of the crime. Deterrence, recidivism, rehabilitation—these factors in sentencing can be studied. But "eye for an eye," "the punishment must fit the crime," the thirst for revenge, cannot be. They are ineradicable sources of uncertainty.

30. In fact the administration of the nation's immigration laws (all federal) is a shambles. For illustrative recent criticism, see U.S. Dept. of Justice, Office of the Inspector General, Evaluation and Inspections Division, *Management of Immigration Cases and Appeals by the Executive Office for Immigration Review* (Oct. 2012). Immigration judges, by the way, though called "judges," are not judges in the sense that Supreme Court Justices, federal court of appeals judges, and federal district judges are. That is, they are not appointed under Article III of the Constitution, which requires presidential appointment and Senate confirmation and confers life tenure and forbids salary reductions. Immigration judges are among the many different types of federal judicial officers, such as the administrative law judges who decide social security disability cases, who are not Article III judges.

That is no excuse for ignoring scientific and social scientific research on crime. One wishes there were more research, but at least there is some. A body of economic research finds for example that forgoing imprisonment as punishment of criminals whose crimes inflict little harm may save more in costs of imprisonment than the cost in increased crime that it creates[31] —a highly relevant consideration in choosing between sentencing a convicted defendant to probation or to prison. A similarly counterintuitive claim[32] is that good-time credits and parole, even though they reduce the length of prison sentences served, may not reduce deterrence and may actually reduce the overall costs of crime and the criminal justice system. Compliance with the conditions for receiving good-time credits or parole and avoiding revocation of parole reduces the utility (the sense of well-being) of the convicts; they would rather misbehave, as otherwise they would not have to be rewarded for good behavior in order to motivate them to behave. If behaving well is a cost, good-time credits and parole may not reduce the disutility of punishment, and hence deterrence, significantly. Good behavior by inmates and shorter time served produce very substantial savings in prison costs, resulting in net social benefits if deterrence is largely unaffected—unless considerable weight is placed on incapacitation as another benefit of imprisonment; if so, the alternative of inducing good behavior not by shortening time served but by providing in-prison privileges to well-behaved inmates may be a better alternative. Tugging the other way, though, is that better behavior by convicts prone to bad behavior may reduce the disutility of imprisonment to other convicts—those who would be victimized by the misbehaving ones.

Few federal judges, or for that matter prosecutors and defense attorneys, are familiar with such studies. Or with studies that raise questions about the length of federal prison sentences;[33] those sentences are so long

31. David S. Abrams, "The Imprisoner's Dilemma: A Cost Benefit Approach to Incarceration," 98 *Iowa Law Review* 905 (2013), is an excellent recent study.

32. Made recently in A. Mitchell Polinsky, "Deterrence and the Optimality of Rewarding Prisoners for Good Behavior" (Stanford Law School Nov. 2012), with extensive reference to supporting studies.

33. Notably American Civil Liberties Union, *At America's Expense: The Mass Incarceration of the Elderly* (June 2012).

that they threaten to pack the prisons with old people. Recently my court decided a case in which a forty-six-year-old sex offender had been sentenced to fifty years in prison (and there is no federal parole).[34] How likely would he be to commit sex offenses (he had no other criminal history) in his eighties and nineties? And how likely is it that his sentence of fifty years, had it been only twenty years, would have undermined deterrence of potential sex offenders? Last year only 1,451 men ages sixty-five and older were arrested for sex offenses (excluding forcible rape and prostitution), which was fewer than 3 percent of the total number of arrests of male sex offenders that year.[35] Only 1.1 percent of perpetrators of all forms of crimes against children (the defendant's victim in our case was a child) are between seventy and seventy-five years old and 1.3 percent between sixty and sixty-nine.[36] How many can there be who are older than seventy-five? It is true that sex offenders are more likely to recidivate than other criminals,[37] because their criminal behavior is for the most part compulsive rather than opportunistic. But capacity and desire to engage in sexual activity diminish in old age. Moreover, when released, a sexual criminal is subject to registration and notification requirements that reduce access to potential victims.[38]

And the costs to prisons of elderly prisoners are great; the average expense of maintaining a federal prisoner for a year is between $25,000 and $30,000,[39] and the expense rises steeply with age because the medical component of a prisoner's expense will rise with his age, especially if he is still

34. *United States v. Craig*, 703 F.3d 1001 (7th Cir. 2012) (per curiam opinion and concurring opinion).

35. FBI, *Uniform Crime Reports: Crime in the United States 2011*, www.fbi.gov/about-us/cjis/ucr/crime-in-the-u.s/2011/crime-in-the-u.s.-2011/tables/table-39 (visited Dec. 3, 2012).

36. U.S. Dep't of Health & Human Services, Children's Bureau, "Child Maltreatment 2010," 76 (2010), http://archive.acf.hhs.gov/programs/cb/pubs/cm10/cm10.pdf (visited Dec. 3, 2012).

37. Virginia M. Kendall and T. Markus Funk, *Child Exploitation and Trafficking*, 310 (2012).

38. Id. at 320.

39. Federal Bureau of Prisons, "Notice," 76 Fed. Reg. 57081 (Sept. 15, 2011), www.gpo.gov/fdsys/pkg/FR-2011-09-15/pdf/2011-23618.pdf (visited Dec. 3, 2012).

alive in his seventies (not to mention his eighties or nineties). It has been estimated that an elderly prisoner costs the prison system between $60,000 and $70,000 a year.[40] Granted, that is not a *net* social cost, because if free these elderly prisoners would in all likelihood receive Medicare and maybe Medicaid benefits to cover their medical expenses. But if freed before they became elderly, and employed, they would have contributed to the Medicare and Medicaid programs through payroll taxes—which is a reminder of an additional social cost of imprisonment: the loss of whatever income the prisoner might lawfully have earned had he been free, income reflecting his contribution to society through lawful employment.

The social costs of imprisonment should in principle be compared with the social benefits of imprisonment, which consist mainly of deterrence and incapacitation. A sentencing judge should therefore consider the incremental deterrent and incapacitative effects of a very long sentence compared to a somewhat shorter one. But to do this he needs data, and a mindset that considers that even criminal sentencing should be evidence-based, not emotion-based or intuitive.

Judicial difficulty in coping with the social scientific literature on crime is illustrated by the Supreme Court's decision in *Roper v. Simmons,*[41] which held that the imposition of capital punishment for murders committed by persons not yet eighteen years old was unconstitutional. In so concluding the Court relied in part on a psychological literature that the Justices in the majority mistakenly believed showed that persons under eighteen are incapable of mature moral reflection.[42] Some are, some aren't. Chronological age does not coincide with mental or emotional maturity; the studies the Court cited don't find that age eighteen is an inflection point at which teenagers acquire an adult capacity for moral behavior. One study the Court cited in support of its decision actually undermines it by stating that "it is not being suggested here that all adolescents are reckless, only that adolescents as a group engage in a disproportionate amount of reckless behav-

40. Kelly Porcella, Note, "The Past Coming Back to Haunt Them: The Prosecution and Sentencing of Once Deadly But Now Elderly Criminals," 81 *St. John's Law Review* 369, 383 (2007).

41. 543 U.S. 551 (2005).

42. Id. at 568–575.

ior." Moreover, the study makes no distinction between persons under and over eighteen and in fact defines adolescence "as extending from puberty to the early 20's."[43] And findings that sixteen- or seventeen-year-olds are less likely to make mature judgments than eighteen-year-olds are statistical rather than individual and don't support a categorical judgment that sixteen- and seventeen-year-olds lack adequate moral insight to realize, for example, that murder is deeply immoral. The Court failed to note that the principal study it cited acknowledges that "the definitive developmental research has not yet been conducted, [and] until we have better and more conclusive data, it would be prudent to err on the side of caution."[44] And it overlooked a study that had concluded that adolescents "may be just as competent as adults at a number of aspects of decision making about risky behavior."[45]

The Impact of Technology

The external complexity that especially—and increasingly—perplexes federal judges and, even more so, jurors is the complexity arising from technological advances. Judges have always had to deal with cases involv-

43. Jeffrey Arnett, "Reckless Behavior in Adolescence: A Developmental Perspective," 12 *Developmental Review* 339, 344, 340 (1992). A similar study discusses "teens" in passing but, like Arnett's study, does not classify them by age. Baruch Fischhoff, "Risk Taking: A Developmental Perspective," in *Risk-Taking Behavior* 133, 142, 148 (J. Frank Yates ed. 1992).

44. Laurence Steinberg and Elizabeth S. Scott in "Less Guilty by Reason of Adolescence: Developmental Immaturity, Diminished Responsibility, and the Juvenile Death Penalty," 58 *American Psychologist* 1009, 1017 (2003). See also id. at 1012–1014. This is an advocacy article that concludes: "The United States should join the majority of countries around the world in prohibiting the execution of individuals for crimes committed under the age of 18." Id. at 1017. The only "study" the Supreme Court cited other than the Arnett and the Steinberg and Scott articles is not a study at all, but an old speculative book by Erik H. Erikson, *Identity: Youth and Crisis* (1968). For other cautionary notes about the uses judges make of psychological studies, see Fischhoff, "Risk Taking," at 148, 152, 157.

45. Lita Furby and Ruth Beyth-Marom, "Risk Taking in Adolescence: A Decision-Making Perspective," 12 *Developmental Review* 1, 36 (1992).

ing technology. But the technology of the steam engine, the railroad, the automobile, a radio or television set from the 1950s, and even the airplane is intuitive, or at least (as in the case of television or the airplane) easily explained; and likewise simple chemistry and biology; old-fashioned commercial banking; two-dimensional diagrams (for example plots of supply and demand); and descriptive statistics presented in tables. That's all yesterday's technology. Judges now have to contend with, among other advanced and advancing technologies, mathematical models of competition that require knowledge of calculus, statistical analysis including multiple regression, and the latest advances in medical diagnosis and treatment, such as "PGD" (pre-implantation genetic diagnosis—the screening of in vitro fertilization embryos for genetic traits, before implantation).[46] They have to contend with the mathematical and statistical techniques employed in modern banking and finance—techniques suggestively termed "financial engineering"—and relatedly with complex financial instruments, such as credit-default swaps, mortgage-backed securities, auction bonds, and collateralized debt obligations, many developed by financial "engineers" who have Harvard PhDs in physics. As these examples show, "technology" must be understood in a broad sense that embraces techniques not usually thought of as scientific even when they are highly mathematized.

There is computer science of course and electrical engineering more generally (along with communications technology) as embodied in cell phones, tablets, and other machines whether or not called computers. There is nutritional biochemistry, which, I have learned from a recent case that I handled involving a patent on a margarine product, can be even more complex than some areas of computer science. There is the immensely complex intersection between antitrust law and high-technology industries.[47]

To their credit, judges have embraced economic analysis of antitrust and other commercial fields of law, enabling serious legal errors based on untutored intuition to be avoided. But like embracing a beauty who turns

46. Kate Wevers, "Prenatal Torts and Pre-Implantation Genetic Diagnosis," 24 *Harvard Journal of Law and Technology* 257 (2010).

47. See, for example, "Antitrust in High-Technology Industries," 8 *Journal of Competition Law & Economics* 449 (2012) (special issue).

out to be a witch, judges are finding economics becoming on the one hand ever more mathematically and statistically complex, and on the other hand ever more complicated as a result of rapid advances in psychology ("behavioral economics").[48] And there is more: arcane practices in such fields of business as marketing, management, executive compensation, debt collection, human resources (personnel management), and institutional structure. Not to mention forensic evidence, surveillance and investigatory techniques, and environmental science (fracking, oil spills, global warming, preservation of wetlands, and so forth). The list goes on and on.

The impact of computerization, and especially the Internet, on American business, culture, privacy, politics, education, knowledge and information, and family and personal (including criminal) behavior, and the technological issues presented by efforts to regulate the monster, cannot be emphasized enough. Consider, as a minor example, how the information flow over the Internet from experienced to new consumers may affect the laws relating to disclosure, or its absence, in consumer contracts.[49]

Not that all complex technology that figures in cases presents a technological challenge to judges. Consider facial-recognition software. It is technologically complex, and if its accuracy were called into question in a case in which police had used it to identify a criminal the court would face a technological issue. But suppose instead that it was a case challenging the use of such software as an invasion of privacy. In such a case the existence and efficacy of such software might be a given and the only issue the court would have to wrestle with would be whether the benefits of the software outweighed its costs in diminished personal privacy, with neither cost being measurable. Privacy, like retribution, is one of those soft variables that judges can't wish away—and don't want to, because most judges are more comfortable with them than with the kinds of variable that science measures.

---

48. See the lucid discussion of these advances in Andrei Shleifer, "Psychologists at the Gate: A Review of Daniel Kahneman's *Thinking, Fast and Slow,*" 50 *Journal of Economic Literature* 1080 (2012).

49. See Shmuel I. Becher and Tal Z. Zarsky, "E-Contract Doctrine 2.0: Standard Form Contracting in the Age of Online User Participation," 14 *Michigan Telecommunications Technology Law Review* 303 (2008).

Consider advances in cognitive neuroscience that by relating cognition and emotion to physiological processes in the brain may someday answer the question whether human beings have free will.[50] Given all the discussion in criminal law opinions about voluntariness, deliberateness, premeditation, willfulness, knowledge, and the like as factors bearing on the proper severity of punishment, one might think that the criminal law, at least, would be heavily dependent on theories of the mind that neuroscience may undermine. Not so. Almost all issues of criminal liability and punishment turn on considerations independent of any but the simplest folk psychology,[51] and perhaps even independent of that, because most of the issues resolve themselves into concern with the dangerousness or destructiveness of the defendant rather than with his mental state. We punish criminals because we fear and (most of us) hate them, not because of what we can find inside their heads. If the defendant's brain is so addled that we think him a victim along with his victim, we no longer hate him but we still fear him, though his punishment may take a slightly different form and not be called "punishment"—incarceration in a prison called a mental institution instead of a prison, quite possibly for a longer time because he may be undeterrable. Or a criminal who is old may be punished with a shorter prison sentence than an otherwise similar young criminal because the risk of recidivism tends to diminish sharply after about the age of forty. The criminal law is concerned with the efficacy of punishment rather than with issues of free will on which neuroscience may some day cast light.

This is not to say that psychology, including neuroscience, has no relevance to law or poses no challenges to judicial understanding. Neuroscience is bringing precision to aspects of penology, as in the use of brain scans to determine personality traits conducive to recidivism.[52] It is also enabling better predictions of violent behavior. Such predictions are relevant

50. See "Neuroscience of Free Will," *Wikipedia*, http://en.wikipedia.org/wiki/Neuroscience_of_free_will (visited Nov. 16, 2012).

51. See Stephen J. Morse, "Lost in Translation?: An Essay on Law and Neuroscience," 13 *Law and Neuroscience: Current Legal Issues 2010*, no. 28, p. 529 (2010).

52. See, for example, E. G. Stalenheim, "Long-Term Validity of Biological Markers of Psychopathy and Criminal Recidivism: Follow-up 6–8 Years after Forensic Psychiatric Investigation," 121 *Psychiatry Research* 281 (2004).

not only to sentence length but also to measures for reducing the likelihood that a person will embark on a criminal career.[53] And, penology to one side, neuroscience may someday—maybe someday soon—provide a much more reliable method of "credibility assessment" than the lie detector.[54]

Technology that figures critically in litigation is placing an especially heavy strain on patent adjudication. In part this is because of the complexity and nonintuitiveness of many inventions (notably software innovations), in part because the Seventh Amendment creates a right to trial by jury of all cases in federal court in which the plaintiff seeks damages other than from the government, and in part because of judges' limited understanding of the economics and technology of innovation. The result is a significant legal and regulatory failure, particularly in regard to information technology (computers), as explained in a recent article that summarizes and extends a rich academic literature:

> The "patent premium" is significant in certain fields of innovative activity, including mechanical devices, pharmaceuticals, chemicals, and biotechnology . . . Few question the general desirability of patents within these industries. One cannot say the same for computer software and the broader field of information technology. Innovators in these industries routinely denounce patents as a major impediment to their work. Some researchers have estimated the patent premium in these areas may be insignificant—even negative. If true, this means that patents are encumbering, rather than spurring, research and development. If this is in fact the case, patents are operating in diametric opposition to the economic rationale that justifies their existence. How can this be? . . .
>
> In the first place, IT innovation is extraordinarily rapid, and characterized by continuous incremental improvements over the prior art.

53. See, for example, Jana L. Bufkin and Vicie R. Luttrell, "Neuroimaging Studies of Aggressive and Violent Behavior: Current Findings and Implications for Criminology and Criminal Justice," 6 *Trauma, Violence, and Abuse* 176 (2005).

54. See John B. Meixner, "Liar, Liar, Jury's the Trier? The Future of Neuroscience-Based Credibility Assessment in the Court," 106 *Northwestern University Law Review* 1451 (2012).

Although some advances are technological "leaps," most innovation is cumulative, achieving modest gains over earlier versions of software or adapting known programming techniques to achieve new functional operations. The sheer pace and scale of innovation in the field quickly renders even initially valuable contributions defunct. For that reason, computer-software patents enforced in court rarely cover what is then a cutting-edge technology . . .

As follow-on innovation pervades the IT sector, providing initial inventors broad exclusive rights over the use, and future improvement, of their software (or other technology) is apt to create undesirable transaction costs that threaten to stymie cumulative invention. Enhancing the initial inventor's incentive to invent through the provision of a strong property right serves to reduce that incentive for future improvers. This trade-off always exists, but with respect to computer software and IT, it is one biased toward improvers, who play a more important role than original inventors.

Second, R&D in the IT field is far less capital intensive than that of pharmaceuticals, biotechnology, and chemistry. The requisite private investment to develop new software, for instance, is relatively modest. One need not pay for expensive laboratory equipment and clinical testing. Although nominally significant, such sums are paltry compared to the sunk costs involved in researching and developing a new drug . . .

Third, inventors in the IT field have multiple avenues through which to appropriate the value of their technological advances. Computer software, particularly when written in nonhuman-readable object code, is relatively difficult to reverse engineer. Given its non-self-disclosing nature, software is hardly a paradigm for the non-excludable quality typically associated with public goods. Furthermore, copyright protects software developers against direct copying. In addition, the first-mover advantage, which is driven by the network effects present in the IT sector, rewards purveyors of new software and other information technologies with a direct pecuniary return. Given the ratio of original-inventor R&D investment to third-party, reverse-engineering costs, IT innovators enjoy significant incentives to invent independent of the patent system.

Fourth, . . . unlike drugs, each one of which tends to be covered by a single patent, products in the IT and computer-hardware industries are invariably subject to dozens, hundreds, or even thousands of patents. Due to a figurative explosion in the number of IT patents that the PTO has issued since . . . 1998, the law charges companies operating in the field with identifying, and inventing around or negotiating a license for, countless patents. To make matters worse, the written claims of IT patents are notoriously indeterminate, such that even those skilled in the art are often unable to make an informed judgment whether a particular patent encompasses a planned product or process.

As a result, large companies in the IT field have accumulated vast patent portfolios, which they largely maintain for purely defensive purposes . . .

Fifth and finally, many observers have criticized the poor quality of IT patents that the USPTO issues. Given the vast number, and indeterminate scope, of patents in the field, many companies instruct their researchers not to search the prior art. Deliberate ignorance of this kind permits companies to avoid willful-infringement liability. Yet, this phenomenon is perverse, not only because it means that IT patents rarely contribute technological knowledge that facilitates ongoing innovation, but because it leads the USPTO to grant some patents that are invalid in light of the prior art. Applicants are under a duty to reveal prior art of which they are aware—the law does not require them to search for anticipatory references. The result is that examiners approve many nonnovel or obvious "inventions" in the IT field.[55]

55. Alan Devlin, "Systemic Bias in Patent Law," 61 *DePaul Law Review* 57, 77–80 (2011) (citations and footnotes omitted). For similar criticisms of our patent system, many focused on the U.S. Court of Appeals for the Federal Circuit, see Michele Boldrin and David K. Levine, "The Case against Patents" (Fed. Reserve Bank of St. Louis, Working Paper 2012-035A, Sept. 2012), http://research.stlouisfed.org/

Judicial Insouciance about the Real

We live "in a world of increasingly complex, fragmented, and ubiquitous information."[56] Federal judges are on the whole not well adapted by training or experience to the technological age that we live in. Consider the Supreme Court. None of its current members has an undergraduate or graduate degree in a technical field; their majors were history, philosophy, political science, literature, and public policy. The Justices have little political or governmental experience, with the principal exceptions of Justices Breyer and Kagan; and I believe that only Justices Alito and Kagan have substantial management experience. Other than Justice Sotomayor, who was a federal district judge for six years, the Justices have I believe little firsthand experience with juries in civil cases (Alito was a federal prosecutor). Only Breyer seems comfortable with technical issues.[57] It is no sur-

---

wp/2012/2012-035.pdf (visited Nov. 26, 2012); Stuart J. H. Graham et al., "High Technology Entrepreneurs and the Patent System: Results of the 2008 Berkeley Patent Survey," 24 *Berkeley Technology Law Journal* 1255 (2009); Dan L. Burk and Mark A. Lemley, "Fence Posts or Sign Posts? Rethinking Patent Claim Construction," 157 *University of Pennsylvania Law Review* 1743 (2009); Kimberly A. Moore, "Markman Eight Years Later: Is Claim Construction More Predictable?" 9 *Lewis and Clark Law Review* 231 (2005); R. Polk Wagner and Lee Petherbridge, "Is the Federal Circuit Succeeding? An Empirical Assessment of Judicial Performance," 152 *University of Pennsylvania Law Review* 1105 (2004); Arti K. Rai, "Engaging Facts and Policy: A Multi-Institutional Approach to Patent System Reform," 103 *Columbia Law Review* 1035 (2003); Rai, "Specialized Trial Courts: Concentrating Expertise on Fact," 17 *Berkeley Technology Law Journal* 877 (2002); also the articles cited in note 80 below. For a powerful argument against patents, period, see Michele Boldrin and David K. Levin, "The Case against Patents," *Journal of Economic Perspectives*, Winter 2013, p. 3. And for an excellent journalistic account of the chaotic situation in software patenting, see Charles Duhigg and Steve Lohr, "The Patent, Mighty as a Sword: Tech Giants' Legal Warfare Takes Toll on Competition," *New York Times*, Oct. 8, 2012, p. A1.

56. Daniel Arbess, quoted in Nick Paumgarten, "Magic Mountain: The World of Power: What Happens at Davos?" *New Yorker*, March 5, 2012, pp. 44, 52.

57. See, for example, *Mayo Collaborative Services v. Prometheus Laboratories, Inc.*, 132 S. Ct. 1289 (2012), praised to the skies (rightly in my view) in Richard H. Stern,

prise that the questions asked and comments made by the current Supreme Court Justices at the oral arguments reveal discomfort with technical issues. "Recent U.S. Supreme Court cases involving technology-related issues indicate that several Justices are embarrassingly ignorant about computing and communication methods that many Americans take for granted. Indeed, some Justices admit they are behind the times."[58] Transcripts of oral arguments before the Court reveal misunderstandings, by a number of the Justices, of the elementary technology of pagers, text messaging, online searching, Internet service providers, V-chips, voicemail, and the Kindle reader. Tendentious and inaccurate use of statistics has also been observed in a number of Supreme Court opinions besides *Roper v. Simmons*.[59] These limitations are of course replicated at the court of appeals and district court level, though most lawyers appointed as district judges do have extensive experience as trial lawyers (though often not in civil cases) and 40 percent of court of appeals judges are former district judges.

Judges can take the legal-doctrinal complexity illustrated by the rules of federal sentencing in stride. Told to calculate the applicable guidelines sentence and then if they want deviate from it (within the limits set by statute or precedent) on the basis of their own ideas about penology, judges can do it. They know "the law" and are comfortable (most of them, anyway) exercising discretion when authorized to do so. Judicial knowledge deficits are great but they primarily involve not the legal doctrines them-

---

"Mayo v. Prometheus: No Patents on Conventional Implementations of Natural Principles and Fundamental Truths," 34 *European Intellectual Property Review* 502 (2012).

58. Mark Grabowski, "Are Technical Difficulties at the Supreme Court Causing a 'Disregard of Duty'?" 3 *Case Western Reserve Journal of Law, Technology & the Internet* 1 (2012). Disturbingly, the article quotes statements by Justices that suggest a considerable degree of complacency about their ignorance of modern technology.

59. See, for example, Charles Seife, *Proofiness: How You're Being Fooled by the Numbers*, 217–222 (2010). A recent example of awkward handling of statistics by Supreme Court Justices is discussed in Nate Silver, "In Supreme Court Debate on Voting Rights Act, a Dubious Use of Statistics," March 7, 2013, http://fivethirtyeight.blogs.nytimes.com/2013/03/07/in-supreme-court-debate-on-voting-rights-act-a-dubious-use-of-statistics/ (visited March 11, 2013).

selves but the real-world activities that give rise to federal litigation. These activities are subjects of specialized bodies of knowledge in or relating to psychology, political science, education, prison administration, religious practices and institutions, statistics, economics, computer science, biochemistry, finance, personnel management, marketing, medicine, epidemiology, collusion between commercial competitors, intellectual property, terrorism, and the status of members of minority groups in foreign countries. Judges can calculate prison sentences that withstand appellate review or post-sentence challenges, but can have no confidence that the sentences are consistent with the facts about criminal behavior. They can puzzle out a legal doctrine but without understanding the activity to which the doctrine is to be applied can't produce reliable reality-based decisions.

That at least is my view; my guess is that most judges don't think they have to know much about the deep factual background of their cases. Either they regard the judicial process as intuitive, and at least if they are experienced judges trust their intuitions; or they believe that legal analysis is essentially semantic—that in a patent case, for example, you have to understand the patent statute but having understood it all you need to do in order to decide the case is to place the facts in the verbal categories that the statute created. And to sentence criminals you just have to have internalized the moral sense of the American community, or maybe the moral sense of the part of the community to which you belong.

Illustrative of judicial insouciance about the real is the Supreme Court's decision that allowing a golfer to ride a golf cart between holes in a PGA tournament (because of a disability) rather than requiring him to walk would not "fundamentally alter the nature" of the PGA's tournament competitions, and therefore prohibiting him from riding violated the Americans with Disabilities Act.[60] The Court's opinion arbitrarily distinguished, without misgivings, between "essential" and "inessential" rules of golf tournaments.[61] Yet how could such a determination be thought within judicial competence? In a similar case considerable evidence had been marshaled that stamina is an important element of championship golf

60. *PGA Tour, Inc. v. Martin*, 532 U.S. 661 (2001).

61. Frederick Schauer, "The Dilemma of Ignorance: PGA Tour, Inc. v. Casey Martin," 2001 *Supreme Court Review* 267 (2001).

and is tested in part by the requirement that the players walk between holes.[62]

An example of judges' outright defiance of empirical reality is the Supreme Court's decision that for a state to prohibit men under twenty-one from buying 3.2 percent beer while permitting women to buy such beer at age eighteen denied equal protection of the law to men.[63] The state presented evidence that young males account for a disproportionate share of arrests for driving while intoxicated and for traffic accidents resulting from intoxication, indicating that young men have more difficulty controlling their intake of alcohol than young women do. The court brushed aside this justification for different treatment of young men and young women on the shockingly anti-intellectual ground that "it is unrealistic to expect either members of the judiciary or state officials to be well versed in the rigors of experimental or statistical technique. But this merely illustrates that proving broad sociological propositions by statistics is a dubious business, and one that inevitably is in tension with the normative philosophy that underlies the Equal Protection Clause. Suffice to say that the showing offered by the appellees does not satisfy us that sex represents a legitimate, accurate proxy for the regulation of drinking and driving."[64] Notice the non sequitur: because judges don't understand statistics, statistics can't prove a systematic behavioral difference between men and women. And does anyone believe that the state law was an invidious discrimination against men—in the 1970s, when discrimination against women was rampant and legal actions against it were sporadic? The real purpose of the decision may have been to show that the Supreme Court would be "even handed" in sex discrimination cases rather than "pro-woman."

The educational backgrounds of Justices and judges reflect a general belief that law is a humanity rather than a science, or even a social science. Some judges think, or at least pretend, that it is a branch of lexicography —that the answers to questions about the meaning of statutes and con-

62. *Olinger v. United States Golf Association*, 205 F.3d 1001, 1006–1007 (7th Cir. 2000), judgment vacated (on the basis of the Supreme Court's decision in *Martin*), 532 U.S. 1064 (2001).

63. *Craig v. Boren*, 429 U.S. 190 (1976).

64. Id. at 204 (footnote omitted).

stitutional provisions are to be found in dictionaries and grammar books and other sources of semantic understanding. Other judges treat law as a branch of rhetoric, or literature—or (without acknowledgment of course) politics. Others treat it as amateur historiography. The dominant methodology of law, as distinct from its doctrinal content, has changed little since A.D. 534, when the Code of Justinian was completed. No profession has changed less in the last 1,478 years than the law, unless it's the clerical profession.

Law is indeed a humanity, and properly so, as I'll argue in Chapter 8. But as practiced by lawyers and most judges it is a *narrow* humanity. Mastery of "the law" in the sense of statutes and cases and treatises and other orthodox sources of law does not equip a judge to deal with sources of complexity that arise even in fields remote from technology. For example, the nation's increasing religious assertiveness has caused litigation involving religion, including litigation over very obscure sects, to surge. How many Americans, for example, have heard of the African Hebrew Israelites of Jerusalem? Who among those who have heard of them can distinguish them from Rastafarians?—a distinction, turning on the Nazirite Vow (and how many judges have heard of that?), central to a recent decision by my court.[65]

Many immigrants who base their claim to be allowed to live in the United States on their status as refugees are seeking asylum from religious persecution. They come from nations that most Americans, including most American judges and administrative officials, know very little about. How many Americans know for example that Eritrea persecutes Jehovah's Witnesses? Who even knew there were Jehovah's Witnesses in Eritrea? And how does a judge verify that an Eritrean applicant for asylum who claims to be a Jehovah's Witness really is one?

The Supreme Court's decisions enforcing the establishment and free-exercise clauses of the First Amendment (especially the former) satisfy no one—including the Justices.[66] I think this is because the Justices have not

65. *Grayson v. Schuler*, 666 F.3d 450 (7th Cir. 2012).
66. See, for example, *Utah Highway Patrol Ass'n v. American Atheists, Inc.*, 132 S. Ct. 12 (2011) (dissent from denial of certiorari) ("Establishment Clause jurisprudence

been able to come up with any alternative to basing those decisions on their fact-free intuitions about religion, which vary with their attitudes toward religion, which in turn derive from their religious beliefs and affiliations, or lack thereof. The perception of the Court as a political court in most constitutional cases and many nonconstitutional ones derives from the fact that the Justices form confident views without any empirical basis for them. In default of empirical or otherwise objective knowledge people rely on their intuition, which is shaped by ideology (including religion), temperament, race and sex, upbringing, and other personal characteristics that differ across judges and Justices. These characteristics provide premises for decision; and when people argue from different premises, there is no basis for agreement. Fact-free constitutional adjudication is abetted by constitutional lawyers (prominently including professors of constitutional law), who "know little about their proper subject matter—a complex of political, social, and economic phenomena. They know only cases. An exclusive diet of Supreme Court opinions is a recipe for intellectual malnutrition."[67]

Federal litigation increasingly involves foreign and international law, not only commercial law but also tort, criminal, and domestic-relations law, as under the Alien Tort Statute[68] and the Hague Convention on the Civil Aspects of International Child Abduction.[69] Because of the size and self-sufficiency and global reach of the United States, and the prevalence

---

[is] in shambles," "nebulous," "erratic," "no principled basis," "Establishment Clause purgatory," "impenetrable," "ad hoc patchwork," "limbo," "incapable of consistent application," "our mess," "little more than intuition and a tape measure"); *Lamb's Chapel v. Center Moriches Union Free School District*, 508 U.S. 384, 398–99 (1993) (concurring opinion) (a "geometry of crooked lines and wavering shapes," a "ghoul in a late-night horror movie" that can't be slain even though "no fewer than five of the currently sitting Justices have, in their own opinions, personally driven pencils through the creature's heart").

67. Richard A. Posner, *Overcoming Law* 208 (1995).

68. Harold Hongju Koh, "Transnational Public Law Litigation," 100 *Yale Law Journal* 2347 (1991).

69. Linda Silberman, "Hague International Child Abduction Convention: A Progress Report," *Law and Contemporary Problems*, Summer 1994, p. 209.

of the English language throughout the world, Americans, including judges, tend to be monolingual, even provincial. Most of us know little about foreign countries, foreign law, or the institutional, procedural, and cultural aspects of foreign legal systems. Some (especially some Supreme Court Justices) have taken to citing foreign judicial decisions as possible guides to American law, a dubious tactic unless the judge understands the cultural and institutional context of a decision.[70]

That few Americans have a good command of a foreign language used not to matter, but now it does because of the effects of globalization on the judicial docket. The astonishing variance across federal appellate courts in reversing denials of asylum[71] must reflect a combination of widespread judicial ignorance of foreign countries and widely different subjective attitudes toward immigration and immigrants, as well as different caseload pressures and differing conceptions of the proper judicial role in reviewing decisions of nonjudicial decision makers, such as the members of the Immigration Court and the Board of Immigration Appeals.

In decisions involving the constitutionality under the First Amendment of legislative restrictions on contributions to political campaigns, the Supreme Court and the lower federal courts have managed to enmesh themselves deeply in the electoral process without understanding it sufficiently well to be able to gauge the consequences of their decisions. The *Citizens United* decision,[72] which removed restrictions on campaign financing by allies and opponents of candidates (provided they are not caught covertly coordinating with their favored candidates), increasingly seems naïve in its denial that massive campaign contributions corrupt the political process, and in its simplistic equation of money to speech.[73] I plead guilty

70. See Richard A. Posner, *How Judges Think*, ch. 12 (2008).

71. Documented in Jaya Ramji-Nogales, Andrew I. Schoenholtz, and Phillip G. Schrag, *Refugee Roulette: Disparities in Asylum Adjudication and Proposals for Reform* (2009).

72. *Citizens United v. Federal Election Commission*, 558 U.S. 310 (2010).

73. Richard A. Posner, "Unlimited Campaign Spending—A Good Thing?" *The Becker-Posner Blog,* Apr. 8, 2012. www.becker-posner-blog.com/2012/04/unlimited-campaign-spendinga-good-thing-posner.html (visited May 17, 2012).

to having written the majority opinion (affirmed by the Supreme Court) upholding Indiana's requirement that prospective voters prove their identity with a photo ID[74]—a type of law now widely regarded as a means of voter suppression rather than of fraud prevention. And the Supreme Court's continued toleration of politically motivated gerrymandering of legislative districts jars against its meticulous insistence that all districts in a state must be so configured as to have almost exactly the same population. I don't understand the Court's toleration for political gerrymandering, a practice that in conjunction with the Court's endorsement of promiscuous campaign donations seems to have poisoned our national politics by filling the House of Representatives with extremists. When gerrymandering makes a district secure for one party, the focus of electoral competition shifts from the general election to that party's primary, where voters are few—the passionate few—and the leverage of rich donors (corporate or individual), motivated to donate generously because of pronounced and often extreme political views, may swing the district to an extremist candidate. That has been the recent experience of the Republican Party in a number of congressional districts.

If scientific (including mathematical and statistical) and technological complexity were the only new and challenging features of the activities that give rise to federal litigation, we might be hopeful that a new generation of judges, improved judicial training, a recommitment to legal realism, and reforms relating to the presentation of evidence at trial would provide in the aggregate a solution to the problem of judges' lack of understanding of complexity. But we must also reckon with the fact that there are many gaps in scientific and technological knowledge. The limits of social science must be acknowledged and improvement sought; the soft variables I mentioned must also be acknowledged. But that leaves a large area in which judges could draw on technical knowledge to improve judicial performance.

Consider what judges do when they don't understand the activity from

74. *Crawford v. Marion County Election Board*, 472 F.3d 949 (7th Cir. 2007), affirmed, 553 U.S. 181 (2008).

which a case before them has arisen. They duck, bluff, weave, change the subject. The principal evasive techniques are, first, deference to lower-level decision makers. Appellate judges defer on many issues to trial judges, invoking such rubrics as clear error or abuse of discretion, and the trial judges in turn hand the ball to the jurors, whose ability to understand technical issues is on average even feebler than that of judges. Thus the "easy" questions are answered by the judge, who rules on motions to dismiss and motions for summary judgment, while the difficult questions, the ones that can't be resolved without a trial, are given to amateurs to answer. Or they are left to be answered by administrative agencies to which judges defer on the often fictitious ground that the agencies have "expertise," even if their adjudicators are poorly trained, horribly overworked, highly politicized, or all these things at once.

Second, appellate courts adopt multifactor tests for the trial courts to apply. Usually the factors are unweighted, which makes the "scoring" of a multifactor test a subjective exercise and so invites appellate deference to the decision by the trial judge or administrative agency. Consider the test for "piercing the corporate veil," which means imposing liability on shareholders for their corporation's torts or breaches of contract, in disregard of the corporation's limited liability—that is, in disregard of shareholders' normal immunity from suit for the corporations' debts, an immunity designed to encourage equity investment by reducing the investor's downside risk. A typical statement of the test is that "courts look at numerous factors in determining whether to pierce the corporate veil. These factors include: inadequate capitalization; failure to issue stock; failure to observe corporate formalities; nonpayment of dividends; insolvency of the debtor corporation; nonfunctioning of the other officers or directors; absence of corporate records; commingling of funds; diversion of assets from the corporation by or to a shareholder; failure to maintain arm's length relationships among related entities; and whether the corporation is a mere facade for the operation of the dominant shareholders."[75] Notice that the list is not

75. *Jacobson v. Buffalo Rock Shooters Supply Inc.*, 664 N.E.2d 328, 331 (Ill. App. 1996) (citations omitted).

exclusive ("These factors include . . ."),[76] that no weights are assigned to the different factors even though their importance differs, and that the last factor ("mere façade") actually embraces and supersedes the others.

If one asks why limited liability should ever be disregarded, the main answer is that it is sometimes used to deceive people into thinking they're dealing with a solvent corporation. The sensible thing would be to apply that standard directly rather than apply a multifactor test. But that would leave less discretion to the trial court and thus make more work for the appellate judges and require of them a deeper understanding of commercial practices.

A third technique that judges use to avoid having to wrestle with complex subject matter is to recast issues in semantic terms. Hence the resort to dictionaries; the obsessive invocation of "plain meaning," which is to say of text devoid of real-world context, because the judges may not understand the context; and the quotation of general language from previous judicial opinions, again neglectful of context, to enable a decision to be based ostensibly on authority rather than on intuition, policy, or judicial psychology. An example of where the semantic fig leaf covering the true ground for a decision is particularly thin is the standard declared by most courts for whether a forum selection clause (a contractual provision that designates the court in which any dispute between the parties arising from the contract must be litigated) can be invoked by or against a nonsignatory of the clause. That is a difficult issue because it involves a trade-off between two types of uncertainty: uncertainty about the scope of the clause if a nonparty can ever invoke or be bound by it, and uncertainty about the clause's

76. A common characteristic of multifactor tests. See, for example, the test laid down by the Tenth Circuit for determining whether the winning party, if the defendant, should be awarded his attorneys' fees in a Lanham Act case (the Act authorizes such an award only in "exceptional cases," 15 U.S.C. § 1117(a)): "No one factor is determinative, and an infringement suit could be 'exceptional' for a prevailing defendant because of (1) its lack of any foundation, (2) the plaintiff's bad faith in bringing the suit, (3) the unusually vexatious and oppressive manner in which it is prosecuted, or (4) *perhaps for other reasons as well.*" *National Association of Professional Baseball Leagues, Inc. v. Very Minor Leagues, Inc.,* 223 F.3d 1143, 1147 (10th Cir. 2000) (emphasis added).

utility if a party can invoke or avoid it by reference to a corporate affiliate. (Suppose a subsidiary was the signatory of the clause; can the parent corporation be bound by it?) Getting the balance right is important because forum selection clauses are important, especially in international transactions because of the difficulty of predicting in which court an international dispute would end up unless the parties had specified a court in their contract.

The standard for applying a forum selection clause to a nonsignatory is whether the nonsignatory is "closely related" to a signatory or to the dispute.[77] Suppose A is the parent of B, and B has agreed with C in a contract (to which A is not a party) that any suit between B and C arising out of the contract must be brought in a French court. Such a dispute arises: C accuses B of a breach of contract and has reason to think that A, B's parent, bears some legal responsibility for B's breach—maybe it ordered B to break the contract, without justification; this would be the tort of intentional interference with contract. C is committed to litigate in the French court with B, but decides to sue A in the United States. If A prefers to litigate in France, it should be allowed to invoke the forum selection clause, and thus make C sue it in France rather than the United States even though it is not a party to it, so that the two closely related cases will not be split between different courts in different countries.

That's a sensible result, but now suppose A and B have totally unrelated disputes with C. A and B are still "closely related"—they are parent and subsidiary—but there is now no reason for allowing A to thwart C's choice of forum by virtue of a contract to which A is not a party. The "closely related" test provides no guidance.

A fourth tactic that judges employ to avoid having to wrestle with complex cases is to wing it, substituting a guess for data. Consider the Supreme Court's opinion upholding a state's ban on partial-birth abortions (late-term abortions in which the fetus is destroyed after the lower extremi-

77. See, for example, *Hugel v. Corporation of Lloyd's*, 999 F.2d 206, 209–210 (7th Cir. 1993); *Holland America Line Inc. v. Wartsila North America, Inc.*, 485 F.3d 450, 455–56 (9th Cir. 2007); *Marano Enterprises of Kansas v. Z-Teca Restaurants, L.P.*, 254 F.3d 753, 757–58 (8th Cir. 2001).

ties, and sometimes the torso, have emerged from the mother's body and only the head remains inside). In partial justification of its holding the Court said: "While we find no reliable data to measure the phenomenon, it seems unexceptionable to conclude some women come to regret their choice to abort the infant life they once created and sustained. See Brief for Sandra Cano et al. as Amici Curiae in No. 05–380, pp. 22–24. Severe depression and loss of esteem can follow. See *ibid.*"[78] The brief on which the Court relied consisted of testimonials of numerous women who had had an abortion and regretted it. No doubt there are many such women. But the brief, sponsored by the ultraconservative Justice Foundation, does not distinguish between partial-birth and conventional abortions and makes no attempt either to estimate how many women regret having had an abortion or to compare such an estimate with an estimate of the number of women who have regretted forgoing an abortion. So the brief provides no support for the Court's ruling. Moreover, the Court's opinion overlooks the difference between regret and mistake. One can regret having done something without thinking it a mistake—the alternative may have been worse. "I regret having to tell you that . . ." is a common expression. The Court also ignored the extensive evidence cited in the dissenting opinion that abortion is no more dangerous to a woman's mental health than having an unwanted child.[79]

Peter Lee provides an analytical framework for my observations concerning the loose judicial regard for accuracy when faced with technical issues.[80] He is struck by the much-noted and much-deplored formalistic

78. *Gonzales v. Carhart*, 550 U.S. 124, 159 (2007).

79. See id. at 183 n. 7.

80. Peter Lee, "Patent Law and the Two Cultures," 120 *Yale Law Journal* 2 (2010). The term "Two Cultures" in the title is a reference to a famous lecture of that title by C. P. Snow in 1959, decrying the gap between the literary and the scientific culture. (Snow was a scientist turned novelist.) The Federal Circuit's formalism has been noted and deplored by many other scholars besides Lee. See, for example, Rochelle Cooper Dreyfuss, "The Federal Circuit: A Continuing Experiment in Specialization," 54 *Case Western Law Review* 769 (2004); Craig Allen Nard, "Toward a Cautious Approach to Obeisance: The Role of Scholarship in Federal Circuit Patent Law Jurisprudence," 39 *Houston Law Review* 667 (2002); Nard and John F. Duffy,

character of the patent jurisprudence of the U.S. Court of Appeals for the Federal Circuit, which has exclusive appellate jurisprudence in patent cases. He sees the judges' formalism as a substitute for understanding inventions and the inventive process. Thinking is costly to the thinker in the sense of being difficult, time-consuming, and frustrating. People economize on the cost of thinking by using shortcuts, deferring to expert opinion (even if that requires an arbitrary choice between competing experts), or changing the subject—in the case of judges, substituting a legalistic approach that they understand for a technologically informed approach that they would find difficult, time-consuming, and frustrating to understand and apply. A psychological literature on which Lee draws[81] describes people as "cognitive misers," and he applies the term to the judges of the Federal Circuit. It can be applied to other judges too when they confront cases that involve technological, social scientific, cultural, or historical issues that baffle them.

Formalism is touted as making law simpler, more definite; yet patent doctrine as formulated by the Federal Circuit is such a tangle that even inventors have great difficulty understanding it.[82]

The creation of the Federal Circuit to be the specialized patent court (it has other jurisdictions as well, but patent law is the most important) has had another bad effect, this one as yet unremarked: it has reduced the ability of the other courts of appeals to deal with technological issues. If they had to wrestle with patent cases those courts would perforce acquire some ability to deal with technological issues in general, and that would improve

---

"Rethinking Patent Law's Uniformity Principle," 101 *Northwestern University Law Review* 1619 (2007). On the strongly (and questionably) pro-patent orientation of the Federal Circuit, see William M. Landes and Richard A. Posner, *The Economic Structure of Intellectual Property Law*, chs. 11–12 (2003); David R. Pekarek Krohn and Emerson H. Tiller, "Federal Circuit Patent Precedent: An Empirical Study of Institutional Authority and Intellectual Property Ideology," 2012 *Wisconsin Law Review* 1177.

81. Summarized in Lee, "Patent Law and the Two Cultures," at 20–29.

82. Mark D. Janis and Timothy R. Holbrook, "Patent Law's Audience," 97 *Minnesota Law Review* 72 (2012).

their ability to deal with such issues in nonpatent cases. Issues involving software are a staple of modern patent law but also arise in a variety of other cases. An example is cases involving searches of computers for child pornography. In a recent case[83] the government had learned of a video, containing such pornography, that had been uploaded to the Internet. The Internet address of the computer from which the video had been uploaded enabled the government to trace the computer to the defendant's home. But it was seven months after the uploading before the government obtained and executed a warrant to search the computer. The search revealed the video along with other child pornography. The defendant argued that there was no probable cause to believe that seven months after the uploading of the video there would still be child pornography on his computer. The evidence, he argued, was "stale," and added that a single video could not establish that he was a "collector" of pornography who could therefore be assumed to retain indefinitely the pornographic images that he had downloaded to his computer.

The government conceded the premise of the defendant's argument—that "stale" computer files are not a permissible basis for a determination of probable cause to search a computer. But it argued that from the single upload it could be inferred that the defendant was indeed a "collector." The parties thus agreed on the importance both of "staleness" and, to a determination of "staleness," of whether the suspect was a "collector"—and in this they were tracking the analysis in numerous cases concerning probable cause to search a computer for child pornography. But the concern with "staleness" and "collecting" reflects a misunderstanding of computer technology. When you delete a computer file it goes into a "trash" folder; and when you "empty" the folder (by clicking on an icon in the folder that says "empty trash" or some equivalent), the contents, including the deleted file in question, disappear. But the files in the trash folder have not left the computer. They have just been placed in a part of the computer's hard drive that you can't access because there is no icon for that part on the computer's

83. *United States v. Seiver*, 692 F.3d 774 (7th Cir. 2012).

screen. Computer experts employed by the FBI and other law enforcement agencies can easily recover a deleted file unless it has been overwritten. And generally a deleted file is overwritten only when the hard drive is full, and this is rare; and even if the hard drive is full, so that overwriting occurs, this doesn't mean that a particular file has been overwritten. Software for rapid overwriting, encryption, and other means of making deleted files inaccessible even to experts can be bought, but apparently are rarely bought by child pornographers.

"Staleness" is relevant to probable cause when the object searched for is perishable or consumable, like cocaine, but not when it is a computer file. No doubt after a *very* long time the likelihood that the defendant still has the computer, and if he does that the file hasn't been overwritten, and if he's sold the computer that the current owner can be identified, drop to a level at which probable cause (that is, a nonnegligible probability of discovering contraband or evidence of crime) to search the suspect's home for the computer, and if the computer is found to search it, can no longer be established. At that point the "collector" inquiry becomes relevant, because to preserve his collection intact the collector may have transferred his pornographic files from the computer he's discarding to his new computer. But seven months is too short a period to reduce the probability that a search of a computer will be fruitful to a level at which probable cause to conduct the search has evaporated.

If you think the relation of judges to lawyers similar to that of regulators or supervisors to doctors, pharmaceutical companies, and crime labs, consider that those regulators or supervisors usually know a lot about the subject matter of the technicians whom they regulate or supervise—not as much as the technicians, but enough. Often this is not the case with judges.

At the root of the refusal of many judges to confront, even to recognize, the challenge of complexity is a professional mind-set that often includes—along with impartiality, conscientiousness, and other traditional attributes of a good judge—lack of curiosity, a feeling of intimidation by science and technology, and a lack of interest in obtaining an empirical rather than merely intuitive grounding for one's beliefs. These attitudes

communicate themselves to the bar, making the problems that judges encounter in coping with technology problems of lawyers as well, with an
unfortunate feedback effect because of the dependence of judges on lawyers in our adversarial legal system. Many lawyers are technologically
challenged, just as the judges are, and so are drawn to the same avoidance
techniques that judges retreat behind, while those who know better are
anxious about deviating from the orthodox methods of legal argument, or
fearful that judges will feel insulted to be spoon-fed appropriately simpli-
fied descriptions of the technological background to a case. I can assure the
reader that we will not be. What *would* anger most judges would be a lawyer's telling them that it's time they dropped the pretense that judicial decisions are based on faithful adherence to statutory and constitutional language and to precedent. That's a fig leaf that almost all judges want to
continue wearing.

Among the technologies about which judges know less than they
should is the "technology" of adjudication itself, and particularly the role
of the jury—the subject of an extensive social scientific literature (see
Chapter 9) with which few judges are familiar. A criticism of this literature
is that it is based to a large extent on experiments with mock juries, but I
don't think it's a powerful criticism. I base this judgment in part on the
heavy use that trial lawyers make of mock juries in preparing for jury trials,
and in part on my experience teaching for several years a clinical course in
evidence and trial advocacy (combined, as they should be—they are inseparable) built on mock trials based on the ingenious case files published
by the Institute for Trial Advocacy. The students in the trials (conducted
in a realistic courtroom in the University of Chicago Law School) played
judge, law clerks, lawyers, witnesses, and jurors. It was remarkable how,
like good actors, they inhabited their roles. One case involved alleged medical malpractice that had resulted in a man's death. His widow was the lead
witness. In each trial of this case the student who played the widow burst
into tears on the stand as she recounted the loss she had experienced from
her (mock) husband's death. And the jurors (whom, in a departure from
realism, I made to deliberate openly rather than secretly) behaved, so far

as I could judge, not like lawyers or law students but like—jurors. That the student participants really did inhabit their assigned roles I could determine from having presided at real trials.

Specialization the Solution?

For a long time it seemed that the answer to external complexity—the complexity of many of the subjects of adjudication—was specialization. If specialists alone can understand some activity that generates legal disputes, the judges of those disputes should be drawn from the ranks of specialists and adapt judicial procedures to the special character of the regulated activity. In other words, for generalist judges substitute experts. That was the dream of the Progressive movement and led to a proliferation of administrative agencies, many of them specialized courts in effect (such as the Federal Trade Commission and the National Labor Relations Board), as well as, though less commonly, to "real" courts with limited jurisdiction, such as the Commerce Court in the 1920s, the U.S. Court of Appeals for the Federal Circuit in 1982, and the Bankruptcy Court (a component of the federal district courts). In state judiciaries we find juvenile courts, domestic relations courts, drug courts, probate courts, the Delaware Court of Chancery, and, increasingly, other business courts.[84]

At the federal level, the specialized court or court-like administrative agency has been a flop, with the principal exception of the Bankruptcy Court[85] (the Tax Court is a partial exception). The deregulation movement shrank or eliminated a number of the federal administrative agencies, with the result that today most nonjudicial federal adjudication is by immigration judges (in asylum cases) and social security judges (in social security disability cases); and these administrative law judges are overworked and many—especially the immigration judges—appear to be underqualified.

84. See John F. Coyle, "Business Courts and Interstate Competition," 53 *William & Mary Law Review* 1915 (2012).

85. See Jeffrey J. Rachlinski, Chris Guthrie, and Andrew J. Wistrich, "Inside the Bankruptcy Judge's Mind," 88 *Boston University Law Review* 1227, 1257 (2006).

Patent disputes might seem an ideal subject for a specialized court, because they so often involve difficult scientific issues. Yet as I have noted already there is deep dissatisfaction with the Federal Circuit's performance and there is also that court's unremarked effect in diminishing the technical sophistication of the judges of the other federal appellate courts.

It seems that because of the American legal culture, the system of appointing federal judges, and other factors, specialized courts just don't "work" in the federal system.[86] They are not, in my opinion,[87] the answer to the problem of complexity. They would make it worse, because of the inveterate tendency of specialists to speak and write in a jargon intelligible only to initiates. Jargon is a species of internal complexity. Specialized judges are unlikely to be deeply knowledgeable about the technical issues that the cases within their specialty present, though they may think they are. Their specialty will be a body of law, rather than of technical knowledge. I shall be urging throughout this book that law should be simple, regardless of the complexity of the issues it grapples with, and judicial opinions simple, and the judicial focus not on solving technical problems, which is for the real techies, but on managing complexity—not adding to it. Jargon, complexification, and tunnel vision are serious dangers in the operation of specialized courts.[88]

86. See Jed S. Rakoff, "Are Federal Judges Competent? Dilettantes in an Age of Economic Expertise," 17 *Fordham Journal of Corporate and Financial Law* 4 (2012); Chris Guthrie, Jeffrey J. Rachlinski, and Andrew J. Wistrich, "The 'Hidden Judiciary': An Empirical Examination of Executive Branch Justice," 58 *Duke Law Journal* 1477 (2009); Richard A. Posner, *The Federal Courts: Challenge and Reform*, ch. 8 (1996).

87. And that of Judge Rakoff, who in "Are Federal Judges Competent?" mounts a compelling series of arguments against specialized courts; I mention only the one that bears most directly on the issue of complexity.

88. At least in the American legal culture—an important qualification. Specialized adjudication may work much better in the inquisitorial legal systems found in much of the world, including Continental Europe and Japan, than it has in our federal judiciary. But I don't know enough about foreign legal systems to be able to explain why that might be so.

Internal Complexity: The Case of the *Bluebook*

If judicial caseload increased with no increase in the complexity of the average case, this would produce internal complexity in the form of a more elaborate, differentiated institutional structure: more judges and staff, hence more interactions and greater need for coordination; more delegation; more specialization; more elaborate screening of appointments. And this type of complexity *has* grown, as a result of the dramatic increase in federal judicial caseloads since about 1960.[89]

But internal complexity can also increase as a result of bureaucratic pressures, illustrated both by the overstaffing of the Supreme Court and by the growth in length of the *Bluebook* and other citation manuals. We might call this form of internal complexity hypertrophy, or in the case of the Supreme Court "imperial overstretch" by analogy to empires that weaken themselves through excessive expansion. Nowadays the word "hypertrophy" is used mainly to denote a class of diseases in which an organ grows to an abnormal size because of the uncontrolled growth of the cells that constitute it. But it is still used occasionally to denote a structure or activity that has grown far beyond any apparent functional need, like the Egyptian pyramids. The pharaohs needed a secure burial place because they were buried with valuable possessions that they believed they'd need in the afterlife. But security didn't require an immense pyramid of stones above the burial place. Not that the elaboration of the pharaonic burial places was mindless; but it served religious and political needs remote from the functional need to secure the burial place against thieves. Supreme Court Justices who face a constant or even declining caseload may nevertheless want more staff, and the publishers of the *Bluebook* want more sales. The Court produces an increase in institutional complexity; the publishers produce a more complex book.

The more complexity grows, the greater its costs become relative to the benefits that it generates. In other words there are declining marginal

89. For a useful and well-titled case study, see Rory E. Riley, "Simplify, Simplify, Simplify—An Analysis of Two Decades of Judicial Review in the Veterans' Benefits Adjudication System," 113 *West Virginia Law Review* 67 (2010).

returns to complexity.[90] I will be suggesting throughout the book (though most concentratedly in Chapter 10) ways of coping with the sources of complexity that beset the federal judiciary. I have already implicitly suggested one way of dealing with the most gratuitous form of it, what I call internal complexity: reducing the size of the Supreme Court's staff. I now suggest another: renunciation of the *Bluebook* and every other manual of citation form.

> The particular faults of the Bluebook . . . place it in the mainstream of American legal thought. Like many of the judicial opinions and law review articles whose citation forms it dictates, the Bluebook is elaborate but not purposive. Form is prescribed for the sake of form, not of function; a large structure is built up, all unconsciously, by accretion; the superficial dominates the substantive. The vacuity and tendentiousness of so much legal reasoning are concealed by the awesome scrupulousness with which a set of intricate rules governing the form of citations is observed.[91]

A system of citation form has two valid functions: to provide enough information about a reference to give the reader a general idea of its significance and whether it's worth looking up, and to enable the reader to find the reference if he wants to look it up. Four goals should guide the design of such a system: to spare the writer or editor from having to think about citation form, to economize on space and the reader's time, to provide information to the reader, and to minimize distraction. There is some tension among these goals, but not a great deal and they are easily implemented. They are disserved by a 511-page tome, the length of the *Bluebook*'s current (2010) edition (the nineteenth).

90. The thesis of Joseph A. Tainter, *The Collapse of Complex Societies* (1988). See also J. B. Ruhl and Harold J. Ruhl, "The Arrow of the Law in Modern Administrative States: Using Complexity Theory to Reveal the Diminishing Returns and Increasing Risks the Burgeoning of Law Poses to Society," 30 *UC Davis Law Review* 405 (1997).

91. Richard A. Posner, "Goodbye to the Bluebook," 53 *University of Chicago Law Review* 1343, 1343–1344 (1986).

Most citations in a law review article, treatise, brief, or judicial opinion are to cases, statutes, treatises, and law review articles, and the format for these citations is familiar to every law student after a month or so of law school. There are esoteric sources, mainly administrative decisions and regulations, but the agencies caption their various promulgations in a way that makes it obvious how to cite them analogously to how judicial decisions and statutes are cited. Increasingly, however, there are citations to foreign and international sources, and the citation of such sources does require guidance.

Notice that my guiding principles do not include "standardization"[92] or, the equivalent, "uniformity." Consistent application of even a very short citation manual will achieve an adequate level of internal consistency. Advocates of uniformity or standardization have a larger ambition—that all legal citations shall be uniform: in short that there shall be a single system of legal citations. The *Bluebook*'s subtitle—"A Uniform System of Citation"—is a bid for monopoly. But a single system of legal citations is no more desirable than a uniform typeface, margins, and paper thickness for all documents of the same general character, such as novels. Within the same document, uniformity is desirable because without it readers will puzzle over whether the differences are accidents or have some intended significance. But across documents slight differences in citation form are untroublesome. The basic legal citation convention of placing volume number before the name of a statute, case, or article, and page number directly after it, is deservedly uniform and likewise the abbreviations of the state case reporters and West's regional reporters. But efforts to impose uniformity beyond the basic conventions encounter rapidly diminishing returns well illustrated by the *Bluebook*'s obsession with abbreviations. An example plucked literally at random from the latest edition is "C.Ag." What does C.Ag. stand for? Why, of course, the Código Águas of Brazil. Now suppose one had occasion to cite the Código Águas. Why would one want to abbreviate it? The abbreviation would be meaningless to some-

92. See Paul Axel-Lute, "Legal Citation Form: Theory and Practice," 75 *Law Library Journal* 148, 149 (1982).

one who was not a Brazilian lawyer, and perhaps to Brazilian lawyers as well—for do *they* abbreviate Código Águas "C.Ag"? The basic rule of abbreviating, ignored by the authors of the *Bluebook*, is to avoid nonobvious abbreviations—don't make the reader puzzle over an abbreviation, as the *Bluebook* does routinely.[93]

One understands why law clerks follow the *Bluebook*. But why a judge would direct his law clerks to do so, or even tolerate their doing so, is a mystery to me. Are judges sheep? Why should they care what kids at the Harvard Law Review consider proper abbreviation? I suspect that the explanation is twofold (threefold, if one includes an ovine factor). First is respect for "authority." For while the *Bluebook* is not authoritative in the sense in which statutes and precedents are, it is the best-known and most venerable guide to legal citations, which gives it a mantle of authority. Second is the passivity, characteristic of judges in an adversarial system—who tend (though sometimes just pretend) to think of themselves as "umpires" who aren't supposed to make rules but just apply them—that inclines them to accept established ways uncritically. In an adversarial system the lawyers present the case, emphasizing authoritative texts, such as statutory provisions and judicial precedents, and the judge sits there, listening to the lawyers expound the authoritative texts, which often are old. A law clerk drafts an opinion, scrupulously bluebooked; the judge hardly notices (the citation form is invisible). How many judges are even aware of such *Bluebook* ukases as: "in law review footnotes, a short form for a case may be used if it clearly identifies a case that (1) is already cited in the *same footnote* or (2) is cited (in either full or short form, including '*Id.*') in *one of the preceding five footnotes*. Otherwise a full citation is required."[94] This reads like a parody, but was not intended to be one. The *Bluebook* contains more than 150 pages of such "rules."

93. As in: Temp. Envtl. L. & Tech. J., ILSA J. Int'l & Comp. L., Emp. Rts. & Emp. Pol'y J., and AIPLA Q.J. These are names of journals. Now try figuring out B.T.A.M. (P-H), A. Ct. Crim. App., A.F. Ct. Crim. App., C.G. Ct. Crim. App., N-M Ct. Crim. App., Ne. Reg'l Parole Comm'n, and Cent. Ill. Pub. Serv. Co.

94. *The Bluebook: A Uniform System of Citation* (19th ed. 2010), at 107 (emphasis in original).

I have put my money where my mouth is, metaphorically speaking. I don't use the *Bluebook* or any other form book in either my judicial opinions or my academic writings. Journals sometimes impose citation forms on me. But the *Federal Reporter* does not; nor do the publishers of most of my books. My judicial and academic writings receive their share of criticism, but no one to my knowledge has criticized them for citation form. Readers are not interested in citation form. Unless the form is outlandish, it is invisible.

The *Bluebook* is generally believed to have been created by Henry Friendly (who still holds the record as Harvard Law School's most brilliant graduate) in 1926 when he was a member of the *Harvard Law Review*.[95] It was twenty-six pages long. When asked many years later what he thought of his creation's progeny—its successively larger editions—he is said to have replied that the law reviews should do with them what the ancient Greeks had done with unwanted infants.

When I was a law student the *Bluebook* was in its tenth edition (published in 1958) and had grown to 124 pages.[96] In the fifty-two years that separate the tenth edition from the nineteenth it has grown by almost 400 percent. Its growth since the first edition has been just a shade under 2,000 percent, which translates to an average annual rate of growth of almost 9.5 percent.

Some increase in length over time was to be expected with the expansion of the legal system, growing interest in foreign law, and the advent of new publication vehicles, such as the World Wide Web. But not the increase that we've seen. The analogy of cancer to the *Bluebook*'s growth comes to mind but also the distinction between the multiplication of cancer cells in the organ in which they first appear and their eventual metastasis to other organs. For the growth of the *Bluebook* has stimulated the creation of supplemental citation and style guides at a number of law reviews, some

95. Actually it's uncertain whether the *Bluebook* was the brainchild of Friendly or of another student at the time, Erwin Griswold, later the long-serving dean of the Harvard Law School and after that Solicitor General of the United States.

96. On the evolution of the *Bluebook* to the early 1990s, see James W. Paulsen, "An Uninformed System of Citation," 105 *Harvard Law Review* 1780, 1782–1785 (1992).

of which dictate compliance with the *Chicago Manual of Style* except as it conflicts with the *Bluebook* or the law review's supplement. In its current edition (the sixteenth), the *Chicago Manual of Style* is a thousand pages long. The *Bluebook* has stimulated something else we don't need, an extensive academic literature on legal citation form.[97] There is even a 180-page book called *Understanding and Mastering* The Bluebook.[98] This is beyond parody.

Earlier in the chapter I mentioned the supplements, such as the Harvard Law Review's *Blackbook,* that codify "common law" elaborations of the *Bluebook.* For it turns out that despite its length, or perhaps because of it, the *Bluebook* does not answer all the questions of form that obsess law review editors. Ad hoc answers, like judicial supplementations of vague or incomplete statutes, are tendered, and because of dread of inconsistency become codified in the supplemental citation form books. All this is absurd almost beyond comprehension, and a distraction to law clerks; but it is invisible to most judges.

I am not alone in criticizing the *Bluebook;* much of the commentary on it is critical.[99] But there is not much root-and-branch criticism. Most critics accept its basic premises, fuss over details, and don't worry that "bluebooking" involves an expenditure of time that would be better spent elsewhere.[100] A *lot* of time wasted, while some students who are not members of law reviews are devoting their free (from class work) time productively to solving legal problems of poor people. Although there a number of alternative systems of legal citation, including some that are much shorter,[101]

97. See the references in the footnotes in Ian Gallacher, "Cite Unseen: How Neutral Citation and America's Law Schools Can Cure Our Strange Devotion to Bibliographical Orthodoxy and the Constriction of Open and Equal Access to the Law," 70 *Albany Law Review* 491 (2007).

98. Linda J. Barris, *Understanding and Mastering* The Bluebook: *A Guide for Students and Practitioners* (2d ed. 2010).

99. See, for example, besides Gallacher's article "Cite Unseen," James D. Gordon III, "Oh No! A New Bluebook!" 90 *Michigan Law Review* 1698 (1992).

100. Gallacher is an exception, and there are others.

101. A good example is Ronald B. Standler, "Legal Research and Citation Style in USA," 2004, www.rbso.com/lawcite.htm (visited Sept. 10, 2010), which combines criticism of the *Bluebook* with alternative suggestions.

the challenger to the *Bluebook* that gets the most attention is even longer than the *Bluebook*—661 pages in its current edition.[102] I want my law clerks to spend their time doing legal research and analysis and criticizing my opinion drafts rather than obsessing over citation form.

So why is the *Bluebook* successful? The prestige of its sponsors (originally the Harvard Law Review, but now also the Yale, Columbia, and Pennsylvania law reviews), and its length (lawyers are suspicious of brevity), are part of the answer; its having been the first published manual of legal citations (or at least the first to have commanded widespread attention) is another part. The desire for uniformity of citation style, misplaced though that desire largely is, gave the *Bluebook* a modest "first mover" advantage, comparable to though weaker than that of being the first telephone company or the first railroad. The more subscribers a telephone company has, the more valuable its service is, and so the first company will have an advantage in signing up new subscribers. And once a railroad is built with a track of a particular gauge, subsequent railroads, wanting to interconnect with the first railroad and each other, will be likely to adopt the same gauge. The more law reviews that use the *Bluebook*'s citation forms, the greater the incentive of a new law review to use those forms as well, less to spare their readers having to adjust to a different form—readers, as I said, generally are indifferent to citation form and anyway accustomed to its differing across publications—than to avoid having to think about citation form or inviting invidious comparison with the elite law reviews that conform to the *Bluebook*. The uniformity advantage is slight, as I have said, or else all legal publishers would use the *Bluebook*, and many do not. My court does not have a citation form book, and the publishers of judicial opinions do not impose a citation style on our opinions. That means that the court reports published by West do not have a uniform citation style—and no one notices, let alone objects.

A puzzle is why the *Bluebook* keeps growing in size. There are reasons for occasional updating, when new types of legal reference material

---

102. Association of Legal Writing Directors and Darby Dickerson, *ALWD Citation Manual: A Professional System of Citation* (4th ed. 2010).

emerge, such as online publications, or, in an earlier day, the *Federal Register*. But the number of new types of material that have emerged since 1926 cannot explain the almost 2,000 percent increase in the *Bluebook*'s length. In part that increase is attributable to the decision of its authors to prescribe an abbreviation for every law review, court reporter, statute book, etc., in the world, so that as these sources proliferate, the lists of abbreviations grow. The nineteenth edition, published just five years after the eighteenth, is 23 percent longer; but the "tables" section, which catalogs legal sources for the United States and a large number of foreign jurisdictions as well, is 38 percent longer, mostly because of additional foreign materials (sources of Iraqi law, for example), all carefully listed and (uselessly) abbreviated. The catalog of sources has value as a guide, but that is the function of a reference book rather than a manual.

The growth in the *Bluebook*'s length is probably attributable in part to the desire, largely financial in origin,[103] to issue new editions at short intervals. Once committed to the *Bluebook* because of the first-mover advantage that it enjoys, law review editors are pretty much forced to buy each successive edition. They would be reluctant to do so if each edition made significant changes in the existing citation forms, as that would undermine the uniformity advantage of the *Bluebook* over competing form books. So adding to the existing forms—listing new legal sources and creating abbreviations for them—is the preferred method of revision from edition to edition, and makes its length grow from edition to edition.

This is not necessarily sound economics. The longer the intervals between editions, the higher the price the *Bluebook* would command, because

---

103. I do not know whether, without revenue from sales of the *Bluebook*, such perks of *Harvard Law Review* editors as monthly open-bar parties at local restaurants, twice-weekly deliveries to Gannett House (the review's premises) of food and snacks via Peapod, daily deliveries of fresh bagels, a television room with a Nintendo Wii, an annual "fall ball" at the New England Aquarium, and a spring banquet at the Harvard Club, would still be possible. In my day—if I may be permitted a moment of old fogyism—the only perks were the banquet, held on the eve of the election of the law review president, and a Friday afternoon cocktail party for the review's officers. The staff of the review, now eighty-eight, was then fifty-six.

buyers would know that the edition they were buying would not become obsolete so soon. Lengthening the intervals would be like increasing the durability and hence value of a light bulb. But updating is so central to legal research that a planned-obsolescence business model works for the *Bluebook*.

The growth in the size and complexity of the *Bluebook* may also reflect the reflex desire of every profession to convince the laity of the inscrutable rigor of its methods. The essence of "profession" as a type of service provider is that it employs esoteric methods that its customers must take on faith. But unlike the genuinely professional methods used by the modern medical profession to diagnose and treat disease, the core method of the lawyer and the judge is "legal reasoning," and it lacks scientific rigor; indeed, at its best, it is uncomfortably close to careful reading, to rhetoric, and to common sense. An unconscious awareness of the limitations of legal "science" drives the search for rigor into unlikely places, such as the form of citations, and has given the profession a recipe for distraction that it does not need.

The *Bluebook* is an absurdity, but it endures, in fact thrives, impervious to criticism and ridicule. The judiciary navigates the sea of modernity, slowed, thrown off course, by the barnacles of legal formalism (semantic escapes from reality, impoverished sense of context, fear of math and science, insensitivity to language and culture, mangling of history, superfluous footnotes, verbosity, excessive quotation, reader-unfriendly prose, exaggeration, bluster, obsession with citation form)—an accumulation of many centuries, yet constantly augmented. There is little desire to give the hull a good scraping. There is fear that the naked hull would be unsightly, even unseaworthy. The fear is overblown. A week after all the copies of the *Bluebook* were burned, their absence would not be noticed.

❧ 4 ❧

FORMALISM AND REALISM IN APPELLATE DECISION MAKING

I now embark on a series of analyses of the decision-making process at the appellate and trial levels of the federal judiciary, beginning with the appellate level. My aim is to explain the process and suggest improvements responsive to the concerns that I have expressed in the preceding chapters, and to other concerns as well. Much of the discussion in this chapter, and also in subsequent chapters, is organized around the tension between formalism and realism (as I explained those terms in the Introduction) as modes of appellate decision making. The implication for the challenge of complexity should be apparent: judges need a return to realism if they are to meet the challenge.

I am an atypical judge in some respects, particularly in my approach to opinion writing, not only in writing my own opinions rather than editing opinions drafted by law clerks but also in matters of style and format and, to a degree, in legal reasoning. Some excellent judges may find my advice about opinion writing (see Chapter 8) unhelpful. I am more confident that my approach to appellate decision making—the judicial vote on the outcome of the case, as distinct from the opinion announcing and defending the outcome—is orthodox and my advice to appellate lawyers (also in Chapter 8) sound. I base this confidence on my long experience of sitting with other judges. We usually react to the cases, and invariably to the lawyers who present them, in the same way even though we have different backgrounds, experience, temperaments, and outlooks.

Judges tend not to be candid about how they decide cases. They like to say they just apply the law—given to them, not created by them—to the facts. They say this to deflect criticism and hostility on the part of losing parties and others who will be displeased with the result, and to reassure the other branches of government that they are not competing with them —that they are not legislating and thus encroaching on legislators' prerogatives, or usurping executive-branch powers. They want to be thought of not as politicians in robes but as technicians, as experts, though some would acknowledge being sometimes compelled by circumstance to legislate from the bench.

Most of the time, judges, such as federal court of appeals judges, who have a mandatory jurisdiction—who cannot pick and choose the cases they hear, as the U.S. Supreme Court does—really are engaged in objective, ideology-free decision making. This may seem counterintuitive. One might think that only if the outcome of an appeal were uncertain would the party that had lost in the trial court bother to appeal. And those would tend to be cases in which the conventional tools of judicial decision making could not resolve the appeal—cases in what I call the "open area." But in fact many cases are appealed that can be and are resolved by conventional legal analysis. The reasons are various: many plaintiffs have no lawyer; many, being emotionally invested in their case, have lost perspective; many are represented by lawyers who are not highly competent (sometimes who are downright incompetent), or are overcommitted and as a result do not devote adequate time to each of their cases, or who have identified with their client and lost perspective or are insufficiently experienced in the area of law that the case involves. Many litigants have nothing to lose by appealing though little to gain. Many have a lot to gain if they win, little chance of winning, but also little to lose in the way of wasted expense by appealing, so that on balance the expected benefit of appealing is positive. Many have strategic reasons to appeal even if they know the appeal is hopeless. And often parties lose in the trial court because of a clear mistake committed by a busy judge; but since defending an appeal is usually pretty inexpensive, the winner in the trial court is more likely to defend the appeal than to throw in the towel; additional reasons are that hope springs eternal (most decisions are affirmed) and that the trial-court judge may be angry if the lawyer for the winning party refuses to defend the judge's decision in the appellate court. Finally, because judicial opinions are often vague or opaque, the law governing an appeal may be clear to the judges but not to the litigants or even their lawyers. In fact lawyers find it difficult to get inside the head of an appellate judge, a problem I address when I discuss appellate advocacy in Chapter 8.

Because most appeals to federal courts of appeals can be decided satisfactorily by straightforward application of known and definite law to the facts of the case, and because most trial judges and intermediate appellate judges take seriously their role as modest law appliers—but also because it takes less time and effort to dispose of a case by application of known law to fact than by forging new law—federal court of appeals judges most of the time do decide appeals formalistically. But it is not always possible. The reasons include the absence of disciplined legislative processes in the American governmental system, as a result of which legislation is often insolubly ambiguous; the difficulty of amending the Constitution and the resulting pressure on federal courts to engage in loose interpretation of it (which, realistically, means making constitutional law); and the breadth of explicitly judge-made law (common law—both state common law, which federal judges frequently must opine on because of the diversity jurisdiction, and federal common law, which federal judges make up). Other reasons the judges can't be just law appliers are the complexity and confusion engendered by a stratified legal system (state statutory law, state common law, state constitutional law, federal statutory law, federal common law, federal constitutional law), and the limitations of human foresight and language. Moreover, playing a legislative as well as a conventionally judicial role as understood in most legal systems outside the Anglo-American sphere is more congenial to judges in a system, such as ours, of lateral entry than it would be in a career judiciary. A lawyer who becomes a judge after another legal career is less likely to kowtow to rules of doubtful soundness than a lawyer who started to climb the judicial ladder right out of law school and learned, as in any bureaucracy, to please his superiors by following rules rather than by bending or replacing them.

The cases in which judges play a legislative role yield the decisions that shape the law. They are not only the most important and most interesting cases but also the most challenging ones. How do they (do we) decide them? What is the predominant judicial approach? What is the best approach?

There is no uniform approach. But there is a spectrum, bounded by extreme formalism at one end and extreme realism at the other, along which American judges can be located. Most federal court of appeals judges cluster in the central portion of the spectrum, with some leaning toward formalism and others toward realism, but none, or very few, being all one thing or all the other. Indeed realism includes formalism as a special case— formalism is the realistic approach to many cases.

The Formalist Judge

I begin with the committed formalist court of appeals judge. He (or she, of course, but "he" as I use it should be understood as unmarked for gender) is, like most American judges, a lateral entrant into the judicial profession. He became a court of appeals judge in early middle age following a career in a law firm or a prosecutor's office, or, less commonly, as a law professor. He may have been a federal district judge for several years but he would have had a nonjudicial career before that. As a practitioner in a law firm or government legal office he would have been operating in a hierarchical environment in which the drafting of briefs and other legal documents was delegated to junior members of the office, often first-year associates. The first draft would be carefully edited by more senior lawyers in the firm, but by the time a member of the firm was ready for a judicial appointment it would have been years since he had written a first draft or even closely edited one—the principal editing was being done by lawyers junior to him. He was an executive, a supervisor, a recruiter of clients, not a writer or even an editor.

His years in practice had habituated him to the conventional norms of the practice of law, which had changed little in centuries (indeed, in millennia). He was accustomed to regard (or at least to pretend to regard) the law as a given and the lawyer's task as applying the law to the particular facts of a case. Judges—mysterious, remote, and, especially if they were federal judges and therefore enjoyed life tenure, almost impossible to court or to intimidate—were to be treated deferentially, and to be assumed to be engaged in a technical, almost an algorithmic, task of law application. Of course some judges were known to be indolent, biased, or "result oriented," but briefing and argument assumed the judge's competence and neutrality, lest the judge feel disrespected. (Notice the tension between assuming that judges are truly disinterested appliers of the law and fearing they'll retaliate against lawyers who don't treat them deferentially.) The judge was assumed to be thoroughly comfortable with—indeed to inhabit—legal jargon, to be knowledgeable about the legal doctrines involved in the cases appealed to him, to have mastered the facts and the commercial or other transaction or activity out of which the case had arisen, to have firm expectations with respect to the style and tone of briefs and arguments, and to be a stickler about format, grammar, spelling, page limits, and citation form, as well as to expect the utmost deference from the lawyers. (The lawyers stand throughout their argument to the court; the judge or judges sit.) If a judge asked a question at argument, and, before the lawyer could answer, the light on the lawyer's podium flashed red, signifying the expiration of the allotted time for the lawyer's argument, he would be expected to ask the judge whether he could answer the question despite having run out of time.[1] The great Learned Hand (not a formalist, however) had famously

---

1. When lawyers ask me that at argument, I used to tell them peevishly that I would not have asked the question had I not wanted it answered. Failing to break their habit (it is *so* hard to change lawyers' habits), I gave up and now answer their question with "yes" or "please."

thrown a brief filed by John Marshall Harlan (when Harlan was a practic-ing lawyer) at him during oral argument because the brief exceeded the Second Circuit's page limit. Hand also liked to swivel his chair 180 degrees when displeased with a lawyer arguing a case before him, thus presenting his back to the lawyer—a rudeness of simian proportions.

The judge's task was understood, as I said, to be the application of law to facts, and the law was to be found in authoritative texts—statutes and other enactments, and judicial decisions. The judge would be assumed to be in quest of "right answers," and the feasibility of the quest was assumed. The lawyer's task was to persuade the judge that, properly interpreted, the authoritative materials yielded the answer that favored the lawyer's client to any legal question presented by the case.

Sophisticated lawyers know better—know that in many cases, and those usually the most important ones, matters aren't that simple. But they are reluctant to allow that knowledge to show in their briefs or oral argu-ments. Effective advocacy is thought to require the lawyer to maintain an elaborate decorum, a sense of propriety of argument based on acceptance of judicial pretensions to neutrality and objectivity. But the norms of advo-cacy are established by the judges, and systemic defects in advocacy are therefore largely attributable to the judges.

The judge appointed to a federal court of appeals from a practice envi-ronment is likely to think that what mainly had changed as a result of his career change is that it is now his task to decide which side's lawyer has done the more persuasive job of applying the law according to the conven-tions of legal analysis. A lawyer is a practicing lawyer one day and a judge the next. As there is no transition, it is natural for the lawyer newly ap-pointed a judge to continue in his accustomed analytical groove. The law-yers offer their competing interpretations of the relevant authoritative texts (statutes, precedents, etc.) and the judge chooses between them. His role is umpireal. He has graduated from contestant to referee. As John Roberts famously (or notoriously) said in his Supreme Court confirmation hearing, the role of a judge, even a Supreme Court Justice, is to call balls and strikes, not to pitch or bat.[2] Cabined by the facts and arguments pre-

2. *Confirmation Hearing on the Nomination of John G. Roberts, Jr. to Be Chief Jus-tice of the United States: Hearing before the Senate Committee on the Judiciary*, 109th

sented by the parties, the judge matches them to the authoritative materials of judicial decision making, such as constitutional and legislative text and the holdings of previous decisions that count as precedents.

The judge may realize that the statutory language applicable to a particular case is hopelessly vague, the legislators' intentions inscrutable, the precedents distinguishable or in conflict, the facts uncertain. But he will strive to resolve indeterminate-seeming cases not by making a legislative judgment but by invoking higher-level rules (rules, some of which I discussed briefly in the last chapter, for resolving disputes over the scope or meaning of a rule), such as a rule requiring deference to a statutory interpretation by the administrative agency charged with enforcing the statute, or a rule disfavoring summary judgment in cases involving issues of intent, or a rule that waivers of sovereign immunity should be construed narrowly, or rules commanding deference to evidentiary rulings by trial judges and to verdicts by juries. The judge thereby minimizes the occasions on which he has to base a decision on his own notions of a sensible resolution of the case, notions that would not produce a "right answer" by reference either to an authoritative text or to the assignment of primary decision-making authority to another tribunal. The formalist judge is loath to base decision on the theories or empirical findings of social scientists; that would strike him as going "outside" the law. Nor would he be adept in using such materials, because they would not have figured largely in his career as a practitioner.

The umpireal conception of the judge breeds the passivity that I noted in earlier chapters. He is paid to look and listen, to choose between contestants. The lawyers make the factual record, make the legal arguments. Legislators, the drafters of constitutions, administrative agencies, and higher and earlier judges make the rules. The judge is an applier of rules made by others to facts generated by others in a contest between others.

To a formalist judge, a "learned," a "scholarly," judicial opinion summarizes the decision of the lower court and the parties' arguments on ap-

---

Cong., Senate Hearing 158, p. 56 (2005). If confirmation hearings were serious inquiries into a candidate's fitness rather than a low form of political theater, Roberts's statement would have been disqualifying.

peal, recites in detail the facts to which the law is to be applied, specifies and explicates the applicable higher-level rules (such as the standard of appellate review), elaborates upon those and other doctrinal materials by copious reference to and quotation of authoritative texts, applies the rules extracted from these materials to each of the nonfrivolous arguments made by the parties, proliferates footnotes in which to place qualifications and discuss side issues (thus striving for completeness), insists on the unquestionable correctness of the decision announced in his opinion, exhibits the specialized vocabulary of the law ("the instant case," *"eiusdem generis,"* "case of first impression," "totality of circumstances," "inferior court," "nexus," etc.) even when synonyms in ordinary English are readily available ("this case," "of the same kind," "novel case," "relevant considerations," "district court" or "lower court," "connection"), conforms scrupulously to the format prescribed for citations by the applicable form book, and maintains a dry, formal, dignified, solemn, elevated, "official" style throughout, eschewing contractions and colloquialisms (and please, no hint of wit—and no maps or pictures!).

And if he encounters an argument that can't be resolved to his satisfaction by reference to authoritative texts or settled second-order rules—that inescapably requires a policy judgment—he will resort to armchair empiricism in lieu of social-scientific analysis, as in *Harrington v. Richter,*[3] which raised the bar for state prisoners seeking federal habeas corpus relief. One question presented by the appeal was whether the state court, in denying relief, should have given some explanation of its reasons—in other words, written an opinion. In the absence of an opinion (which would not have had to be long, or formal, or published), the federal court to which the prisoner had turned after losing in the state court could have no idea whether that court had based its decision on an unreasonable application of U.S. Supreme Court precedents, in which event federal habeas corpus would entitle the prisoner to a new trial or failing that to release from prison.[4] But to the argument that therefore state courts would be encouraged not to

3. 131 S. Ct. 770 (2011).
4. 28 U.S.C. § 2254(d)(1).

write opinions when affirming criminal convictions, because that would make it difficult for the prisoner to obtain federal habeas corpus, the Court responded that

> opinion-writing practices in state courts are influenced by consid-
> erations other than avoiding scrutiny by collateral attack in federal
> court. Cf. *In re Robbins*, . . . 959 P. 2d 311, 316, n. 1 ([Cal.] 1998) (state
> procedures limiting habeas are "a means of protecting the integrity
> of our own appeal and habeas corpus process," rather than a device
> for "insulating our judgments from federal court review" (emphasis
> deleted)). At the same time, requiring a statement of reasons could
> undercut state practices designed to preserve the integrity of the case-
> law tradition. The issuance of summary dispositions in many collat-
> eral attack cases can enable a state judiciary to concentrate its re-
> sources on the cases where opinions are most needed.[5]

The statement quoted from the California Supreme Court is self-serving, unrealistic about human nature—especially judicial human nature in states in which judges are elected and so cannot afford to be thought "soft on crime"[6]—and unsubstantiated. To give credence to such a statement, as the U.S. Supreme Court did, is indicative of a weak sense of fact. Frivolous cases, or cases presenting grounds that have already been rejected, can usu-ally be decided without a statement of reasons. But *Richter* was not such a

5. 131 S. Ct. at 784.

6. There is abundant evidence that elected judges lean strongly against crimi-nal defendants, especially near election time. See, for example, Carlos Berdejó and Noam Yuchtman, "Crime, Punishment, and Politics: An Analysis of Political Cycles in Criminal Sentencing" (forthcoming in *Review of Economics and Statistics*); Herbert M. Kritzer, "Law Is the Mere Continuation of Politics by Different Means: American Judicial Selection in the Twenty-first Century," 56 *DePaul Law Review* 423, 461–465 (2007); Paul R. Brace and Melinda Gann Hall, "The Interplay of Preferences, Case Facts, Context, and Rules in the Politics of Judicial Choice," 59 *Journal of Politics* 1206, 1221, 1223 (1997); Stephen B. Bright and Patrick J. Keenan, "Judges and the Pol-itics of Death: Deciding between the Bill of Rights and the Next Election in Capital Cases," 75 *Boston University Law Review* 759, 792–796 (1995).

case; "the integrity of the case-law tradition" requires the issuance of opinions in nonfrivolous cases, since case law consists of rules and standards stated in or inferred from judicial opinions; and no showing was made that if compelled to write opinions in nonfrivolous cases the California courts would be overwhelmed.

Richter quotes from an earlier statement that "federal habeas review of state convictions frustrates both the States' sovereign power to punish offenders and their good-faith attempts to honor constitutional rights."[7] But the state has no "sovereign power" to punish offenders by procedures that violate the Constitution. Even more puzzling is the notion that federal habeas corpus "frustrates" states' "good-faith attempts to honor constitutional rights." If a trial court denies a constitutional challenge and the appellate court reverses, how does this frustrate the trial court's attempt to honor constitutional rights? It wasn't attempting hard enough, at least in the appellate court's view. Why for that matter is good faith the point? Even judges whose good faith is not questioned are often reversed, simply because they made a mistake or a higher court has a different take on the case. The practical reason for extending federal habeas corpus to convicted persons (an extension without basis in the historical understanding of habeas corpus) is that the federal constitutional rights of state criminal defendants have been created for the most part not by the framers of the Constitution but by the U.S. Supreme Court. Most of the Bill of Rights "applies" to state action only by virtue of the Court's strained interpretation of the due process clause of the Fourteenth Amendment. (It is strained because in the Bill of Rights itself "due process of law" is merely one clause of one of ten constitutional amendments.) It is natural for state judges, who had no part in the creation of what amounts to a detailed federal code of criminal procedure applicable to state prosecutions, to take a narrower view of criminals' rights than the Court does—especially elected state judges.[8]

7. 131 S. Ct. at 787, 787, quoting *Calderon v. Thompson,* 523 U.S. 538, 555–556 (1998).

8. See Berdejó and Yuchtman, "Crime, Punishment, and Politics"; Kritzer, "Politics by Different Means"; Brace and Hall, "The Interplay of Preferences"; Bright and Keenan, "Judges and the Politics of Death."

The aim of the formalist judge is to appear not to legislate from the bench, and is achieved, or at least furthered, by deploying the kind of evasive rhetoric that one finds in *Richter,* as in decisions at all levels of the judiciary. The judge may know in his heart of hearts that formalist methods don't work in cases in which neither the orthodox materials of decision nor the higher-level rules for filling gaps in those materials point to a "correct" outcome. But he will decide the case somehow because a judge's inescapable duty is to decide. When the orthodox materials of judicial decision making run out, life experience, personal-identity characteristics such as race and sex, temperament, ideology (often influenced by personal-identity characteristics, religion, and party loyalties), ideas of sound public policy whether or not ideologically inflected, considerations of administrability and workload, moral beliefs, collegial pressures, public opinion, family background, reading, sentiment and aversions, even indifference, will fill the void. The outcome in *Richter* is more plausibly explained by the hostility of conservative judges to collateral attacks on criminal convictions (that is, attacks mounted after the conviction has been upheld on appeal or has otherwise become final), and the affront to state sovereignty (power) that collateral attacks of state convictions in federal courts present, than by the reasons given in the opinion.

Yet nowadays references to social policy, economic efficiency or welfare, and judicial economy and administrability are considered legitimate by most judges and Justices. Even formalists acknowledge the legitimacy of bringing policy considerations to bear in cases in which the judge can't escape having to make a choice, rather than being compelled to a result by a force akin to logic. We shall see in Chapter 7 even Justice Scalia—the arch-formalist of statutory and constitutional interpretation—foundering in his efforts to ground interpretation in an "objective" methodology of purely semantic analysis with heavy emphasis on dictionary definitions. The modern formalist acknowledges such low-level practical concerns as whether correcting a minor error is worth prolonging an already protracted proceeding or whether a rule regulating police conduct, say, will be too complicated for the police to administer. Even formalist judges need and acknowledge tiebreakers when the formalist algorithms give out.

So modern formalism is better described as a tendency than as a dogma. It is a tendency constantly veering into absurdity. Consider the judicial elaboration of the sensible rule that debts "for willful and malicious injury by the debtor to another entity or to the property of another entity" cannot be discharged in bankruptcy.[9] So a con man ordered to pay restitution to his victims may not escape the obligation by declaring bankruptcy. But that is an extreme cases; to decide less extreme ones the courts have to assign meaning to the term "willful and malicious." Doubtless it should cover criminal activity and intentional torts but exclude torts of simple negligence; whether it should include torts involving reckless conduct is uncertain. I can't think of what more can usefully be said to flesh out the term "willful and malicious."

But judges will not leave well enough alone. They are determined to elaborate the statutory term, as in the examples of "serious bodily injury" and "proximate cause," discussed in the last chapter. The Second Circuit for example has defined the word "malicious" in the term "willful and malicious" as "wrongful and without just cause or excuse, even in the absence of personal hatred, spite, or ill-will."[10] The Fifth Circuit equates "willful and malicious injury" to "either an objective substantial certainty of harm or a subjective motive to cause harm."[11] The Sixth Circuit used to define "willful" to mean "deliberate or intentional," and "malicious" to mean "in conscious disregard of one's duties or without just cause or excuse; it does not require ill-will or specific intent to do harm."[12] But after the Supreme Court held in *Kawaauhau v. Geiger*,[13] resolving the doubt I noted, that recklessness was not "willful and malicious" within the meaning of the Bankruptcy Code, the Sixth Circuit, without retracting its earlier definition, said

9. 11 U.S.C. § 523(a)(6).

10. *Ball v. A.O. Smith Corp.*, 451 F.3d 66, 69 (2d Cir. 2006), quoting *Navistar Financial Corp. v. Stelluti*, 94 F.3d 84, 87 (2d Cir. 1996).

11. *Williams v. International Brotherhood of Electrical Workers, Local 520*, 337 F.3d 504, 509 (5th Cir. 2003), quoting *Miller v. J.D. Abrams, Inc.*, 156 F.3d 598, 603 (5th Cir. 1998).

12. *Wheeler v. Laudani*, 783 F.2d 610, 615 (6th Cir. 1986).

13. 523 U.S. 57 (1998).

that the debtor "must will or desire harm, or believe injury is substantially certain to occur as a result of his behavior."[14] The Eleventh Circuit continues to use a formula almost identical to that in the Sixth Circuit's earlier opinion: "'Malicious' means wrongful and without just cause or excessive even in the absence of personal hatred, spite or ill-will. To establish malice, a showing of specific intent to harm another is not necessary."[15] The Seventh Circuit had quoted the Sixth Circuit's original formula approvingly,[16] but had not revisited the issue after the Supreme Court's *Kawaauhau* decision until 2012, in a decision I discuss below.[17]

The Eighth Circuit deems conduct "malicious" only if it is "certain or almost certain . . . to cause harm."[18] The Ninth Circuit requires for willfulness a showing "either that the debtor had a subjective motive to inflict the injury *or* that the debtor believed that injury was substantially certain to occur as a result of his conduct," while "a 'malicious' injury involves '(1) a wrongful act, (2) done intentionally, (3) which necessarily causes injury, and (4) is done without just cause or excuse.'"[19] The Tenth Circuit has fused "willful" and "malicious," saying that "willful" means "the debtor must 'desire . . . [to cause] the consequences of his act or . . . believe [that] the consequences are substantially certain to result from it,'"[20] while "malicious" requires "proof 'that the debtor either intend the resulting injury or intentionally take action that is substantially certain to cause the injury.'"[21]

Notice the redundancies—"deliberate and intentional," "objective . . .

14. *Markowitz v. Campbell*, 190 F.3d 455, 465 n. 10 (6th Cir. 1999).

15. *Maxfield v. Jennings*, 670 F.3d 1329, 1334 (11th Cir. 2012) (per curiam) (internal quotations and citations omitted).

16. See *In re Thirtyacre*, 36 F.3d 697, 700 (7th Cir. 1994).

17. See *Jendusa-Nicolai v. Larsen*, 677 F.3d 320 (7th Cir. 2012).

18. *Fischer v. Scarborough*, 171 F.3d 638, 643 (8th Cir. 1999), quoting *Johnson v. Miera*, 926 F.2d 741, 743–44 (8th Cir. 1991).

19. *Petralia v. Jercich*, 238 F.3d 1202, 1208–09 (9th Cir. 2001) (emphasis in original).

20. *Panalis v. Moore*, 357 F.3d 1125, 1129 (10th Cir. 2004), quoting *Mitsubishi Motor Credit of America, Inc. v. Longley*, 235 B.R. 651, 657 (10th Cir. BAP 1999), quoting in turn *Restatement (Second) of Torts*, § 8A (1965).

21. Id., quoting *Hope v. Walker*, 48 F.3d 1161, 1164 (11th Cir. 1995).

certainty,"[22] "subjective motive," "will or desire," "wrongful act . . . done without just cause or excuse." Notice the ambiguity of a phrase like "specific intent to do harm"—how does that differ from "intent to do harm," the latter being required by the *Kawaauhau* decision? And what does "*necessarily* causes injury" mean? (Certain to cause injury? But why would that be required?) And is "objective substantial certainty of harm" really intended to substitute for intent to harm, or is the point rather that if harm was certain to result we disbelieve that it was inflicted accidentally?

Notice that the Eighth Circuit, in defining "malicious" as "certain or almost certain . . . to cause harm," confused a state of mind (malice) with the consequence of an act (harm). Notice finally that each federal court of appeals has been content to go its own way, without attempting to reconcile its verbal formulas with those of the other circuits.[23] With the baroque complexity of the formulas that I've been quoting compare the simplicity of the following definition in a recent opinion: "a willful and malicious injury, precluding discharge in bankruptcy of the debt created by the injury, is one that the injurer inflicted knowing he had no legal justification and either desiring to inflict the injury or knowing it was highly likely to result from his act. To allow him to shirk liability by discharging his judgment debt in those circumstances would undermine the deterrent efficacy of tort law without serving any policy that might be thought to inform bankruptcy law."[24]

Verbosity masquerading as precision is well illustrated by a test enunciated by one of the courts of appeals for when government can be held liable for depriving a person of life, liberty, or property without due process of law by placing the person in a position of danger: "To make out a proper danger creation claim, a plaintiff must demonstrate that (1) the

---

22. Certainty *is* objective; "subjective certainty" is an oxymoron—the proper term is "certitude," which means confidence, often misplaced, in the correctness of one's belief.

23. Another example of gratuitous judicial verbosity yielding inconsistent legal standards is discussed in *Nightingale Home Healthcare, Inc. v. Anodyne Therapy, LLC,* 626 F.3d 958 (7th Cir. 2010).

24. *Jendusa-Nicolai v. Larsen,* 677 F.3d at 324.

charged state entity and the charged individual actors created the danger or increased plaintiff's vulnerability to the danger in some way; (2) plaintiff was a member of a limited and specifically definable group; (3) defendants' conduct put plaintiff at substantial risk of serious, immediate, and proximate harm; (4) the risk was obvious or known; (5) defendants acted recklessly in conscious disregard of that risk; and (6) such conduct, when viewed in total, is conscience shocking."[25]

Notice in this formula—a common result of legal verbosity—the contradiction in stating that the risk can be "obvious" rather than "known" but that the defendant must act in "conscious disregard" of it, which entails knowing that there is a risk. Notice the confusion injected by requiring that the defendant not only have acted recklessly, but have shocked the conscience—whatever that means. The expression has been part of the legal lexicon at least since 1804,[26] and was picked up by the Supreme Court a half century later,[27] though its first modern appearance, and its most influential, was in Justice Frankfurter's opinion for the Supreme Court in *Rochin v. California*,[28] where he used the phrase to classify a police search for illegal drugs by means of a stomach pump as a violation of due process. I don't know what the expression means, or what it adds to indifference to a known risk of injury.

It should be quite enough, eschewing the jargon of "proximate harm" and "conscious disregard" and "conscience shocking," to say that government employees acting within the scope of their employment violate the due process clause when they commit a reckless act that causes injury, provided that the act is directed at or with reference to the victim (or a group to which the victim belongs) rather than being an allocative judgment that results in injury, as where the judgment of the police in allocating more police resources to one part of town than to another part is challenged. Without the qualification that liability does not extend to allocative judgments federal judges would become deeply involved in the allocation of

25. *Currier v. Doran*, 242 F.3d 905, 918 (10th Cir. 2001).
26. See *Coles v. Trecothick*, 9 Ves. Jun. 234, 246 (Ch. 1804).
27. See *Byers v. Surget*, 60 U.S. 303, 311 (1856).
28. 342 U.S. 165, 172, 173 (1952).

public funds and services. Lacking any guidance in the Constitution to making such judgments, they would be at large, usurping traditional legislative and executive functions. Yet the test that I quoted from the *Currier* opinion, despite its six components, leaves out the qualification.

The Realist Judge

Let me elaborate slightly on the definition of the realist judge that I offered in the Introduction. Such a judge understands the limitations of formalist analysis, does not (a related point) have a "judicial philosophy" that generates outcomes in particular cases, wants judicial decisions to "make sense" in a way that could be explained convincingly to a layperson, and is a "loose constructionist," which means he believes that interpretation should be guided by a sense of the purpose of the text (contract, statute, regulation, constitutional provision) being interpreted, if the purpose is discernible, rather than by the literal meaning of the text if purpose and literal meaning are at odds with one another. The realist judge has a distaste for legal jargon and wants judicial opinions, as far as possible, to be readable by nonlawyers, wants to get as good a handle as possible on the likely consequences of a decision one way or the other, has an acute sense of the plasticity of American law, is acutely conscious too of the manifold weaknesses of the American judicial system and wants to do what he can to improve it. He does not draw a sharp line between law and policy, between judging and legislating, and between legal reasoning and common sense. Realism, like formalism, has implications for the language and structure of the judicial opinion and not merely for outcome, but I largely reserve discussion of those implications for Chapter 8.

When Holmes said that "general propositions do not decide concrete cases. The decision will depend on a judgment or intuition more subtle than any articulate major premise,"[29] he was exaggerating in order to vivify the proposition that legal principles tend to be stated with a generality that transcends the circumstances of the particular case. That generality is nec-

29. *Lochner v. New York*, 198 U.S. 45, 76 (1905) (dissenting opinion).

essary not only to provide guidance for future disputants but also and relatedly because we instinctively think of particulars as instantiations of generalities. But there is danger in appealing to generalities to decide cases. A human being is an animal, but a sign forbidding animals in a restaurant should not be interpreted to ban humans. One cannot safely apply a rule on the basis of its grammatical structure and the meaning of the words that compose it; one has to have a sense of what the rule is concerned with. The realist tries to dispel ambiguity by digging beneath the semantic surface of the applicable rule for the practical considerations that motivated its adoption, and then by restating the rule in a modern idiom and with a clear indication of the rule's limits as derived from its purpose. Most legal rules, provided they are not allowed to balloon to their semantic outer limits, have at least a kernel of practical sense. Finding and exhibiting that kernel (and maybe limiting the rule to it) is a goal of realist analysis.

When legislative purpose (including the purposes behind constitutional provisions, a form of legislation) is discernible, the realist judge is an interpreter or perhaps a helper. But often it is not discernible, and then the judge is the legislator and has to base decision on his conception of sound public policy within the limits the legislators have set. And when that is the case the judge must, like other legislators, consider among other things the likely consequences of a decision one way or the other. I don't agree with Justice Scalia that indifference to hundreds of deaths that might result from the Supreme Court's embracing a broad interpretation of the Second Amendment is the sign of a good judge.[30] If deaths are a consequence of deciding a case one way rather than another, that's something for the judge to consider along with the other consequences. The main reason for dissatisfaction with the limited facticity of the typical judicial proceeding—with its heavy emphasis on live testimony, its ungrounded faith in the ability of judges or jurors to determine "credibility" from the body language and voice tones and hesitations of a witness,[31] and its discomfort with empirical methodology—is that the way in which litigation processes and presents

30. *District of Columbia v. Heller,* 554 U.S. 570, 634–635 (2008). I discuss the *Heller* decision in Chapter 7.

31. See note 33 and accompanying text.

facts makes it difficult for judges to gauge the consequences of deciding a case one way or the other when the unavailability or inadequacy of legalist methods of decision making makes consequences a proper consideration for the judge—as it does in a great many cases.

A nonjudge asked to resolve a dispute between two people will seek a "reasonable" resolution in a sense shaped by notions that he would be likely to call fairness, common sense, or customary understandings. A realist judge is likely to approach a case in much the same way but with a sharper focus on consequences in order to discipline his thought, including systemic consequences that would not occur to a layperson. Those consequences, as I noted in the Introduction, include the effect a decision is likely to have on the stability of legal rules and decisions and on legislators' thought processes if judges ignore clearly written statutes without having a compelling reason to do so; for then legislators won't know what they're legislating—they'll merely be producing putty for the judges to shape. "Knowledge of objectives is helpful, often vital, in interpreting and applying rules. But objectives must not be confused with criteria. Where certainty is at a premium, sound law-making requires the setting forth of clear and definite criteria rather than a general directive to decide each case in the manner that will maximize the attainment of the law's objectives. The latter approach, carried to the extreme, would reduce all law to an admonition to do what's right."[32]

The consequences of judicial action are often difficult to predict. But attention to consequences has disciplinary force, slowing the rush to an emotional judgment. It also motivates judges, aided by lawyers and social scientists, to investigate consequences systematically. Judges' belief that they don't make law dulls their critical faculties, even as the slow pace of legal change (a consequence of trying to maintain stability in law) locks obsolete legal doctrines in place too long.

Responsible realist judges who acknowledge and embrace a legislative function for the judiciary will confine its exercise to areas not only in which formalist methods fall short, but which judges understand. They

---

32. *Herrmann v. Cencom Cable Associates, Inc.*, 999 F.2d 223, 226 (7th Cir. 1993).

must avoid the temptation to legislate from the bench in a field about which they know little, whether the field is gun control, legislative apportionment, the administration of public schools, or campaign finance. These are examples of areas in which a dose of "judicial self-restraint" would be salutary (see Chapter 6).

Legislating from the bench should be distinguished from careful, even aggressive, appellate review of decisions by lower courts and especially decisions by administrative agencies. A strong norm of deference to the decisions of administrative agencies is the fossil remnant of an era in which judges were excessively hostile to agencies and in which "progressives" had boundless faith in the potential of agencies as agents of reform. The progressives prevailed in the New Deal. Deferential standards of appellate review of agency decisions, such as "substantial evidence" and "abuse of discretion," ensued and persist, producing many injustices. First-line decision makers, including the judicial officers and review boards of administrative agencies, often do have significant advantages over reviewing judges in knowledge of technical fields. But it is unrealistic for appellate judges to accord the same deference to decisions of immigration and social security judges, each of whom conducts hundreds of hearings a year, as to administrative law judges of the National Labor Relations Board, who conduct far fewer hearings. We judges see the differences in the opinions. (We also see many more social security and immigration opinions than opinions of other agencies, which may have given some of us an unduly jaundiced view of the administrative process.) Must we ignore the differences and accord equal deference to all administrative decisions? The realist judge thinks not. The realist judge thinks that deference is earned, not bestowed.

No legal catchphrase is more often repeated than that determinations by a trial judge (or jury) whether to believe or disbelieve a witness can be overturned on appeal only in extraordinary circumstances. The reason is said to be the inestimable value, in assessing credibility, of seeing and hearing the witness rather than reading a transcript of his testimony, since the transcript eliminates clues to veracity that are supplied by tone of voice, hesitation, body language, and other nonverbal expression. This is one of those commonsense propositions that may well be false.[33] Nonverbal clues to veracity are unreliable and distract a trier of fact (or other observer) from the cognitive content of the witness's testimony. Yet it would occur to few judges to question the proposition that the trial judge has superior ability to judge credibility than the appellate judge, because nothing in the culture of the law encourages its insiders to be skeptical of oft-repeated propositions accepted as the age-old wisdom of the profession, and because appellate judges (indeed all judges) usually are happy to hand off responsi-

33. See Michael J. Saks, "Enhancing and Restraining Accuracy in Adjudication," 51 *Law and Contemporary Problems*, Autumn 1988, pp. 243, 263–264. The frequent unreliability of the evidence on which judges and jurors rely is the subject of a large literature. See Amina Memon, Aldert Vrij, and Ray Bull, *Psychology and Law: Truthfulness, Accuracy and Credibility* (2d ed. 2003); Scott Rempell, "Gauging Credibility in Immigration Proceedings: Immaterial Inconsistencies, Demeanor, and the Rule of Reason" 25 *Georgetown Immigration Law Journal* 377 (2011); D. Michael Risinger and Jeffrey L. Loop, "Three Card Monte, Monty Hall, Modus Operandi, and 'Offender Profiling:' Some Lessons of Modern Cognitive Science for the Law of Evidence," 24 *Cardozo Law Review* 193 (2002); Dale A. Nance, "Reliability and the Admissibility of Experts," 34 *Seton Hall Law* Review, 191 (2003); Edward J. Imwinkelried, "The Relativity of Reliability," 34 *Seton Hall Law Review* 269 (2003); Jonathan M. Golding et al., "Big Girls Don't Cry: The Effect of Child Witness Demeanor on Juror Decisions in a Child Sexual Abuse Trial," 227 *Child Abuse and Neglect* 1311 (2003); Peter J. Graham, "The Reliability of Testimony," 61 *Philosophy and Phenomenological Research* 695 (2000); Jeremy A. Blumenthal, "A Wipe of the Hands, A Lick of the Lips: The Validity of Demeanor Evidence in Assessing Witness Credibility," 72 *Nebraska Law Review* 1157 (1993; Olin Guy Wellborn III, "Demeanor," 76 *Cornell Law Review* 1075 (1991). As summarized by Max Minzer, "Detecting Lies Using Demeanor, Bias, and Context," 29 *Cardozo Law Review* 2557, 2566 (2007), "demeanor cues do not lead to accurate lie detection." Appellate judges' credulity about "demeanor cues" is of a piece with the credulity of many trial judges and jurors about eyewitness evidence, on which see, for example, Stuart Rabner, "Evaluating Eyewitness Identification Evidence in the 21st Century," 87 *New York University Law Review* 1249 (2012); Sandra Guerra Thompson, "Beyond a Reasonable Doubt? Reconsidering Uncorroborated Eyewitness Identification Testimony," 41 *UC Davis Law Review* 1487 (2008); Nancy Steblay et al., "Eyewitness Accuracy Rates in Police Showup and Lineup Presentations: A Meta-Analytic Comparison," 27 *Law and Human Behavior* 523 (2003).

bility for deciding to another adjudicator. No longer, however, are they technologically constrained to do so. Witnesses' testimony could be video-taped, and the videotapes of their testimony made available to an appellate judge who thought demeanor important in assessing the truthfulness of testimony.

Not that there aren't reasons for appellate deference to credibility de-terminations by the trier of fact, who spends much more time on a case than the appeals court does and so may have a better feel for the facts. And anyway the primary job of appellate courts is to repeat, restate, correct, and maintain uniformity of legal doctrines; correcting erroneous factual determinations is incidental to that primary responsibility. That is a good reason for deference but not as appealing a one as the dubious claim that trial judges are in a much better position to determine facts than appellate judges are.

The realist judge wants the law to be grounded in reality but also to conform as far as possible to lay intuitions. I can illustrate with a case in which a prison inmate was complaining that improper treatment in the im-mediate aftermath of his stroke amounted to cruel and unusual punish-ment.[34] To be permitted to bring a federal civil rights suit, an inmate has to exhaust "available" grievance procedures offered by the prison. The plain-tiff claimed that he'd been unable to file a timely grievance because of his stroke. The deadline for filing was sixty days from the date of the event giving rise to the grievance. The grievance procedures allowed for a late filing if "good cause" for its untimeliness was demonstrated, but did not define "good cause" and the state refused to concede that physical incapaci-tation was "good cause." But how could it not be? The implication if it were not would be that an inmate who was in a coma for the sixty days after the event giving rise to his claim would have failed to exhaust his prison remedies and so would be barred from access to a federal court. A layper-son would think it obvious that a prison remedy so cropped was not "avail-able" to the inmate. A judge should not dismiss the lay intuition out of hand as irrelevant to interpreting the term "available." So strong a lay intu-

34. *Hurst v. Hantke*, 634 F.3d 409 (7th Cir. 2011).

ition should require a lot of formalist gymnastics to overcome in the name of "the law."

There are two principal concerns about realism in judging. The first is that judges may be mistaken about the "real world," especially if asked to consider scientific, statistical, or otherwise technical data; they may be bamboozled. That is a danger, but one they can be armed against by proper training in the management of technical issues, which is different from having technical expertise; I address that matter in later chapters. The second concern is that the law will be less predictable if it is at the whim of changing understandings of the real world. This concern is groundless. Think back to the case *(United States v. Seiver)*, discussed in the last chapter, on deletion of pornographic materials from personal computers. If the rule adopted in that case, which would eliminate "staleness" and "collector status" as criteria for a warrant to search a computer for evidence of receipt, possession, or distribution of child pornography, catches on, the decision will have established a precedent to guide future cases. The precedent will stand until and unless changes in law or technology make it obsolete. No greater certainty can reasonably be expected of law. Law must change as technology changes.

Advice to New Appellate Judges

I have gone on at length about the differences between formalist and realist judges, but most federal judges nowadays, at all levels, are as I said hybrids even though their realism tends to be hidden by formalist rhetoric.[35] And much of the advice that might be imparted to new federal court of appeals judges on how to approach decision making would be independent of the mixture of the formalist and the realist in their judicial outlook. For example, I am convinced that a court of appeals judge who has never been a trial judge should volunteer to conduct trials, including jury trials, in the district

35. "Perhaps we have good Realist reasons to be skeptical about the surface of judicial opinions, with their feigned supine posture before the force of the law and legal reasoning." Brian Leiter, "In Praise of Reason (and Against 'Nonsense' Jurisprudence)," 100 *Georgetown Law Journal* 865, 877 (2012).

courts of his circuit from time to time. An appellate judge who lacks a trial-court judge's perspective on the litigation process will be handicapped in reviewing rulings by district judges. Not understanding the context of such rulings, the appellate judge with no trial experience may give the rulings too much or too little weight.

Many judges can do better than they are doing in managing their law clerks.[36] The challenge of managing a tiny staff should not be too great for judges to overcome, although like other lawyers judges tend not to be very good managers. One thing too few judges do is ask their law clerks in advance of oral argument not only to read the briefs but also to make a preliminary study of the record, and if it is obvious that the decision will turn on key cases or statutory provisions to make sure the judge has copies of those critical materials to study before, and take with him to, the oral argument. The law clerks should also do background research, if time permits. A realist judge's law clerks should Google the parties and do other online research (see next chapter) to help them and their judge understand the parties, the commercial or scientific or other context of the case, and the activities of the parties or others that gave rise to the case.

Most judges assign only one of their law clerks to help them prepare for each oral argument, at which the judge would (in my court) hear either six or nine cases. That's a mistake. One clerk should take the lead, based on his background or interests, in preparing for discussion of the case, but all three or four should participate in the preparation and discussion. Their views may diverge in interesting ways helpful to the judge. And exposure to a wide range of cases increases the speed with which the clerks become familiar with a wide range of legal areas, making them better law clerks, making the job more interesting for them, and preparing them better for their careers as lawyers. But law clerks should not be required to write bench memos. That is time-consuming and reduces the time they have for research.

Because I don't think law clerks should write judicial opinions, it may

36. There is a helpful literature on law clerks. See, for example, besides the references in Chapter 2 of this book, Aliza Milner, *Judicial Clerkships: Legal Methods in Motion* (2011).

seem that I hold them in low esteem. Not at all. I regard them as invaluable, not only as researchers but as critics. I require my law clerks to call me by my first name despite the difference in our ages and status because I want them to be *entirely* candid and direct with me (brutally so if they want); I want them to treat me as an equal, not as a superior. If they think I'm wrong about something, I want them to tell me I'm wrong, with no pussy-footing. Often I *am* wrong, because my law clerks are very smart, and know things that I don't know; and because there are three of them and only one of me, so that they spend more time on each case than I do; and because their priors often are different from mine.

When formality prevails in a judge's office (his "chambers," as it is archaically termed—I call it my "office"), the law clerk is likely to try to anticipate the judge's reaction to a case, and to see his own role as that of defending the judge's take on the case. If he writes opinion drafts (as the vast majority of law clerks do nowadays, though not mine), they will be like lawyers' briefs; in effect they will be briefs in support of the judge's votes. The judge in a hurried post-argument conference with the other judges may cast his vote on the basis of an intuition, feeling unjustifiably confident by dint of experience (a common self-delusion, as psychologists have shown[37]), and if he is assigned to write the majority opinion his law clerks will scramble to make the best case they can for the outcome they've been told to justify.

Needless to say I think judges should eschew the "Becker model" of managing a judge's office, which I discuss at greater length in Chapter 8 along with the important distinction between management and managerialism. The Becker model interposes a senior law clerk between the judge and

37. David G. Myers, *Intuition: Its Powers and Perils* (2002); Lee D. Ross, "The Intuitive Psychologist and His Shortcomings: Distortions in the Attribution Process," 10 *Advances in Experimental Social Psychology* 173 (1977); Kenneth S. Bowers et al., "Intuition in the Context of Discovery," 22 *Cognitive Psychology* 72 (1990); Tony Bastick, *Intuition: How We Think and Act* (1982); Robert E. Nisbett and Lee Ross, *Human Inference: Strategies and Shortcomings of Social Judgment* (1980); Amos Tversky and Daniel Kahneman, "Extensional Versus Intuitive Reasoning: The Conjunction Fallacy in Probability Judgment," 90 *Psychological Review* 293 (1983).

the other law clerks, creating an unnecessarily hierarchical structure for so small a staff and diminishing the enthusiasm and contributions of the other clerks. I can see however how a weak judge would find the model irresistible, as it would provide him with in effect an assistant judge. Given the roughly 5,000 to 1 ratio of American lawyers to federal court of appeals judges, one might think it would be a rarity to appoint a weak judge, though some strong judges are bound to weaken with age. But federal judges are appointed by politicians, so a uniform high quality of appointees cannot be assumed—which is not to suggest, however, that a purely meritocratic system of selecting federal judges would be an improvement. I don't think it would be. It would sacrifice diversity of experience and insight and tend to create a judicial mandarinate that had too limited an understanding of the larger society.

A judge should be aggressive at oral argument. The prepared remarks of the lawyers rarely add much to what is in their briefs; only through questioning does the judge learn more about the case than he knows already. And tendentious questioning—questioning that indicates how the judge is leaning with regard to the merits of the appeal—is an important method of communication with the other judges on the panel. The deliberations that follow oral argument often are stilted. The judges speak in a prescribed order (junior to senior or senior to junior, depending on the court), and for the sake of collegiality often pull their punches in stating their view of how the case should be decided. Once a judge has indicated his vote in the case, even if tentatively, concern with saving face may induce him to adhere to the vote in the face of the arguments of the other judges, who moreover may be reluctant to press him to change his mind, fearing they'll offend him by doing so.

When trying to make up his mind about which way to vote, a judge should remind himself of his limitations (limitations that all judges have) —the limitations of his knowledge of the law, the limitations of his knowledge of the case at hand, the limitations of his knowledge of the real-world context of the case, and the limitations (or distortions) of his thinking that result from the biases that all judges bring to judging. Not that it is wrong, let alone possible, to judge without biases. The neutral term is "priors"—

the expectations, formed by background, experience, and temperament, that every decision maker brings to a dispute that he is asked to resolve. My colleagues and I read the same briefs, hear the same oral argument, yet sometimes react quite differently, either because of different priors, which can dominate the posterior probability (the probability one attaches to a decision one way or another after gathering evidence), or because of different weightings of the same evidence.

A judge must try to be aware of his priors, so that they do not exert an excessive influence on his decisions. The judge might have a soft spot for animals, and for environmental values generally; for the police; for paramedics; for asylum seekers; for people with serious mental illnesses; and for marginal religious sects. He may have a range of antipathies as well, such as to the Internal Revenue Service or insurance companies (these were common judicial antipathies when I first became a judge, though I didn't share them and neither do my current colleagues), litigious people, hypersensitive people, and people consumed by *pleonexia*—Aristotle's word for wanting more than one's due. Through self-awareness and discipline a judge can learn not to allow his sympathies or antipathies to influence his judicial votes—unduly. But the qualification in "unduly" needs to be emphasized. Many judges would say that nothing outside "the law," in the narrow sense that confines the word to the texts of formal legal documents, influences *their* judicial votes at all. Some of them are speaking for public consumption, and know better. Those who are speaking sincerely are fooling themselves.

Formalists like to say that realists go outside law in deciding cases. That is question begging. It assumes that law is what formalists understand by the word. Not so; whatever judges do within their jurisdiction is law[38]— whether good or bad law is a different question.

38. This was Hans Kelsen's concept of law. See his *Pure Theory of Law* (Max Knight trans. 1967). I defend the concept in my book *Law, Pragmatism, and Democracy* 251–265 (2003).

❧ 5 ❧

THE INADEQUATE
APPELLATE RECORD

Factual assertions in briefs tend to be of two kinds: names, dates, and other background facts likely to be encountered in any narrative but rarely significant to the decision of a case; and facts similar to facts that have appeared in previous cases, the cases the parties will have cited as precedents. All too often, facts that are important to a sensible decision are missing from the briefs, and indeed from the judicial record. If it is a commercial case, the judge needs to understand why the transaction at issue was configured as it was; if it is a criminal case in which the defendant is accused (for example) of reckless endangerment by firing a gun into the air, the realist judge wants to know such things as the height, occupancy, density, and proximity of surrounding buildings, the time of day or night, and pedestrian density within the range of the bullet. The reason for the judge's wanting to get deep into the weeds in a case is that, by hypothesis, it is a case that is indeterminate from a formalist perspective.

The reckless-endangerment case is a real one, in which we upheld the district judge's finding of reckless endangerment. Here is the opinion's summary of the facts:

> At 3:00 A.M. one morning, the defendant and his girlfriend left the Guvernment Bar and Lounge, a nightclub in downtown Indianapolis. The club was on the verge of closing for the night and other patrons were leaving, though we do not know how many. The front entrance to the club is on Market Street, and the couple left by that entrance and walked to an "alley" behind the club, though the satellite photograph appended to this opinion suggests that it is actually a parking lot. While there the defendant fired six shots from a gun described in the record only as an FN Herstal pistol that holds 20 rounds of ammunition that can "penetrate up to 14 levels of body armor." The shell casings were found in the parking lot. No one was injured. The club is only a couple of blocks from Monument Circle, the Times Square of Indianapolis (but a very tame and quiet Times Square), and is situated among buildings. There is no indication of the bullets' trajectory or where they landed, though it seems undisputed that the defendant fired the shots into the air. The club has a rear entrance, but there is conflicting evidence on whether anyone was using it when or just before the defendant was shooting, and the judge made no finding.[1]

The satellite photograph was not in the record; nor the club's distance from Monument Circle. Nor was anything said about the pistol beyond what is summarized in the paragraph I just quoted—and it was not enough (as the defendant, however, failed to argue), because it left open the possibility that while the pistol could fire armor-piercing ammunition, maybe it

1. *United States v. Boyd*, 475 F.3d 875, 876–877 (7th Cir. 2007).

could fire less lethal ammunition as well (maybe the armor-piercing ammunition is sold only to police). I looked up "FN Herstal" in Google and discovered from the manufacturer's marketing material that the FN Herstal (presumably the reference was to the FN Herstal Five-seveN Pistol, the only pistol Herstal makes that holds twenty rounds) "fires the SS190 5.7x28mm ball round. This projectile will perforate any individual protection on today's battlefield including the PASGT kevlar helmet, 48 layers of kevlar body armor and the CRISAT target (titanium and kevlar)."[2] The implication is that the model is designed for that bullet, though notice that it is advertised as penetrating forty-eight, rather than fourteen (the number in the record), layers of body armor.

The opinion goes on to criticize the parties' development of the facts:

> We are . . . distressed at the sloppiness with which the case has been handled by both sides. Neither party attempted to quantify the risk created by the defendant's conduct; and vague words such as "substantial" are not a satisfactory substitute for data . . . Less forgivably—for the enormous variety of the circumstances in which random shooting occurs may defeat efforts to estimate the probability that a given incident would result in injury—no satellite photo (available free of charge from Google) was placed in evidence to indicate the physical surroundings. Nor does the record specify the model FN Herstal that the defendant was using or the type of ammunition the gun contained. The judge made no finding concerning the number of persons on the streets near the shooting (another conflict in the evidence that she did not try to resolve) or whether any persons were in the parking lot when and where the shooting took place. There was also no evidence on whether there are apartment buildings as well as office buildings in the vicinity of the shooting . . . [But despite the gaps in the evidence,] we are reasonably confident that the Indiana courts would hold that firing multiple shots from a high-powered gun

2. Id at 877.

in downtown Indianapolis for no better reason than an excess of animal spirits creates a substantial risk of bodily injury within the meaning of the Indiana statute.[3]

Internet Research by Judges

The Internet, and particularly the World Wide Web, have made it much easier for judges to conduct their own factual research, as in the Herstal gun case, rather than having to rely entirely on what the lawyers serve up to them. And because it is easier, judges (and their law clerks) are doing more of it, and this has given rise to controversy.[4] Lawyers have criticized me for including in my opinions, as in the *Boyd* opinion that I have just been discussing, facts drawn from Web research conducted by me or my law clerks. My response is that the lawyers should do the Web research and spare me the bother. The Web is an incredible compendium of data and a potentially invaluable resource for lawyers and judges that is underutilized by them.

The focus of controversy is citations to just one Web source, namely *Wikipedia*.[5] It is an important source, and, though it has to be used with

3. Id. at 878–879.

4. See, for example, Elizabeth G. Thornburg, "The Curious Appellate Judge: Ethical Limits on Independent Research," 28 *Litigation Review* 131 (2008); D. McKechnie, "The Use of the Internet by Courts and the Judiciary: Findings from a Study Trip and Supplementary Research," 11 *International Journal of Law and Information Technology* 109 (2003); Lee Peoples, "The Citation of Wikipedia in Judicial Opinions," 12 *Yale Journal of Law and Technology* 1 (2009); Peoples, "The Citation of Blogs in Judicial Opinions," 13 *Tulane Journal of Technology and Intellectual Property* 39 (2010); William R. Wilkerson, "The Emergence of Internet Citations in U.S. Supreme Court Opinions," 27 *Justice System Journal* 323 (2006); Coleen M. Barger, "On the Internet, Nobody Knows You're a Judge: Appellate Courts' Use of Internet Materials," 4 *Journal of Appellate Practice and Process* 417 (2002).

5. See, for example, Peoples, "The Citation of Wikipedia," and "The Citation of Blogs."

caution, on the whole a reliable one,[6] but there are many other reliable on-line sources of information locatable by a Google search, as well.

Not long ago I heard a case involving an appeal by a woman convicted of knowingly harboring an illegal alien.[7] She had allowed her boyfriend, an illegal alien, to live with her. Although there was no evidence that in doing so she was trying to make it more difficult for the government to apprehend him, the government asked us to define "to harbor" to mean merely to house a person. We rejected the suggested definition, though it can be found in dictionaries, and directed the defendant's acquittal. We ruled that the statutory term means providing a person with a secure haven, a refuge, a place to stay in which the authorities are unlikely to be seeking him, rather than just providing him with a place to stay or just cohabiting with him.

Our reasons were several, but one was the result of a Google search of the number of hits on several terms in which the word "harboring" appears. The search, which was based on the supposition that the number of hits on each term would be a rough index of the frequency of its use, revealed the following:

"harboring fugitives": 50,800 hits
"harboring enemies": 4,730 hits
"harboring refugees": 4,820 hits
"harboring victims": 114 hits
"harboring flood victims": 0 hits
"harboring victims of disasters": 0 hits
"harboring victims of persecution": 0 hits
"harboring guests": 184 hits
"harboring friends": 256 hits (but some involve harboring Quakers—

6. As pointed out in the majority and concurring opinions in *Fire Ins. Exchange v. Oltmanns*, 285 P. 3d 802 (Utah App. 2012). The opinions mount a powerful defense of judicial citation to the Web.

7. *United States v. Costello*, 666 F.3d 1040 (7th Cir. 2012). Harboring an alien known by the harborer to be illegal is made a crime by 18 U.S.C. § 1324(a)(1)(A)(iii).

"Friends," viewed in colonial New England as dangerous heretics)

"harboring Quakers": 3,870 hits

"harboring Jews": 19,100 hits[8]

From these results we inferred that the word "harboring," as it is actually used, connotes deliberately safeguarding a person or persons from detection or seizure by the authorities, whether the safeguarding takes the form of concealment, movement to a safe location, or physical protection. This connotation enables one to see that a hospital may not be "harboring" an alien when it renders emergency treatment even if he stays in the emergency room overnight, that giving an alien a lift to a gas station because his car has a flat tire may not be harboring, that driving an alien to the local office of the Department of Homeland Security to apply for an adjustment in status to that of lawful resident may not be harboring, that inviting an alien for a "one night stand" may not be attempted harboring, and finally that living with him because he's your boyfriend may not be harboring either.

What is true is that an appeals court should not make its decision turn on a fact found outside the court record unless the fact is incontestable. I think the number of Google hits on a word or phrase can fairly be regarded as incontestable, and likewise, in the *Boyd* case, the club's distance from Monument Circle. And often what is left out of the briefs but readily found online is just background material (for example, the basic facts about a corporate defendant, such as what its business is—a fact sometimes omitted even from briefs in employment discrimination cases!) that would be less likely to affect our decision than just to reassure us that we understood the real-world setting of the case.

The broader point is that a judge is required to observe a distinction among three types of fact. The first type consists of "adjudicative facts," which if contested can (it is believed) be established with the requisite reliability only by the adversary process of a trial, involving testimony and

8. 666 F.3d at 1044.

exhibits that are made admissible in evidence by the rules of evidence. Expert witnesses are allowed to rely on hearsay, even if it would be inadmissible if testified to by a nonexpert witness, provided it's the kind of hearsay on which reputable practitioners in their field of expertise rely in forming an expert opinion. Other witnesses are limited to testifying to facts within their personal knowledge. Adjudicative facts tend to be the critical facts, the facts on which the outcome of the case is likely to depend; hence the emphasis on trying to get them just right.

The second type of fact consists of facts of which a judge can take "judicial notice" because they are incontestable. To say that they're incontestable is to say that they don't need to be established by evidence to be taken as true.

The third type of fact consists of "legislative facts." These are facts that bear on the formulation or interpretation of legal doctrines. Judges are permitted to rely on such facts without evidence and without having to satisfy the conditions for taking judicial notice of a fact.

These are the conventional categories of facts in litigation. But there are also background facts—facts (I've given some examples) designed to increase the reader's understanding of a case by placing the adjudicative facts in an illuminating context—and what might be called "coloring-book" facts, by which I mean facts designed to make a judicial opinion come alive. Such facts if critical to the outcome might have to be proved, but if they're not critical it doesn't matter whether they've been established with the same rigor required of adjudicative facts. There are also visual aids, such as a map or a photograph, that can enhance understanding by clarifying the facts in a case.[9] I will give a couple of examples shortly.

Of particular significance are background facts concerning the technological or commercial setting of a case. One of the remarkable features of the Internet is the explanatory *range* of the entries. Recently, for example, I have written opinions in cases involving the feasibility of remote wiping of cell phones and of recovering deleted files on laptops,[10] and in both cases

9. See, for example, *Grayson v. Schuler*, 666 F.3d 450, 452 (7th Cir. 2012).

10. *United States v. Flores-Lopez*, 670 F.3d 803 (7th Cir. 2012); *United States v. Seiver*, 692 F.3d 774 (7th Cir. 2012), discussed in Chapter 3.

(and in others as well) I was able to find technically sophisticated but lucid explanations of the relevant technology online.

Lawyers want the term "adjudicative fact" to be broadly construed because they want to control litigation. (This is one of the hidden tensions between bench and bar; there are others.) They are unhappy when appellate judges go outside the record that the lawyers have shaped. They think they should be warned whenever an appellate judge is minded to inject something into an opinion that they hadn't thought to argue, though if judges were required to warn the lawyers, the appellate process would be protracted beyond endurance, depending on how curious, how thirsty for knowledge, the judge was. Appellate judges are permitted to go outside the record without the lawyers' permission—only adjudicative facts are off limits. The reluctance of most judges to do so may reflect the passivity that the umpireal conception of the judge induces and habits of thought that the judge acquired when he was a trial lawyer, if he was one.

My recourse to Internet research drew public criticism in the case of "Brother Jim,"[11] who sued a college in Indiana that had refused to let him give a speech on the lawn of the college's library; he claimed that the college's refusal violated his freedom of speech. Like *Boyd*, Brother Jim's case illustrates lawyers' failure to anticipate and answer questions that are likely to occur to appellate judges who are bothered, as judges of realist inclination are apt to be, by gaps in the lawyers' narrative of a case. (Lawyers have surprising difficulty figuring out how judges react to cases—how they think. That is a theme of Chapter 8 of this book.)

One gap in the Brother Jim case was the nature of a "disturbance" that had led to his earlier expulsion from the college grounds; asked at the oral argument what the nature of the disturbance was, neither side's lawyers knew. (They should have known! They should have realized it was a loose end that one or more of the judges might want tied up.) Another mystery was the layout of the college, specifically why Brother Jim thought the walkway in front of the student union, which the college had offered him as an alternative site for his speech, an inadequate venue for preaching to

11. *Gilles v. Blanchard*, 477 F.3d 466 (7th Cir. 2007).

the college community. A third was the nature of the college—Vincennes University, which none of the judges on the panel (two judges from Chicago and one from Milwaukee) knew anything about.

Internet research did not reveal the nature of the "disturbance," but it probably was related to Brother Jim's intense hostility to homosexuality, which I discovered from being led by a Google search to his website. I did not mention that hostility in my opinion, but I did mention an earlier case dealing with a disturbance involving his appearance at another college; the opinion in that case had remarked his "confrontational style." Nor did I mention—another bit of information, this one from the website of Vincennes University—that the branch of its campus in Vincennes is actually a two-year college, though I did mention that all the students at the campus are undergraduates. None of my gleanings from the Web influenced our decision.

But the opinion does mention some of the gleanings, which I thought enriched the opinion. An article about judicial research on the Internet criticizes me for having done that:

> The opinion starts with a thumbnail history of Vincennes University. It then describes how the plaintiff, James Gilles ('Brother Jim'), experienced his epiphany at a Van Halen concert and became the itinerant preacher with the mission of bringing the gospel to college campuses across the country. Judge Posner found many of the facts for that story on Brother Jim's website . . . And before turning to the legal analysis, Judge Posner's opinion graphically illustrates the area of Vincennes University in dispute with a satellite photo of the campus downloaded from the Internet . . . The line between adjudicative facts and nonadjudicative facts can be devilishly hard to discern, and it can be fairly debated whether Judge Posner stayed on the right side of that line in *Gilles*.[12]

---

12. Charles D. Knight, "Searching for Brother Jim: Improving Appellate Advocacy with the Internet," *Circuit Rider*, Apr. 2010, pp. 12–13.

I am unrepentant. The facts that I had obtained from the Web about Vincennes University and about Brother Jim's epiphany (which is either moving or amusing, depending on the reader's religious views), and subsequent career as an itinerant preacher on college campuses, were included for background and color; they played no role in the decision and so it doesn't matter what side of an indiscernible line I was on. The satellite photo did support Brother Jim's contention that the library lawn was a superior venue for preaching or other speechifying than the cramped walkway to which he was confined by the university authorities (in fact the library lawn appears to be the only open area on the campus), as also shown in the photo. But since the university won the case anyway, our photographic assist to Brother Jim could not be thought to have had a prejudicial effect.

Of course Web research can result in errors. But no one should be so naïve as to believe that the determination of facts by the familiar adversary process at a trial is proof against error—that witnesses dare not violate their oath to tell the truth, the whole truth, and nothing but the truth, so help them God, for fear of divine retribution, that cross-examination is an infallible or even a reliable tool for exposing lies and mistakes, that all expert testimony is reliable and intelligible, that all trial lawyers are competent at obtaining, evaluating, and presenting evidence, that judges and jurors are skilled at evaluating the credibility of witnesses, or that the rules of evidence are single-mindedly designed to produce truth rather than to serve other, and inconsistent, goals as well, such as protecting people's privacy, limiting executive power, and conserving judicial resources.

The limitations of the conventional judicial record are acute in two fields in which the "judicial" record is actually a record compiled by an administrative law judge. The two fields, both of which I mentioned in Chapter 3, are asylum law and social security disability law. The immigration judges are heavily overworked,[13] and the immigration bar is weak because

13. See "Improving the Immigration Courts: Effort to Hire More Judges Falls Short: Report of the Transactional Records Access Clearinghouse at Syracuse University," July 2008, http://trac.syr.edu/immigration/reports/189/ (visited Dec. 19, 2011).

most illegal immigrants (including asylum seekers) have very little money and because immigrants tend to gravitate to lawyers of the same ethnic background regardless of the lawyer's competence. The federal courts of appeals, to which denials of asylum are appealable, reverse these denials at a very high rate, often because the immigration judges and the Justice Department's lawyers display an appalling ignorance of foreign countries— of facts about them that should be common knowledge and not require "proof" in the normal legal sense of the word: such facts as the difference between being denationalized when a country is split in two (so citizens of Czechoslovakia had to choose between Czech and Slovakian citizenship when Czechoslovakia dissolved) and when a country revokes the citizenship of a despised minority (as Nazi Germany did to German Jews); that poor African countries do not have as elaborate a system of official documentation as the United States; that African husbands are less likely than American husbands to discuss their business dealings with their wives; and so on.[14]

In reviewing decisions denying applications for social security disability benefits by people who claim to be physically or mentally incapable of full-time employment—decisions made by overworked administrative law judges of the Social Security Administration (confronted, like the immigration judges, by a weak bar, because social security disability practice is not lucrative)—the courts of appeals encounter all too often ignorance (hiding behind medical and legal jargon) of disease and disability, especially mental disease and disabling pain.[15]

The Internet is not going away. The quality and quantity of online material that illuminates the issues in federal litigation will only grow. Judges

14. See *Haile v. Holder*, 591 F.3d 572, 573 (7th Cir. 2010); *Soumahoro v. Gonzales*, 415 F.3d 732, 734–35 (7th Cir. 2005); *Apouviepseakoda v. Gonzales*, 475 F.3d 881, 894–897 (7th Cir. 2007) (dissenting opinion).

15. For a particularly disturbing example of administrative incompetence in social security disability adjudication, see *Bjornson v. Astrue*, 671 F.3d 640 (7th Cir. 2012). See also *Hughes v. Astrue*, 705 F.3d 276 (7th Cir. 2013); *Martinez v. Astrue*, 630 F.3d 693, 694–74 (7th Cir. 2011); *Spiva v. Astrue*, 628 F.3d 346 (7th Cir. 2010); *Parker v. Astrue*, 597 F.3d 920 (7th Cir. 2010); *Kohler v. Astrue*, 546 F.3d 260 (2d Cir. 2008); *Kangail v. Barnhart*, 454 F.3d 627 (7th Cir. 2006).

must not ignore such a rich mine of information. Nor can they ignore a related phenomenon that I do not discuss: the rise of the law blog, now rivaling and threatening the conventional legal journals.[16]

All this said, I acknowledge that there is a problem of reliability when judges go outside the record—though, as I have already suggested, the reliability of the record (the admissible evidence that was admitted) cannot be assumed either, despite rules of evidence intended to make it reliable. The problem of reliability is not serious with respect to background or "coloring book" facts, or pictures, maps, or diagrams included in a judicial opinion merely for clarification. But it can be serious, and not only when it involves adjudicative facts but also when it involves legislative facts, as in the *Roper* case discussed in the last chapter, or the *Parents Involved* case discussed in the next—both cases in which Justices relied heavily on extra-record materials, largely statistical, to justify their constitutional views. There are of course ways of assessing the reliability of statistical studies, as well as of other scientific or quasi-scientific evidence, but those ways may be opaque to judges. Appellate judges don't conduct *Daubert* hearings to filter out junk science, as district judges are required to do (see Chapter 9). There is a danger that judicial recourse to secondary literature, and to the Internet more broadly, will often be rhetorical rather than substantive. I have no solution to this problem—other than to suggest trying through judicial training and other means to increase the intellectual sophistication of the judiciary.

Judicial timidity about conducting Internet research has a negative feedback effect. Appellate lawyers naturally focus their briefs and oral arguments on what the judges have the easiest access to, which are the decision of the lower court or agency, relevant statutory material, precedents, treatises, and the record compiled in the lower court or agency. Often the record is quite skimpy, especially when the appeal is from a court rather than an agency, since the vast majority of court cases these days are disposed of summarily rather than after a trial. If judges don't do online re-

16. See J. Robert Brown, Jr., "Law Faculty Blogs and Disruptive Innovation" (University of Denver Sturm College of Law, Aug. 13, 2012).

search, the lawyers are unlikely to do so, thinking it disfavored; and if the lawyers don't do it judges are unlikely to do it, because of their traditional reluctance to "go outside the record." If judges lead the way, lawyers will follow, however reluctantly, and the knowledge base of appellate adjudication will expand.

A genuine worry about the use of the Internet in litigation is its use by jurors; I discuss that problem, which is different from the problem I've been discussing of judges' use of the Internet, in Chapter 9.

Is a Word Really Worth a Thousand Pictures?

Sticklers will object that maps and satellite photos—any photos, for that matter—are unreliable evidence because they are not continuously updated. (The satellite photo in Brother Jim's case had actually been taken after the incident that gave rise to the case.) That matters very little if the map or the photo is offered to illustrate uncontested facts. And in the unusual case in which the map or photo is inaccurate, someone is likely to notify the court of its error and the opinion will be corrected; and provided that the map or photo was used for illustrative purposes rather than as a source of adjudicative facts, the correction will not affect the outcome. I have included maps and pictures in my opinions more than other judges have (maybe more than any other judge), and have never received a complaint that the map or picture was inaccurate.

Yet so disfavored are pictures, maps, objects, and diagrams in appellate briefs (a reflection of the semantic emphasis that a formalist orientation breeds) that I've said that some lawyers think a word is worth a thousand pictures.[17] Cases involving the alleged infringement of pictorial trademarks provide compelling examples of when a verbal comparison is no substitute for a picture. This was brought home to me in a case I heard many years ago involving two professional football teams.[18] The owner of the Balti-

17. *Coffey v. Northeast Illinois Regional Commuter R.R. Corp.*, 479 F.3d 472, 478 (7th Cir. 2007); *United States v. Barnes*, 188 F.3d 893, 895 (7th Cir. 1999).

18. *Indianapolis Colts, Inc. v. Metropolitan Baltimore Football Club Limited Partnership*, 34 F.3d 410 (7th Cir. 1994).

more Colts had moved the Colts to Indianapolis and renamed the team the Indianapolis Colts. A Baltimore businessman responded to this loss by acquiring a Canadian Football League team for Baltimore that he named the Baltimore CFL Colts.[19] Both the new Baltimore team and the Indianapolis Colts sold various items of clothing, such as hats and T-shirts, with the team logo on it. The Indianapolis Colts sued the Baltimore CFL Colts, charging trademark infringement. The briefs contained no photos of the merchandise sold by either team, but only labored verbal descriptions from which it was difficult to infer whether consumers were likely to think that merchandise marked with the Baltimore CFL Colts' logo had actually been sponsored by the Indianapolis Colts.

At the oral argument I asked the lawyer for the Indianapolis Colts whether he had any of the disputed merchandise with him. He seemed startled by the question, but answered that he did and went over to counsel's table and fished from his briefcase a pair of hats, one from each team, and showed them to the judges—and (without knowing it) won the case then and there.

Years later we had a spate of cases involving alleged copyright and trademark infringement of Beanie Babies, and we had to cope with, among other things, doctored photos of infringing beanbag toys, and absurd arguments of which my favorite, made by an infringer's lawyer, was that the reason that his client's beanbag pig resembled Ty's Beanie Baby pig was that both had been copied from nature. So in my opinion I included photos of the beanbag pig and a real pig.[20] The resemblance, needless to say, was very slight.

Trademarks are an obvious example of the utility of pictures in appellate litigation. Far less obvious is their utility in cases involving alleged violations of the minimum wage or overtime provisions of the Fair Labor Standards Act, but here is a recent example of my court's use of a picture in

19. See John F. Steadman, *From Colts to Ravens: A Behind-the-Scenes Look at Baltimore Professional Football* 52–54 (1997).

20. *Ty, Inc. v. GMA Accessories, Inc.*, 132 F.3d 1167, 1174–75 (7th Cir. 1997). It was also a doctored-photo case and the doctored photos are also reproduced in the opinion.

such a case.[21] A provision of the act excludes, from the time during which an employee is entitled to be compensated at the minimum hourly wage (or, if it is overtime work, at 150 percent of his hourly wage), "any time spent in changing clothes . . . at the beginning or end of each workday which was excluded from measured working time . . . by the express terms

21. The case is *Sandifer v. United States Steel Corp.,* 678 F.3d 590, 592 (7th Cir. 2012), cert. granted, 133 S. Ct. 1240 (2013).

of or by custom or practice under a bona fide collective-bargaining agreement applicable to the particular employee."[22] The collective-bargaining agreements between U.S. Steel and the steelworkers union had always excluded clothes-changing time. But the steelworkers who were the plaintiffs in the case argued that the work clothes they change in and out of at the plant are not "clothes" within the meaning of the statute but rather safety equipment. Unfortunately the statute does not define "clothes."

The alleged "clothes" consisted of flame-retardant pants and jacket, work gloves, metatarsal boots (work boots containing steel or other strong material to protect the toes and instep), a hard hat, safety glasses, ear plugs, and a "snood" (a hood that covers the top of the head, the chin, and the neck). These work "clothes" were in the record, and on the theory that a picture is worth a thousand words, our opinion includes a photograph of a man (one of my law clerks), dressed in the "clothes."

We concluded for a variety of reasons unnecessary to dwell on here that the outfit was better characterized as work clothes than as safety equipment. I think it was a help to the judges but also to the reader of the opinion to see the items of clothing or equipment that we discussed and the ensemble formed by the items. The picture helped to make the verbal description and analytic discussion intelligible.

A final example, from another recent decision of my court, regarding the utility of pictorial assists in judicial opinions, concerns the lawfulness of an arrest for criminal trespass

> to "state-supported" land, and occurred shortly after [the plaintiff, Kevin Sroga, suing for false arrest] left a police station upon being released from police custody following still another arrest but not one challenged in this case . . . He left by the front door of the police station and walked past a sign that reads "No Loitering No Trespassing" into a parking lot marked with signs that said "Parking Police Personnel Only." A police officer noticed him walking between the rows of police cars peering inside each car. Realizing that he was being ob-

22. 29 U.S.C. § 203(o).

served, Sroga struck up a conversation with an officer who was sitting in one of the cars. He claims she was an old friend, but she offered her handcuffs to another officer to fasten on Sroga.

***

Illinois law, so far as concerns that arrest, forbids anyone to enter land "supported in whole or in part with State funds" and "thereby [to] interfere[] with another person's lawful use or enjoyment" of the land, 720 ILCS 5/21-5(a), provided that he has been warned off by "a printed or written notice forbidding such entry . . . [that] has been conspicuously posted or exhibited at the main entrance to such land or the forbidden part thereof." *Id.*, § 5/21-5(b).

This aerial photo shows the scene:

Sroga explains that he walked through the police parking lot because it was the quickest way for him to get from the police station, which is at the southeast corner of Grand Avenue and Central Avenue (at the top of the photo), to a nearby train station to catch a ride home. The parking lot is immediately behind the police station and is accessible by a public sidewalk that runs along the police station's east side (on the right, as one faces the photo). South of its intersection with Grand

Avenue, Central Avenue crosses the railroad tracks on a bridge, and an exit from the police parking lot at the lot's southwest corner, underneath the Central Avenue overpass just before the tracks, brings one to Armitage Avenue; and just to the west, on Armitage, is the train station that Sroga says he was trying to get to. He could have gotten from the police station to the train station by walking west on Grand Avenue after leaving the police station, turning south on Central Avenue, and then taking stairs down to Armitage, without going through the police parking lot, but the route he took was a little shorter and didn't involve stairs.

The mere fact that a piece of land is "supported" by the government doesn't make a person who enters it a trespasser. Otherwise one couldn't use streets or sidewalks. There has to be something in its appearance or layout (a fence for example), or informative signs, to indicate that the public is barred. All that the signs indicated was that only police cars could park in the lot.

So the police didn't have probable cause to arrest Sroga simply because he took a shortcut through their parking lot. It was Sroga's shenanigans in the lot—his peering into the police cars and his pestering the officer whom he found sitting in her police car—that gave the police probable cause to believe that he was interfering with the lawful use of the land.[23]

Without the aerial photo, it would have been difficult to understand how the plaintiff could have thought it permissible to walk through the police parking lot.

23. *Sroga v. Weiglen,* 649 F.3d 604, 605–606, 608–609 (7th Cir. 2011). Other opinions that would be difficult to understand without the Google maps included in them are *Parvati Corp. v. City of Oak Forest,* 709 F.3d 678 (7th Cir. 2013); *Guth v. Tazewell County,* 698 F.3d 580 (7th Cir. 2012); and *Vodak v. City of Chicago,* 639 F.3d 738 (7th Cir. 2011).

❧ 6 ❧

COPING STRATEGIES FOR APPELLATE JUDGES I

Judicial Self-Restraint

I have been arguing that in the face of mounting complexity, appellate judges should become more realistic, less passive, more fact- and policy-oriented. There was once a passive alternative, called "judicial self-restraint" or just "judicial restraint," that appealed to judges in constitutional cases. No longer.[1] Yet it deserves to be taken seriously, and is the subject of this chapter. In the next chapter I take up another passive strategy—textual originalism—thought by some judges to provide an escape from the need to grapple with the complexity of today's world. I also discuss in that chapter an activist interpretive strategy that offers judges still another escape route from having to confront that complexity. Only if

1. For empirical evidence of the decline of judicial self-restraint, see Lee Epstein and William M. Landes, "Was There Ever Such a Thing as Judicial Self-Restraint?" 100 *California Law Review* 557 (2012).

there is no escape can judges be expected to confront it; I argue in this and the next chapter that there is no escape.

The term "judicial self-restraint" is a chameleon. Of the many meanings that have been assigned to it,[2] three have the best claims to be taken seriously. The first is that judges apply law, they don't make it. That is formalism—"the law made me do it." The second is that judges defer, to a very great extent, to decisions by other officials—appellate judges to trial judges and administrative agencies, all judges to legislative and executive decisions. This is "modesty," or "institutional competence," or "process jurisprudence." I gave examples in Chapter 3 and will give additional examples when I discuss trial courts in Chapter 9. It is a wobbly compass; when the judge has to choose between deferring to one court, agency, or branch of government and refusing to defer to another, the restrained course may be unclear.

The third form of judicial self-restraint, and the focus of this chapter, is a marked reluctance to invalidate legislation on constitutional grounds; I call this version of judicial self-restraint "constitutional restraint." It is in tension with the first concept of self-restraint, "the law made me do it." The Constitution is the supreme law; reluctance to override a statute or executive decision must give way to it. Yet that reluctance is the core of constitutional restraint. Like deference based on notions of comparative institutional competence, constitutional restraint has internal tensions. The doctrine that statutes should be interpreted to avoid raising constitutional questions reduces the frequency with which statutes are held unconstitutional, but does so by reducing the scope of legislation—interpreting it

2. See J. Harvie Wilkinson III, *Cosmic Constitutional Theory: Why Americans Are Losing Their Inalienable Right to Self-Governance* (2012); Stefanie A. Lindquist and Frank B. Cross, *Measuring Judicial Activism* (2009); John Daley, "Defining Judicial Restraint," in *Judicial Power, Democracy and Legal Positivism* 279 (Tom Campbell and Jeffrey Goldsworthy eds. 2000); Bradley C. Canon, "A Framework for the Analysis of Judicial Activism," in *Supreme Court Activism and Restraint* 385 (Stephen C. Halpern and Charles M. Lamb eds. 1982). Judge Wilkinson, of the U.S. Court of Appeals for the Fourth Circuit, is today the leading proponent of judicial self-restraint.

narrowly to skirt constitutional objections—and thus the power of legis-latures.[3]

Thayer and His Epigones

The best-known and best-developed version of constitutional restraint be-gins with an 1893 article by Harvard law professor James Bradley Thayer which argued that a statute should be invalidated only if its unconstitution-ality is "so clear that it is not open to rational question."[4] (He seems not to have been concerned with challenges to the constitutionality of executive action; the executive branch was much smaller when he wrote than it has since become.) Judges in a number of the cases that Thayer cited in support of his formula had gone so far as to say that a law should not be invalidated unless its unconstitutionality was clear "beyond reasonable doubt."[5]

Thayer was borrowing an approach that is found in a variety of adju-dicative settings, such as appellate review of a trial judge's findings of fact, or of rulings on objections to the admission of evidence, or of manage-ment decisions, such as deciding whether to limit the number of witnesses at trial; he derived his specific formula for constitutional restraint from the

3. Judge Easterbrook has argued persuasively that it is, on balance, an activist doctrine. Frank H. Easterbrook, "Do Liberals and Conservatives Differ in Judicial Activism?" 73 *University of Colorado Law Review* 1401, 1405–1409 (2002).

4. James B. Thayer, "The Origin and Scope of the American Doctrine of Con-stitutional Law," 7 *Harvard Law Review* 129, 144 (1893). The fullest discussion that I have found of Thayer's approach, its antecedents, and its sequelae is Sanford Byron Gabin, "Judicial Review, James Bradley Thayer, and the 'Reasonable Doubt' Test," 3 *Hastings Constitutional Law Quarterly* 961 (1976) (as slightly amplified in Gabin's book *Judicial Review and the Reasonable Doubt Test* [1980]). Also very good is Evan Tsen Lee, *Judicial Restraint in America: How the Ageless Wisdom of the Federal Courts Was Invented* (2011). See also *One Hundred Years of Judicial Review: The Thayer Centennial Symposium*, 88 *Northwestern University Law Review* 1 (1993).

5. See, for example, references in Thomas M. Cooley, *Treatise on the Constitu-tional Limitations Which Rest upon the Legislative Power of the States of the American Union* 182 nn. 2–3 (1868).

standard for reversing a judgment entered on a jury verdict.[6] Thus judges should not invalidate a law "merely because it is concluded that upon a just and true construction the law is unconstitutional," but only "when those who have the right to make laws have not merely made a mistake, but have made a very clear one."[7] A "law made me do it" restraintist, in contrast, would condemn the statute, believing that his duty was to apply the law as he understood it even if he acknowledged to himself that his understanding might be imperfect. To allow doubt to change his decision would be to allow something that is not law to influence a judicial outcome. Thayer's "conception of judicial self-restraint has nothing to do with the virtue of fidelity to law. Indeed, since Thayerism requires judges to defer to legislative judgments of constitutionality that they disbelieve, a strict policy of fidelity to law actually seems inconsistent with Thayerism."[8]

Thayer's immediate successor as the leading advocate of constitutional restraint was Holmes, who had practiced law with Thayer for a time. Then came Louis Brandeis (a former student of Thayer), then Felix Frankfurter (a friend and acolyte of both Holmes and Brandeis)—the most emphatic expositor of self-restraint in Thayerian terms[9]—and then Alexander Bickel (a former law clerk of Frankfurter). There are others in this lineage but these are the main figures.[10]

A number of scholars and judges who have been skeptical of the competence (in the sense either of legitimacy or ability) of courts to decide difficult or consequential cases have not, however, looked to Thayer for inspiration. One provocatively titled piece—it has "Thayerian" in the title, but is not Thayerian in spirit—argues for giving Congress an institutional

6. Jay Hook, "A Brief Life of James Bradley Thayer," in *One Hundred Years of Judicial Review: The Thayer Centennial Symposium*, at 5.

7. Thayer, "The Origin and Scope of the American Doctrine," at 144.

8. David Luban, "Justice Holmes and the Metaphysics of Judicial Restraint," 44 *Duke Law Journal* 449, 459 (1994).

9. See, for example, *West Virginia State Board of Education v. Barnette*, 319 U.S. 624, 667–670 (1943) (Frankfurter, J., dissenting).

10. See Luban, "Justice Holmes and Metaphysics," at 451.

makeover so that it can perform better, which might obviate the need for *any* judicial second-guessing.[11] Thayer himself did not discuss institutional design, nor did the Thayerians whom I've mentioned.

Skeptics of judicial competence often are strict constructionists, in the sense of hewing close to the semantic level—the literal meaning—of statutes.[12] That is a passive strategy—I discuss the currently most influential variant of it in the next chapter—but it is not the passive strategy of the Thayerians, who were, as we'll see, loose constructionists.

In support of his concept of constitutional restraint, Thayer argued:

1. Authorizing courts to invalidate laws enacted by the national legislature was an innovation with only a thin basis in the constitutional text, and was still controversial when he wrote. This argued for prudential restraint; courts must be wary of going head to head with the other branches of government.

2. Often a law goes into effect years before the courts get a case in which its constitutionality is challenged or is ripe for adjudication. Thayer argued that this implied that the legislature had to make an independent constitutional judgment—especially the federal legislature, because federal courts refuse to issue advisory opinions and so Congress has to decide for itself whether a statute that it wants to enact would be constitutional. He reinforced this argument by reference to Article VI, clause 3, of the Constitution, which requires the members of Congress, among others, to take an oath to support the Constitution. Thayer thought Congress a kind of constitutional court. The English had gone so far as to deem Parliament the nation's supreme court—an act of Parliament had the force of a constitutional amendment.[13] Thayer was advocating a modified version of the English approach.

3. Questions relating to the power of the different branches of govern-

11. Elizabeth Garrett and Adrian Vermeule, "Institutional Design of a Thayerian Congress," 50 *Duke Law Journal* 1277 (2001).

12. See Adrian Vermeule, *Judging under Uncertainty: An Institutional Theory of Legal Interpretation* 57–59 (2006), discussed in Richard A. Posner, *How Judges Think* 214–216 (2008). "Literalists" would be a better term than "strict constructionists."

13. Philip Hamburger, *Law and Judicial Duty*, ch. 8 (2008).

ment are inescapably political, and so courts have perforce to use political, rather than just legal, criteria to answer them. Thayer thought that such criteria would favor restraint.[14]

4. Most important to Thayer (and implied by his first two points) was his belief that if courts enforced constitutional limitations to the hilt, legislators would stop thinking about the constitutionality of proposed legislation and just think about how the courts would react. Legislative deliberations would be bobtailed and legislatures trivialized: "The checking and cutting down of legislative power, by numerous detailed prohibitions in the constitution, cannot be accomplished without making the government petty and incompetent . . . Under no system can the power of courts go far to save a people from ruin; our chief protection lies elsewhere."[15] Or as he later put it, "The tendency of a common and easy resort to this great function [judicial review of legislation], now lamentably too common, is to dwarf the political capacity of the people, and to deaden its sense of moral responsibility. It is no light thing to do that."[16] We might compare this to one of the traditional arguments for deferential appellate review of factfindings by trial courts: it encourages trial judges to be more thoughtful. The analogy is imperfect, however, because appellate review of trial-court determinations of pure legal issues is plenary (that is, the appellate court gives no weight to the trial court's resolution of them) rather than deferential, that is, giving weight to that resolution. It's the difference between reversing a trial court's ruling or finding because the appellate court thinks it erroneous and reversing only if the appellate court thinks it *clearly* erroneous.

Thayer seems to have had a high opinion of legislative deliberation if the courts didn't disrespect it by giving insufficient weight to the products of that deliberation.[17] These are separate points: one can think that legisla-

---

14. Thayer, "The Origin and Scope of the American Doctrine," at 152.

15. Id. at 156.

16. James Bradley Thayer, *John Marshall* (1901), in *James Bradley Thayer, Oliver Wendell Holmes, and Felix Frankfurter on John Marshall* 3, 86 (1967).

17. The "pro-legislature" aspect of Thayer's article is emphasized in Robin West, "The Aspirational Constitution," 88 *Northwestern University Law Review* 241 (1993).

tures do a good job, and so shouldn't be penned in tightly by the courts, without thinking that legislators are like judges and deliberate in a responsible and creative fashion about the constitutionality of proposed legislation. Thayer believed both things. Both beliefs appear to be mistaken, or at least weakly supported. (More on this later.) So Thayerism got off to a shaky start.

Holmes was Thayer's first and most illustrious successor in the School of Thayer. In private correspondence he claimed not only that he was a follower of Thayer but that his concept of judicial restraint had been derived from and was identical to Thayer's.[18] And it is true that he used Thayer's formula (the reasonableness test) in opinions; I'll give an example later. But he didn't buy Thayer's premises. He didn't admire legislatures, or the "liberal" laws they kept churning out, such as the antitrust laws and other regulations of business. He didn't think legislators had the potential to be thoughtful interpreters of the Constitution. Indeed he didn't think that legislators reasoned. Legislation was merely a litmus paper that revealed the balance of political power in a society. Thayer had thought political considerations inescapable when a court was dealing with constitutional issues, but that those considerations would push judges toward upholding even statutes that they thought probably unconstitutional. This was the opposite of Holmes's thinking; he believed that judges who thought in political terms when they were adjudicating a constitutional case would be prone to invalidate rather than uphold a challenged law if their political ideology diverged from the legislature's.

Holmes's opinions on the Massachusetts court upholding the rights of unions,[19] and his later, more famous opinions for the U.S. Supreme Court dissenting from decisions that invalidated social-welfare legislation on "liberty of contract" grounds, are generally thought the apogee of judicial self-restraint because of the derisive comments that he made about such legislation in his private correspondence. He kept saying that he was com-

18. See Letter from Oliver W. Holmes to James B. Thayer, Nov. 2, 1893, reprinted in Luban, "Justice Holmes and Metaphysics," at 462 n. 34.

19. See his dissenting opinions in *Plant v. Woods*, 57 N.E. 1011 (Mass. 1900); *Vegelahn v. Gunter*, 44 N.E. 1077 (Mass. 1896), and *Commonwealth v. Perry*, 28 N.E. 1126 (Mass. 1891).

pelled by his conception of the proper judicial role to vote to uphold laws he abhorred. I am skeptical. He was far from uniformly conservative—think of his free speech and habeas corpus opinions, and his dissent in the wiretapping case (*Olmstead*, discussed later in this chapter). These are not closely reasoned opinions, but sharp reactions to illiberal government actions that he found abhorrent. He cannot be politically typecast.

More important, "the law made me do it" protestations that pepper his correspondence obscure the Darwinian streak that is so pronounced in his free-speech dissents[20] and in *Buck v. Bell* ("three generations of imbeciles are enough"). For Holmes, political struggle was closely analogous to natural selection—perhaps even an exemplification of it. The strongest would win. Not that they necessarily *deserved* to win, though he wanted the "imbeciles" to lose by not being allowed to reproduce, and though he contemplated the Darwinian character of the social struggle with unmistakable relish.[21] Darwinism is a theory of adaptation, not of improvement. Judicial rulings invalidating modern liberal legislation might be wise or foolish, but in either case they would merely delay the inevitable. "The first requirement of a sound body of law is, that it should correspond with the actual feelings and demands of the community, whether right or wrong."[22] So judges should get out of the way of the struggle between unions and employers, socialists and capitalists, no matter which side the judges wanted to prevail. The democratic political process was merely the civilized, because nonviolent, method of registering the relative strength of the competing forces in society—a substitute for civil war in much the same way that settlement is a substitute for trial. "All that can be expected from modern improvements is that legislation should easily and quickly, yet not too quickly,

20. See Vincent Blasi, "Holmes and the Marketplace of Ideas," 2004 *Supreme Court Review* 1 (2004).

21. Holmes "believed that revering dominant social forces, like hurling oneself into duty, is part of the joyful affirmation of life as we actually find it. At bottom, we affirm the dominant inclinations of society because the promptings of vital force require no warrant and we know in our bones that in the end no warrant for them is to be found." Luban, "Justice Holmes and Metaphysics," at 507.

22. O. W. Holmes, Jr., *The Common Law* 41 (1881).

modify itself in accordance with the will of the *de facto* supreme power in the community . . . The more powerful interests must be more or less reflected in legislation, which, like every other device of man or beast, must tend in the long run to aid the survival of the fittest."[23] Holmes's Darwinian conception of legislation, remote from Thayer's, best explains his restrained posture in cases involving claims of deprivation of property or economic liberty in violation of due process.

Brandeis, so often bracketed with Holmes, differed from him without being much like Thayer. Like Holmes he was a legal realist *avant la lettre*, but unlike Holmes he was political to his fingertips—a Jeffersonian with a Southerner's hostility to strong central government (he was from Kentucky, after all, though he was not your typical Kentuckian) and a marked hostility to finance, chain stores, and big business in general. These antipathies were shared by many state legislators, who were on the whole more liberal than most federal judges, as was Brandeis. Finding himself on an activist conservative Court, he embraced constitutional restraint—adopting, advocating, and amplifying doctrines, such as standing, ripeness, and avoidance of constitutional rulings where possible, that eliminate or at least postpone (and sufficient unto the day is the evil thereof) occasions on which a federal court deems itself authorized to declare a legislative or executive measure unconstitutional. None of these doctrines can be found in the constitutional text or its English antecedents; they are the invention of American judges[24]—some are Brandeis's own inventions.[25] No more than Holmes was he uniformly restrained. He joined Holmes's opinion in *Buck v. Bell*. His dissent in *Olmstead* was activist in locating a constitutional limitation on wiretapping in a right of privacy nowhere hinted at in the constitutional text. And he participated in decisions that invalidated New Deal

---

23. Anonymous [Oliver Wendell Holmes, Jr.], "The Gas-Stokers' Strike," 7 *American Law Review* 582, 583 (1873).

24. John A. Ferejohn and Larry D. Kramer, "Independent Judges, Dependent Judiciary: Institutionalizing Judicial Restraint," 77 *New York University Law Review* 962, 1004–1015 (2002).

25. See, for example, *Fairchild v. Hughes*, 258 U.S. 126 (1922); Lee, *Judicial Restraint in America*, at 39–40, 68–76.

legislation and that by doing so got the Supreme Court into political trouble in the 1930s.

Both Holmes and Brandeis defended judicial restraint on the further ground that it would enable the states to function as policy laboratories. They would experiment with different policies, and the experiments, being limited in scope (because confined to individual states), would do little harm even when they produced bad policies; when they produced good ones they would be laying empirical foundations for nationwide social reform. But the two Justices embraced the theory of state experimentation on different grounds—Brandeis because he wanted to generate field evidence about which policies worked and, more important, to protect the liberal policies enacted in many states, Holmes because (I conjecture) he saw an analogy to variation, which is a precondition of evolution.

When avoidance tactics failed and deciding a constitutional question became inescapable, Brandeis sought to demonstrate the reasonableness of challenged legislation that he favored by piling on factual details gleaned less from the judicial record than from official investigations and social science research.[26] Holmes, in contrast, not having an empirical bent, was usually content to assert the reasonableness of challenged legislation and leave it at that, as when he said in his dissent in *Lochner* "I think that the word liberty in the Fourteenth Amendment is perverted when it is held to prevent the natural outcome of a dominant opinion, unless it can be said that a rational and fair man necessarily would admit that the statute proposed would infringe fundamental principles as they have been understood by the traditions of our people and our law. *It does not need research to show* that no such sweeping condemnation can be passed upon the statute before us. A reasonable man might think it a proper measure on the score of health. Men whom I certainly could not pronounce unreasonable would uphold it as a first instalment of a general regulation of the hours of work."[27] Whether or not research was needed to establish the reasonableness of the law, it wasn't going to be supplied by Holmes.

26. Wallace Mendelson, "The Influence of James B. Thayer upon the Work of Holmes, Brandeis, and Frankfurter," 31 *Vanderbilt Law Review* 71, 74–75 (1978).

27. *Lochner v. New York*, 198 U.S. 45, 76 (1905) (dissenting opinion) (emphasis added).

Frankfurter, who like Brandeis was political to his fingertips, advocated Thayerism with a noisy passion unequaled by any other Thayerian. Brilliant but neither thoughtful nor empirical, he innocently deemed legislators experts and shared the Progressive movement's excessive regard for government by experts and Thayer's high regard for legislatures. He even thought (absurdly) that legislators could be shamed into reapportioning their legislatures—into reapportioning themselves out of a job, in other words. He tacked on to Thayer's formula, and elaborated, Brandeis's procedural restraints, which under the rubric of "political questions" figured in his dissent in *Baker v. Carr*, the case that held legislative malapportionment unconstitutional.[28]

Many of Frankfurter's restrained decisions are explicable without reference to judicial self-restraint, including his famous dissent in the second flag-salute case.[29] The American equivalent of a "court Jew" (monarchs of ethnically diverse nations, such as Austria-Hungary, where Frankfurter was born, sometimes valued educated Jews because of their cosmopolitanism—their lack of attachment to any of the local tribes), Frankfurter was intensely patriotic. He couldn't understand why any American would refuse to salute the American flag, which has a symbolic significance for Americans that far exceeds that of the national flag in other nations—the Union Jack for example. He displayed no restraint when it came to the Fourth Amendment and the equal protection clause; he was a strong supporter of declaring public school segregation unconstitutional.[30]

Although Alexander Bickel considered himself a Frankfurter avatar, and made frequent approving references to Thayer,[31] his version of judicial self-restraint was really Brandeis's. Bickel had a political program—the kind of mild liberalism one associates with the current liberal members of the Supreme Court—that he thought the Court could put over on society

28. 369 U.S. 186, 266 (1962).

29. *West Virginia State Board of Education v. Barnette*, 319 U.S. at 647.

30. These features of Frankfurter's jurisprudence are well described in Melvin I. Urofsky, *Felix Frankfurter: Judicial Restraint and Individual Liberties* (1991).

31. Notably in Alexander M. Bickel, *The Least Dangerous Branch: The Supreme Court at the Bar of Politics* 35–46 (1962).

by clever deployment of tactical devices, some original with him. Bickel talked a lot about "principles" but his principles were political ideas, and he thought the Supreme Court had to move cautiously in imposing them on the nation because other institutions would fight back. For Bickel and his latter-day judicial avatar, Guido Calabresi, the Supreme Court is always in a tense political competition with the elected branches of government.[32] This is the view of political scientists as well, and has merit; Bickel was offering tactical advice to the Court to help it prevail over the other branches.

For example, he wanted the Court to avoid giving the imprimatur of constitutionality to "bad" legislation that it did not yet dare to condemn (the Court should deny certiorari in such cases), lest the laity treat a decision upholding a statute's constitutionality as an endorsement; Bickel thought laypersons incapable of distinguishing between legislation that is constitutional and legislation that is good. In other cases he wanted the Court to engage legislatures in a coercive "dialogue."[33] Really bad state legislation would be invalidated, but on narrow grounds that gave the states the illusion that if only they did a better job of articulating the concerns underlying the legislation, or at least expressed their desire for it more forcefully, it might survive.[34] It would be a Bickellian Court's hope that the legislators would have their eyes opened by the Court's tutorial or that efforts at reenactment would founder on the inertia that makes it difficult to enact legislation, including reenactments. Bickel had a higher opinion of legislatures than Holmes but a lower one than Thayer, for he thought legislators merely educable, rather than competent even without a Bickellian Court's tutorials.

32. See, for example, *Quill v. Vacco*, 80 F.3d 716, 738–743 (2d Cir. 1996) (Calabresi, J., concurring), reversed, 521 U.S. 793 (1997); *United States v. Then*, 56 F.3d 464, 469 (2d Cir. 1995) (Calabresi, J., concurring); Guido Calabresi, "The Supreme Court, 1990 Term: Foreword: Antidiscrimination and Constitutional Accountability (What the Bork-Brennan Debate Ignores)," 105 *Harvard Law Review* 80, 103–108 (1991).

33. Alexander M. Bickel, "The Supreme Court, 1960 Term: Foreword: The Passive Virtues," 75 *Harvard Law Review* 40, 47–58 (1961).

34. Id. at 58–64.

Bickel criticized the Connecticut birth-control statute (which forbade the use of contraceptives, without an exception even for married couples) that the Supreme Court invalidated a few years later in the *Griswold* decision. Nothing in the Constitution or in the Court's previous decisions seemed to bear on such a statute; family and sex law had long been thought prerogatives of the states. But Bickel didn't want the Court to uphold such a bad statute and so he advised its invalidation on the narrow ground that because it was not being enforced it should be deemed abandoned.[35] Such a ruling would allow the state to reenact the statute. But because it is much more difficult to enact a statute than to leave it on the books unenforced (or weakly enforced, as in the case of the Connecticut birth-control law), probably the statute would not be reenacted (reenactment of a statute being equivalent, in point of difficulty, to its original enactment); and so Bickel's goal would be achieved without the Court's making a frontal assault on state power to regulate contraception.

For Bickel, then, judicial self-restraint was prudential. Bickel, and he hoped the Justices as well, were ahead of public opinion, and so had to maneuver cautiously if his and their views were to become durable constitutional law. The approach diverges from Thayer's because it rests on a patronizing attitude toward legislatures (and the public at large) and assigns a role of moral leadership to the Supreme Court.

With Bickel's death in 1974 the main Thayerian tradition comes to an end,[36] though the doctrines of justiciability decisively shaped by

35. "A device to turn the thrust of forces favoring and opposing the present objectives of the statute toward the legislature, where the power of at least initial decision properly belongs in our system, was available to the Court, and it is implicit in the prevailing opinion [in *Poe v. Ullman*, 367 U.S. 497 (1961)]. It is the concept of desuetude." Bickel, "The Supreme Court, 1960 Term," at 61. But the Court in *Griswold* invalidated the Connecticut statute not on grounds of desuetude but as an infringement of a constitutional "right of privacy" (an Aesopian term meaning, in Supreme Court discourse, sexual freedom). *Griswold v. Connecticut*, 381 U.S. 479, 485–486 (1965). Actually the statute *was* enforced, though only against birth control clinics.

36. The precipitous decline in interest in Bickel's ideas in the decade following his death is remarked in Anthony T. Kronman, "Alexander Bickel's Philosophy of Prudence," 94 *Yale Law Journal* 1567 (1985).

Brandeis survive. The terms "judicial restraint" and "judicial self-restraint" survive too—but only as vague all-purpose compliments, routinely intoned in Senate confirmation hearings, where they serve as rhetorical camouflage, while "judicial activism" survives as a vague, all-purpose pejorative.[37] There are few academic Thayerians any more[38] and no apostles of restraint on the current Supreme Court.[39] The last indisputably restrained Justice (yet imperfectly so, from a Thayerian perspective) was the second Justice Harlan, who retired three years before Bickel's death. The "rational basis" criterion of constitutionality, a legacy of Thayer, has dropped away, becoming another Aesopian formula, this one standing for the Court's lack of interest in applying constitutional norms to statutes restricting property rights, though interest in doing that is reviving as the Court moves to the right.

The Decline of Self-Restraint

The decline of judicial self-restraint as a doctrine is shown graphically in the following Ngram chart of the terms "judicial self-restraint" and "judicial activism" (Google's Ngram Viewer program was explained in the Introduction):

I begin the chart in 1930 because the terms were not used before then, although the concepts were fully formed in the nineteenth century. Notice how "judicial self-restraint" enters the legal vocabulary in 1935, as criticism

37. See Easterbrook, "Do Liberals and Conservatives Differ," at 1401–1403. I use "activism" to denote rejection of constitutional restraint. On the history of the term, see the interesting discussion in Craig Green, "An Intellectual History of Judicial Activism," 58 *Emory Law Journal* 1195 (2009).

38. Two, Mark Tushnet and Robin West, are cited in Richard H. Fallon, Jr., *Implementing the Constitution* 142 n. 41 (2001). Fallon himself, however, rejects judicial self-restraint. Id. at 9–10. Tushnet and West are well to the left in the political spectrum, and one wonders whether they would be Thayerians if the Supreme Court had a liberal majority. Another neo-Thayerian, however, Adrian Vermeule (see Vermeule, *Judging under Uncertainty*, ch. 8), is well to the right.

39. David A. Strauss, "The Death of Judicial Conservatism," 4 *Duke Journal of Constitutional Law and Public Policy* 1, 7–10 (2009); Easterbrook, "Do Liberals and Conservatives Differ," at 1409. Justice Ginsburg comes closest.

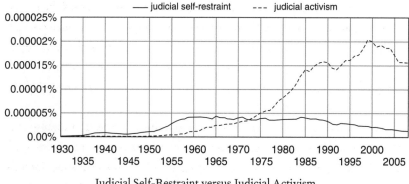

Judicial Self-Restraint versus Judicial Activism

of the conservative activism of the anti-New Deal Supreme Court surged, and peaks in the 1960s, when the Warren Court's liberal activism peaked, igniting sharp criticism from conservatives. The term then began a gradual but inexorable decline to its present low level. The negative term, "judicial activism," had a later start, but like its converse surged in the 1960s, and continued rising, peaking at the end of the 1990s, and then dropping but to a level far above that of "judicial self-restraint." "Judicial activism" remains an all-purpose term of opprobrium, but unsurprisingly lost some ground when "judicial self-restraint" ceased to be a rallying cry.

Thayer has at least two remaining epigones on the federal courts of appeals, though neither is an orthodox Thayerian (there are no orthodox Thayerians). One is Judge Clifford Wallace of the Ninth Circuit, the author of a thoughtful article, somewhat Thayerian in character, though imperfectly so and he doesn't mention Thayer.[40] I think he makes a mistake in defending judicial restraint by reference to democracy, which he argues requires that the judges give the widest possible latitude to legislative choice. For by pitching his defense of judicial restraint on democracy he plays into the hands of constitutional theorist John Hart Ely, who defended the activist decisions of the Warren Court on the ground that they made American government more democratic:[41] for Ely, judicial activism in defense of democracy trumped judicial restraint grounded in respect for democracy.

40. J. Clifford Wallace, "The Jurisprudence of Judicial Restraint: A Return to the Moorings,"50 *George Washington Law Review* 1 (1981).

41. John Hart Ely, *Democracy and Distrust* 74–75 (1980).

The most interesting thing in Wallace's article is his refreshingly precise formula for restrained judicial decision making. When a case is in doubt, he says, the judge should

(1) Clarify only as much of the statute as is necessary to decide the case before the court.
(2) Clarify the statute in the fashion that the legislature probably would have, had the ambiguity been brought to its attention.
(3) Follow common-law principles of statutory construction.[42]
(4) Clarify the statute in a manner that innovates the least against the background of prior law—especially in regard to extending causes of action.[43]

But these are not Thayerian precepts. They are techniques for interpreting statutes narrowly. Narrow interpretation curtails the scope of legislation. That is very un-Thayerian.

The most restrained of well-known current judges is J. Harvie Wilkinson III[44] of the Fourth Circuit, who is notable for opposing not only *Roe v. Wade*, abhorred by conservatives, but also *District of Columbia v. Heller*, abhorred by liberals.[45] But Wilkinson's opposition to both decisions, although consistent with Thayerism because neither decision satisfies Thayer's standard for invalidating legislation, is not Thayerian in spirit. Wilkin-

42. That may sound like an oxymoron, but we'll see in the next chapter that it's not.

43. Wallace, "The Jurisprudence of Judicial Restraint," at 9.

44. Rated the most restrained of the 142 current federal court of appeals judges for which the author had data, in Corey Rayburn Yung, "Flexing Judicial Muscle: An Empirical Study of Judicial Activism in the Federal Courts," 105 *Northwestern University Law Review* 1, 42, 55 (2011). Yung's concept of activism, however, goes further than just rejection of restraint in invalidating statutes; his measure of a judge's activism is the ratio of reversals based on a plenary standard of appellate review to reversals based on a deferential standard. The idea is that the former type of reversal bespeaks a lack of deference.

45. See J. Harvie Wilkinson III, "Of Guns, Abortions, and the Unraveling Rule of Law," 95 *Virginia Law Review* 253 (2009), and his recent book *Cosmic Constitutional Theory*.

son does not adopt Thayer's formula. And apart from his emphasis on the effect of the *Roe* and *Heller* decisions on policy experimentation by states[46] (assuming, as he correctly did, that the Supreme Court would extend its ruling in *Heller* to the states), his criticisms, like Judge Wallace's, are based on a preference for democratic decision making over judicial.[47] That's not the same thing as Thayer's belief that aggressive judicial review of legislation infantilizes legislators. Wilkinson doesn't appear to think that judicial self-restraint would make legislators responsible deliberators on constitutional questions.

Among noted lower-court judges of the past, Learned Hand qualified as a Thayerian, yet went further than Thayer, urging that most of the Bill of Rights be regarded as not justiciable at all.[48] But Henry Friendly, the greatest judge of the last half century and accused by no one of being an "activist" in the pejorative sense of that abused term—on the contrary, he was a trenchant critic of the activist excesses of the Warren Court—was not a Thayerian. For consider this passage from one of his notable essays: "A great constitutional decision is not often compelled in the sense that a contrary one would lie beyond the area of rationality. I shall not insist that *Erie* was the rare exception. But it provided a far better fit with the scheme of the Constitution as that had developed over the years than do the assertions that the 'necessary and proper' clause empowers Congress to establish substantive law for the federal courts in fields otherwise reserved to the states, or that federal courts themselves may do so—thereby not merely permitting but insuring unequal justice under law."[49] The first two sen-

46. See Wilkinson's article "Of Guns, Abortions, and the Unraveling Rule of Law," at 307–309, 318–320.

47. As when he says, rejecting constitutional theory, that "convinced that they possess pre-articulated frameworks that dictate unassailable results, theory-driven judges and scholars have forgotten that wisdom lies simply in knowing the limits of one's knowledge, that good sense is more often displayed in collective and diverse settings than in a rarefied appellate atmosphere, and that the language, structure, and history of law serve best as mediums of restraint rather than excuses for intrusion." Wilkinson, *Cosmic Constitutional Theory*, at 115.

48. Learned Hand, *The Bill of Rights* 65–66 (1958).

49. Henry J. Friendly, "In Praise of *Erie*—and of the New Federal Common Law," 39 *New York University Law Review* 383, 398 (1964).

tences in this passage, if spoken by a Thayerian, would compel the conclusion that the Court should have upheld the constitutionality of Congress's prescribing rules of decision for federal diversity cases. Instead Friendly goes on to defend the *Erie* decision (written by Brandeis, who based it partly on earlier dissents by Holmes), which held the contrary, in the process wiping out a host of precedents.

The Rise of Constitutional Theory

The evanescence of constitutional restraint, both generally and in its Thayerian form, is related to the rise of constitutional theory—a rise stimulated by the conservative backlash against the Warren Court and the follow-on rulings of the Burger Court, such as *Roe v. Wade*—of a kind remote from Thayer's theory. (Robert Bork is a key figure here.) Modern constitutional theories—whether Bork's or Scalia's originalism, or Ely's representation reinforcement, or Breyer's active liberty, or the Constitution as common law, or the living Constitution, or the unwritten Constitution (see next chapter), or the invisible Constitution, or living originalism, or the moral reading of the Constitution, or libertarianism, or the Constitution in exile, or anything else—are designed to tell judges, particularly Supreme Court Justices, how to decide cases correctly rather than merely sensibly or prudently. And if there is a demonstrably right answer to even the most difficult constitutional question, it is natural to think it's the answer the judge *must* give, that any other answer would be lawless. Modern constitutional theory gives the theorists the required certitude, emboldening them to ignore Holmes's dictum that certitude is not the test of certainty. So "Scalia and Thomas insist that the apparent tension between their sharp demands for restraint in some areas and their sweeping exercise of activism in others is resolved by the written Constitution itself."[50] They make prudence seem a cop-out (one is put in mind of William Blake's definition of prudence: a rich, ugly old maid courted by incapacity). As Wilkinson puts it, modern constitutional theories "have given rise to nothing less than competing schools of liberal and conservative judicial activ-

50. Thomas M. Keck, "Activism and Restraint on the Rehnquist Court: Timing, Sequence and Conjuncture in Constitutional Development," 35 *Polity* 121, 139 (2002).

ism, schools that have little in common other than a desire to seek theoretical cover for prescribed and often partisan results."[51]

The precondition to a judge's embrace of Thayer's standard is thus to have no theory of how to decide whether a statute or an executive action violates the Constitution. For if he has such a theory he will feel lawless in failing to apply it. So it's no surprise that none of the Thayerians had any idea how legal analysis would yield an answer to a question arising under one of the many vague or archaic provisions of the Constitution. "Everyone essentially believed that the Constitution could and should be interpreted using the same, open-ended process of forensic argument that was employed across legal domains—marshalling (as applicable, and in a relatively unstructured manner) arguments from text, structure, history, precedent, and consequences to reach the most persuasive overall conclusion."[52]

One might have thought that Thayerians would be strict constructionists, as strict construction of the Constitution would limit the frequency with which statutes would be invalidated. But the Thayerians were loose constructionists,[53] including Thayer himself.[54] And loose construction, when applied to a provision of the Constitution, is not a theory, but rather a license to read into the provision a judge's views of sound policy responsive to modern problems. It is when judges have such a license that there is pressure for a doctrine of judicial self-restraint.

But can a judge really decide a case without a theory of how to decide

51. Wilkinson, *Cosmic Constitutional Theory*, at 4.

52. Larry D. Kramer, "Judicial Supremacy and the End of Judicial Restraint," 100 *California Law Review* 621, 624 (2012).

53. See, for example, Thayer, *John Marshall*, in *James Bradley Thayer, Oliver Wendell Holmes, and Felix Frankfurter on John Marshall*; Oliver Wendell Holmes, "John Marshall," in id. at 129, 131 (remarking the "fortunate circumstance that the appointment of Chief Justice fell to John Adams, instead of to Jefferson a month later, and so gave it to a Federalist and loose constructionist to start the working of the Constitution"); Felix Frankfurter, "John Marshall and the Judicial Function," in id. at 135, 145 (remarking the "decisive influence [of] Marshall's experience at Valley Forge" on his work on the Supreme Court).

54. Thayer, "The Origin and Scope of the American Doctrine," at 138; Bickel, *The Least Dangerous Branch*, at 36, 43–44.

it correctly? Paradoxically the answer is that he can—in fact that he may have to. Faced with a case that doesn't yield to conventional legal reasoning, a judge can't throw up his hands and say "I can't decide this case because I don't know what the right answer to the question presented by it is." He has to decide it, using whatever tools are at hand. Judges who don't insist that a legalistic algorithm will decide every case tend to be "pragmatists," not in some pretentious philosophical sense (though there are affinities with pragmatic philosophers, such as Charles Sanders Peirce, a friend of Holmes, and John Dewey, an admirer of Holmes) but in the sense of an approach to decision making that emphasizes consequences over doctrine, or, stated otherwise, fits doctrine around consequences. Thayer and his followers were pragmatists. Wilkinson misses this point, describing pragmatism as antithetical to judicial self-restraint.[55]

Holmes was famously skeptical about conventional legal reasoning— about legal formalism in other words—especially in constitutional cases, where the orthodox materials of decision quickly run out and judges' ideologies and emotions are engaged and often are decisive in shaping their votes. The discussion of constitutional methodology in Holmes's opinions is remarkably casual compared to current Supreme Court opinions, which fairly pant with erudition. His opinions are almost barren of references to constitutional text, the framers' understanding of it, or principles of interpretation. The great dissent in *Lochner* is only a page long and consists of Thayer's standard of reasonableness (asserted, not defended) plus brief invocations of a handful of cases in which the Supreme Court had—in conflict with *Lochner* itself, it seemed—limited the scope of substantive due process. Holmes cited these cases to refute any claim that "a rational and fair man would admit that [the maximum-hours statute at issue in *Lochner*] would infringe fundamental principles as they have been understood by the traditions of our people and our law." He conducted no analysis of the statute's actual or probable effects ("It does not need research to show . . ."), though one might think them highly relevant to its reasonableness.

Holmes's activist free-speech dissent in *Abrams* combined the prag-

<hr />

55. Wilkinson, *Cosmic Constitutional Theory*, at 87–88.

matic epistemology of Charles Sanders Peirce (his friend) and Darwinism (a pervasive influence, as I have suggested, on Holmes, who reached adulthood in the same year that *The Origin of Species* was published): truth is the body of ideas that has thus far survived the competitive struggle in the intellectual marketplace. "Thus far" is important; in Peirce's epistemology there are no absolute or, in all likelihood, permanent truths. And Holmes's activist dissent in *Olmstead* rested on a baldly stated claim that for the government to obtain evidence of criminal guilt illegally is worse from a moral (maybe an aesthetic) standpoint than by excluding the evidence to let the criminal escape the law's clutches.[56] There is very little conventional legal reasoning in these opinions—none in the *Olmstead* dissent. Yet they are among Holmes's most notable opinions.

In private correspondence Holmes described his approach to constitutional decision making as being based on an unwillingness to invalidate a statute unless it made him want to puke.[57] He didn't repeat the formula in an opinion or article, but it's as good a description as any of his approach. It is further evidence that he was not an orthodox Thayerian despite his appropriation of Thayer's test of reasonableness in opinions such as *Lochner*, and his generous (albeit private) acknowledgment of Thayer's influence. "Thayer's is a one-way approach, Holmes's a two-way. Thayer's approach limits—it never expands—judicial review. Holmes's approach

---

56. "There is no body of precedents by which we are bound, and which confines us to logical deduction from established rules. Therefore we must consider the two objects of desire both of which we cannot have and make up our minds which to choose. It is desirable that criminals should be detected, and to that end that all available evidence should be used. It also is desirable that the government should not itself foster and pay for other crimes, when they are the means by which the evidence is to be obtained. If it pays its officers for having got evidence by crime I do not see why it may not as well pay them for getting it in the same way, and I can attach no importance to protestations of disapproval if it knowingly accepts and pays and announces that in future it will pay for the fruits. We have to choose, and for my part I think it a less evil that some criminals should escape than that the government should play an ignoble part." *Olmstead v. United States*, 277 U.S. 438, 470 (1928) (dissenting opinion).

57. *Holmes-Laski Letters: The Correspondence of Mr. Justice Holmes and Harold J. Laski*, vol. 2, p. 888 (Mark DeWolfe Howe ed. 1953).

allows judges to stretch the constitutional text when necessary to avoid extreme injustice. Holmes's Constitution has no gaps—it is noteworthy how rarely his constitutional opinions quote the constitutional text."[58] Thus, "a[n orthodox] Thayerian would disapprove of [*Griswold v. Connecticut*] because the [Connecticut birth-control statute] was not unconstitutional beyond a reasonable doubt; indeed, it is difficult to find a provision of the Constitution on which to hang one's hat in a case about contraception. A Holmesian might find the statute so appalling (not only because of its theocratic cast, but also because its only practical effect was, by preventing birth control clinics from operating,[59] to deny poor married couples access to contraceptive devices other than condoms) that he would vote to invalidate it despite the difficulty of grounding his vote in the constitutional text."[60]

Brandeis liked to pile up facts to show that a challenged statute passed Thayer's test of reasonableness. But this is to say that for Brandeis constitutional law devolved into policy analysis. The idea that he shared with Holmes of the states as laboratories in which to conduct policy experiments was sensible, but was weakened by the fact that a federal statute might if upheld end experimentation yet restraint might require the Justices to uphold it.

Frankfurter's judicial approach is illustrated by his declaration that for police to use a stomach pump to obtain evidence of crime is "conduct that shocks the conscience"[61] and thus violates "the general requirement that States in their prosecutions respect certain decencies of civilized conduct. Due process of law, as a historic and generative principle, precludes defining, and thereby confining, these standards of conduct more precisely than to say that convictions cannot be brought about by methods that offend 'a sense of justice.'"[62] Apparently despairing of finding a guide other than "a

58. Richard A. Posner, *How Judges Think* 288 (2008).

59. Richard A. Posner, *Sex and Reason* 205 (1992); Mark A. Graber, "False Modesty: Felix Frankfurter and the Tradition of Judicial Restraint," 47 *Washburn Law Journal* 23, 24–26 (2007).

60. Posner, *How Judges Think*, at 288–289.

61. *Rochin v. California*, 342 U.S. 165, 172 (1952).

62. Id. at 173.

sense of justice" to deciding constitutional questions, Frankfurter hoped that punctilious observance of procedural formalities, coupled with exhaustive judicial deliberation, would generate sound decisions.[63] That is wrong. Procedural nitpicking can reduce the occasions on which the Supreme Court considers itself free to decide the constitutionality of a statute, but it cannot give content to such empty phrases as "a sense of justice" offered as constitutional doctrine. And judicial deliberation is overrated as a means of bringing about agreement on issues that divide judges deeply, as constitutional issues often do.[64]

And finally there is Bickel's stab at a theory of constitutional decision making: "The function of the Justices—and there is no question but what this accords with the great authoritative body of opinion on the subject—is to immerse themselves in the tradition of our society and of kindred societies that have gone before, in history and in the sediment of history which is law, and, as Learned Hand once suggested, in the thought and the vision of the philosophers and the poets. The Justices will then be fit to extract 'fundamental presuppositions' from their deepest selves, but in fact from the evolving morality of our tradition."[65] The phrase "fundamental presuppositions" is from a similarly ethereal passage by Frankfurter.[66] The number of Justices and judges who would have passed Hand's high-culture immersion test was small when he wrote; in today's busy, philistine culture it is minuscule.

Less remarked than the vulnerability of Thayerism to attack by constitutional theorists, but to me a more serious weakness, is its naïveté about the legislative process (not shared by Holmes, however, whose view of the process, which I quoted earlier, was cynical). Think for example of how a

---

63. See also Henry M. Hart, Jr., "The Supreme Court, 1958 Term: The Time Chart of the Justices," 73 *Harvard Law Review* 84 (1959).

64. See Lee Epstein, William M. Landes, and Richard A. Posner, *The Behavior of Federal Judges: A Theoretical and Empirical Study of Rational Choice*, ch. 7 (2013); Posner, *How Judges Think*, at 382 (index references to "Deliberation").

65. Bickel, *The Least Dangerous Branch*, at 236.

66. See *Sweezy v. New Hampshire*, 354 U.S. 234, 266–267 (1957) (concurring opinion).

Thayerian might defend *Brown v. Board of Education*. Frankfurter, an enthusiastic supporter of *Brown*, could have argued that the legislatures that had enacted public school segregation in the southern and border states were not authentic popular bodies because the large black populations in those states had been effectively disfranchised. (A parallel argument could be made in defense of *Baker v. Carr* about malapportioned legislatures: malapportionment entrenches electoral minorities.) But once one begins to question Thayer's sunny view of legislatures, one is embarked on a journey without an end. The U.S. Senate is malapportioned. The American political process at all levels is corrupted by money, interest groups, public ignorance and apathy, and inherent limitations of representative democracy, in which people vote for persons rather than policies. Holmes was a realist in the tradition of Thrasymachus in Plato's *Republic*: in a democracy, as in any other form of government, might ultimately prevails; judges, Holmes argued, had best get out of the juggernaut's path, though on occasion a piece of legislation might be so revolting that they must take a stand. Holmes's view of the legislative process is overdramatized, but comes closer to the truth than Thayer's view of legislators as constitutional deliberators who if left alone by judges would legislate as statesmen. Frankfurter shared Thayer's exaggerated view of legislators' ability and high-mindedness while Bickel naively thought them educable by Justices who shared his values.

Thayerism's Death and Legacy

I have explained the vulnerability of Thayerian theory (it might better be called a rhetoric than a theory), but I have not explained its death. It died on two fronts: in the academy (except for the handful of hyper-Thayerians), as I have explained, but also in the courts. Its judicial demise preceded its academic demise and is attributable to the exuberant activism of the Warren Court, which in the 1950s and 1960s powered a major, left-leaning expansion of constitutional law. The doctrine of "incorporation," pushed very hard by the liberal Justices (led in this domain by Justice Black), was the antithesis of judicial self-restraint because it imposed uniform rules on the states and could not be thought compelled by the Constitution. It not only preempted state legislative decisions but ended experimentation at the state level in the preempted areas.

Not that the Warren Court was the first activist Court; the Court had been activist in the *Lochner* era, and in earlier eras as well. But the Thayerian Justices on the *Lochner* Court, Holmes and Brandeis, had accrued considerable prestige as exponents of constitutional restraint, and beginning in the late 1930s the Court had rapidly dismantled the *Lochner* era's jurisprudence, by then broadly regarded as aberrant. The only notably restrained Justice of the Warren Court was Harlan—and not consistently so, or as celebrated a judicial figure as Holmes or Brandeis. The fizz had gone out of constitutional restraint, perhaps for good, as there has been no consistent exponent of judicial self-restraint on the Court since Harlan. One reason is that the conservative successors to the Justices of the Warren Court were not about to embrace a ratchet theory of judicial restraint (urged, naturally, by liberals): unrestrained liberals expand constitutional rights; restrained conservatives preserve the expanded rights by complying scrupulously with precedent in order to limit their own judicial discretion. That would be nonsensical, and is not implied by Thayerism.

One can imagine judicial self-restraint as an equilibrium and judicial activism as another equilibrium, but it's hard to imagine alternation, in which periods of activism and periods of restraint succeed one another, as an equilibrium.[67] Alternation would require a degree of self-abnegation that could not realistically be expected of Supreme Court Justices. It's no fun to be the conservator of a constitutional tradition one abhors, especially when the overruling of activist decisions can be defended as restoring a true judicial restraint,[68] rather than a misnamed restraint that gives

---

67. Aziz Z. Huq, "When Was Judicial Self-Restraint?" 100 *California Law Review* 579 (2012), provides evidence both for and against this conjecture.

68. As argued in Wallace, "The Jurisprudence of Judicial Restraint," at 15–16. On *Heller* as "payback" for *Roe v. Wade*, see Wilkinson, "Of Guns, Abortions, and the Unraveling Rule of Law," at 274. For explicit rejection of Thayerism by a prominent conservative constitutional theorist, see Steven G. Calabresi, "Thayer's Clear Mistake," 88 *Northwestern University Law Review* 269, 275–277 (1993).

controlling weight to activist precedents. Increasingly after Reagan's appointments to the Supreme Court, conservative Justices rolled back several major initiatives of the Warren Court, and having done so—and with the bit thus between their teeth—have kept moving rightward (with a boost from appointments by the two President Bushes), as in the handgun-possession and campaign-finance decisions.

One might have expected that the rightward turn which began in the 1980s and has accelerated since the Roberts and Alito appointments would give rise—as in the era of conservative judicial activism that lasted from Thayer's day to its abrupt end in 1937 when the Supreme Court, frightened by Roosevelt, threw in the towel—to a robust liberal revival of the doctrine of judicial self-restraint. Not so; for that would imply a repudiation of the doctrine of incorporation and the Supreme Court's landmark Warren-era decisions. In liberal quarters the search has been for a theory of judicial review that would legitimate those decisions while delegitimizing the growing conservative activism of the modern Court. The search has failed. The liberal academic theories of constitutional decision making, widely derided as mush, have little appeal even to liberal Justices. They have been unable to project a coherent vision of a liberal constitutional jurisprudence, while the right has gotten away with garbing its activism in legalistic rhetoric. Judicial self-restraint has ceased to be a contender.

Left and right each have a constitutional agenda. And because the Constitution is so old, and in critical respects so vague, it is plastic, creating another problem for Thayerism, perhaps the fatal one: given the Constitution's interpretive plasticity, a full-throated commitment to judicial self-restraint, the kind of commitment urged by Judge Wilkinson but shared by few other judges, would shrink constitutional law to very small dimensions. The doctrines of constitutional law are the creation of the Supreme Court by loose interpretation of the actual document. An immense body of doctrine in such areas as free speech, prisoner rights, religious rights and establishments, privacy, sexual freedom, gun ownership (as we'll see in the next chapter), civil and criminal procedure, and the regulation of commerce is the cumulative product of generations of freewheeling, anti-Thayerian judicial innovation.

But though dead, Thayerism has left a legacy. Most of the premises of the Thayerians, though not of Thayer himself, have enduring value: limitations on justiciability; Brandeis's desire to study the real-world impact of challenged legislation; and the desirability of preserving opportunities for state-level experimentation—well illustrated by the Supreme Court's decision refusing to invalidate school vouchers for parochial schools[69] and notably absent from its decision nationalizing the extravagant interpretation of the Second Amendment[70] discussed in the next chapter. Additionally supportive of judicial restraint in an approximately Thayerian sense are the arguments for judicial timidity in constitutional adjudication in general: Justices usually are competent lawyers, but rarely more; judicial decisions can be rich in unintended consequences; the scope of the Constitution is vast and the Justices operate on limited information; because there are no sensible algorithmic methods of deciding difficult cases, most constitutional decisions have only weak claims to objective validity; the parts of the Constitution that generate litigation at the Supreme Court level are too old and general to be directive; the issues presented in constitutional cases tend to be both emotional and momentous and the decisions resolving them inescapably reflect the Justices' personal values, psychology, background, peer pressures, political anxieties, professional experiences, ideological inclinations, and other nonlegalistic factors, often operating unconsciously; unrestrained courts produce unrestrained backlash (so compare the Warren and Roberts Courts); and courts have limited tools and as a result their "legislative" efforts can often be undone by the other branches. Unintended consequences of Supreme Court decisions abound. For example, Congress and many states reacted to the Warren Court's liberalization of criminal procedure by raising minimum and maximum prison sentences, so that, as far as anyone knows, while probably fewer innocent people are convicted nowadays, those who are serve longer terms, though sometimes they are exonerated before completion of their terms and released.

I have said that we need evidence-based law; and if we had it, there

---

69. *Zelman v. Simmons-Harris*, 536 U.S. 639 (2002).
70. *McDonald v. City of Chicago*, 130 S. Ct. 3020 (2010).

would be less need for a tiebreaker, because there would be fewer ties; and less need therefore for a doctrine of judicial self-restraint. But we do not have it, and I gave in Chapter 3 an example of where we are unlikely to get it: in factoring retribution into criminal sentences. Judges will continue to do this, on no better ground than emotion.

Because constitutional theory has failed to make constitutional law objective—because that law remains to an alarming degree political and ad hoc—there is an argument for a renewal of some approximation to Thayer's theory of constitutional restraint. Consider as just one of many examples of the need for such a theory the Supreme Court's decision in *Parents Involved in Community Schools v. Seattle School District No. 1.*[71] Two school districts, in two different states, used race as a factor in assigning students to public schools in an effort to achieve a degree of racial balance; without a racial "tiebreaker," the schools were apt because of residential patterns to remain segregated. The Supreme Court held, five (conservative Justices) to four (liberal Justices), that the school districts' use of race in this manner was a denial of equal protection of the laws to whites. The majority, concurring, and dissenting opinions sprawl over two hundred pages in the *U.S. Reports.* Justice Breyer's ninety-five-page dissenting opinion marshals considerable empirical evidence regarding the likely consequences of the racial-tiebreaker approach, but concurring opinions by Justices in the majority present contrary evidence.

The Justices in the majority, with the exception of Justice Kennedy, appear to believe that any use of racial classifications is unconstitutional, a doctrinaire position with no basis in the equal protection clause. The clause does not require that everyone be treated the same; it does not require for example that either everyone be in prison or no one be in prison; that everyone receive the identical entitlements from government; or that all public school teachers be paid the same salary. It can't, in short, be taken literally. It can only sensibly be understood to prohibit invidious, hurtful, arbitrary discrimination, and it is not obvious that a slight favoring of black children, who face an uphill battle in American society without fault on

71. 551 U.S. 701, 803 (2007).

their part, is invidious, hurtful, or arbitrary. Maybe it is, because it certainly does disadvantage innocent white children, and maybe it isn't, because the disadvantage probably is slight and a greater degree of social and economic equality may be important to the nation's overall welfare. Given these uncertainties, and the usual lack of guidance provided by vague, antiquated constitutional language, there was a strong argument for allowing the school districts in *Parents Involved* to experiment with a limited form of reverse discrimination. It is in so indeterminate a case as that—and indeterminate cases are legion in constitutional cases that the Supreme Court decides to hear—that Thayer's theory comes into its own. What a pity that today no Justice of the Supreme Court and precious few judges of any other court pay any heed to it.

❧ 7 ❧

COPING STRATEGIES FOR
APPELLATE JUDGES II

Interpretation

Originalism is just the search for a convenient past.

Leon Wieseltier

Nowadays the most ambitious efforts to free judges from having to understand empirical reality parade under the banner of interpretation. A linked pair go by the names "textualism" and "originalism"—in other words literalism and historicism. Together they constitute textual originalism, whose votaries purport to "look for meaning in the governing text, ascribe to that text the meaning that it has borne from its inception, and reject judicial speculation about both the drafters' extratextually derived purposes and the desirability of the fair reading's anticipated consequences."[1] So all that judges have to do and all they should do when faced with an issue of statutory or constitutional interpretation is apply the relevant statu-

---

1. Antonin Scalia and Bryan A. Garner, *Reading Law: The Interpretation of Legal Texts* xxvii (2012).

tory or constitutional text to the facts of the particular case. The escape from empirical reality is then complete.

In form, textual originalism is a celebration of judicial passivity; in practice, it is a rhetorical mask of political conservatism. At the other end of the political spectrum we encounter a freewheeling imaginative approach—one of rampant activism, so obviously unanchored as to be shunned even by liberal judges. I begin in this chapter with textual originalism as described and defended in a recent book by Justice Antonin Scalia and legal lexicographer Bryan Garner and then turn to the ungrounded liberal imagination on display in a recent book by Yale Law Professor Akhil Amar. I close with a brief discussion of an alternative approach that may be all there is between the extremes illustrated by the Scalia-Garner and Amar books.

The Spirit Killeth, but the Letter Giveth Life

The purest form of textualism derives the meaning of a statute or other legally operative document from dictionaries,[2] disregarding Learned Hand's warning that while "of course it is true that the words used, even in their literal sense, are the primary, and ordinarily the most reliable, source of interpreting the meaning of any writing: be it a statute, a contract, or anything else . . . [,] it is one of the surest indexes of a mature and developed jurisprudence not to make a fortress out of the dictionary; but to remember that statutes always have some purpose or object to accomplish, whose sympathetic and imaginative discovery is the surest guide to their meaning."[3] And as Judge Easterbrook, though himself a self-declared textualist,[4]

2. See Note, "Looking It Up: Dictionaries and Statutory Interpretation," 107 *Harvard Law Review* 1437 (1994); Phillip A. Rubin, "War of the Words: How Courts Can Use Dictionaries in Accordance with Textualist Principles," 60 *Duke Law Journal* 167 (2010).

3. *Cabell v. Markham*, 148 F.2d 737, 739 (2d Cir. 1945), affirmed, 326 U.S. 404 (1945). See also *Bartok v. Boosey & Hawkes, Inc.*, 523 F.2d 941, 947 (2d Cir. 1975).

4. Frank H. Easterbrook, "Textualism and the Dead Hand," 66 *George Washington Law Review* 1119, 1121, 1126 (1998). And see his foreword to Scalia and Garner, *Reading Law*, at xxi.

has added, "the choice among meanings [of words in statutes] must have a footing more solid than a dictionary—which is a museum of words, an historical catalog rather than a means to decode the work of legislatures."[5] Another commentator has said that "it makes no sense to declare a unitary meaning that 'the dictionary' assigns to a term. There are a wide variety of dictionaries from which to choose, and they usually provide several entries for each word. The selection of a particular dictionary and a particular definition is not obvious and must be defended on some other grounds of suitability. This fact is particularly troubling for those who seek to use dictionaries to determine ordinary meaning. If multiple definitions are available, which one best fits the way an ordinary person would interpret the term?"[6]

Dictionary definitions are acontextual, but the meaning of words and sentences depends critically on context, including background understandings. A sign in a park that says "Keep off the grass" is not properly interpreted to forbid the grounds crew to cut the grass. "One can properly attribute to legislators the reasonable minimum intention 'to say what one would ordinarily be understood as saying, given the circumstances in which it is said.' This principle, it should be noted, does not direct interpreters to follow the literal or dictionary meaning of a word or phrase. To the contrary, it demands careful attention to the nuances and specialized connotations that speakers of the relevant language attach to particular words and phrases in the context in which they are being used."[7] Although this was said by a textualist, it is rejected by Scalia and Garner in considering a similar hypothetical question of interpretation—the meaning of an ordinance which states that "No person may bring a vehicle into the park."[8]

5. Frank H. Easterbrook, "Text, History, and Structure in Statutory Interpretation," 17 *Harvard Journal of Law and Public Policy* 61, 67 (1994). See also A. Raymond Randolph, "Dictionaries, Plain Meaning, and Context in Statutory Interpretation," 17 *Harvard Journal of Law and Public Policy* 71, 72 (1994).

6. See Note, "Looking It Up," at 1445 (footnote omitted). See *United States v. Costello*, 666 F.3d 1040 (7th Cir. 2012).

7. John F. Manning, "The Eleventh Amendment and the Reading of Precise Constitutional Texts," 113 *Yale Law Journal* 1663, 1704 (2004).

8. Scalia and Garner, *Reading Law*, at 36.

Does this include an ambulance that enters the park to save a person's life? The authors answer "yes."[9] An ambulance is a vehicle. Any dictionary will tell you that. End of analysis. The result is perverse but to the authors' way of thinking perverse results are an acceptable price to pay for the objectivity that the authors think textual originalism offers—new dictionaries for new texts, old dictionaries for old ones. Had the draftsmen of the ordinance wanted to make an exception for ambulances, they should have said so. Maybe they will be more careful next time. Yet later we'll see Scalia and Garner retreat in the ambulance case, a retreat consistent with a pattern of equivocation exhibited throughout their book.

A recent empirical study of the Supreme Court's increasing reference to dictionaries has yielded devastating conclusions: "The Court's tendency to rely on one or at most two dictionaries per case, the wide variation in dictionary brand preferences among the justices, the fact that even justices with 'preferred' dictionaries are far from consistent in usage across individual cases, and the absence of a coherent approach to the time period distinction between statutory enactment and lawsuit filing, combine to suggest that this comparatively novel interpretive resource is being applied in strikingly subjective ways."[10] "In the Rehnquist and Roberts eras, dictionaries have become a principal resource for determining the meaning of statutes. Dictionary usage has risen from 3.3% of all decisions during the final five years of the Burger Court to 33.3% of our dataset decisions for the last three Roberts Court terms. Throughout this period of dramatically higher usage, the Court has failed to engage with interested legal audiences who have expressed skepticism regarding the justices' subjective, standardless, and seemingly impulsive dictionary practices. The justices also have not engaged with one another on the increased role played by dictionaries."[11]

A judge who wants to illustrate the meaning of a word doesn't have to

9. Id. at 39.

10. James J. Brudney and Lawrence Baum, "Oasis or Mirage: The Supreme Court's Thirst for Dictionaries in the Rehnquist and Roberts Eras" 5 (Fordham University School of Law, Jan. 2013), http://ssrn.com/abstract=2195644 (visited Feb. 7, 2013).

11. Id. at 91 (footnote omitted).

cite a dictionary. All he has to do is use the word in a sentence that readers would recognize as a correct English sentence. In an opinion holding that to "oppose" racial discrimination does not require "resistance" to racial discrimination (that is, taking steps to prevent or eliminate the discrimination), there was no need to look up "oppose" in a dictionary, as the Court did;[12] all the Court need have said was that "To say I oppose racial discrimination but I have done nothing to prevent or eliminate it is a proper use of the verb to 'oppose.'"

Justice Scalia is one of the most politically conservative Supreme Court Justices of the modern era—anyone doubting this should read his vitriolic partial dissent in *Arizona v. United States*[13]—and he is the intellectual leader of the conservative Justices on the current Supreme Court. Yet he claims that his judicial votes are generated by an objective interpretive methodology (the only objective methodology, he claims) and that because it is objective, ideology, including his own fervent ideology, plays no role. Obviously statutory text itself is not inherently liberal or conservative. But *textualism* is conservative. A legislature is thwarted when a judge refuses to apply its handiwork to an unforeseen situation that is encompassed by the statute's aim but does not make a smooth fit with its text. Ignoring the limitations of foresight, and also that a statute is a collective product that may leave many questions of interpretation to be answered by the courts because the enacting legislators didn't agree on the answers, the textual originalist demands that the legislature think through myriad hypothetical scenarios and provide for all of them explicitly rather than rely on courts to be sensible. Textual originalism is "gotcha" jurisprudence.

It is notable that legislators do not accept the Scalia-Garner prescriptions (such as the "last-antecedent canon" and the "series-qualifier canon" discussed later in this chapter); for if they did they would write their statutes to conform to them, and they don't. The best argument for textual originalism might seem to be that it would encourage legislators to make

12. See *Crawford v. Metropolitan Government of Nashville and Davidson*, 555 U.S. 271, 276 (1990).

13. 132 S. Ct. 2492, 2511 (2012). See in particular the anti-immigrant rant at p. 2522, which I discuss later in this chapter.

statutes crystalline, but there is no evidence that it has had such an effect despite its influential sponsorship by Scalia and other prominent conservatives on and off the bench. The collective nature of the legislative product makes such an aspiration infeasible. Textualism hobbles legislation—and thereby tilts toward "small government" and away from "big government," a tilt that in today's America, as distinct from Thomas Jefferson's America, is a conservative preference.

Scalia and Garner say that "the canons influence not just how courts approach texts but also the techniques that legal drafters follow in preparing those texts"[14] but provide no evidence; and in fact it appears that judges are appallingly ignorant of how statutes are actually drafted. An evolving empirical literature contradicts Scalia and Garner's confident assertion about the effect of judicial approaches to interpretation on the legislative process; the literature emphasizes for example the substantial weight that, *contra* Scalia and Garner, drafters of statutes give to legislative history.[15]

In a preemptive rebuttal to accusations that textual originalism is political, the Scalia-Garner treatise gives examples of liberal decisions that Scalia has written or joined.[16] There are indeed a number of them, which is no surprise—he must have voted in at least two thousand cases as a Justice of the Supreme Court. The book gives the example of his vote to hold a federal statute forbidding the burning of the American flag unconstitutional.[17] It is a curious example for a textualist to give, however, because the relevant constitutional provision—"Congress shall make no law abridging . . . the freedom of *speech*" (emphasis added)—does not speak to nonverbal

14. Scalia and Garner, *Reading Law*, at 61.

15. Abbe R. Gluck and Lisa Schultz Bressman, "Statutory Interpretation from the Inside—An Empirical Study of Congressional Drafting, Delegation and the Canons: Part I" (Part I forthcoming 65 *Stanford Law Review* (May 2013); Part II forthcoming 66 *Stanford Law Review* (2014); Victoria F. Nourse, "A Decision Theory of Statutory Interpretation: Legislative History by the Rules," 122 *Yale Law Journal* 70 (2012); Nourse and Jane C. Schacter, *The Politics of Legislative Drafting: A Congressional Case Study* 77 *New York University Law Review* 575 (2002).

16. Scalia and Garner, *Reading Law*, at 17.

17. *United States v. Eichman*, 496 U.S. 310 (1990). See also *Texas v. Johnson*, 491 U.S. 397 (1989).

forms of political protest and because burning cloth is not a modern invention. Scalia and Garner insist that legal terms be given their original meaning: "In their full context, words mean what they conveyed to reasonable people *at the time they were written*—with the understanding that general terms may embrace later technological innovations."[18] It is an insistence inconsistent with interpreting "speech" to encompass flag burning. As explained by Blackstone, whom Scalia and Garner revere as an authority on American law at the time of the Constitution though Blackstone's *Commentaries* preceded the Bill of Rights by a quarter of a century, "Neither is any restraint hereby laid upon freedom of thought or enquiry: liberty of private sentiment is still left; *the disseminating, or making public,* of bad sentiments, destructive of the ends of society, is the crime which society corrects."[19] That English people had a right of virtually unlimited public free speech was not recognized until the creation of the Speakers' Corner of Hyde Park in 1872, and English plays remained subject to censorship until 1968. In this country, the Sedition Act, passed as one of the Alien and Sedition Acts of 1798, seven years after the ratification of the Bill of Rights, made it a crime to publish "false, scandalous, and malicious writing" defamatory of the government or of certain government officials. A number of people were convicted of violating the Sedition Act. The Alien and Seditions Acts expired by their terms in 1801 without having been held to be unconstitutional.

Another curious feature of Scalia's defense of his judicial votes as being untainted by political ideology is that most of the liberal judicial votes that he mentions (though not his votes in the two flag-burning cases) are

18. Scalia and Garner, *Reading Law,* at 16 (emphasis added). See also id. at 86. The phrasing on page 86 is damaging to the authors' thesis: "Drafters of every era know that technological advances will proceed apace and that the rules they create will one day apply to all sorts of circumstances that they could not possibly envision." True, and among the "circumstances that they could not possibly envision" many are not technological yet have as strong a claim as technological advances to being allowed to modify original understanding.

19. William Blackstone, *Commentaries on the Laws of England,* vol. 4, p. 152 (1770) (emphasis added).

dissents from conservative decisions, and so have no impact on the conservative result. In a similar vein William Eskridge has pointed out that although Scalia emphatically denounces the use of legislative history as a tool of statutory interpretation—with characteristic bluntness he has called it "garbage"[20]—he joins conservative although not liberal opinions that invoke legislative history.[21]

The decisive objection to the quest for original meaning, even when conducted in good faith, is that judicial historiography rarely dispels ambiguity. Judges are not competent historians. Even real historiography is frequently indeterminate, as real historians acknowledge.[22] A dubious form of historical analysis endorsed however by some originalists is speculation about how people who lived long ago would have answered a question that had never been put to them, and could not have been because it concerned a practice or concept or technology that did not exist and was not foreseen during their lifetime. Scalia accepts this approach with respect to technological change. (He has to; otherwise the Second Amendment—see next paragraph—would create a right to keep and bear only eighteenth-century weapons.) Yet no historian could give a responsible answer to the question how an eighteenth-century mind would react to twenty-first century technologies of surveillance, criminal investigation, marketing, financial regulation, mass media, and so forth.[23] To put to judges questions that are unan-

20. Transcript of Reuters interview with Antonin Scalia and Bryan A. Garner, p. 20, Sept. 17, 2012, http://newsandinsight.thomsonreuters.com/uploadedFiles/Reuters_Content/2012/09_-_September/Scalia_Reuters_transcript.pdf (visited Oct. 3 2012).

21. William N. Eskridge, Jr., "The New Textualism and Normative Canons," 113 *Columbia Law Review* 531, 567 n. 183 (2013). In addition, though Scalia and Garner are particularly derisive of "purposive" interpretations of statutory text (see index references to "purpose" and "purposivism" in Scalia and Garner, *Reading Law,* at 550–551), Scalia joined a frankly purposive, anti-textualist conservative dissent in *NASA v. Federal Labor Relations Authority,* 527 U.S. 229, 253–254 (1999). He also, we'll see, sometimes uses legislative history in his own opinions; I discuss a notable example shortly.

22. Georg G. Iggers, *Historiography in the Twentieth Century: From Scientific Objectivity to the Postmodern Challenge,* 8–9 (1997).

23. See Leonard W. Levy, *Original Intent and the Framers' Constitution* (1988);

swerable is to evoke "motivated reasoning," the form of cognitive delusion that consists of credulous acceptance of the evidence that supports a pre-conception and peremptory rejection of evidence that contradicts it.[24]

Let's look at how in *District of Columbia v. Heller*,[25] which held that the Second Amendment creates a right to own a handgun for self-defense, Justice Scalia used history to derive that interpretation. The amendment states: "A well regulated Militia being necessary to the security of a free State, the right of the people to keep and bear Arms, shall not be infringed." All that this seems to mean is that since a militia, provided that it is well regulated, is a very good thing for a state to have, the federal government must not be allowed to castrate it by forbidding the people of the United States to possess weapons. For then the militia would have no weapons, and an unarmed militia would be an oxymoron—and the federal government would be too powerful in relation to the states. Scalia and Garner quote approvingly Justice Joseph Story's analysis of statutory preambles—"the preamble of a statute is a key to open the mind of the makers, as to the mischiefs, which are to be remedied, and the objects, which are to be accomplished by the provisions of the statute."[26] But both the Scalia-Garner book and the *Heller* opinion ignore Story when it comes to the preamble of the Second Amendment ("A well regulated Militia being necessary to the security of a free State"), though the preamble implies that the Second Amendment is not about personal self-defense but about forbidding the federal government to disarm state militias. The *Heller* opinion treats the preamble dismissively, contrary to the favorable treatment of preambles in the Scalia-Garner book, where they are subsumed under "canon of construction" 34 (that is,

---

Peter Novick, *That Noble Dream: The "Objectivity Question" and the American Historical Profession* (1988).

24. See Daniel C. Molden and E. Tory Higgins, "Motivated Thinking," in *The Cambridge Handbook of Thinking and Reasoning* 295–317 (Keith J. Holyoak and Robert G. Morrison eds. 2005). See also *Special Issue: Political Dogmatism*, in *Critical Review: A Journal of Politics and Society*, vol. 24, no. 2 (2012).

25. *District of Columbia v. Heller*, 554 U.S. 570 (2008).

26. Scalia and Garner, *Reading Law*, at 218, quoting Joseph Story, *Commentaries on the Constitution of the United States* 326 (2d ed. 1851).

number 34 of the seventy rules of statutory interpretation that the book discusses), the "prefatory-materials canon." The book nowhere mentions the preamble to the Second Amendment.

The preamble has a history. Americans in the late eighteenth century feared a standing army. They thought it much more likely than a citizen militia to become an instrument of tyranny and to entangle the nation in foreign wars. They feared centralized government (as found in Britain), and on both counts wanted to make sure that the states could retain their militias. Fear that without such a provision in the Bill of Rights the provision in Article I of the Constitution authorizing Congress to organize, arm, discipline, and call into service "the Militia" (a term that embraces the state militias, because the same provision reserves the right to train and officer "the Militia" to the respective states) would enable Congress to disarm them was expressed in the debates over the ratification of the original Constitution and was the motivation for the Second Amendment. Whether read in isolation or in the light of the concerns that actuated its adoption, the amendment has no reference to the private possession of handguns for defense of person or property. "The original understanding of the Second Amendment was neither an individual right of self-defense nor a collective right of the states, but rather a civic right that guaranteed that citizens would be able to keep and bear those arms needed to meet their legal obligation to participate in a well-regulated militia."[27]

Most professional historians consider the weight of the historical evidence to be against the existence of a common law right, elevated to constitutional status by the Second Amendment, to have weapons in the home

---

27. Saul Cornell, *A Well-Regulated Militia: The Founding Fathers and the Origins of Gun Control in America* 2 (2006). See also Paul Finkelman, "'A Well Regulated Militia': The Second Amendment in Historical Perspective," 76 *Chicago-Kent Law Review* 195, 213–214 (2000); Don Higginbotham, "The Federalized Militia Debate: A Neglected Aspect of Second Amendment Scholarship," 55 *William & Mary Quarterly* 39, 47–50 (1998); Roy G. Weatherup, "Standing Armies and Armed Citizens: An Historical Analysis of the Second Amendment," 2 *Hastings Constitutional Law Quarterly* 961, 994–995 (1975).

for purposes unrelated to militia duty.[28] Fourteen of the eighteen history professors who signed amicus curiae briefs in the *Heller* case sided with the District of Columbia. Scalia doubtless believes that historians disfavor *Heller* because as humanities professors they tend to be liberals, and liberals tend to support gun control. Fair enough—but if history is such a mushy discipline that historians' political views shape their professional views, history is not a good candidate for bringing objectivity to constitutional decision making.

The majority opinion in *Heller* emphasizes not only the supposed existence of a preexisting right to keep and bear arms for personal defense but also, and critically, what the words of the Second Amendment would have meant to late eighteenth-century readers.[29] But to extract the desired meaning from those words required Scalia to ignore the preamble. No other right conferred by the Bill of Rights comes with a preamble. Imagine if the cruel and unusual punishments clause in the Eighth Amendment were prefaced by: "Drawing and quartering having been used by the English monarch to intimidate political and religious dissenters. . . ." That would affect how broadly courts interpreted the phrase "cruel and unusual punishments."

Scalia acknowledges in *Heller* that allowing people to keep handguns in their home cannot help the militias, because modern military weapons are not appropriate for home defense. Yet the opinion also says that the only weapons the Second Amendment entitles civilians to possess are ones that are not "highly unusual in society at large."[30] Modern military weapons are highly unusual in society at large. So by creating a privilege to own guns of no interest to a militia, the opinion decouples the amendment's two clauses.

The Court justified this decoupling by arguing that the word "people" in the expression "the right of the people to keep and bear Arms" (the

---

28. Cornell, *A Well-Regulated Militia,* at 2–4, 58–65; Lois G. Schwoerer, "To Hold and Bear Arms: The English Perspective," 76 *Chicago-Kent Law Review* 27, 34–38 (2000); Don Higginbotham, "The Second Amendment in Historical Context," 16 *Constitutional Commentary* 263, 265 (1999).

29. *District of Columbia v. Heller,* 554 U.S at 577–592.

30. Id. at 627.

amendment's second clause) *must* comprehend more than just militiamen because eighteenth-century militias enrolled only able-bodied free men— a mere subset of the people of the United States. But obviously the framers did not mean to confer even a prima facie constitutional right to possess guns on slaves, criminals, lunatics, and children, none of whom were thought eligible for militia service. The purpose of the first clause of the amendment, the militia clause, is to narrow the right that the second clause confers on the "people."

Undoubtedly the framers and ratifiers believed that the right of militiamen to keep and bear arms entitled them to keep muskets in their homes. For members of a militia were required to *provide* the muskets with which to arm themselves when on militia duty. The muskets were their personal property rather than that of state governments. But to use this historical understanding as the ground of a constitutional right of members of the National Guard (as the state militias are now collectively termed) to keep military weapons (machine guns, hand grenades, mortars, etc.) in their homes would be preposterous, and is disclaimed in the opinion. Properly interpreted, the Second Amendment allows private ownership of guns only if required for militia duty.

There is an unrecognized tension between Justice Scalia's angry disdain for legislative history as an aid in interpreting statutes and his enthusiastic mining of what by contrast with most statutory legislative history is ancient history when it comes to interpreting the eighteenth-century Constitution. If eighteenth-century history can be reconstructed by a judge and his law clerks, why not the twentieth- or twenty-first history of a modern statute? And if history is a treacherous guide to modern statutes, how can it be the vade mecum to understanding old constitutional provisions?

One reason for Scalia's criticism of the use of legislative history to interpret statutes is that a legislature is a hydra-headed body whose members may not agree on the resolution of the interpretive issues raised by a statute they've voted for. He goes too far.[31] But when he looks for the original

---

31. See Christian E. Mammen, *Using Legislative History in American Statutory Interpretation*, ch. 9 (2002); Nourse, "A Decision Theory of Statutory Interpretation."

meaning of constitutional provisions, he is doing legislative history of enactments of a hydra-headed body—a constitutional convention, a Congress, ratifiers (state conventions or state legislatures)—bodies often with more heads than a legislature has.

True, if "legislative history" just means the drafting history of a provision, his use of legislative history in *Heller*[32] was limited. But that is too narrow an understanding of the term. Scalia's coauthor defines legislative history as "the background and events leading to the enactment of a statute, including hearings, committee reports, and floor debates."[33] The term "cruel and unusual punishments" in the Eighth Amendment was taken verbatim from the English Bill of Rights of 1689, more than a century before the ratification of the Eighth Amendment; but would Scalia deny that the English original was part of the amendment's legislative history? The "background and events leading to the enactment" of the Second Amendment are the very focus of the *Heller* opinion. Scalia's quest for original meaning took him to a variety of English and American sources from which he distilled the existence of a common law right of armed self-defense that, he argued, had been codified in the Second Amendment. Some of the English sources were medieval.

In so questing, Scalia had been engaged in what is derisively called "law office history." The derision is deserved. Lawyers are advocates for their clients; and judges and especially their law clerks tend to be advocates for whichever side of the case the judge has decided to vote for. The judge sends his law clerks scurrying to the library for bits and pieces of historical documentation. When the clerks are the numerous and able clerks of Supreme Court Justices, enjoying the assistance of the able staffs of the Supreme Court library and the Library of Congress, and when dozens or sometimes hundreds of amicus curiae briefs have been filed, many bulked out with the fruits of their authors' own tendentious law office historiography, it is a simple matter to compose a plausible historical defense of a result desired on undisclosed grounds. (Sanford Levinson, a liberal professor

32. See *District of Columbia v. Heller*, 554 U.S. at 598–599, 603–605.

33. "Legislative History," *Black's Law Dictionary* 983 (Bryan A. Garner, editor in chief, 9th ed. 2009).

of constitutional law, has acknowledged that the most important reason for *his* support of a constitutional right of private possession of handguns is that opposition to the right is harmful to the electoral prospects of the Democratic Party.)[34] Actually it wasn't *so* simple in *Heller*, so Scalia and his staff labored mightily to produce a long opinion (the majority opinion is almost twenty-five thousand words long) that would convince, or perhaps just overwhelm, doubters. The range of historical references in the majority opinion is breathtaking, but it is not evidence of disinterested historical inquiry; it is evidence of the ability of well-staffed courts to produce snow jobs.

This is strikingly shown by the opinion's lengthy discussion of how the Second Amendment has been interpreted. Scalia quotes a number of statements in the past two centuries to the effect that the amendment guarantees a personal right to possess handguns. But they are statements by lawyers or other advocates, including legislators and judges and law professors dabbling in history, rather than by disinterested historians—more law-office history, in other words. Moreover, those statements had had no traction before *Heller*. For more than two centuries the "right" supposedly created by the Second Amendment of private possession of handguns for purposes of personal protection had lain dormant. Constitutional rights often do lie dormant, spectral subjects of theoretical speculation until some change in the social environment creates a demand for their vivification and enforcement. But nothing had changed in the social environment to justify giving the Second Amendment a new life discontinuous with its old one: a young new wine in a decidedly old wineskin. There is no greater urgency about allowing people to possess handguns for self-defense or defense of property today than there was thirty years ago when the

34. Sanford Levinson, "Democratic Politics and Gun Control," *Reconstruction*, Spring 1992, p. 137. Misuse of history is not a monopoly of conservative judges; it is thoroughly bipartisan. See Neil M. Richards, "Clio and the Court: A Reassessment of the Supreme Court's Uses of History," 13 *Journal of Law and Politics* 809 (1997); William M. Wiecek, "Clio as Hostage: The United States Supreme Court and the Uses of History," 24 *California Western Law Review* 227 (1988); Alfred H. Kelly, "Clio and the Court: An Illicit Love Affair," 1965 *Supreme Court Review* 119.

prevalence of violent crime was greater, or for that matter a hundred years ago.

Judge Wilkinson, whom we encountered in the last chapter fighting a rearguard action in defense of judicial self-restraint, argues that since historical analysis of the right to keep and bear arms for personal protection is at best inconclusive from the standpoint of advocates of interpreting the amendment to create such a right, judicial self-restraint dictated that the District of Columbia's ordinance not be invalidated.[35] His argument derives support from a surprising source: Judge Easterbrook's foreword to the Scalia-Garner tome. The foreword lauds the book to the skies, but toward the end plants the following deeply subversive thought: "Words don't have intrinsic meanings; the significance of an expression depends on how the interpretive community alive at the time of the text's adoption understood those words. The older the text, the more distant that interpretive community from our own. At some point the difference becomes *so* great that the meaning is no longer recoverable reliably."[36] And what should a court do when that happens? It should, Easterbrook contends, "declare that meaning has been lost, so that the living political community must choose."[37] The "living political community" in *Heller* consisted of the voters and officials of the District of Columbia. "When the original meaning is lost to the passage of time . . . the justification for judges' having the last word evaporates. The alternative is choice through the Constitution's principal means of decision: a vote among elected representatives."[38] Scalia

35. See J. Harvie Wilkinson III, "Of Guns, Abortions, and the Unraveling Rule of Law," 95 *Virginia Law Review* 253, 264–275 (2009).

36. Easterbrook, Foreword to Scalia and Garner, *Reading Law*, at xxv (emphasis in original).

37. Id. See also "A Dialogue with Federal Judges on the Role of History in Interpretation," 80 *George Washington Law Review* 1889, 1915 (2012) (remarks of Frank H. Easterbrook).

38. Easterbrook, Foreword, at xxvi. See also Joshua D. Hawley, "The Most Dangerous Branch," *National Affairs*, Fall 2012, pp. 29, 39. Judge Easterbrook also takes a "more relaxed" view than Scalia of the use of legislative history to illuminate statutory meaning, as pointed out in Neil Duxbury, *Elements of Legislation* 221 n. 192 (2013), citing an opinion (*Board of Trade v. SEC*, 187 F.3d 713, 720 (7th Cir. 1999)) and

and Garner seem to endorse a version of the doctrine of judicial self-restraint when they say that the unconstitutionality of a statute must be "clearly shown."[39] But they do not practice what they preach.

Still another problem with Scalia's analysis—again one internal to textual originalism—is disregard for the interpretive conventions of the legal culture in which the Second Amendment was drafted and ratified. The reigning theory of legislative interpretation in the early years of the United States was flexible—"loose"—construction, as famously articulated by Chief Justice Marshall in numerous opinions, such as *United States v. Fisher,*[40] where he wrote

> that the consequences are to be considered in expounding laws, where the intent is doubtful, is a principle not to be controverted; but it is also true that it is a principle which must be applied with caution, and which has a degree of influence dependent on the nature of the case to which it is applied. Where rights are infringed, where fundamental principles are overthrown, where the general system of the laws is departed from, the legislative intention must be expressed with irresistible clearness to induce a court of justice to suppose a design to effect such objects. But where only a political regulation is made, which is inconvenient, if the intention of the legislature be expressed in terms which are sufficiently intelligible to leave no doubt in the mind when the words are taken in their ordinary sense, it would be

---

several articles (for example, "Text, History, and Structure in Statutory Interpretation," 17 *Harvard Journal of Law and Public Policy* 61, 64 (1994)) by Easterbrook.

39. Scalia and Garner, *Reading Law,* at 345. See also id. at 410 n. 24.

40. 2 Cranch (6 U.S.) 358, 389–390 (1805). For other examples from the period, see *Kerlin's Lessee v. Bull,* 1 Dall. (1 U.S.) 175, 178 (1786); *Woodbridge v. Amboy,* 1 N.J.L. 213 (Sup. Ct. 1794); James Madison, *Federalist 37* (1788). For a comprehensive analysis, see William N. Eskridge, Jr., "All About Words: Early Understandings of the 'Judicial Power' in Statutory Interpretation, 1776–1806," 101 *Columbia Law Review* 990 (2001). See also the essays by Thayer, Holmes, and Frankfurter on John Marshall in *James Bradley Thayer, Oliver Wendell Holmes, and Felix Frankfurter on John Marshall* (1967).

going a great way to say that a constrained interpretation must be put upon them, to avoid an inconvenience which ought to have been contemplated in the legislature when the act was passed, and which, in their opinion, was probably overbalanced by the particular advantages it was calculated to produce.

Flexible interpretation is particularly appropriate to a constitutional provision ratified more than two centuries ago, dealing with a subject greatly affected in the intervening period by social and technological change, including urbanization and a revolution in weapons technology. Because of the difficulty of amending the Constitution, it has from the beginning been loosely construed so that it would not become a straitjacket. The older the constitutional provision and the more the relevant circumstances have changed since enactment, the more appropriate loose construction is. There are few more antiquated constitutional provisions than the Second Amendment, concerned with state militias at a time when the militias' weapons were stored in the militiamen's homes; like the Third Amendment, which limits the quartering of troops in people's homes, the Second Amendment is a fossil.

Having labored to produce an originalist justification for a right to possess handguns for self-defense, Scalia in *Heller* jettisons originalism by listing permissible restrictions on gun ownership—withholding it for example from felons and from people who are mentally ill, barring it from sensitive places (no doubt including the Supreme Court building), forbidding especially dangerous guns. These are sensible restrictions, but the Court makes no effort to root them in eighteenth-century thought.

So despite the pretense of engaging in originalist interpretation (but originalism stripped of the original understanding of how a constitutional provision should be interpreted), the *Heller* decision is an example of motivated thinking. As when the Supreme Court in a series of decisions held in the teeth of the language of the Fourteenth Amendment that the amendment "incorporates" (and thus makes applicable to action by states) almost all of the provisions of the Bill of Rights, *Heller* presents an exercise of judicial discretion as historically determined. The true springs of the *Heller* decision must be sought elsewhere than in the majority's declared commitment to originalism. (Another example of motivated reasoning may be the conservative Justices' expansive interpretation of the free-speech clause of the First Amendment to limit regulation of campaign financing.)[41]

There is an important difference, which though obvious is often overlooked, between using loose construction to make and to prevent making the Constitution a straitjacket. In a decision rendered shortly before *Heller* the Supreme Court had held that to execute a person who rapes a child but does not kill her violates the cruel and unusual punishments clause of the Eighth Amendment.[42] That was a loose construction that tied the hands of the states and the federal government, and Justice Scalia and the other conservative Justices dissented. But in *Heller* it was the liberal Justices dissenting from a decision that tied the hands of the federal government, and of the states as well when the Supreme Court decided three years later, in *McDonald v. City of Chicago,* that the Second Amendment constrains state as well as federal action.[43] That was a remarkable extension of *Heller.* For the Second Amendment places no limitations on state government, only on the federal government, which the amendment forbids to disarm the state militias. The Second Amendment protects state rights. Or rather used to.

Compare the *Zelman* case[44] mentioned briefly in the last chapter, where the Court had upheld, against a challenge based on the establishment clause of the First Amendment, the funneling of public monies to private schools by means of vouchers that parents could use to pay for their kids' tuition. Most private schools are Catholic parochial schools. The interpretation of the establishment clause that permitted the use of public moneys to finance parochial schools rejected the imposition on government of a constitutional restraint that the liberal Justices wanted to impose, thus reversing the positions of the liberal and conservative Justices in *McDonald*. *McDonald* limited state experimentation with the regulation of guns; *Zelman* expanded the right of states to experiment with private education.

41. *Citizens United v. Federal Election Commission,* 558 U.S. 310 (2010).

42. *Kennedy v. Louisiana,* 554 U.S. 407 (2008).

43. 130 S. Ct. 3020 (2010).

44. *Zelman v. Simmons-Harris,* 536 U.S. 639 (2002).

Similar too is the *Kelo* decision, in which the Supreme Court held that the takings clause of the Fifth Amendment does not forbid a state to condemn private property and, having thus seized it, turn it over to a private developer.[45] The decision provoked outrage by conservatives, who oppose condemnation because it infringes property rights. Yet all that the Court had done was unshackle state governments from a potential constitutional constraint. And sure enough in the wake of the decision a number of states curtailed their eminent domain powers. Similarly, had the Supreme Court kept its hands off gun regulation it would not have been outlawing the private possession of guns but merely leaving gun control to legislatures. The proper occasion for using loose construction to enlarge constitutional restrictions on government action is when the group seeking the enlargement does not have good access to the normal political process to protect its interests, as gun advocates did and do.

Constitutional interpretations that relax rather than tighten the Constitution's grip on the legislative and executive branches of government are especially welcome when there are regional or local differences in relevant circumstances or public opinion, and a uniform rule is neither necessary nor appropriate. It is in such cases that federalism, which conservatives claim to venerate, comes into its own. *Heller* and *McDonald* give short shrift to the values of federalism, and the related values of cultural diversity, local preference, and social experimentation. If Washington D.C. (or Chicago or New York) wants to ban handguns, why should the views of a national majority control? Is that democracy, or is it Rousseau's forced conformity to an elite's hypostasis of the "popular will"? It is true that a member of a national majority can be a member of a minority within a local area: gun buffs in Washington, D.C., for example. But a person who is a member of a local minority but of a national majority can relocate to a part of the country in which the national majority rules. A resident of Washington can move a few hundred yards to northern Virginia.

Scalia and Garner's book on interpretation, though its focus is on stat-

---

45. *Kelo v. City of New London*, 545 U.S. 469 (2005).

utory rather than constitutional interpretation, is among other things Scalia's response to the critics of textual originalism in general and the critics of *Heller*—at once his best known and most criticized decision[46]—in particular. Let's see how convincing the response is.

The authors get off on the wrong foot by arguing that textual originalism was the dominant method of interpretation until the middle of the twentieth century.[47] The only evidence they tender consists of quotations from distinguished judges and jurists, such as William Blackstone, John Marshall, and Oliver Wendell Holmes, all of whom wrote before 1950 and none of whom, while respectful of statutory and constitutional text, as any responsible lawyer would be, was a textual originalist; all were famously loose constructionists. Think of Marshall's opinion in *Fisher*, quoted earlier, and recall my discussion of Holmes in the last chapter. And think of Holmes's encomium to Marshall, whom Holmes could not "separate . . . from the *fortunate* circumstance that the appointment of Chief Justice fell to John Adams, instead of to Jefferson a month later, and so gave it to a Federalist and *loose constructionist* to start the working of the Constitution."[48]

Scalia and Garner call Blackstone "a thoroughgoing originalist."[49] They say he "made it very clear that original meaning governed."[50] Yet they quote without demur Blackstone's famous statement that "the fairest and most rational method to interpret the will of the legislator, is by exploring his intentions at the time when the law was made, by *signs* the most natural and probable. And these signs are either the words, the context, the

---

46. For biting criticism by a conservative originalist—criticism not of the result in *Heller* but of Scalia's opinion—see Nelson Lund, "The Second Amendment, *Heller*, and Originalist Jurisprudence," 56 *UCLA Law Review* 1343 (2009).

47. Scalia and Garner, *Reading Law*, at xxvii–xxviii.

48. Oliver Wendell Holmes, "John Marshall," in *The Essential Holmes: Selections from the Letters, Speeches, Judicial Opinions, and Other Writings of Oliver Wendell Holmes, Jr.* 206–207 (Richard A. Posner ed. 1992) (emphasis added). On Holmes as a loose constructionist, see Duxbury, *Elements of Legislation*, at 144.

49. Scalia and Garner, *Reading Law*, at 79.

50. Id. at 404.

subject matter, the effects and consequence, or the spirit and reason of the law."[51] That passage should be wormwood to Scalia and Garner.

It is possible to glean from judges who are loose constructionists the occasional paean to textualism (a modern example is Justice Kennedy).[52] But it is naïve to think that judges believe everything they say. They tend systematically to deny the creative—the legislative—dimension of judging, important as it is in our system. They don't want to give the impression that they're competing with "real" legislators or indeed are engaged in anything but the politically unthreatening activity of objective, literal-minded interpretation, using arcane tools of legal analysis. The fact that loose constructionists sometimes publicly endorse textualism is evidence only that for strategic reasons judges are, like other people, especially other officials, not always candid.

A profound embarrassment for textual originalists is that one of the most esteemed judicial opinions in American history, *Brown v. Board of Education,* is nonoriginalist. In 1868, when the Fourteenth Amendment was ratified, the provision forbidding states to deny to any person the "equal protection of the laws" meant that states—the former states of the Confederacy being the particular target, of course—must not deny legal protection to the newly freed slaves and to blacks more generally. In particular states could not without facing legal retribution turn a blind eye to the Ku Klux Klan's campaign of intimidation of blacks and carpetbaggers. Had the provision been thought to forbid racial segregation of public schools it would not have been ratified. And "separate but equal" is consistent at the textual originalist level with "equal protection." Yet Scalia and Garner claim that "recent research persuasively establishes that this [the ruling in *Brown* that separate but equal is not equal] was the original understanding of the post-Civil War Amendments." They cite for this proposition a sin-

51. Id. at 369, quoting Blackstone, *Commentaries on the Laws of England,* vol. 1, p. 59 (emphasis in original). They do not quote Blackstone's further statement that "The most universal and effectual way of discovering the true meaning of a law, when the words are dubious, is by considering the reason and spirit of it; or the cause which moved the legislator to enact it." Id. at 61.

52. Quoted in Scalia and Garner, *Reading Law,* at 347. See also id. at 212.

gle law review article[53] and omit to mention a powerful criticism of the article by a leading legal historian,[54] which the author of the article they cite is not, although he is a distinguished constitutional law professor and former federal judge. Scalia and Garner embrace his analysis even though it is based on the legislative history of the Fourteenth Amendment, though legislative history is anathema to Scalia and Garner—moreover, the analysis is based almost entirely on bills and floor debates in Congress *after* 1868, when the Fourteenth Amendment was ratified; and post-enactment legislative history is an especially unreliable guide to meaning. Scalia and Garner don't even mention post-enactment legislative history in their book; they must think it wholly beyond the pale.

Omission to mention contrary evidence, of which I've just given examples, is Scalia and Garner's favorite rhetorical device. Repeatedly they cite cases (both state and federal) as exemplars either of textual originalism or of a disreputable rejection of it, while ignoring critical passages that show the judges neither ignoring text nor tethered to textual originalism. I will give some examples.[55]

They applaud a decision that said that the word "sandwiches" does not include burritos, tacos, or quesadillas because Merriam-Webster's dictionary defines "sandwich" as "two thin pieces of bread, usually buttered, with a thin layer (as of meat, cheese, or savory mixture) spread between them."[56] Scalia and Garner stop there, as if that dictionary reference were the court's entire decision and therefore establishes the utility and propriety of judges' using dictionaries as a guide to the meaning of legal docu-

53. Scalia and Garner, *Reading Law*, at 88, citing Michael W. McConnell, "Originalism and the Desegregation Decisions," 81 *Virginia Law Review* 947 (1995).

54. Michael J. Klarman "*Brown*, Originalism, and Constitutional Theory: A Response to Professor McConnell," 81 *Virginia Law Review* 1881 (1995).

55. Among other examples that I could give are their discussions (on pp. 229, 230–231, and 275–276, respectively) of *State v. Hudson*, 470 A.2d 786 (Me. 1984), *Babbitt v. Sweet Home Chapter of Communities for a Great Oregon*, 515 U.S. 687 (1995), and *United States v. Persichilli*, 608 F.3d 34, 37–38 (1st Cir. 2010).

56. Scalia and Garner, *Reading Law*, at 54–55. The decision is *White City Shopping Center, LP v. PR Restaurants, LLC*, 2006 WL 3292641 (Mass. Super. Ct. Oct. 31, 2006).

ments. But the court had not stopped with the dictionary; it had begun there.

A company called PR Restaurants had leased space to operate a sandwich shop in a shopping center. Its lease forbade the shopping center to rent space to a store that derived more than 10 percent of its sales revenue from sales of sandwiches. PR claimed that the shopping center had violated the lease by renting space to a Mexican-style restaurant that sold burritos, tacos, and quesadillas. After noting Merriam Webster's definition of "sandwich," the court bolstered its rejection of PR's claim by a series of points unrelated to dictionary definition: "PR has not proffered any evidence that the parties intended the term 'sandwiches' to include burritos, tacos, and quesadillas. As the drafter of the exclusivity clause, PR did not include a definition of 'sandwiches' in the lease nor communicate clearly to White City during lease negotiations that it intended to treat burritos, tacos, quesadillas, and sandwiches the same. Another factor weighing against PR's favor is that it was aware that Mexican-style restaurants near the Shopping Center existed which sold burritos, tacos, and quesadillas prior to the execution of the Lease yet, PR made no attempt to define, discuss, and clarify the parties' understanding of the term 'sandwiches.'" These are more persuasive points than the dictionary's definition of "sandwich."

And as is often the case, the court got the definition wrong—Scalia and Garner miss this, too. A sandwich does not have to have two slices of bread; it can have more than two (a club sandwich), and it can have just one (an open-faced sandwich). The slices of bread do not have to be thin, and the layer between them does not have to be thin either. The slices do not have to be slices of bread: a hamburger is generally regarded as a sandwich, as is also a hot dog—and some people regard tacos and burritos as sandwiches, and a quesadilla is even more sandwich-like. Dictionaries are mazes in which judges are soon lost. A dictionary-centered textualism is hopeless.[57]

57. An historical investigation of the sandwich would have been more fruitful. For a profound analysis of that history, see Woody Allen, "History of the Sandwich," *American Konspiracy*, June 21, 2011, http://amkon.net/showthread.php/34058-History-of-the-Sandwich-Woody-Allen (visited Oct. 19, 2012). I am indebted to Anthony D'Amato for this invaluable reference.

In another obeisance to the dictionary, Scalia and Garner commend a court for having ordered the acquittal of a person who had fired a gun inside a building yet been charged with the crime of shooting "from any location into any occupied structure."[58] They say the court correctly decided the case on the basis of the dictionary definition of the word "into." They are wrong. The court said that the *entire* expression "from any location into any occupied structure" was ambiguous, because while "into" implied that the shooter was outside, "from any location" implied that he could be anywhere and therefore inside.[59] The court decided the case on other grounds.

Scalia and Garner ridicule a decision by the supreme court of Kansas which held that cockfighting did not violate a law against cruelty to animals.[60] They say the decision illustrates that "courts have sometimes ignored plain meaning in astonishing ways," because in defiance of dictionary definitions the court "perversely held that roosters are not 'animals.'"[61] What the court actually said was that "biologically speaking a fowl is an animal," but that roosters (cocks) are not in the class of animals protected by the statute. The court gave several reasons for this conclusion—all ignored by Scalia and Garner. One reason was that many Kansans thought of chickens as birds in contradistinction to animals. The court's most cogent reason was that the Kansas legislature had passed a statute forbidding cockfighting on Sundays, implying that it was permissible the rest of the week, and had later repealed the statute, implying that cockfighting was again permissible on *any* day of the week—and in fact cockfighting was an open and notorious sport in Kansas (to the surprise and disgust of the judges).

Scalia and Garner commend, as illustrating the error of the Kansas court, a decision holding that a goldfish is an "animal" within the meaning of a statute that said that "No person shall offer or give away any live animal as a prize or an award in a game, contest or tournament involving skill

---

58. Scalia and Garner, *Reading Law*, at 71–72.

59. *Commonwealth v. McCoy*, 962 A.2d 1160, 1167 (Pa. 2009).

60. *State ex rel. Miller v. Claiborne*, 505 P. 2d 732 (Kan. 1973).

61. Scalia and Garner, *Reading Law*, at 72–73.

or chance." But in contrast to the Kansas case, no reason had been given for rejecting the dictionary definition of "animal."[62]

Another case discussed by Scalia and Garner involved a man charged with contributing to the delinquency of a "juvenile," defined as "any child under the age of seventeen."[63] The girl was sixteen but married (to someone else), and Scalia and Garner applaud the court's ruling exonerating the defendant on the ground that the word "child" does not include an "emancipated minor."[64] They describe this as a "technical meaning," since obviously in ordinary speech a child bride is a child. Technical meanings abound in law (for example, "person" as including a corporation), but the example is inapt. The court's ruling was based on a statute that defined "emancipation" of married women to mean they could make contracts without permission of their husband or a judge.[65] This had nothing to do with the meaning of "juvenile" or "child" in the criminal statute. If children were forbidden to drink liquor, would the court have made an exception for married children? It would not have; but that is the logic of the opinion commended by Scalia and Garner.

They denounce a court that held that the word "family" in a rent-control statute that prohibited a landlord from dispossessing a "member of the deceased tenant's family who has been living with the tenant," but did not define the word "family," included "a cohabiting nonrelative who had an emotional commitment to the deceased tenant."[66] The decision may be right or wrong, but it is odd that Scalia and Garner failed to mention that the "family" in question was a homosexual couple at a time when homosexual marriage was not recognized in New York and that the two men had been living together just like spouses and had been accepted as such by their families.

---

62. *Knox v. Massachusetts Society for Prevention of Cruelty to Animals*, 425 N.E.2d 393 (Mass. App. 1981), discussed in Scalia and Garner, *Reading Law*, at 72–73.

63. *State v. Gonzales*, 129 So. 2d 796 (La. 1961).

64. Scalia and Garner, *Reading Law*, at 73–74.

65. La. Stat. Ann. tit. 9, § 101.

66. *Braschi v. Stahl Associates Co.*, 543 N.E.2d 49 (N.Y. 1989), discussed in Scalia and Garner, *Reading Law*, at 90.

The authors applaud a decision holding that a refusal to rent a house to an unmarried couple (this one heterosexual) did not violate a statute forbidding discrimination in rentals because of (among other things) "marital status," not defined in the statute. The court based its decision on a statute forbidding fornication.[67] One may doubt whether the statute was what motivated the decision, given the statement in the majority opinion (not quoted or mentioned by Scalia and Garner)—remarkable for 1990—that "it is simply astonishing to me that the argument is made that the legislature intended to protect fornication and promote a lifestyle which corrodes the institutions which have sustained our civilization, namely, marriage and family life."[68] In the next sentence the judge invoked the statute's legislative history.

After the landlord's refusal to rent to the couple but before the court's decision, the state had amended its antidiscrimination law to define "marital status" as "whether a person is single, married, remarried, divorced, separated, or a surviving spouse." The man and woman who had wanted to rent were both single, a protected marital status. And on the page following the discussion of the case Scalia and Garner remark "that the meaning of an ambiguous provision may change in light of a subsequent enactment" unless "the ambiguous provision had already been given an authoritative judicial interpretation."[69] The original statute had not defined "marital status," thus leaving the term ambiguous, and the term had not been given an authoritative judicial interpretation before the legislature defined it. That definition should have provided a basis, consistent with textual originalism, for a different outcome in the cohabitation case. Scalia and Garner discuss none of this.

A provision of federal immigration law allowed the wife of a naturalized American citizen to be admitted to the United States for treatment in a hospital without being detained as an alien. The noncitizen wife of a native-born, as distinct from a naturalized, American citizen was denied

67. *State by Cooper v. French*, 460 N.W.2d 2 (Minn. 1990), discussed in Scalia and Garner, *Reading Law*, at 253–254.

68. 460 N.W.2d at 8.

69. Scalia and Garner, *Reading Law*, at 254–255.

entry for treatment, and the Supreme Court upheld the denial.[70] Garner and Scalia applaud the result, which gave more rights to the wife of a naturalized citizen than to the wife of a native-born citizen, while calling it "admittedly absurd."[71] They recognize a doctrine of "absurdity" that permits interpretive deviations from literal readings, but declare it inapplicable because a provision relating to native-born Americans would be out of place in an immigration statute, which is about aliens. But the wife who was denied entry *was* an alien.

They fail to mention that the Supreme Court seems to have agreed with the alternative interpretation of the statute by the court of appeals. That court had noticed that the statute by its terms applied only if the marriage had taken place after the husband was naturalized, and thus was limited to cases in which, as a result of the marriage, the wife had become an American citizen even though she was living abroad—for the immigration law provided that "any woman who is now or may hereafter be married to a citizen of the United States, and who might herself be lawfully naturalized, shall be deemed a citizen." But because the wife happened to be of Chinese ethnicity, she could not, under the immigration law as it then stood, become an American citizen despite being married to a native-born American citizen; had she been a citizen, she could of course have entered the country for hospital treatment without detention. The Supreme Court said that it was "inclined to agree with [the] view" of the court of appeals[72]—the view, which saved the statute from absurdity while amplifying its offensiveness, that the statute was based on the different status of citizen and noncitizen wives rather than on any difference between native-born and naturalized citizens. It was only after stating its inclination to agree with the court of appeals' sensible interpretation that the Court had, it seems reluctantly, embraced the alternative ground that the right of entry without detention did not apply to alien wives of native-born Americans.

There is a common thread to the cases that Scalia and Garner discuss. Judges do discuss the meanings of words and sometimes look for those

70. *Chung Fook v. White*, 264 U.S. 443 (1924).

71. Scalia and Garner, *Reading Law*, at 238–239.

72. 264 U.S. at 445.

meanings in dictionaries, but they don't stop there. Even judges who consult dictionaries against the advice of Judge Easterbrook and others consider the range of commonsense nontextual clues to meaning that come naturally to readers trying to solve an interpretive puzzle. Judges are eclectic rather than doctrinaire when it comes to interpreting statutes.

This is suggested by the following Google Ngram, which traces the relative frequency since 1920 of the terms "textualism," "originalism," "canons of construction," "legislative history," and "legislative intent." The first three terms connote approaches congenial to Scalia and Garner; the latter two are anathema to them. The first three terms were virtually unmentioned before the mid-1980s, but began a gradual rise then, in the period in which Scalia was appointed to the Supreme Court and in which the Federalist Society was growing rapidly in the favorable climate of the Reagan presidency. Soon "legislative history," on which the Supreme Court had been relying heavily, began a sharp drop in mentions; "legislative intent" declined as well. Yet both terms remain far more frequently mentioned than "textualism," "originalism," or "canons of construction."[73] "Legislative history" alone is mentioned far more often than all three of Scalia-Garner-favored terms combined; "legislative intent" is mentioned about as many times as all three terms combined.

These are mentions in books rather than in judicial opinions; but a study of statutory interpretation in decisions of the Supreme Court yielded results similar to those in my Ngram.[74] Most Justices and judges refuse to make a wholehearted commitment to textual originalism.

Not even Justice Scalia. For among the fifty-seven "canons of construction" that he and Garner approve is *eiusdem generis* (which lawyers misspell as *ejusdem generis* because that's how English judges spelled it ages ago). The term literally means "of the same kind" but is used in law to mean that when a homogeneous list of specific terms ends with a general term, the general term should be interpreted as being limited to things sim-

73. That is, interpretive principles—the term "canons of construction," with its ecclesiastical overtones, is legalism at its silliest.

74. Frank B. Cross, *The Theory and Practice of Statutory Interpretation*, ch. 6 (2009).

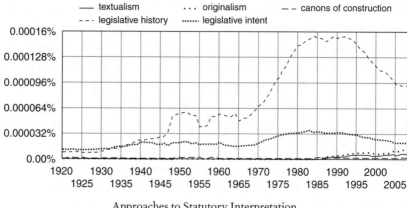

Approaches to Statutory Interpretation

ilar to the specific terms. Scalia and Garner give an example from an opinion by Justice Holmes,[75] whom, we recall, they want to enlist in the ranks of the textual originalists. They summarize the opinion tersely: "'automobile, automobile truck, automobile wagon, motor cycle, or any other self-propelled vehicle not designed for running on rails'—held not to apply to an airplane."[76] The summary distorts Holmes's analysis. The statute in question criminalized the transportation in interstate commerce of a "motor vehicle" known to have been stolen. Not mentioning the statutory term "motor vehicle," Scalia and Garner consider only whether an airplane is the same kind of thing as an automobile, an automobile truck, etc. For Holmes the question was whether an airplane is a "motor vehicle," and while he alludes to without naming the principle of *eiusdem generis* his principal ground for reversing the defendant's conviction was that in common speech an airplane is not a motor vehicle and—here alluding to the "rule of lenity" (another canon of construction approved by Scalia and Garner)—that a conviction for a poorly defined crime should not be allowed to stand. Holmes also mentioned legislative history in support of his interpretation. All this Scalia and Garner ignore.

Another canon of construction that the authors approve is the "series-qualifier canon" (new to me): "When there is a straightforward, parallel

75. *McBoyle v. United States*, 283 U.S. 25 (1931).
76. Scalia and Garner, *Reading Law*, at 200.

construction that involves all nouns or verbs in a series, a prepositive or postpositive modifier normally applies to the entire series."[77] In *Amaral v. St. Cloud Hospital,*[78] a state statute allowed doctors access to hospital records if they were "requesting or seeking through discovery data, information, or records relating to their medical staff privileges." The question was whether "through discovery" modified just "seeking," or also "requesting." The court held that it modified both, consistent with the series-qualifier canon, and Scalia and Garner applaud.[79] But the court did not mention the canon; nor was it the basis of its decision. It said: "In the face of statutory language that lacks clarity and a less than illuminating legislative history, we turn for guidance to the purposes underlying the enactment of review organizations statutes in order to determine how the provider data exception [the access provision in the statute] fits within those purposes."[80] That is, giving up on text, the court resorted to legislative purpose, a no-no move for Scalia and Garner, as they fail to mention. The doctors were seeking access to peer review reports about themselves. The court concluded that the legislature didn't want them to have access to materials of that sort except in a litigation in which the materials were sought in pretrial discovery.

Another case the authors discuss[81] involved interpretation of a provision in an insurance policy that covered "any infringement of copyright or improper or unlawful use of slogans in your advertising." The question was whether "in your advertising" modified just "improper or unlawful use of slogans" or also "infringement of copyright"; if the latter was the correct interpretation the policy would cover copyright infringement only if the infringing material was in an advertisement. The court held that "in your advertising" modified just "slogans," a result contrary to the series-qualifier canon. Scalia and Garner defend the result by invoking the rule

77. Id. at 147
78. 598 N.W.2d 379 (Minn. 1999).
79. Scalia and Garner, *Reading Law,* at 150.
80. 598 N.W.2d at 386.
81. *Phoenix Control Systems, Inc. v. Insurance Co. of North America,* 796 P. 2d 463 (Ariz. 1990), discussed in Scalia and Garner, *Reading Law,* at 150–151.

that ambiguities in a contract should be resolved against the party that drafted it. But the court did not mention that rule. Nor the series-qualifier canon. Instead it invoked the "last-antecedent canon": "that a qualifying phrase be applied to the word or phrase immediately preceding as long as there is no contrary intent indicated."[82] Oddly, the last-antecedent canon not only is approved by Scalia and Garner; they discuss it directly before the series-qualifier canon. Failure to mention it in reference to the insurance case is puzzling because the two canons contradict each other. Scalia and Garner nowhere attempt to dispel the apparent contradiction, or even mention it.

They might attempt to defend their misreading of case after case after case by saying that all they're interested in is the particular canon that a particular case illustrates: the fact that the court gave other grounds for its decision, ignoring the applicable canon, is irrelevant. But the second-deepest fallacy of textual originalism is the suggestion that a *single* canon of construction can decide more than a tiny handful of cases; no single canon can decide most of the cases that Scalia and Garner discuss. The deepest fallacy is the proposition that the fifty-seven approved canons are all consistent with textual originalism (which is why they're approved). Many of them, as we'll see shortly, are neither textual nor originalist.

Another blot on Scalia and Garner's defense of textual originalism is their disingenuous characterization of other interpretive theories, as in their statement that textual originalism is "the only objective standard of interpretation even competing for acceptance. Nonoriginalism is not an interpretive theory—it is nothing more than a repudiation of originalism, leaving open the question: How does a judge determine when and how the meaning of a text has changed? To this question the nonoriginalists have no answer—or rather no answer that comes even close to being an objective test."[83] But "nonoriginalism" is not the name of an alternative approach to statutory and constitutional interpretation. Nor is what they call "so-called *consequentialism*"—that is, "Is this decision good for the 'little guy'?"[84] With their airy dismissals of alternatives to textualism contrast the

82. 796 P. 2d at 466.
83. Scalia and Garner, *Reading Law*, at 89.
84. Id. at 352 (emphasis in original).

eclectic approach of William Popkin, whose treatise on statutory interpretation,[85] while attentive to the canons, takes in the other approaches to statutory interpretation. Popkin discusses almost 150 terms that have been used in statutory interpretation, most related not to the canons of construction (although the major ones are discussed) but to other theories of interpretation, such as "author and audience," "holistic interpretation," "background consideration," "change," "pragmatism," and "purposivism."

Discrediting Scalia-Garner's entire approach is the absence of an actual commitment to textual originalism. The fifty-seven "canons of construction" that they endorse (thirteen others they reject)—most of which are not textualist—provide them with all the running room needed to generate whatever case outcome conforms to Justice Scalia's strongly felt views on such matters as abortion, homosexuality, illegal immigration, states' rights, and the death penalty. The authors are not even consistent in their application of the canons. Many they approve of are not just nontextual but antitextual, which limits the scope and utility of textualism as an interpretive method. Consider canon 38—"A statute should be interpreted in a way that avoids placing its constitutionality in doubt."[86] In other words, the text can be bent to avoid the court's having to wrestle with a constitutional question. The authors ground the canon in "judicial policy"[87] rather than in textual originalism.

They say that "a fair system of laws requires precision in the definition of offenses and punishments,"[88] implying that judges may use a concept of "fairness" to interpret statutes creating offenses and punishments. How is that to be squared with textual originalism?

They say that "textualism, *in its purest form,* begins and ends with what the text says and fairly implies."[89] Yet they are not committed to the "purest

---

85. William D. Popkin, *A Dictionary of Statutory Interpretation* (2007), cited once, in passing (at p. 203), but not discussed, in the Scalia-Garner book.

86. Scalia and Garner, *Reading Law*, at 247. Recall from note 3 in Chapter 6 that Judge Easterbrook regards this as an activist doctrine.

87. Scalia and Garner, *Reading Law*, at 249.

88. Id. at 301.

89. Id. at 16 (emphasis added).

form," for they say that "determining what is *reasonably* implied [by the words of a statute] takes some judgment."[90]

Scalia and Garner even endorse as I noted the "rule of lenity"—that ambiguities in criminal statutes should be resolved in favor of the criminal defendant—a rule that isn't even interpretive, let alone textualist. Legislators are more concerned with stopping up loopholes by defining criminal acts broadly than with avoiding ambiguity in criminal statutes. The rule of lenity is a judicial counterweight to legislative intent. For consider this remarkable passage in *Federalist No. 78* (Hamilton) concerning the type of judicial action illustrated by the rule of lenity:

> But it is not with a view to infractions of the Constitution only, that the independence of the judges may be an essential safeguard against the effects of occasional ill humors in the society. These sometimes extend no farther than to the injury of the private rights of particular classes of citizens, by unjust and partial laws. Here also the firmness of the judicial magistracy is of vast importance in mitigating the severity and confining the operation of such laws. It not only serves to moderate the immediate mischiefs of those which may have been passed, but it operates as a check upon the legislative body in passing them; who, perceiving that obstacles to the success of iniquitous intention are to be expected from the scruples of the courts, are in a manner compelled, by the very motives of the injustice they meditate, to qualify their attempts. This is a circumstance calculated to have more influence upon the character of our governments, than but few may be aware of.

The rule of lenity is a judicial invention calculated to "mitigat[e] the severity and confin[e] the operation" of "unjust and partial laws." The judge, an independent official interposed between a democratic legislature that cannot be entirely trusted and the citizens subject to the legislative whim, shaves off some of the hard points of legislation.

The lenity canon is an example of a canon limited to a particular sub-

90. Id. at 193 (emphasis in original).

ject matter, in that case criminal law. An oddity of the Scalia-Garner treatise is that they ignore most such canons; other examples are that ambiguities in the Bankruptcy Code are to be construed in favor of debtors rather than creditors and that laws relating to American Indian tribes are to be construed favorably to the tribes.

They say that what they call (and commend) "fair reading" "requires an ability to comprehend the *purpose* of the text, which is a vital part of its context." But they also say that "the purpose is to be gathered only from the text itself, consistently with the other aspects of its context."[91] Later they do an about-face, saying that "a sign at the entrance to a butcher shop reading 'No dogs or other animals' does not suggest that only canines, or only four-legged animals, or only domestic animals are excluded."[92] That is certainly correct. But it is correct not by virtue of anything textual but because of the principle that meaning includes what "would come into the reasonable person's mind,"[93] or what we know an author has "in mind" in writing something.[94] On this ground a sign that says "No dogs, cats, and other animals allowed" includes totally unrelated animals (contrary, however, to the principle of *eiusdem generis*) because "no one would think that only domestic pets were excluded, and that farm animals or wild animals were welcome."[95] Right again! But right because textualism is wrong.

Regarding that old chestnut—a medieval statute that punished whoever "draws blood in the streets"—Scalia and Garner point out that the phrase could mean either attacking someone or treating a sick person (as by applying leeches)—and "the former was obviously meant."[96] Indeed so, but once again this is allowing judges to go outside statutory text to base decision on what was intended rather than what was said; for what was said encompassed the application of leeches. And likewise when the authors endorse a presumption against the implied repeal of state statutes by federal statutes, they do not base their endorsement on anything to do with textu-

91. Id. at 33 (emphasis in original).
92. Id. at 206.
93. Id. at 208.
94. Id. at 199.
95. Id. at 212.
96. Id. at 357.

alism. They base it "on an assumption of what Congress, in our federal system, would or should normally desire."[97] What Congress *would* desire? *Should* desire? *That's* textualism too?

And remember how, early in the book, the authors had said that forbidding an ambulance to enter a park closed to vehicles even to save a person's life was entailed by textual originalism? Now, several hundred pages later, we learn that the ambulance is not prohibited from entering the park after all, owing to the "common-law defense of necessity," which the authors allow to override statutory text,[98] though just a few pages later they remark that except in "select fields such as admiralty law, [federal courts] have no significant common-law powers."[99] Elsewhere they express approval of an opinion in which Justice Kennedy (not a textual originalist) stated that "the Sherman Act's use of 'restraint of trade' invokes the common law itself ... not merely the static content that the common law had assigned to the term in 1890."[100] In other words, restraint of trade had at the time of enactment of the Sherman Act a specific meaning (namely "restraints on alienation," in which typically the seller of a business agrees not to go into competition with the buyer for a stated period of time—such restraints figure almost not at all in modern antitrust law) that courts feel free to alter in conformity with commercial changes and the teachings of modern economics. Yet thirteen pages after endorsing that heresy Scalia and Garner state that "federal courts do not possess the lawmaking power of common-law courts," here ignoring the fact that most of the concepts deployed not only in antitrust law but also in federal criminal law—such as *mens rea*, conspiracy, attempt, self-defense, and necessity—are common law concepts.

They indicate their agreement with old cases that held that an heir who murders his parents or others from whom he expects to inherit is not disqualified from inheriting[101] despite the common law maxim that no per-

---

97. Id. at 293.

98. Id. at 309.

99. Id. at 313.

100. *Leegin Creative Leather Products, Inc. v. PSKS, Inc.,* 551 U.S. 877, 887–888 (2007), discussed in Scalia and Garner, *Readling Law,* at 96.

101. Id. at 100.

son shall be permitted to profit from his wrongful act. (Notice how common law wafts unpredictably in and out of their analysis.) They call these cases "textually correct" though awful, and are happy to note that they've been overruled by statute. Yet just before registering their approval of the cases they had applauded the rule that allows statutes of limitations to be tolled (delayed) "because of unforeseen events that make compliance impossible."[102] The tolling rule is not statutory; it's a graft on statutes that don't mention tolling. Why is that okay but not a rule disqualifying a murdering heir? They don't say, though the question is not entirely rhetorical. As noted in one of the cases they cite, inheritance statutes had been interpreted to displace common law principles, and forfeiture of property was no longer a recognized punishment for crime.[103] By not mentioning these distinctions between the murdering-heir cases and the tolling cases, Scalia and Garner render their discussion of common law grafts on statutes incoherent.

I mentioned that they defend the principle that judges should avoid interpreting a statute in a way that will render it unconstitutional as representing "judicial policy,"[104] even though judicial policy making is the antithesis of textual originalism. In a similar vein they note that "many established principles of interpretation are less plausibly based on a reasonable assessment of meaning than on grounds of policy adopted by the courts" —and they applaud these principles too.[105] They approve the "canon" that statutes dealing with the same subject should "if possible be interpreted harmoniously" on the ground that it's "based upon a realistic assessment of what the legislature *ought* to have meant," which in turn derives from the "sound principles . . . that the body of the law *should* make sense, and . . . that it is the responsibility of the courts, within the permissible meanings of the text, to make it so."[106] In other words, judges should be realistic, should impose right reason on legislators, should in short clean up after them.

---

102. Id. at 99.
103. *Wall v. Pfanschmidt*, 106 N.E. 785 (Ill. 1914).
104. Scalia and Garner, *Reading Law*, at 249.
105. Id. at 30–31.
106. Id. at 252 (emphasis added).

Over Scalia's partial dissent the Supreme Court held that a federal statute which provided that no state could require that a statement relating to smoking and health be placed on a cigarette package, other than the statement required by the statute, did not preempt state tort suits charging cigarette advertisers with concealing the health hazards of smoking.[107] The ruling was consistent with the canon approved by Scalia and Garner that I mentioned earlier—that a federal statute is presumed to supplement rather than displace state law. The majority held that suits based on the state's view of the health hazards of smoking were preempted (and this part of the decision Scalia concurred in) but not suits based on general obligations imposed by tort law to avoid fraud. Scalia and Garner ignore the distinction between the two types of suit—one based on a disagreement with the federally prescribed warning, the other based on general principles of tort law rather than anything specific to cigarette advertising or labeling. They say instead that "when Congress has explicitly set forth its desire, there is no justification for not taking Congress at its word."[108] But the statute was not explicit about overriding all state tort suits that might relate to cigarette advertising, even those not based on any state regulation inconsistent with federal regulation, so the canon against implied federal preemption of state law should have carried the day for Scalia.

The basic fallacy of textual originalism can be understood with the help of the distinction in contract interpretation between "intrinsic ambiguity" and "extrinsic ambiguity." An intrinsic ambiguity is an ambiguity apparent just from reading the contract; the phrase "from any location into any occupied structure," discussed earlier, is an example of such an ambiguity in a statute. But sometimes a contract unambiguous if you just read it (unambiguous "on its face") is ambiguous if you understand its real-world context. In the famous case of *Raffles v. Wichelhaus*,[109] the plaintiff agreed to sell the defendants a quantity of cotton, at a specified price, to be shipped

107. *Cipollone v. Liggett Group, Inc.* 505 U.S. 504 (1992). The Court held other tort claims to be preempted, and Scalia agreed with that part of the decision.

108. Scalia and Garner, *Reading Law*, at 293.

109. 2 H. & C. 906, 159 Eng. Rep. 375 (Ex. 1864). See A. W. Brian Simpson, "Contracts for Cotton to Arrive: The Case of the Two Ships Peerless," 11 *Cardozo Law Review* 287 (1989).

from Bombay to Liverpool by a ship named *Peerless*. There was no ambiguity on the face of the contract. But there happened to be two ships named *Peerless* sailing from Bombay to Liverpool a few months apart. The cotton was shipped on the second *Peerless*, and—the price of cotton having fallen in the meantime—the defendants argued that it should have been shipped on the first one. Nothing in the contract indicated which ship *Peerless* the parties had agreed that it would be shipped on and the court ruled that therefore the contract was hopelessly ambiguous—though perfectly clear on its face.

In many cases of extrinsic ambiguity, though not *Raffles v. Wichelhaus*, extrinsic evidence—trade usage, prior dealings by the parties, testimony by the negotiators, other negotiating history, or the nature of the goods or services involved in the transaction (were cotton a perishable good, it might have been inferable that the parties intended it to be shipped by the first *Peerless* to sail)—may enable the ambiguity to be resolved and the contract enforced. It's the same with statutes. Often, expanding the scope of inquiry beyond the bare text reveals what the statute meant but through the legislators' oversight failed to say.

The analogy to contractual ambiguity brings out another fallacy of textual originalism. To say that a text is ambiguous "on its face," that is, intrinsically ambiguous, is to say that the reader is unsure what the author meant because the text can be read in different ways; maybe it uses words with more than one meaning or the word order is confusing or the text ungrammatical. Principles of interpretation do not dispel ambiguity; rather they impose a meaning on an ambiguous text. Sometimes ambiguity can be dispelled by consideration of the circumstances of enactment or the likely consequences of alternative interpretations; often it cannot be but since the case must be decided the court gives the statute a meaning that makes the statute make practical sense. In all this, textual originalism plays very little, maybe no, role. Which is why most of the fifty-seven approved "canons" are not textualist or originalist, but are tie-breakers used when textual originalism gives out.

Justice Scalia has called himself a "faint-hearted originalist," illustrating the point by saying that he would hold that flogging was forbidden by the cruel and unusual punishments clause of the Eighth Amendment, even though it was considered neither cruel nor unusual when the Bill of Rights was ratified.[110] Textual originalism in his and Garner's hands is mush—and he isn't even committed to textual originalism. To repeat, most of the interpretive principles he endorses are not textualist or originalist, and some, like the rule of lenity, are not even interpretive.

Scalia's *faux* originalism is well illustrated by his opinion for the Court in *United States v. Jones*,[111] which involved a search effected by attaching a GPS device to the underside of a suspect's car without the suspect's knowledge. The opinion holds that since the car was the suspect's property, and thus his "effect" within the meaning of the Fourth Amendment, the attachment of the device was a trespass, and a search enabled by a trespass violates the amendment. Yet given the technology of electronic surveillance, the same "search" could have been conducted without committing a trespass, just as wiretapping is a method of search that does not involve (ordinarily) a trespass. The search effected by the GPS should not have been considered a violation of the Fourth Amendment because of a trespass that caused no damage to the property trespassed upon and that the owner of the property wasn't even aware of, but because it was an unauthorized search. The trespass was irrelevant. The Fourth Amendment does not mention trespass. A search need not be a trespass, or a trespass a search. Scalia's analysis, as pointed out in the concurring opinion of Justice Alito, is an escape from having to decide the limits that the Fourth Amendment should be understood to place not only on electronic surveillance but on remote identification generally, an area of rapid technological advance.[112]

I have dwelt at such length on Scalia's theory of interpretation because it so strikingly illustrates what I called in Chapter 3 "internal complexity,"

110. Antonin Scalia, "Originalism: The Lesser Evil," *57 University of Cincinnati Law Review* 849, 864 (1989). Why he has qualms about flogging, when he has no qualms about capital punishment, eludes me.

111. 132 S. Ct. 945 (2012).

112. See, for example, the book-length article by Laura K. Donohue, entitled "Technological Leap, Statutory Gap, and Constitutional Abyss: Remote Biometric Identification Comes of Age," *97 Minnesota Law Review* 497 (2012). A simple example of remote biometric identification is facial recognition; of immediate biometric identification, fingerprint evidence.

that is, complexity that is internal to the legal system. The canons of construction were not invented by Tim Berners-Lee (generally regarded as the inventor of the World Wide Web), whose invention has challenged the judiciary from outside, but by judges and lawyers. Their invention has made law more complex, but not more accurate, predictable, or sensible. Juggling canons produces confusion in some judges while enabling others to mask the beliefs or emotions that actually drive their "interpretive" decisions.

Scalia and Garner defend the canons by quoting a statement by Justice Frankfurter that "insofar as canons of construction are generalizations of experience, they all have worth."[113] The quotation is accurate but the context is ignored and as a result the meaning distorted. For Frankfurter goes on to say that "in the abstract [the canons of construction] rarely arouse controversy. Difficulties emerge when canons compete in soliciting judgment, because they conflict rather than converge. For the demands of judgment underlying the art of interpretation, there is no vade-mecum." And in the preceding paragraph Frankfurter had said: "Nor can canons of construction save us from the anguish of judgment. Such canons give an air of abstract intellectual compulsion to what is in fact a delicate judgment, concluding a complicated process of balancing subtle and elusive elements. All our three Justices [Holmes, Brandeis, and Cardozo] have at one time or another leaned on the crutch of a canon. But they have done so only rarely, and with a recognition that these rules of construction are not in any true sense rules of law."[114]

The canons don't discipline Justice Scalia's judicial votes, which appear

113. Scalia and Garner, *Reading Law*, at 61, quoting Felix Frankfurter, "Some Reflections on the Reading of Statutes," 47 *Columbia Law Review* 527, 544 (1947). The critical literature on the canons of construction is vast. For a useful synthesis, see James J. Brudney and Corey Ditslear, "Canons of Construction and the Elusive Quest for Neutral Reasoning," 58 *Vanderbilt Law Review* 1 (2005).

114. For additional criticisms of *Reading Law*, see Professor Eskridge's review, "New Textualism," which relies on a large body of academic work, much of it empirical, on the legislative process, and on statutory interpretation by the Supreme Court, that both falsifies Scalia and Garner's claims and more fully documents the political character of Scalia's opinions in cases involving statutory interpretation than I have attempted to do.

to reflect his personal beliefs more than they do any politically neutral analytical system. For compare his partial dissent in the *Arizona* immigration case, which I mentioned earlier, with his vote to join the majority opinion in the *McDonald* case, which, remember, held that the Second Amendment as interpreted by *Heller* applies to the states as well as to the federal government. In the *Arizona* case Scalia voted to allow states in effect to enforce federal immigration law, saying that "Arizona bears the brunt of the country's illegal immigration problem. Its citizens feel themselves under siege by large numbers of illegal immigrants who invade their property, strain their social services, and even place their lives in jeopardy. Federal officials have been unable to remedy the problem, and indeed have recently shown that they are unwilling to do so. Thousands of Arizona's estimated 400,000 illegal immigrants—including not just children but men and women under 30—are now assured immunity from enforcement, and will be able to compete openly with Arizona citizens for employment."[115] This is not only inappropriately emotional, but a prime example of evidence-free as distinct from evidence-based law. "Arizona bears the brunt"? Arizona is only one of the states that border Mexico, and if it succeeds in excluding illegal immigrants these other states will bear the brunt, so it is unclear what the net gain to society would have been from Arizona's efforts, now partially invalidated by the Supreme Court. The assertion that illegal immigrants in Arizona are invading Americans' property, straining their social services, and even placing their lives in jeopardy is sufficiently inflammatory to call for a citation to some reputable source of such hyperbole. Scalia cites nothing to support it. Maybe Arizona's illegal immigrants are more violent, less respectful of property, worse spongers off social services, and otherwise more obnoxious than the illegal immigrants in other states, but one would like to see some evidence of that. The estimate he gives for the number of illegal immigrants in Arizona amounts to 6 percent of the Arizona population. Doubtless most of them work. Mexicans are famously hard workers. What would it do to the Arizona economy if these workers suddenly vanished? On the basis of Alabama's experience with cracking down on illegal

115. 132 S. Ct. 2522.

immigrants, one can predict that Arizona's economy would be seriously harmed.[116]

So passionate a paean to states' rights as Justice Scalia's opinion in the *Arizona* case is hard to square with his joining the *McDonald* case. If ever there was a strong argument for states' rights, it is the argument for allowing states to determine rights of handgun ownership. Not only is there enormous cultural variance among states in attitudes toward guns, and no reason for national uniformity, but the diversity of state policies is a precondition for learning which policies are best. The states are the indispensable laboratories for evidence-based solutions to the problems posed by widespread gun ownership and high levels of gun homicides, suicides, and accidental deaths. I don't understand how Scalia's votes in these two cases can be reconciled on any grounds other than his personal values—a liking for guns (he's an enthusiastic hunter, though *Heller* and *McDonald* are about handguns rather than hunting rifles) and an intense dislike of illegal immigrants.

Dreaming a Constitution

The opposite of textual originalism is the subjection of constitutional text (or it could be statutory text, but the emphasis is on the Constitution because of liberals' dismay at constitutional interpretations by the conservative Roberts Court) to flights of imaginative fancy that nevertheless purport to be interpreting, not creating. That is the approach taken by Akhil Amar in his book *America's Unwritten Constitution*.[117]

The problem the author confronts is that the Constitution of 1787, even as altered and augmented by amendments, is not a democratic docu-

---

116. See Margaret Newkirk and Gigi Douban, "Alabama Immigration Law Has Surprise Result," *Bloomberg Businessweek: News from Bloomberg*, Sept. 24, 2012, www .businessweek.com/news/2012-09-24/africans-relocate-to-alabama-to-fill-jobs-after-immigration-law (visited Dec. 24, 2012).

117. Akhil Reed Amar, *America's Unwritten Constitution: The Precedents and Principles We Live By* (2012). For criticisms different from those I offer, see David A. Strauss, "Not Unwritten, After All," 126 *Harvard Law Review* 1532 (2013).

ment. Amar is a liberal democrat and therefore needs to update the Constitution to put it in sync with his ideology; that appears to be the aim of most constitutional theorists. (I confess to being cynical about constitutional theory.) His method is that used by the Roman Catholic Church in interpreting the Bible: supplementation from equally authoritative sources. The Church believes that a Pope receives divine inspiration that enables him to proclaim dogmas that are infallible and thus have equal authority with the Bible. Jesus Christ's mother does not play a prominent role in the New Testament but she became a focus of Catholic veneration and in 1854 the Pope proclaimed the dogma of Mary's Immaculate Conception (that is, that she had been born without original sin).

That is the line taken by Amar. Alongside the written Constitution is an unwritten Constitution. The two are consubstantial. Like the teachings of the Catholic Church, *the* Constitution is a composite of a founding document and a variety of supplementary practices and declarations (many of course in writing also). No matter how wild Amar's constitutional views may seem, he claims they are all in this two-in-one Constitution; he didn't put them there.

But despite the book's title it is not two in one—it is twelve in one. For he lists, and discusses at length, eleven unwritten Constitutions. They are an "implicit" Constitution, a "lived" Constitution, a "Warrented" Constitution (the reference is to Earl Warren), a "doctrinal" Constitution, a "symbolic" Constitution, a "feminist" Constitution, a "Georgian" Constitution (the reference is to George Washington), an "institutional" Constitution, a "partisan" Constitution (the reference is to political parties, which are not mentioned in the written Constitution), a "conscientious" Constitution (which, for example, permits jurors and judges to ignore valid law), and an "unfinished" Constitution that Amar is busy finishing. All these unwritten Constitutions, in Amar's view, are authoritative. And, miraculously, when correctly interpreted they all cohere both with each another and with the written Constitution.

If instead of invoking unwritten Constitutions Amar were content to note and describe the multifarious influences on judicial formation of constitutional doctrine, he would be on solid ground. But he takes the notion of unwritten Constitutions literally, and the results are bizarre—even more so than those of *The Invisible Constitution* (2008) by Amar's Harvard counterpart Laurence Tribe, another liberal tilting at the originalist windmill. Tribe was able to conjure only six invisible (not to him of course) Constitutions, all beginning—a remarkable coincidence—with the letter g (they include a geodesic Constitution and a gyroscopic one). Amar has more putty to knead and shape: eleven unwritten constitutions to Tribe's six invisible ones.

Amar's method is illustrated by his discussion of the right of women to serve on juries (really a duty, since jurors are conscripts rather than volunteers). The Nineteenth Amendment provides that the right of an American citizen to vote shall not be denied by either the federal government or any state on account of sex. The amendment was ratified in 1920. Many years later the Supreme Court held that it is a denial of equal protection of the laws (and hence a violation of the Fourteenth Amendment, ratified in 1868) to forbid women to serve on juries. Amar argues that this cannot be right, because the equal protection clause of the Fourteenth Amendment cannot apply to voters. The reason is that like the due process clause in the same amendment, but unlike the amendment's privileges and immunities clause ("No State shall make or enforce any law which shall abridge the privileges or immunities of citizens of the United States"), the equal protection clause protects "persons" rather than only American citizens—and no one thinks that foreigners have a constitutional right to vote in American elections. But the Nineteenth Amendment, Amar argues, guarantees the right of women to vote as jurors as well as in political elections because voting is voting—it is not limited to elections—and by further implication the amendment guarantees as well the right to serve on a jury, since jurors arrive at a verdict by voting. Amar calls these two extensions of the Nineteenth Amendment "a simple implication of [women's] right to vote generally."[118] (I would substitute "fantastic" for "simple.") They thus illustrate both the "implicit" Constitution, one of his eleven unwritten Constitutions, and the "feminist" Constitution, another. A further implication of

118. Id. at 288. Can he really have meant "simple"?

Amar's interpretation of the Nineteenth Amendment is that since it is not only not limited to voting in political elections, or indeed in elections of any sort, but also not limited to voting in a governmental setting, such as a jury trial, it should entitle women to vote in apartment-building cooperatives and indeed in men's clubs, even men's clubs that are not in violation of antidiscrimination law.

Amar's reasoning implies a weird understanding of the equal protection clause—that if voting were not categorically excluded from it (excluded by Amar's interpretation of the clause), foreigners would have a constitutional right to vote in American elections because they are persons. Amar appears actually to believe this: why otherwise his categorical exclusion of voting from that clause? (Because that would make the Fifteenth and Nineteenth Amendments superfluous? But they could be limited to voting in elections, leaving the equal protection clause to protect rights in other contexts, such as jury trials, in which votes are cast.) As sensibly interpreted, the equal protection clause forbids only arbitrary or deeply hurtful differences in treatment; it would be senseless if thought to forbid *all* differences in treatment. There is nothing arbitrary or offensive about limiting the right to vote in American elections to American citizens, or for that matter to adult American citizens.

This isn't the only place where Amar gets into trouble by moving a decision he likes from one part of the Constitution to another. He applauds *Griswold v. Connecticut*,[119] the case, which I mentioned in the last chapter, that invalidated Connecticut's prohibition of the use of contraceptives, including their use by married couples. But he says the decision should have been based not on the due process clause (the Court's ground) but on the privileges and immunities clause, because he thinks a citizen's constitutionally protected privileges and immunities are derived from "what [citizens] do, what they say, what they believe"[120]—that is, from the "lived" Constitution. But since the privileges and immunities clause confers rights only on citizens, this leads to the absurdity that married foreigners in Connecti-

119. 381 U.S. 479 (1965).
120. Amar, *America's Unwritten Constitution*, at 120.

cut could be forbidden to use contraceptives. (And what about a foreigner married to a citizen? Could the citizen be entitled to use a contraceptive but not the foreigner?)

Amar's most outlandish riff on the Nineteenth Amendment comes when he compares its enactment to the prosecution of the Nazi leaders at Nuremberg and argues that both proceedings dispensed justice retroactively in order to make amends for past enormities. The Nuremberg Tribunal punished the Nazi leaders for violating principles of international law that had not been widely recognized previously, and Amar argues that the Nineteenth Amendment, or its amplification by the unwritten feminist Constitution, authorized judges to invalidate interpretations of the written Constitution that might have been influenced by the exclusion of women from playing any role in the Constitution's ratification. Hence the decision in which the Supreme Court invalidated provisions of the Violence Against Women Act as exceeding Congress's authority to regulate interstate commerce was wrong, Amar argues, because the Nineteenth Amendment implicitly invalidates any interpretation of earlier constitutional provisions, such as the commerce clause of Article I, that harms women, since women had no opportunity to participate in the drafting or ratification of those provisions. Similarly, Amar argues, the Supreme Court could have invalidated the laws against abortion as soon as the Nineteenth Amendment was ratified, holding that they would be valid "only if reenacted by a legislature elected by women voting equally alongside men."[121] (He calls this "retrospective democracy.")[122] By this logic the Twenty-Sixth Amendment, ratified in 1971, which gave eighteen-year-olds a constitutional right to vote, invalidated all earlier interpretations of the Constitution adverse to eighteen- to twenty-year olds. (That would be pursuant to the "children's Constitution," another unwritten Constitution, unaccountably omitted from Amar's list of unwritten Constitutions.)

Not until the 1970s did the Supreme Court strike down laws outside the scope of the Nineteenth Amendment that discriminated against women. It

121. Id. at 292.
122. Id. at 282.

did so on the authority of the equal protection clause. Amar thinks that it could have done it on the authority of three of his unwritten Constitutions: the feminist Constitution of course, the implicit Constitution, and also the lived Constitution. The proposed Equal Rights Amendment to the Constitution would, had it been ratified, have decreed that "equality of rights under the law shall not be denied or abridged by the United States or by any State on account of sex." Congress proposed the amendment in 1972 but it was never ratified. No matter; the "broad popular support" for the amendment "was entitled to interpretive weight as a popular gloss on the Fourteenth Amendment and the Ninth Amendment, in keeping with the principles of America's lived Constitution."[123] In other words, in Amar's conception of constitutional law, to fail to ratify a proposed constitutional amendment is merely to deposit it in an unwritten Constitution, making it, by that roundabout route, a part of *the* Constitution without having to be ratified.

Amar is troubled by the fact that although Article I of the written Constitution empowers Congress to "raise and support Armies" as well as to "provide and maintain a Navy," it nowhere states that Congress can *create* an army. "Raise" seems in context a synonym for "create," and anyway the necessary and proper clause of Article I would, one would think, authorize the creation of an army, as would—I would have expected him to argue— the Constitution's preamble. The preamble, which he deems a source of constitutional rights, lists as one purpose of the Constitution "to provide for the common defense."

But he contends that given the hostility of the Constitution's framers to standing armies, the phrase "raise . . . Armies" may originally just have meant temporarily mobilizing the state militias for national service. He thinks the term acquired its modern meaning only with Reconstruction. Congress had created a large national army to fight the Civil War, and afterward that army (much shrunken of course) occupied the former Confederate states for years. Amar argues that the fact that the national army rather than state militias were assigned to administer Reconstruction "gave

123. Id. at 296.

the Union Army prominent pride of place over the militia" and by doing so confirmed "the lawfulness today of a national draft, regardless of what the framers may have expected or intended,"[124] because the North had used conscription, though it had been immensely unpopular and fewer than 10 percent of Union soldiers had been conscripts.

On the same day that the Supreme Court in *Brown v. Board of Education* outlawed states' racial segregation of schools, the Court in *Bolling v. Sharpe*[125] held that the District of Columbia could not segregate its public schools either. The case is an embarrassment to textualists (it is not mentioned in the Scalia-Garner book), because the equal protection clause, which was the basis of *Brown,* is applicable only to states. The pragmatic justification of the *Bolling* decision is twofold: *Brown* would have lacked credibility had the Court exempted its own domicile; and it would make no sense to allow the federal government to practice racial discrimination while forbidding the states to do so. Amar's justification for the decision is that although the Fourteenth Amendment (the only part of the Constitution that contains an equal protection clause) purports to apply only to actions by states, it actually binds the federal government as well. For he reads section 5 of the Fourteenth Amendment as authorizing Congress to create new constitutional rights. That's not what it says; it says: "The Congress shall have power to *enforce,* by appropriate legislation, the *provisions* of this article" (emphasis added). No matter; Amar considers the Fourteenth Amendment a veritable cornucopia of unenumerated but binding constitutional rights. "Americans in the 1860s should be understood as having given birth to a new constitutional principle, albeit one that did not explicitly appear in the Fourteenth Amendment's text. Under this new unwritten principle, the federal government would properly enjoy sweeping authority to hold state governments to the highest contemporary standards of democratic inclusiveness."[126]

Amar's penultimate Constitution (the "conscientious Constitution") authorizes defiance of all the other Constitutions, beginning with the writ-

124. Id. at 94.
125. 347 U.S. 497 (1954).
126. Amar, *America's Unwritten Constitution,* at 81.

ten one, in the name of conscience. In the chapter (entitled "Doing the Right Thing") that expounds this unwritten Constitution, Amar argues that judges and juries have constitutional authority to nullify laws on the basis of conscience alone. He wants the judge to tell the jurors in a criminal trial that they're authorized (required?) to acquit the defendant even if they think him guilty, if they disapprove of the punishment, even if the punishment is lawful. Judges and jurors can suspend the Constitution and laws ad hoc.

Yet after the wild ride that I have but sketched, the reader ends Amar's book with a feeling of anticlimax, realizing that Amar doesn't actually need any of his unwritten Constitutions to achieve his ambitious goals, because he reads the written Constitution promiscuously. He reads the provision in Article IV that guarantees every state "a Republican Form of Government" as having created *all* the rights thought important in a modern democracy—even the right to a properly apportioned legislature; he says that this right "forms the bedrock of the American system of government,"[127] though it was unrecognized until the 1960s and implies that the United States does not have a Republican form of government because the Senate is malapportioned. He believes that all the rights of criminal defendants can be inferred from either Article III (the article that creates the judicial branch, but says nothing about rights) or the Constitution's preamble ("We the People of the United States, in Order to form a more perfect Union, establish Justice, insure domestic Tranquility, provide for the common defence, promote the general Welfare, and secure the Blessings of Liberty to ourselves and our Posterity, do ordain and establish this Constitution for the United States of America"). All that was needed to outlaw the Jim Crow laws, he believes, was the provision in Article I of the Constitution that forbids the federal government and the states to grant "titles of nobility," because racial discrimination made southern whites de facto aristocrats. (If I had to pick the single most preposterous claim in his book, a distinction with many contenders, that would be it.) He adds that although the Constitution of 1787 presupposes slavery (for example in the fugitive slave clause of Article IV), "When read generously, with idealistic

127. Id. at ix.

attention to both letter and spirit, the original Constitution thus seemed to condemn a legalized racial hierarchy."[128] (Actually it presupposed and ratified it.) The idea that the Constitution was a compromise does not enter Amar's mind. He claims that everything that modern liberals like was in the Constitution from the beginning.

Everything, it seems, except election of the President by popular vote. He regards the election of the President by the Electoral College as "downright un-American,"[129] but invokes the "unfinished Constitution" to substitute election by popular vote without need for a formal amendment. His brief discussion illustrates a characteristic of constitutional theorizing that chimes with my concern with the legal profession's neglect of complexity: a lack of interest (notable in Scalia's jurisprudence as well, as we've seen) in facts.

The hostility of liberals to the Electoral College is based on the fact that it enables a candidate to become President even though another candidate got more popular votes, as happened in the 2000 election, where Bush beat Gore with more electoral votes but fewer popular votes. But there are grounds for preferring the electoral-vote system that deserve consideration and that Amar ignores. One is that while a dispute over the outcome of an Electoral College vote is possible—it happened in 2000—it's less likely than a dispute over the popular vote because the winning candidate's share of the Electoral College vote invariably exceeds his share of the popular vote. In the November 2012 election, for example, President Obama received 61.7 percent of the electoral vote compared to only 51.3 percent of the popular votes cast for him and for Romney (I ignore the scattering of popular votes that were not counted for either candidate). Because almost all states award electoral votes on a winner-take-all basis, even a very slight plurality in a state creates a landslide electoral-vote victory in that state. A tie in the nationwide electoral vote is possible because the total number of votes—538—is an even number, but it is highly unlikely; it has not occurred since 1800.

Of course a tie in the number of popular votes in a national election in

128. Id. at 144 (footnote omitted).
129. Id. at 463.

which more than a hundred million votes are cast is even more unlikely. But if the difference in the popular vote is small, then if the winner of the popular vote were deemed the winner of the presidential election the losing candidate would have an incentive to seek a recount in every state in which he thought he would gain more votes from the recount than his opponent would. The candidates' lawyers would go to work in state after state to try to obtain a judicial or legislative determination that the votes be recounted, and the result would be debilitating uncertainty, delay, and conflict—remember the turmoil that a dispute limited to one state, Florida, engendered in 2000.

The Electoral College method of selecting a President requires a candidate to have trans-regional appeal. No region (South, Northeast, etc.) has enough electoral votes to elect a President. So a solid regional favorite has no incentive to campaign heavily in the states of that region, for he gains no electoral votes by increasing his plurality in states that he knows he will win. This is a desirable result because a candidate with only regional appeal is unlikely to be a successful President. The residents of the other regions are likely to feel disenfranchised—to feel that their votes didn't count, that the new President will have no regard for their interests, that he really isn't *their* President. (Even Obama, though unpopular in the South, won important Southern states—Florida and Virginia—in the 2012 election.)

It's true that the Electoral College method of selecting the President may turn off potential voters for a candidate who has no hope of carrying their state. Knowing their vote will have no effect, they have less incentive to pay attention to the campaign than they would if the President were picked by popular vote, for then the state of a voter's residence would be irrelevant to the weight of his vote. But though no individual voter's vote swings a national election, about half the eligible American population does vote in presidential elections, and most of these voters are not in battleground states. The national media keep them interested and attentive.

The winner-take-all method of awarding electoral votes induces the candidates—as we saw in the 2012 election—to focus their campaign efforts on the toss-up states; that follows directly from the candidates' lack of inducement to campaign in states they are sure to win. Voters in toss-up states are more likely to pay close attention to the campaign—to really *listen* to the competing candidates—knowing they're going to decide the election. They are likely to be the most thoughtful voters on average (and for the further reason that they'll have received the most information and attention from the candidates), and the most thoughtful voters *should* be the ones to decide the election. Also, the Electoral College restores some of the weight in the political balance that the populous states lose by virtue of the malapportionment of the Senate decreed in the Constitution. This may seem paradoxical, given that electoral votes are weighted in favor of less populous states. Wyoming contains only about one-sixth of 1 percent of the U.S. population, but its three electors (of whom two are awarded only because Wyoming has, like every state, two senators) give it slightly more than one-half of 1 percent of total electoral votes. But winner take all gives a slight increase in the popular vote a much bigger electoral-vote payoff in a large state than in a small one—imagine the difference in payoff in electoral votes from winning New York by a thousand votes versus winning Wyoming by the same margin. So other things being equal, a large state gets more attention from presidential candidates in a campaign than a small states does.

And finally the Electoral College contrivance avoids the problem of elections in which no candidate receives a majority of the votes cast. For example, Nixon in 1968 and Clinton in 1992 both had only a 43 percent plurality of the popular votes, while winning a majority in the Electoral College (301 and 370 electoral votes, respectively). There is pressure for run-off elections when no candidate wins a majority of the votes cast; that pressure, which would greatly complicate the presidential election process, is reduced by having the election decided in the Electoral College.

Opposites Attract and Repel

Amar's book and the Scalia-Garner treatise, despite being in most respects polar opposites, have three points of overlap. One is sheer bulk (567 pages for Scalia-Garner, 615 for Amar), illustrating the hypertrophic tendencies of legal writing. Remember that Scalia and Garner organize their analysis around fifty-seven good "canons of construction," that is, interpretive principles, and thirteen "false" ones; Amar has his twelve Constitutions (one written, eleven unwritten), Tribe his seven (the written Constitution plus the six invisible ones—though in fairness Tribe's book is much shorter than the other two books). Second is indifference to empirical reality. Third is the authors' pretense that their interpretive approach is not only objective and nonideological but also democratic because the Constitution is democratic and therefore any limitations that courts place on government in the name of the Constitution are ipso facto democratic as well.

Amar's book is more aggressive in regard to the Constitution's democratic pedigree than Scalia and Garner's book. He harps incessantly on the Constitution of 1787 as a charter of "popular sovereignty," a charter adopted by "We the People," indeed "enacted by the American people,"[130] enacted by "America's supreme legislature, the people"[131]—"the people themselves ratified the original Constitution and all its textual amendments"[132]—hence a democratic charter. In fact the Constitution was ratified by state conventions rather than by popular vote, and although the delegates were elected, the suffrage was extremely limited. Slaves, Indians, free blacks in the South, women, indentured servants, and propertyless men (except in Pennsylvania) had no right to vote. As a result probably no more than 10 percent of the adult population could vote for delegates to the state conventions.

Amar seems oblivious to how closely the Constitution of 1787 tracked Britain's less-than-democratic eighteenth-century governmental system. Although there are many differences, the U.S. Constitution allocates the traditional powers of the English monarch—such as enforcing the laws, appointing high officials, commanding the armed forces, conducting diplomacy, and pardoning—to the President. It allocates the essential powers of the House of Commons to the House of Representatives, and of the House of Lords to the Senate, and it models the federal judiciary on the British judiciary. Under the Constitution of 1787 only the House of Representatives was to be popularly elected, underscoring the resemblance of the House of Representatives to the House of Commons; and like the House

130. Id. at 10.

131. Id. at 15.

132. Id. at 103. Similar sentiments are expressed, though less breathlessly, in Scalia and Garner, *Reading Law,* for example at p. 88.

of Commons, the suffrage was limited, as we have seen. In addition, senators were to be appointed by state legislatures, and the President and Vice President were to be elected not by the "People" but by an Electoral College whose members would be selected in the manner directed by each state legislature; there was (and is) no requirement that the electors be selected by popular vote. The Senate was radically malapportioned. Judges were appointed, and for life. All officials of the executive branch, other than the President and Vice President, were appointed rather than being elected whether directly or indirectly.

So while the Constitution was republican, it was not democratic. (To this obvious point, Amar is blind.) And because it is so difficult to amend, it can hardly be considered to have been the product of an exercise of popular sovereignty by any people living today, or for that matter any people who reached adulthood after 1787.

"Here, the people would rule," says Amar.[133] No: here, as everywhere, a governing class would rule, but some members of the class would be directly or indirectly elected by a fraction of the adult population for fixed terms of office and would thus be competing for popular favor and therefore be answerable to public opinion.[134] That was an advance over existing political systems, including Britain's, but popular democracy it was not. Besides the restricted suffrage and a preference for indirect over direct election, the Constitution does not authorize initiatives, referenda, or recalls. There is no direct democracy. The republican model was Rome, not Athens.

Realist Interpretation

The extremes presented by textual originalism and unanchored imagination are equally unacceptable—which leaves us with interpretation understood in realistic, commonsensical terms.[135] Interpretation is a natural

133. Amar, *America's Unwritten Constitution*, at 168.

134. See Joseph A. Schumpeter, *Capitalism, Socialism, and Democracy* 269–273 (1942); Richard A. Posner, *Law, Pragmatism, and Democracy*, ch. 5 (2003).

135. As in Kent Greenawalt, *Statutory and Common Law Interpretation*, pt. 1 (2013).

mental activity. It is also ubiquitous. It is not improved by rules of interpretation. Literature professors and literary critics address daunting problems of interpretation in classics of literary modernism without benefit of canons of construction. Does anyone think they are worse at interpreting difficult texts than judges are?

One point should be uncontroversial: interpretation is relative to the nature of the document being interpreted. In the case of constitutional provisions Judge Easterbrook may be right that if the meaning of a provision has been lost through passage of time judges should not invalidate a practice challenged as violating it. In the case of statutory provisions, common sense tells us to pay attention to the meaning of the words, certainly, and to the importance of distinguishing between what the provision means and what the judge would like it to mean, and between what a provision says and what a legislator may have said it meant. But common sense also teaches us to be realistic about the legislative process—to understand the importance of compromise and the ambiguities that compromise frequently exacts, and to understand that legislators have a short horizon (the next election) and rarely try to anticipate and specify the entire range of possible applications of a statute, and that in light of that understanding the judicial duty is to devise interpretations that make sense.

Interpretation is not necessarily improved by being made self-conscious. Not that it isn't rule-governed: linguistics has exposed the vast structure of implicit rules that constitute the actual grammar of speech. But one doesn't become a better reader by bringing the rules to the surface. One becomes a better reader by studying the works that are to be interpreted, in their fullest context, rather than by studying "interpretation."[136]

In a comprehensive empirical study of statutory interpretation in the Supreme Court and (to a lesser extent) the courts of appeals, Frank Cross concludes that none of the interpretive theories invoked by judges actually constrains judicial discretion.[137] Judges are interpretive opportunists (he uses a more polite term—"interpretive pluralists"). They invoke textual-

136. See Richard A. Posner, *Law and Literature* 276 (3d ed. 2009).
137. Cross, *The Theory and Practice of Statutory Interpretation*.

ism, legislative history, the canons of construction, and so forth as rhetorical rather than interpretive tools. They are powerful rhetorical tools. They have convinced Professor Lawrence Rosenthal that "originalism is ascendant."[138] But his article goes on to argue persuasively that, as substance, originalism is fake.

Both Amar and Scalia-Garner might with profit have pondered the following passage from a book written by a distinguished legal realist many years ago. It shows how one can be sensible about interpretation without having a theory, just as one can walk upright without having a theory of bipedalism:

> In addition to the power to hold legislative acts invalid, a written constitution confers another and perhaps as great a power. It is the power to disregard prior cases . . . A change of mind from time to time is inevitable when there is a written Constitution. There can be no authoritative interpretation of the Constitution. The Constitution in its general provisions embodies the conflicting ideals of the community. Who is to say what these ideals mean in any definite way? Certainly not the framers, for they did their work when the words were put down. The words are ambiguous. Nor can it be the Court, for the Court cannot bind itself in this manner; an appeal can always be made back to the Constitution. Moreover, if it is said that the intent of the framers ought to control, there is no mechanism for any final determination of their intent. Added to the problem of ambiguity and the additional fact that the framers may have intended a growing instrument, there is the influence of constitution worship. This influence gives great freedom to a court. It can always abandon what has been said in order to go back to the written document itself. It is a freedom greater than it would have had if no such document existed . . . A written constitution, which is frequently thought to give rigidity to a system, must provide flexibility if judicial supremacy is to be permit-

138. Lawrence Rosenthal, "Originalism in Practice," 87 *Indiana Law Journal* 1183 (2012).

ted . . . A written constitution must be enormously ambiguous in its general provisions. If there has been an incorrect interpretation of the words, an amendment would come close to repeating the same words. What is desired is a different emphasis, not different language. This is tantamount to saying that what is required is a different interpretation rather than an amendment.[139]

I note finally the light cast by this and the preceding chapter on the issue of complexity in the judicial process. Judges have never much wanted to immerse themselves in the study of the real-world activities out of which litigation arises. They have been ingenious in deploying avoidance strategies, including interpretive approaches that emphasize the semantics of legislative and constitutional provisions. These are unacceptable alternatives to basing legal decisions on a realistic understanding of the full factual context of a litigation. Textual originalism is a particularly bad alternative because it is so complex—and at the same time indefinite and manipulable. Living, hidden, unwritten, invisible constitutions—they're a joke. Theories of statutory and constitutional interpretation are clutter and the last thing our courts need is more clutter.

A realistic approach to interpretation is an approach that is analytically simple, that shifts the judicial focus to factual inquiry and gives the judge time for such inquiry by excusing him from having to learn dozens of canons of construction and in cases such as *Heller* from trying to survive the rip tide that engulfs any judge who finds himself swimming in eighteenth-century history. Justice Scalia makes judging difficult for himself and his acolytes without bringing himself or them any closer to understanding what is needed to decide cases sensibly. The realist judge's approach is that if the statute is clear, fine; if it's not clear, let's try to figure out what the legislature's general aim or thinking was and interpret the statute to ad-

139. Edward H. Levi, *An Introduction to Legal Reasoning* 58–59 (1948) (footnote omitted). That the Constitution may be too vague even to be justiciable is powerfully argued in Eric J. Segall, *Supreme Myths: Why the Supreme Court Is Not a Court and Its Justices Are Not Judges* (2012). He is in tune with the skeptics of judicial competence, such as Adrian Vermeule, whom I mentioned in the preceding chapter.

vance that aim. And there may be clues in the legislative history. If we can't figure out what the aim is, we'll have no alternative but to assume the role of pro tem legislators and impose some reasonable meaning on the statute. That's what the courts have done for example with the antitrust laws, and no one seems to complain. That's realist interpretation. Amar, Tribe, Balkin, and the other advocates of the unbridled imagination throw off Scalian shackles so violently that what they are left with can't be called interpretation, realist or otherwise.

Brian Butler distinguishes my approach from Scalia's by describing mine as "information producing" and his as "information excluding."[140] Scalia's approach is semantic, though in practice he ranges beyond the statutory or constitutional text, so that his advice to other judges might be said to be "do as I say, not as I do." But clearly he doesn't want to base statutory or constitutional interpretation on data, whereas realistic interpretation insists on consideration of context in a full factual sense in a wide spectrum of cases.

Scalia makes judging too difficult by telling judges to master and apply a baffling and ultimately fruitless system for avoiding engagement with reality. He is a complexifier, though it is less likely that complexity guides his judicial votes (and those of others of his school of thought) than that it conceals the biases that actually generate those votes. Amar, on the other hand, makes judging too easy. A judge who takes Amar's book seriously will have free rein to decide any case any way he wants.

Amar says early in his book: "We are all textualists; we are all living constitutionalists."[141] Thank goodness not.

140. Brian E. Butler, "Law, Pragmatism and Constitutional Interpretation: From Information Exclusion to Information Production," 3 *Pragmatism Today* 39 (2012). Other commentators have described my interpretive approach as pragmatic, a characterization that I accept. See John F. Manning, "Statutory Pragmatism and Constitutional Structure," 120 *Harvard Law Review* 1161 (2007); Martha Minow, "Religion and the Burden of Proof: Posner's Economics and Pragmatism in *Metzl v. Leininger*," 120 *Harvard Law Review* 1175 (2007); Calvin TerBeek, "Pragmatism in Practice: An Evaluation of Posner's Pragmatic Adjudication in First Amendment and Fourth Amendment Cases," *48 South Texas Law Review* 472 (2006).

141. Amar, *America's Unwritten Constitution*, at xiii.

❧ 8 ☙

MAKE IT SIMPLE, MAKE IT NEW

Opinion Writing and Appellate Advocacy

Ideas come from writing as much as writing comes from ideas.
Stephen J. Pune

Badly written judicial opinions might seem a distinctly peripheral concern of a legal system struggling to cope with the modern technical world. But that is not so. My concern is not with philistinism but with lack of clarity, which is a product of jargon, verbosity, and excessive delegation to law clerks and an important source and example of gratuitous internal complexity—of judges distracted from wrestling with the complexity of modernity by producing judicial opinions that further complexify law. Because opinion writing at the appellate level (the level on which I focus) is significantly influenced by appellate advocacy, I include in this chapter a brief discussion of that as well.

The Signs of Bad Judicial Writing

More than a decade ago I summarized my reservations about the quality of judicial opinion writing:

First, there is a noticeable lack of candor and, *second* and related, a notable lack of concreteness, in judicial opinions . . .

Third, there is an overuse of jargon, one of the marks of what I've called elsewhere the "pure" style of judicial opinion-writing. It is a style self-consciously professional; its antithesis, what I call the "impure" style, is simple, nontechnical, colloquial, narrative, essayistic.

Fourth is a lack of economy of expression—lack of considerateness for the audience for judicial opinions. Under this rubric can be grouped the tendency to overkill, to repetition, to tedium, and the clutter of citations, facts, quotations, and boilerplate, which are such characteristic features of judicial prose.

Fifth is the preoccupation with trivia that is so marked a characteristic of the legal mind. It is the hypertrophy of the high degree of verbal *care* that is a genuine asset of the well-trained lawyer.

Sixth is a surprising reluctance to use pictures in cases . . . The aversion to the visual is of limited significance in judicial writing but it is an excellent example of the flight from concreteness to abstractness that is such a pronounced feature of the legal professional's style of thinking and writing.

Seventh and last is the pall that "political correctness" casts over judicial writing, particularly with respect to gender; insistence on gender neutrality of pronouns is a recipe for stilted prose.

The underlying problems are an exaggerated formalism, which is to say a desire to make a judicial opinion seem rigorous, logical, technical, even esoteric (not the everyday practical reasoning that judicial decision-making, much of the time, really is); a sheer lack of knowledge of, experience in, and aptitude for good writing; an excess of specialization related to the rise of law clerks and ghostwriting generally, which has made writing seem an eminently delegable component of judicial performance; the absence of a national culture of rhetoric, such as England had until recently; and, closely related, the philistine character of American culture, in which writing well, along with other aspects of humane culture, is not highly valued.

... The decline of the humanities is likely to continue as more and more educational emphasis is placed on computers and other aspects of technology, as the rise of ethnic diversity engenders ever greater anxiety over the traditional cultural hegemony of "dead white European males," and as literature continues to lose ground to electronic communication and entertainment. The trend bodes ill for judicial writing. At the same time, variance in the quality of judicial prose is likely to decline as judicial writing is brought ever more under the aegis of ghostwriters (the law clerks and staff attorneys) drawn from the best law schools.[1]

I stand by these points, but I would cite another source of bad judicial writing as well: the unusual situation of an author (sometimes a judge, more commonly a law clerk) who knows that he will be published and read regardless of the taste and preferences of his audience. West Publishing does not refuse to publish any of the opinions that federal judges submit to it for publication, and lawyers and judges must read the relevant judicial opinions whether readable or not, interesting or not, well written or not. Not having a publisher, or an audience, that must be pleased, judges tend not to think about whom they are writing for. They tend to write above the heads of laypersons (such as the litigants) but to write down to their professional audience, when they could communicate effectively with both by writing simply and directly.

The Writer Model versus the Manager Model

The initial decision that an appellate judge must make about opinion writing is not how to write, but whether to write his opinions or instead to edit

---

1. Richard A. Posner, "Legal Writing Today," 8 *Scribes Journal of Legal Writing* 35–36 (2001–2002) (footnotes omitted; emphasis in original).

law clerks' opinion drafts. The choice is between two models of the appellate judge: the writer model, which prevailed before judges had law clerks, and for a time after that before they had as many law clerks (and other staff, such as interns and externs) as they have now, and the manager model, which is dominant today.

As judges' staffs have expanded, hierarchy has increased; and as hierarchy increases, the judge, who is at the top of the hierarchy, increasingly defines his role as that of a manager. The management model of a court of appeals judge's job has been taken to its furthest extreme in the "Becker model," invented by the late Judge Edward Becker of the Third Circuit and adopted (though often in a dilute form) by a number of federal appellate judges. In that model the judge hires a former law clerk (not necessarily one of *his* former law clerks), who has additional legal experience besides the clerkship, to be his senior law clerk. The senior clerk assigns opinion writing, editing, and other duties to the judge's other clerks in accordance with his evaluation of their strengths and weaknesses, and these junior law clerks report to him rather than to the judge, with whom indeed they may have little face-to-face contact. The staff may include unpaid interns or externs, who report to the clerks. Sometimes the senior clerk is permanent while the junior law clerks serve the usual one-year term; sometimes some or all of the clerks are permanent, though for budgetary reasons court of appeals judges are no longer permitted to have more than one permanent law clerk (but those who had more when the rule of only one was adopted can keep them).[2] After an opinion drafted by one of the junior clerks is edited by the senior clerk (perhaps by the other junior clerks as well), it is submitted to the judge for final editing, which, depending on the judge, may be perfunctory at one extreme or, at the other extreme, come close to rewriting the opinion from scratch.

Notice that the Becker model involves delegation by the judge not only

2. Law clerks' salaries increase with experience. Most federal appellate law clerks are hired right out of law school and for only one year, and thus at the lowest salary. The salary range in Chicago (law clerks' salaries are adjusted for cost of living) is $63,000 to $91,000, though a very few experienced clerks are eligible to be paid $106,000. Given the range, career clerks are substantially more expensive than clerks hired right out of law school and for just one year.

of opinion drafting but also of opinion editing. This delegation is also found in the offices of many judges who have not gone all the way to the Becker model. There is a certain logic to this further delegation of what once was thought the judge's work: a clerk who writes well enough to be entrusted with drafting a judicial opinion is likely to be a competent editor of another clerk's draft.

A decision to write the first draft of the opinion, and thus to reject the management model, is difficult for the judicial appointee who has spent many years in a managerial role in a law firm or government legal service; as a writer of first drafts, he is rusty. He may not realize that editing is no substitute for writing from scratch. The writer of the first draft controls the final product to a degree an editor is apt not to realize. "Opinion drafting places a great deal of responsibility on the clerk, because the first draft influences everything that follows. Even though judges work with drafts to make them their own, they often adopt the authorities, organization, and language from their clerks' drafts."[3] The judge-editor also may not realize that the process of writing, which means searching for words, for sentences, in which to express meaning, is a process of discovery rather than just of expressing preformed ideas; that it reveals analytical gaps; that it gives rise to new ideas;[4] and that fluency in writing comes largely from—writing. There are the problems with clerk-drafted opinions that I mentioned in Chapter 2: the lack of the judge's personal voice, the voice of experience (the law clerk has no experience); and the likely incomplete understanding of, and greater likelihood of forgetting, a document written by someone else. And related is a lack of commitment: the judge who did not actually compose a critical argument in an earlier opinion may not notice or even care when a contrary argument appears in "his" opinion in a new case, written by a new law clerk. Some judges, as I said, though requiring

3. Mary L. Dunnewold, Beth A. Honetschlager, and Brenda L. Tofte, *Judicial Clerkships: A Practical Guide* 216 (2010). I would insert "most" between "though" and "judges."

4. "Writing is 'thinking in ink.' The actual process of writing helps the writer analyze the subject at hand and draw conclusions. Thus, as you write, new ideas will bubble up that you should incorporate into the analysis." Id. at 91. Notice that "you" in this passage is a law clerk, not a judge.

their law clerks to draft an opinion, rewrite it almost from scratch. But that is an inefficient way of working, productive of needless delay.

In the "Posner model," emulated I fear by few if any other judges, the judge, being an experienced writer of judicial opinions if he's been a judge for even just a few years (for he may be writing fifty or more opinions a year), writes a serviceable if rough draft shortly after the judges confer following the argument and the opinion assignments are made. He gives his draft to one of his law clerks, indicating mainly by bracketed directions in the draft what further research he wants the clerk to do. That further research is likely to be both legal and factual—and factual in the broadest sense, including not only facts in the record but also background facts gleaned from the Internet and elsewhere, and what in Chapter 5 I called "coloring book" facts, and also facts unearthed in scientific and social scientific research. The clerk understands that he's also to check all the facts in the draft carefully, delve into the record for key facts that the judge may have overlooked, criticize the form and substance, tone and clarity, of the judge's opinion, suggest ideas, suggest style and word changes, and propose and if feasible pursue additional lines of research or ask the judge whether they are worth pursuing.

The clerk presents the results of his work on the judge's first draft in the form of comments either inserted in the draft, if short, or if not then in a separate memorandum. The judge then rewrites the draft. The cycle of judge-clerk interaction may be repeated several times before the opinion is ready to be cite checked by another law clerk (who is also welcome to make suggestions for further improvements) and then reworked a final time by the judge and finally circulated to the other judges on the panel. The judge may also show part or all of his draft to another judge, soliciting suggestions, in advance of completion and circulation. The entire process should not take more than three or four weeks unless the case is exceptionally complex or the judge or law clerks busy with other opinions. The aim is for the opinion to be issued within a month or six weeks after oral argument, though surges in caseload or the unusual difficulty of a particular case, which may delay approval by the other judges on the panel or provoke a dissenting or concurring opinion, may slow down the process.

Notice in this unorthodox model of judge-clerk interaction the inversion of the judge's and the clerk's respective roles in the dominant model, in which the clerk writes the opinion draft and the judge edits it. In the "Posner model" the clerk's work importantly includes making editorial suggestions on the judge's draft. There is a long tradition of editors' improving authors' work. Think of Maxwell Perkins's editing of Thomas Wolfe's novels, or Ezra Pound's editing of T. S. Eliot's great poem *The Waste Land*. What would have been perverse would have been for Wolfe to ask Perkins to write the first draft of Wolfe's novels (that is, novels that would be published under Wolfe's name) or Eliot to ask Pound to write the first draft of *The Waste Land*.

The judge who works from a law clerk's draft must wait not only for the clerk to complete his research but also for this inexperienced opinion writer to write an opinion draft—and not a rough draft either, but a polished draft that will impress the judge. The conscientious judge is unlikely to be entirely satisfied with the law clerk's draft. He is likely to ask the law clerk to conduct additional research, to trim here and expand there, to alter tone or focus or emphasis, and he may ask his other clerks to go over the draft as well. So a cycle is initiated much as when the judge writes the first draft—but the cycle begins later because the law clerk will have labored for a longer time to produce his first draft than a judge to produce *his* first draft. And the judge who is not just an editor, but a rewriter, may find himself spending as much time rewriting the law clerk's draft as he would have spent writing the first draft himself.

Delay is a serious problem in federal courts even when caseload is not very heavy. Some court of appeals judges take almost a year, on average, to issue a published opinion. The reason may be indecision, procrastination, difficult colleagues (who may themselves be procrastinators, or indecisive)—or, in many cases I suspect, poor management, which means not using staff efficiently. Still another common reason for delay is inability to prioritize. Suppose a judge on the same day is assigned two cases, and only one clerk is available to work on them, the judge's other clerks being busy with other cases. One of the two cases, which I'll call *A*, will require four weeks' work from argument to publication; the other, *B*, will require only two weeks' work. If it makes no difference to the overall length of the litigation which case is decided first (it will make a difference if, for example, in one case the court will be remanding for further proceedings in the district court and in the other it will be affirming a judgment for one of the parties and thus terminating the litigation), the judge assigned to do the two opinions should do *B* first. If the decision in *B* is completed and issued first, and *A* second, then the combined elapsed time from argument to decision of the two cases will be eight weeks, *B* being decided after two weeks and *A* four weeks later (so *A* will have taken six weeks to decide). If the decision in *A* is completed and issued first, the combined elapsed time will rise from eight to ten weeks—the decision in *A* will be issued four weeks after the argument and *B* two weeks later, hence six weeks after argument.[5] How many judges are aware of the significance of the order in which opinions are prepared, or would make any adjustment in work schedules if told about it?

When I was the chief judge of my court (1993–2000), I suggested to newly appointed judges that they write their own opinions and let the law clerks do the research, criticize the opinions, etc. but not write them. I said that maybe at first the judge, if not coming from a branch of the legal profession of which writing was a central component (academia is the main example), would find it tough sledding to write a decent opinion. But practice makes perfect; opinion writing would become easier as the years rolled by (maybe months not years, considering how many opinions a "writing" federal court of appeals judge would write every year), but eventually the judge would develop a proficiency that no law clerk, working for only one year, could develop. The time of law clerks would be freed up for criticizing the judge's drafts—indeed even for editing the drafts, if the clerks are good editors—as well as for conducting research in greater depth than

5. To make the example clearer, suppose that both cases are argued on November 1. If *A* is done first, the opinion in it will be issued on November 28, four weeks later. Then work on *B* will start, and the opinion in *B* will be issued two weeks after that, on December 12, which is six weeks after the argument. If *B* is done first, the opinion in it will be issued on November 15, after two weeks, and the opinion in *A* on December 12, six weeks after argument. So in the first sequence the two opinions take ten weeks from argument to be done, and in the second sequence only eight.

is possible when clerks are charged with writing judicial opinions, since the clerks (unless permanent, or nearing the end of their one-year term) are inexperienced opinion writers, laboring painstakingly, fearful of the judge's criticism. The judge who does not write his own opinions and therefore does not become an experienced opinion writer, and who hires new law clerks every year, must either adopt the Becker model or spend his judicial career editing fledgling lawyers with no previous experience in writing judicial opinions.

Realism requires acknowledgment that since judges appoint law clerks while politicians appoint judges, many newly appointed law clerks are better judicial writers than some judges will ever be, however diligently the judge works to improve his speed and fluency. Even in such cases my tendency is to prefer the judge-written opinion for its greater authenticity, and hence the greater insight that the opinion provides the bench and the bar into the judge's thinking and likely future judicial votes.

The delegation of opinion writing to inexperienced law clerks is one reason for delay in deciding cases, but a more fundamental reason, which is a cousin to judges' lack of a sense of an audience for which they're writing, is that delay imposes no cost on the *judges* unless it becomes so extreme that they're criticized. The litigants' lawyers rarely dare to complain. The costs of judicial delay to them, to parties similarly situated to the litigants, and to judges having similar cases are costs to which most judges seem oblivious. Those costs deserve emphasis. Appellate decisions resolve, or at least advance the resolution of, the underlying litigation and thus eliminate or reduce uncertainty, a result that is almost always desirable from a social-welfare standpoint. The decisions also provide information for the guidance of other persons in situations similar to that of the litigants in the present case, and other courts having or soon to have similar cases. That is valuable information too, and the sooner it is disseminated the greater its value.

The umpireal conception of the judge's role, which retains a strong grip on the judicial imagination, is a further discouragement to efforts to speed up the judicial process. An umpire isn't responsible for speeding up the play. But the judge is the manager of the case, as well as the umpire; he makes many of the rules. He doesn't just apply them—and he fixes the length of the game. He can't avoid management. He has a staff; it's small but it has to be managed. As manager he should be worrying about moving the case along and, if the decision is to remand it for further proceedings in the district court, providing as much guidance as possible to the district judge, to expedite the completion of the case and if possible avert another appeal.

Management versus Managerialism

There is a distinction to be drawn between management and managerialism. By the latter term I mean an organizational culture, best illustrated in the federal judiciary by the Becker model, in which leadership takes second place to management, which is to say to work assignment, delegation, and hierarchy. In the typical appellate judge's "chambers" the basic work of drafting a bench memo in advance of oral argument, and, if the judge is assigned the majority opinion to write (or decides to write separately), preparing the first draft of the opinion, is assigned to the lowest rung of the office hierarchy, a law clerk or perhaps an intern or extern, or sometimes a member of the staff attorney pool (law clerks not hired by or assigned to particular judges). The drafter's work is reviewed by the senior law clerk, and maybe by the other clerks as well, and eventually a polished, maybe a consensus, product is submitted for the judge's approval. The managerial model minimizes error, but tends also to bleach creativity and individuality from the final product, as well as to generate delay. The clerks may also review draft opinions submitted for their judge's approval, along with petitions for panel rehearing and petitions for rehearing en banc, prepare drafts of the judge's speeches, assist him with judicial committee work—and in all these ways place him at a further distance from the essential inputs into the decisional process. Managerialism is a risk-averse strategy that yields a safe, conventional product. Judges whose work habits have been shaped by a similar culture in a law firm or government legal agency find the managerial approach to judging congenial. Especially in large law firms, briefs tend to be committee products, and committee composition subordinates originality and imagination to the need for compromise. The intellectual passivity fostered by such a culture, because of the extensive delegation that it involves, is further encouraged by the judge's embrace of the umpireal role.

But the decline of first-draft opinion writing by judges reflects more than managerialism and the resulting tendency of experienced lawyers to be editors and supervisors rather than draftsmen. It also reflects the decline of the literary culture in America. As a result of the spread of popular entertainment, the growth of science, social science, and technology relative to the humanities, the supplantation of letter writing by email, and the decline in the prestige of highbrow literature (mainly because so little of it is being created, though there's a chicken-and-egg problem—supply may be following demand down), writing is no longer considered a skill relevant to high office. Presidents and other politicians don't even pretend to write their own speeches, though most judges who don't write their own opinions remain reluctant to acknowledge this publicly. Nowadays only a few fusspots, like me, care that judges delegate opinion writing to their law clerks, though some judges feel a twinge of conscience and offer excuses. Justice Ginsburg has been quoted as saying that she would like to "write all my opinions myself, but there is just not enough time to do that."[6] Instead, she says, she edits heavily. Her claim not to have enough time to write opinions puzzles me given how few opinions Supreme Court Justices write. Over the past six complete terms of Court (the 2006 through 2011 terms), Justice Ginsburg produced a total of ninety-six opinions (forty-six majority or plurality opinions, the rest—more than half the total—concurring or dissenting ones). That is an average of sixteen per term. Suppose it would take her four hours to write the first draft of an opinion, on average. That may be a generous estimate. Supreme Court opinions don't have to

6. Todd C. Peppers, "The Modern Clerkship: Ruth Bader Ginsburg and Her Law Clerks," in *In Chambers: Stories of Supreme Court Law Clerks and Their Justices* 391, 397 (Todd C. Peppers and Artemus Ward eds. 2012).

be long, since the Court usually grants certiorari to decide only one or two issues[7] and doesn't have to worry about lower-court case law. Parkinson's Law, applied to a Court in which size of staff is inverse to number of decisions, offers the best explanation for the inordinate length of the modern Supreme Court opinion.

Four hours of drafting each of sixteen opinions would add up to sixty-four hours a year. If Justice Ginsburg works two thousand hours a year, then writing her own opinions would require reallocating only 3 percent of her time from other judicial tasks—tasks that include editing her law clerks' drafts, which must be time-consuming; so the net increase in the time spent in opinion writing/editing would be less than 3 percent. Even those of us who write our own opinions do editing—self-editing—but that is less time-consuming than editing someone's writing, and more gratifying. If you're Manet, do you want to put the finishing touches on Thomas Couture's *Les Romains de la décadence,* or on your own *Olympia?*

This is not written in a spirit of criticism of Justice Ginsburg. Her opinions are meticulous and her input into them seems very considerable; indeed I imagine that she's a rewriter and not just an editor, and makes the opinions fully her own. Her recent separate opinion in the "Obamacare" case[8] is a masterpiece and must have taken very considerable time and effort to compose. I am wondering merely whether her method is efficient, a question that is part of the larger question of whether judges are good managers, able optimally to allocate work between themselves and their law clerks.

I'm also not meaning to suggest by reference to highbrow culture that

7. Justice Stevens has said that "the most helpful and persuasive petitions for certiorari to this Court usually present only one or two issues, and spend a considerable amount of time explaining why those questions of law have sweeping importance and have divided or confused other courts," *O'Sullivan v. Boerckel,* 527 U.S. 838, 858 (1999) (dissenting opinion). See also Stewart A. Baker, "A Practical Guide to Certiorari," 33 *Catholic University Law Review* 611, 613 (1984).

8. *National Federation of Independent Business v. Sebelius,* 132 S. Ct. 2566, 2609 (2012).

judges who write their own opinions should be imitating Henry James, James Joyce, or Gertrude Stein. Better models are the great *clear* writers, like Hemingway and Orwell—the latter said his aim was to write prose as transparent as a pane of glass. And anyway the issue isn't models; it's simply that people who write well tend to be people who have read a great deal of classy prose, and there are fewer and fewer such people. To write with flair is a gift vouchsafed to few judges (to few people, period). But any intelligent person can teach himself to write clearly; and it's clarity that is needed in an age of complexity, clarity for example in being able to explain technical matters in a way that judges and lawyers of very limited technical knowledge can understand and emulate in their own opinions and briefs. Clarity is of course not the only characteristic of good writing, and a judge (or law clerk) ambitious to write well and not merely intelligibly can be helped by guides to writing prose. They need not be guides to writing legal prose; the two best that I know are not.[9]

The Formalist Opinion

The judge's decision whether to be a writer or an editor does not determine the form of the judicial opinion, with the important qualification that a law clerk's opinion draft is almost certain to be formalist because most law clerks are formalists. They are formalists because what they bring to the job of being a law clerk (with the occasional exception of valuable background knowledge, for example in a technical field—if their judge values such knowledge in a law clerk) is mainly what they learned in law school. And what they learned—in part because it was what they expected

9. Stephen J. Pune, *Voice & Vision: A Guide to Writing History and Other Serious Nonfiction* (2009); Helen Sword, *Stylish Academic Writing* (2012). Both books emphasize rhetorical devices for getting and holding a reader's attention; in this they reflect the competitive nature of the book and article (including academic book and article) market—readers have many choices. But because lawyers are compelled to read judicial opinions, judges and law clerks tend to be indifferent to devices for attracting and holding readers; they have a captive audience. It is still another cause of bad judicial writing.

to learn—was the conventional sort of legal analysis that consists of fitting the facts of a case to a legal rule usually found in a statute or constitutional provision or in a judicial opinion. That was not all they were taught; at the better law schools, from which most federal law clerks come, most of the professors are not formalists. But it is what the students came to believe, from the style of most of the judicial opinions they read, that judges would expect from them as law clerks. Students are fed a steady diet of judicial opinions in law school, and not only are judges on average more formalist than law professors but judicial opinions are more formalist than the judges who are their nominal authors.

Years ago, teaching a course at the University of Chicago Law School in judicial opinion writing, intended for students planning to clerk, I was struck by the difference between their taste in judicial opinions and mine. The students liked pedestrian clerk-written opinions and disdained opinions by great judicial writers such as Holmes and Hand. They were positively affronted by opinions of Judge Alex Kozinski of the Ninth Circuit— an excellent writer!

Managerialism has an affinity to formalism. The decision to delegate opinion writing to law clerks encourages a judge to adopt a formalist conception of the judicial role, since that role facilitates such delegation, given the tendency of law clerks to write formalist opinions. And it makes life easier for the clerks. Not only does it allow them to write in the mode that comes naturally to them as a result of their legal education ("law clerks may write well but—in speaking for another—they employ a safely formulaic mode usually learned in editing a law review"[10]); also, the materials out of which to fashion a formalist opinion can all be found either in the parties' briefs or in publications readily available and familiar to the law clerks—statutes and cases of course but also treatises and law review articles. So judge and clerk can remain enclosed in a sealed compartment lined with distinctively legal documents from which to generate a "right answer."

10. Michael Boudin, "Judge Henry Friendly and the Craft of Judging," 159 *University of Pennsylvania Law Review* 1, 13 (2010).

The results of this stylistic formalism can, to a fastidious writer, seem pretty ghastly. Clerk-written opinions abound in superfluous names and dates; superfluous procedural details; superfluous Latinisms (such as "ambit," *"de minimis,"* *"eiusdem generis,"* *"sub silentio"*); legal clichés (such as "plain meaning," "strict scrutiny," "instant case," "totality of circumstances," "abuse of discretion," "facial adequacy," "facial challenge," "chilling effect," "canons of construction," "gravamen," and "implicates" in such expressions as "the statute implicates First Amendment concerns"); legal terms that have an ambulatory rather than a fixed meaning (such as "rational basis" and "proximate cause"); incurably vague "feel good" terms such as "justice" and "fairness"; pomposities such as "it is axiomatic that"; insincere verbal curtsies ("with all due respect," or "I respectfully dissent"); and gruesome juxtapositions (such as *"Roe* and its progeny," meaning *Roe v. Wade* and the subsequent abortion-rights cases). To this add: timid obeisance to clumsy norms of politically correct speech; unintelligible abbreviations gleaned from the *Bluebook;*[11] archaic grammatical rules (for example, don't begin a sentence with "However" or "Moreover" —these words are "postpositives"—and never say "on the other hand" without having first said "on the one hand"); archaic rules of punctuation, especially placement of commas; and offenses against good English ("choate" for "not inchoate," "pled" for "pleaded" when referring to a complaint or other pleading, "proven" as a verb instead of "proved," "absent" and "due to" as adverbs, "habeas claim" for "habeas corpus claim," "he breached his contract" for "he broke his contract") or against good Latin (*"de minimus"* for *"de minimis"* and *"ejusdem generis"* for *"eiusdem generis"*).

Where stylistic formalism reigns, there is a fussy preoccupation with trivial forms of "correctness," so law clerks spend a lot of time proofreading and bluebooking opinions drafts lest a typographical error or an error

11. Recall the examples from Chapter 3: Temp. Envtl. L. & Tech. J., ILSA J. Int'l & Comp. L., Emp. Rts. & Emp. Pol'y J., AIPLA Q.J., B.T.A.M. (P-H), A. Ct. Crim. App., A.F. Ct. Crim. App., C.G. Ct. Crim. App., N-M Ct. Crim. App., Ne. Reg'l Parole Comm'n, and Cent. Ill. Pub. Serv. Co.

of citation form end up in a published opinion. Time-consuming attention to unimportant detail is characteristic of legal practice, and is no doubt related to the custom (tenacious though at last eroding) of hourly billing, and to a certain insecurity that legal reasoning is really as cogent as formalists pretend. The accuracy and consistency of the judicial opinion at the formal level, along with length and detail and citations and quotations and professional jargon, serve as signals, though false ones, that the analytical content of the formal envelope is reliable. The judicial obsession with picky details may also reflect judges' weaknesses as managers; they do not know how to prioritize.

A formalist opinion will usually start with a detailed recitation of "the facts," many of them irrelevant as well as uninteresting (dates, for example, where nothing turns on the date of a particular occurrence), yet with much left out that is both interesting and important and could be found in a five-minute search of the Web. For often a case involves obscure business practices, arcane foreign customs, rare medical mishaps, and other esoterica that the lawyers do not bother to explain to the judges.

After the statement of facts (at once too many and too few) comes an unnecessary summary of the lower court's opinion and of the parties' contentions, and a statement of the standard of review. There really are only two standards of appellate review: plenary and deferential. Conventionally there are four basic standards (with many variants), which in ascending order of deference to the trial court or administrative agency are de novo, clearly erroneous, substantial evidence, and abuse of discretion. But the last three are, in practice, the same, because finer distinctions are beyond judges' cognitive capacity. The multiplication of unusable distinctions is a familiar judicial pathology.

At long last, after much huffing and puffing, comes the analysis in the opinion, often well concealed in quotations from previous judicial opinions (quotations often taken out of context, in defiance of Holmes's dictum quoted in Chapter 5 that "general propositions do not decide concrete cases"), in bromides that do not describe actual judicial practice (such as "we start from the words of the statute"—which judges never do; judges always start from some general sense of what the statute is about), in strings of citations that would be seen not to support the decision if anyone bothered to read the cited cases, and in vacuous appeals to "plain meaning" or made-up legislative "intent." The opinion will be decked out in unnecessary section headings and ornamented with unnecessary footnotes.

The aim of such drafting, to the extent it has an aim rather than being a product of habit and convention, is to make the opinion seem learned, comprehensive, orthodox, and exact, and to make the outcome seem to follow ineluctably from prior authoritative pronouncements with no addition from the writer, who pretends merely to have displayed the authorities that make the outcome an inevitability.

The sheer *strangeness* of much judicial prose needs to be remarked. Consider the following passage, from an opinion in a criminal case in which the defendant was complaining that because of his diabetes he was unlikely to survive his sentence, and that therefore the sentence should be shortened. (He lost the appeal.) The abstract character and lofty tone of the passage mark it as formalist:

> There is a worthy tradition that death in prison is not to be ordered lightly, and the probability that a convict will not live out his sentence should certainly give pause to a sentencing court. Wurzinger's [Wurzinger is the defendant] key argument is not the nonstarter that "age per se is a mitigating factor" (though he does attempt that argument as well), but that a sentence of death in prison is notably harsher than a sentence that stops even a short period before. Death is by universal consensus a uniquely traumatic experience, and prison often deprives defendants of the ability to be with their families or to otherwise control the circumstances of death. A sentence that forces this experience on a prisoner is quantitatively more severe than a sentence that does not consume the entirety of a defendant's life, inflicting greater punishment and creating a stronger deterrent effect. See, e.g., *United States v. Patriarca*, 948 F.2d 789, 793 (1st Cir. 1991) (holding that an increase in penalty that ensured death in prison would likely deter bail jumping). Additionally, of course, the physical constraints of a dying

illness will incapacitate some defendants as effectively as imprisonment, making such a long sentence unnecessary.[12]

The paragraph begins oddly by implying, obviously unintentionally,
that the defendant has been ordered to die in prison ("death in prison is not
to be ordered lightly"). It then states without explanation that age can't be
a mitigating factor in sentencing, though it can be, as the sentencing guidelines recognize,[13] since, as I noted in Chapter 3, recidivism is less likely the
older the defendant. A strange clause follows: "Death is by universal consensus a uniquely traumatic experience." The reader doesn't have to be
told what death is, and anyway what the court is talking about is not death
itself but rather the prospect of imminent death that accompanies dying. A
dying person would rather be at home with his family than in a prison, and
his family would want this too. But that is not, the court neglects to mention, a basis for shortening an otherwise appropriate sentence. Rather it is a
basis for releasing dying prisoners, whatever the length of their sentences
—a civilized practice unless one is dealing with a monster, which Wurzinger, a middle-aged meth dealer, was not.

The next sentence in the paragraph—"A [prison] sentence that forces
this experience on a prisoner [death in prison] is quantitatively more severe
than a sentence that does not consume the entirety of a defendant's life, in-
flicting greater punishment and creating a stronger deterrent effect"—is no
improvement. The word "quantitatively" does not belong; "consume the
entirety of a defendant's life" is labored; and "creating a stronger deterrent
effect" sounds as if not releasing a dying prisoner may be an appropriate
way of making a long sentence more painful and so achieving greater deterrence—an uncivilized mode of jacking up punishment if I am right that
releasing dying prisoners would be a civilized practice. And finally there is
the mysterious parenthetical remark that the *Patriarca* case had held that
"an increase in penalty that ensured death in prison would likely deter bail

12. *United States v. Wurzinger,* 467 F.3d 649, 652 (7th Cir. 2006) (citations, with
the exception of *Patriarca,* omitted).

13. U.S.S.G. § 5H1.1. See also *United States v. Johnson,* 685 F.3d 660, 661–662
(7th Cir. 2012), and studies cited there.

jumping." What could that *mean?* You have to go to *Patriarca* to find out, and you discover there that all the court meant was that a defendant would be unlikely to jump bail if he knew that the consequence were he caught might be a sentence so long that he would die in prison.

If judges can't or won't write clearly and simply, I don't see how they (how we) can cope with the complexities of modernity. If a judge can't articulate a complex issue clearly, it probably means he doesn't understand it and that most of his readers will not understand it. The struggle to be clear is inseparable from the struggle to understand. The tendency of formalism is to opt out of both struggles.

Yet the formalist opinion is in the ascendant. The evolution of articulation of judicial thought has gone into reverse. Today's typical appellate opinion is more formalist than the typical opinion of a half century ago. The change reflects the growth of managerialism but is also a defensive reaction to criticisms of the freewheeling style and liberal results of the decisions of the Supreme Court in the 1960s, and an attempt to camouflage the continued judicial activism of both Left and Right. The growth of managerialism also reflects the increased role of law clerks in the judicial system and ultimately the heavier caseloads of the appellate courts, since heavier caseloads beget more clerks (except in the Supreme Court, where as we know the increase in law clerks has been correlated with a decrease in caseload). The alternative to more clerks—more judges—would not only be more costly but also more clumsy, because of the increased difficulty of coordination. The number of judges has grown of course but much less than it would have had to grow had the ratio of law clerks to judges remained unchanged. Hierarchy is an economizing method of organization.

Judge Kozinski, in an essay surprisingly denouncing legal realism (he is a legal realist), thinks that law clerks keep judges honest (by which he means formalist): "You have to give them reasons [for the decision you favor], and those reasons better be pretty good—any law clerk worth his salt will argue with you if the reasons you give are unconvincing."[14] This is not

14. Alex Kozinski, "What I Ate for Breakfast and Other Mysteries of Judicial Decision Making," 26 *Loyola of Los Angeles Law Review* 993, 994 (1993).

true, unless very few law clerks are "worth [their] salt." Especially if the judge has come from a hierarchical practice environment, and given the age difference between law clerks and judges and that law clerks are on average sharper analytically than their judge, law clerks are reluctant to argue with the judge. Judges have been known to fire law clerks: Judge Kozinski is one of those judges.

A further point *contra* Kozinski is that law clerks who draft opinions don't have much time to study cases and other materials in advance of oral argument, because drafting judicial opinions intended for publication is a daunting task for just-graduated law students and consumes the bulk of the clerk's time. A clerk's doubts about the soundness of his judge's take on the case are likelier to crystallize after the case has been argued and a tentative vote taken by the judges, when in drafting the opinion the clerk discovers a problem that neither he nor his judge had noticed. That will usually be too late. The clerk will be tempted to paper over the problem rather than admit to his judge that he had failed to provide accurate advice before the argument and the vote. His job now is to defend the vote. That is probably the judge's expectation as well. If he's a former advocate, it is natural for him to regard the opinion as a brief in support of the outcome.

Rules of Good Opinion Writing

But enough of my complaining; I want to be constructive. I believe that both formalist and realist, and whether judge or law clerk, can write a better, a more readable, and also a more honest opinion by heeding a few simple rules (I realize that some of these will stick in the formalist's craw):

1. Don't be a *jargonista*. Legal jargon obfuscates, and deceives the legal writer into thinking he's writing with precision, when he's simply writing anachronistically. Some technical language is inescapable; the judge cannot simply rename legal doctrines that have established, even if opaque, names, such as "consideration," "promissory estoppel," "res ipsa loquitur," and "burden of production." But the examples I gave earlier of fusty legalisms can be replaced with plain English.

2. Pretend to be writing for an intelligent lay audience. That will help

you avoid jargon, turgid prose, footnotes, long quotations, tedious repetitions, and the other earmarks of conventional legal writing.

3. State the purpose, unless obvious, of any doctrine on which the opinion relies. This is a check against invoking doctrines that make no sense—maybe they did once but they have since succumbed to mindless repetition.

4. Put off announcing the decision (affirmed, reversed, dismissed, etc.) until the end of the opinion. When as is common it is laconically announced at the beginning, the impression conveyed is that what follows is simply the rationalization of a result reached on undisclosed grounds. My suggestion is "rhetorical" because of course the outcome *will* have been determined, at least tentatively, before the opinion was written. But it is not dishonest rhetoric to put the conclusion after rather than before the analysis that supports it, and by doing so make the opinion, at least, less dogmatic. (A compromise is to say at the outset, "For reasons to be explained, the judgment of the district court is affirmed [reversed, etc.].")

5. In a case in which the panel is split, avoid referring in the majority opinion to the dissenting opinion, a practice that has become common in Supreme Court opinions. Such references invite the reader to interrupt his reading of the majority opinion to see what the author is responding to (often heatedly), or to suspend belief pending the reading of the dissenting opinion. The way to deal with arguments in the dissenting opinion that are worth replying to is to state them without attribution and then refute them if you can.

6. Avoid acronyms and abbreviations other than the obvious ones, such as FBI or etc. They are ugly and distracting, as well as often being opaque to the reader. Even if the opinion writer spells out the acronym or abbreviation when first using it, readers may have difficulty keeping the meaning in mind as they read on.

7. Eschew footnotes, and not only ones dueling with dissenters. A judicial opinion is not a scholarly article. Footnote material peripheral to the opinion can be deleted; if important it can be worked into the text.

8. Ask yourself—about every comma, every word, every sentence, every parenthetical phrase or clause, every paragraph, in the opinion you're

about to circulate to the other judges on the panel—what work does this word, this sentence, etc., *do?* If the answer is "nothing," it should be deleted. Facts, names, dates, procedural details—how often they merely pad out an opinion! Must every opinion list the parties' contentions? For that matter, must all the *parties* be mentioned? No, because often the caption of a case will list parties that have dropped out or were supernumerary from the beginning. Must every opinion include a detailed summary of the district court's or administrative agency's opinion? Repeat the standard of review? Assure the reader that the court has given "careful" consideration to the issues? (An empty, self-congratulatory flourish.) Demonstrate, in short, that the literary culture in America is indeed dead?

9. Be sure to read every case, statute, regulation, article, treatise, etc., cited in the opinion. A judge shouldn't trust the law clerk who found the item and inserted it (or, if the judge writes his own opinions, who suggested that the judge do so) to have characterized it correctly. Not that the judge will always have time to read the entire case, statute, regulation, article, treatise, etc.; but he should read the material, within the cited work, that his opinion cites and enough of the text before and after the key passages in the cited material to be sure he understands the context.

These are rules for the realist as well as for the formalist. But the realist needs two additional rules:

10. Eschew solemnity and pomposity in your opinions but include everything you're conscious of having influenced the decision—so more dicta, more attention to the real-world background and consequences of the decision, and receptivity to the light that other fields of thought can cast on law.

11. Part of being realistic is to be practical and candid, and part of sounding realistic is to be informal—so write without pretense or adornment, striving for the "impure" style that I have argued elsewhere is superior to the "pure" style of the formalist opinion.[15] The impure style is the style epitomized by Justice Robert Jackson, who "rarely seemed to be searching for the proper 'judicial' stance or tone in his opinions. Instead,

---

15. Richard A. Posner, *Law and Literature*, ch. 9 (3d ed. 2009).

he appeared capable of expanding the stylistic range of opinion writing to accommodate his human reactions . . . In such moments the distance between judges and mortals was suddenly shortened."[16] Other highly regarded judges and Justices, including John Marshall, Oliver Wendell Holmes, Benjamin Cardozo, Learned Hand, and Roger Traynor, were practitioners of the "impure" style as well (the impression of Cardozo's style as being overripe is based on his books and essays, not on his opinions). Yet they are not considered to have "lowered" the tone of the judiciary by writing as they did. As Holmes once said, a judge's opinions don't have to be heavy in order to be weighty.

William Popkin, who in his book on judicial opinions terms what I am calling the "impure" style the "personal voice," singles out Holmes's opinions as "provid[ing] the best examples of a personal judicial voice . . . Holmes's language is direct, unadorned, and without artifice, neither magisterial nor professional. He uses language shared by a community that includes both the judicial author and the public audience."[17] Popkin also describes Holmes's personal voice as authoritative and contrasts it with what he calls a "personal/exploratory" style, which he illustrates with quotations from opinions of mine,[18] explaining:

A judge who adopts an exploratory tone shares with the audience the difficulty of reaching a decision, rather than speaking down to the reader by adopting an authoritative tone. There are three ways in which Posner opinions are exploratory. The first is that he admits doubts about how to find the right answer. The second is that the opinion reads as though the author is thinking out loud about how to work through the issues—often speculating about questions that turn

16. G. Edward White, *The American Judicial Tradition: Profiles of Leading American Judges* 185 (3d ed. 2007).

17. William D. Popkin, *Evolution of the Judicial Opinion: Institutional and Individual Styles* 146–147 (2007).

18. See id. at 153–169.

out not to be essential to dispose of the case but that are part of the judge's thought process.

The third way relates to the substantive criteria used to reach a decision. Posner rejects clear-sounding rules for deciding a case, such as textualism in statutory interpretation. Instead, he prefers more fuzzy standards (often the purpose of the underlying rule) or rules-with-exceptions, except when there are good pragmatic reasons for adopting a simple-to-apply rule.[19]

Popkin justifies the approach as follows:

The public projection of judicial authority through an authoritative institutional and individual style of presenting judicial opinions has always existed in tension with the internal professional reality that the development of the law is a messy task, fraught with conflict and uncertainty. And this has placed tremendous pressure in the Anglo-American tradition on the judicial opinion, which must implement the dual external and internal goals of preserving judicial authority and developing judicial law. That pressure has only increased in the modern legal culture where judges acknowledge the intersection of law and politics, reject the older tradition of judges authoritatively declaring law derived from legal principle, and consider an institutional base for judging to be insufficient support for justifying judicial law in a legal system where democratic legislation is now the dominant source of law. The judge is no Hercules.

This leaves modern judges with the difficult task of appealing to an external source of substantive law, without the protective armor of authoritative legal principle or a completely secure institutional base. My suggestion for responding to this difficulty . . . is to make greater use of a personal/exploratory style of presenting judicial opinions, as illustrated by Posner's approach. This style implements

19. Id. at 159.

what I call "democratic judging," which is suited to a legal culture where law and politics are clearly related and in which a democratic process is essential to maintaining the authority of government institutions.[20]

The *Morris* Opinion

I may be able to make my reservations about formalist opinion writing clearer by discussing a representative formalist opinion of the U.S. Court of Appeals for the District of Columbia, one of the best federal courts of appeals. It is the opinion in a case called *United States v. Morris.*[21] I reprint it in full at the end of this chapter—along with the opinion I would have written had I been the assigned judge. The court's opinion is 3,237 words long; my version is 602 words long.

The main issue in *Morris* was whether the defendant had used a gun "during and in relation to a drug trafficking offense." The jury found that he had. He appealed, challenging both that conviction and his conviction for the underlying drug offense. The appellate opinion, after stating that "we reject both challenges and affirm the judgment below" (not a good start, in my view), proceeds to a description of the crimes and the course of the trial. The defendant had been arrested in a one-bedroom apartment in which the police also found one hundred small ziplock bags containing cocaine, plus three loaded pistols. Two of the guns were found under the cushions of the living room couch on which Morris was sitting when the officers entered, and the third in a nightstand in the bedroom. The bags of cocaine were hidden in ducts in the bedroom ceiling. The reader is told the date on which Morris was arrested and his apartment searched—even the street address of the apartment. These details of time and place are extraneous.

Then comes a brief, unexceptionable, but also unnecessary statement of the standard of appellate review—unnecessary because it is well known

20. Id. at 168–169 (footnotes omitted).
21. 977 F.2d 617 (D.C. Cir. 1992).

and because nothing in the case turns on it. Next is a discussion of Morris's opening gambit in the appeal: that there was not enough evidence to convict him of possession of the drugs. "Possession, of course, can be either actual or constructive," the opinion states. Actually "constructive possession" is at best a tricky concept. This exposes the "of course" as bluster. It is no help to be told that constructive possession "requires evidence supporting the conclusion that the defendant had the ability to exercise knowing 'dominion and control.'" What does the archaic word "dominion" add to "control"? And why should ability to control, divorced from control, count as—control, and therefore possession? Or is possession somehow different from control?

Nor is it a help to be told that "a jury is entitled to infer that a person exercises constructive possession over items found in his home." The opinion reviews the facts and finds "ample evidence from which the jury could infer that Morris lived alone in the apartment and exercised constructive possession over its contents." The "ample" is superfluous, as are most adjectives and adverbs in judicial opinions—they add needless emphasis and often strike the reader as exaggerations, even as whistling in the dark.

One begins to sense that an elephant gun is being discharged against a mouse. Morris was found in an apartment fairly bursting with drugs, and there was plenty of evidence that he was the only resident. He testified, it is true, that he was just a visitor—that he had in fact by an unhappy coincidence showed up just a few minutes before the police raid. The jury did not have to believe this and obviously did not. It believed he was the tenant, so the drugs must have been his, since no theory was advanced as to who else might have owned them if Morris was the tenant. There is really no more that the opinion needed to say about the drug conviction.

The foray into "constructive" possession was as confusing as it was needless. What can "constructive" possession of the contents of one's own apartment mean? Morris was sitting on his couch when the police entered. Was he in merely "constructive" possession of the couch? If so, what is "actual" possession? Does one "actually possess" a gun only when one is holding it in one's hand? In fact, does "constructive possession" do any work in law? I think not, once one recognizes that "possession" does not just mean holding something in one's hand. Actual versus constructive possession is one of the many unhelpful distinctions in legal analysis; it should be retired. It would be so refreshing if from time to time judges stopped and asked themselves what the stock phrases of judicial discourse actually mean and do.

The bulk of the *Morris* opinion is given over to the defendant's challenge to his conviction for the distinct offense of having used or carried a gun during and in relation to his drug dealings. The opinion says that the court is going to analyze this as a "use" case rather than a "carry" case. But a footnote toys with the alarming possibility—the sort of thing that makes the laity wonder about the legal mind—that Morris could have been found to be "carrying" the two guns found under the couch on which he was sitting when the officers entered the apartment. And here is a warning against footnotes in judicial opinions: although the "carry" footnote says that the guns were under the couch, the statement of facts earlier in the opinion had said they were in the couch, under the seat cushions.

In the text of the opinion we're told that the test for the "use" offense is whether "the gun facilitated or had a role in the trafficking offense" (and what is the difference between "facilitating" and "having a role"?) and that to help in applying the test "this court has identified a number of factors . . . We discuss only some of them here, recognizing that courts have identified and will identify others." This is also alarming, since, as I noted in Chapter 3, multifactor tests are difficult to apply objectively. And when the factors are numerous, unweighted, and open-ended ("and will identify others"), a multifactor test is an invitation to the exercise of uncanalized discretionary authority.[22]

The first factor in the multifactor test invoked by the court is possession. But while stressing the importance of possession, the opinion also ex-

22. Similar criticisms are made in *Nightingale Home Healthcare, Inc. v. Anodyne Therapy, LLC*, 626 F.3d 958 (7th Cir. 2010); *Menard, Inc. v. Commissioner of Internal Revenue*, 560 F.3d 620, 622–623 (7th Cir. 2009); *Reinsurance Co. of America v. Administratia Asigurarilor de Stat*, 902 F.2d 1275, 1283 (7th Cir. 1990) (concurring opinion); and Michael D. Cicchini, "Dead Again: The Latest Demise of the Confrontation Clause," 80 *Fordham Law Review* 1301 (2011).

presses puzzlement about how someone could use a gun that he didn't possess. The obvious answer, overlooked by the court, is that he could threaten to use a gun that was not his—and that he would never have tried to grab —but that was within his reach, making his threatening gesture credible.

The opinion states that "mere possession of a gun even by a drug trafficker does not violate the statute" but that the statute does reach (as the court had already said) "any case in which the gun facilitated or had a role in the trafficking offense." This means that "the defendant's possession of the gun is an important factor," and "possession, of course [of course], encompasses joint, as well as constructive possession." It begins to look as if, despite the initial denial, the court thinks that mere possession of a gun by a drug dealer *is* use during and in relation to the drug offense. (That would be strange: does a police officer "use" his gun every day, by virtue of the fact that he wears it in a holster on his belt every day?) But maybe not, if the gun is in a safe-deposit box, for "a gun kept close at hand is more likely being used for protection than a gun packed away in a hard-to-reach spot." But most drug dealers, like most other handgun owners, have no use for their guns other than protection, so why would they ever pack them away in hard-to-reach places?

The opinion discusses other elements of the multifactor test, such as the "proximity of the gun to the drugs." It is true that the closer the gun is to the drugs, the likelier that the use that the possessor is making of the gun and the drugs is conjoint. So the reader is surprised to find the court saying that proximity can cut either way. The court gives the curious example of a case in which the gun and the drugs were found together in the pocket of a raincoat in the defendant's closet; the inference was therefore that the gun was intended only to be used for some future sale, when the defendant put on his coat and went outside. But it wasn't the proximity of the gun to the drugs that tended to show that the gun was not intended for use in connection with a current sale; it was the fact that both the gun and the drugs were in a closet.

The next factors discussed are "whether the gun is loaded" and "the number and type of guns." But these two, really three, factors actually are irrelevant. For the opinion makes clear that one unloaded gun of ordinary design accessible to Morris would have been quite enough for his conviction to be sustained, especially since the government's expert witness testified to "the well-nigh universal use of guns to protect such [drug-trafficking] operations."

The least meaningful factor discussed in the opinion is whether the gun is on "open display." If it is, this suggests "a deterrent to poachers . . . This is not to say, however, that a gun that is within reach, though out of sight, does not also strongly suggest its intended use for protection of the drugs." So heads the government wins, tails the defendant loses—which makes "open display" not merely the "least meaningful" factor, but meaningless. (A distressing feature of judicial opinions is how often they include meaningless statements. In the otherwise unrelated case of *Consumer Product Safety Commission v. GTE Sylvania, Inc.*, for example, the Supreme Court said—and it has repeated this in subsequent cases, as have lower courts—that "absent a clearly expressed legislative intention to the contrary, [the language of the statute] must ordinarily be regarded as conclusive."[23] The word "ordinarily" renders the statement meaningless. Even if there is no "clearly expressed legislative intention" that contradicts the statutory language, adherence to that language is required only "ordinarily." "Ordinarily" one applies a statute as written; that is the default interpretation. The entire challenge of statutory interpretation consists in identifying and applying the exceptions; the *Sylvania* formula ducks the challenge and as a result says nothing worth saying.)

I grant that judicial verbosity and redundancy have a rhetorical function, though an unworthy one. Reciting truisms and trudging patiently through a host of factors mentioned in previous cases convey an impression of irrefutability, deliberateness, moving patiently, step by step, leaving no stone unturned. It is a reassuring style, not only because it signals (sometimes misleadingly) thoroughness but also because it enables the opinion to be padded with a number of unexceptionable propositions. The greater the number of truthful statements in a judicial opinion, the more truthful the opinion seems, even if the truthful statements are platitudes.

23. 447 U.S. 102, 108 (1980).

Judges understandably are uncomfortable issuing opinions to the effect that "we have very little sense of what is going on in this case. The record is poorly developed, and the lawyers are lousy. We have no confidence that we have got it right. We know we're groping in the dark. But we're paid to decide cases, so here goes." Yet that is the subtext of countless appellate opinions. The simplest cases are not brought, or not appealed, or are decided in unpublished opinions (sometimes with no opinion—just the word "affirmed"). A substantial fraction of published appellate opinions are found in close cases, and another substantial fraction in cases that do not seem close but that are in a muddle of one sort of another. The unnecessary details and truisms that stud judicial opinions create a soothing façade of facticity.

To return to the gun case: Americans love guns and fear violent crime. Many law-abiding Americans, including law-abiding residents of big-city slums, keep loaded guns in their homes to protect themselves from intruders. Some residents of slums are not law-abiding yet keep loaded guns in their homes for reasons unrelated to their illegal activities—in fact for the same reason as the law-abiding people. The challenge to the courts in administering the "use or carry" statute is, one might have thought, to distinguish between having a gun for self-protection and having it for the protection of one's drug business, or of oneself in one's capacity as a drug dealer.

Morris does not relate the factors in its multifactor test to the task of distinguishing between these two possible inferences from a defendant's having loaded guns lying about. The relation is not obvious. It would be absurd to suppose, for example, that the concept of "possession" could help distinguish between a gun kept for self-protection and a gun kept for the defense of illegal drugs; or that whether the gun was loaded, working, accessible to the owner, and strategically placed for defense of self and property could do so. As the size of the arsenal grows, as the arsenal takes on a more "professional" character, as the proximity of the arsenal to the drugs increases, the inference that the guns are being used to defend drugs rather than (just) person or other property grows. The decisive factor in Morris's case was that he had stuffed two guns under the cushions of his living-room couch—an extraordinary location for a home defense arsenal but a good one if the resident sells drugs in his living room. Rather than zero in on this critical fact the court actually forgot it in the "carry" footnote.

The style of the opinion had retarded the search for meaning. With its tedious marshaling of factors and facts and its dense citation of previous cases (twenty-five in all, mostly concerned with the gun charge), the opinion tries to sweep the reader to a confident conclusion that Morris was guilty of the gun offense as well as of the drug offense. It is the style that comes naturally to the pen of a person who is legally trained. I have not been picking on a weak opinion, or a heterodox one.

I am guessing that the opinion was written by a law clerk, and edited but not rewritten extensively by the judge who was its nominal author.[24] The opinion has the exhaustiveness of the anxious novice author and the impersonality one also expects when a clerk is the author—he is hardly likely to want to inject his personality, and would likewise think it impertinent to try to inject the judge's. Readers of judge-written opinions, in contrast, learn much about the authors as a result of experiencing the unmediated encounter of judge with case.

The *Morris* opinion also occasions reflection on the issue of candor and self-knowledge in judicial opinions. Candor should be distinguished from honesty. A judge may believe that everything in his opinion is true, at least so far as he can determine truth, yet be holding back some of the considerations that (as he is aware) inclined him to vote to decide the case the way he did. I would call such an opinion honest but uncandid. A candid opinion would state all the considerations that the judge was conscious of having influenced his judicial vote. Yet to the extent the judge was unaware of all those considerations, the opinion, though candid, would be incomplete. The best opinion—the most authentic and most informative—would be a

24. The judge acknowledged generally working from opinion drafts by her law clerks. Patricia M. Wald, "How I Write," 4 *Scribes Journal of Legal Writing* 55, 59–61 (1993). Judge Wald, by the way, has had an extremely distinguished legal career; after retiring from the court of appeals in 1999 she became a prominent figure in international law and adjudication. I am not picking on an average, let alone below-average, judge. See "Patricia Wald," *Wikipedia*, http://en.wikipedia.org/wiki/Patricia_Wald (visited Dec. 25, 2012).

candid opinion by a judge who was aware of all the considerations that moved him: an opinion combining candor with self-knowledge.

Virtually no official public document is *fully* candid, or should be. It's an instrument of government rather than a communication from the heart. In the case of an appellate opinion, other than a dissent or concurrence joined in by no other judge, the author may need to compromise his views or blunt the opinion's rhetorical thrusts in order to persuade other judges to join it. And concern with preserving collegiality, as well as consideration for the feelings of litigants and their lawyers, may properly induce a judge to turn down his rhetorical volume.

So "let it all hang out" is not a good judicial motto. Yet a judicial opinion can be decorous yet candid, even if not quite 100 percent candid. When one reads an opinion by Holmes, or Learned Hand, or Robert Jackson, or Henry Friendly, one has the sense (and it is confirmed by biographical information) that everything or almost everything that influenced the judge's judicial vote is set forth in the opinion; that one has therefore a complete and accurate account of the decisional process, or at least a close approximation to such an account. In contrast, reading an opinion by Frankfurter one often senses both that it contains statements that he could not have believed (generally these are exaggerations rather than outright falsehoods) and that the opinion does not contain all the drivers of the result. We sense that he is not leveling with the reader, or indeed with himself. And that is true of many judges, indeed probably of most judges in at least some, and often many, cases.

That was implicit in my analysis in Chapter 4 of the realist and the formalist judge. I said that most judges are hybrids but that you wouldn't gather this from judicial opinions because most opinions, even in cases that can be adequately explained only in realist terms, are formalist in style. The realism is concealed, and a good deal of research may be required to determine the motivation for the decision, or indeed for an entire body of case law.[25] This is unfortunate, because it can mislead the people to whom the law is addressed and their lawyers.

25. See Matthew C. Stephenson, "Legal Realism for Economists," *Journal of Economic Perspectives,* Spring 2009, pp. 191, 197–199.

And so another rule of good judicial opinion writing is that before circulating an opinion draft to the other judges on the panel the judge should ask himself whether he believes everything in his draft and if the answer is "no" he should delete the portions he doesn't believe. He should also ask himself whether there may be something lurking at the back or bottom of his mind that has influenced his analysis and conclusion, and if so he should state it.

The last rule I propose is that the judge (or law clerk, if the judge has delegated opinion writing to his law clerks) write clearly in the special sense of writing in a way that makes the opinion intelligible to nonlawyers. Recently a law professor (I don't recall the law school) told me to my surprise that "law students believe that Judge Posner must love law students." She explained that even entering law students could understand my opinions, but not (or not often) those of other judges, and that the students infer that since I would doubtless prefer to write like other judges, only love could have motivated me to write so that students could understand what I was saying. I do *like* law students, although I would not go so far as to say that I *love* them; and I *would* like them to be able to understand my opinions and I would like nonlawyers—the few who might be inclined to read a judicial opinion occasionally—to be able to read them too. But my main reason for trying to write clearly (and I do *try*—I am not a naturally clear writer) is that unless I reduce a case to its simplest possible terms I can't be confident that I actually understand it and that my decision is right, or at least sensible (often one can't be sure what the correct outcome is). One test of whether a decision is sensible is whether, if it were explained to an intelligent layperson, he or she would think it correct rather than stalk off mumbling "Mr. Bumble in *Oliver Twist* was right: if this decision is compelled by the law, the law is a ass."

Not that "sensible" and (legally) "correct" are synonyms. Legal justice is not synonymous with justice perceived in lay terms; adjudication by a professional judge is not to be equated to the resolution of a dispute by a nonlawyer acquaintance of the disputants. The judge is an institutional actor hedged in by restrictions on his exercise of discretion to do "what is right"—restrictions that include the authority of legislators, the force of precedent, and "the rule of law" (a misunderstood term: it properly means deciding cases without regard to the relative attractiveness, social status, or other idiosyncratic features of the particular litigants). But before voting for an outcome deformed by institutional constraints one wants to be sure that those constraints really do require a decision that no layperson would think sensible.

Some Tips on Appellate Advocacy

Opinion writing is intimately related to the briefs and oral argument of appellate advocates, so I end this chapter with a short discussion of appellate advocacy—short because the subject has recently been exhaustively, and very sensibly, addressed in another book by Justice Scalia and Mr. Garner.[26]

What is most important for the appellate advocate to understand is that a sense of the audience is the key to rhetorical effectiveness.[27] The advocate must think his way into the brains of the audience. And so the key to effective appellate advocacy is to imagine oneself an appellate judge. If one does that one will see immediately that the judge of such a court labors under an immense disadvantage. He has little time to spend on each case and is therefore bound to know far less about the parties, the product or service involved, and the context than the advocate does. And in all likelihood he is a generalist, lacking specialized knowledge of most of the fields of law that generate the cases that come before him. The advocate, in contrast, probably is a specialist, unless his "specialty" is appellate advocacy. Most appeals, however, are argued by the trial lawyer.

The judge's knowledge deficit is apt to be particularly acute in cases that present technical issues, as I have been emphasizing throughout this book. But not only in those cases; for unless the court is hearing a criminal

---

26. Antonin Scalia and Bryan A. Garner, *Making Your Case: The Art of Persuading Judges* (2008)—a book as good as their book on interpretation that I discussed in the last chapter is deficient. The earlier literature on this subject is catalogued in Kathryn Stanchi, "Persuasion: An Annotated Bibliography," 6 *Journal of the Association of Legal Writing Directors* 75 (2009).

27. See Richard A. Posner, *Overcoming Law*, ch. 24 (1995).

appeal, the judge is unlikely, because of the vastness of the jurisdiction of the federal courts, to have a deep or comprehensive knowledge of the law applicable to the appeal. This will vary from judge to judge depending on the judge's background and interests. But the advocate may not be told which judges of the court of appeals will be hearing his case until it is too late for him to change his brief, or even his oral-argument strategy unless he's very nimble.[28]

The judge in such a situation is badly in need of the advocates' help—something few advocates seem to understand. Legal education is partly at fault. The law schools naturally focus on imparting the vocabulary and rhetoric of legal rules and standards, without which one cannot function as a lawyer. And with the rise of law and economics (economic analysis of law), law schools increasingly provide students with pretty sophisticated policy analyses of those rules and standards. What they do not much do is take the next step and impart a realistic understanding of the judicial process and of how in light of that understanding to present cases most effectively to judges and juries. Maybe they're afraid of inducing premature skepticism in students or of angering judges.

So my essential advice to the appellate advocate is to put yourself in the judge's shoes. That will enable you to grasp the key differences between judge and advocate. It will also help if you understand that most judges are practical people, even the former academics among us. Don't be fooled by the formalist cast of most judicial opinions. It reflects the formalism of the clerk authors, which exceeds that of the judges. In cases not governed by clear statutory text or precedent, judges are interested not only in the words of the rule the advocate is invoking but also in its purpose; and not only in the facts that have been developed in an evidentiary hearing but also in the nonadjudicative facts that illuminate the background and con-

28. My court does not announce the panel until the morning of the oral argument. Most courts give the parties more notice, consistent with my suggestion in the text. The argument for my court's approach, which on balance I find compelling, is that the coherence of the court's law is undermined if the briefs and oral argument in each case are directed to a particular subset of the court's judges, focusing on their previous opinions, their priors, their idiosyncrasies.

text of a case and the law itself. Unless a case is cut and dried, the advocate shouldn't just state a rule and note a semantic correspondence between it and the facts of the case.

A related point is that the advocate should make his brief as far as possible self-contained. He should explain not only what the case is about and what the background law is but also why the case is important (or unimportant)—what if anything turns on the outcome, either for the parties or for some larger community. If for example the amount in controversy in a civil appeal is only $50, the first question the judge will ask himself is: What on earth has impelled the parties to bear the expenses of litigation over such a trivial sum? The advocate should anticipate the question and answer it in his brief. The brief should tie up loose ends rather than, by leaving them hanging, make the judge approach oral argument with furrowed brow. Do not waste your time at argument dispelling mysteries that a sentence in your brief could have cleared up.

In other words, make everything *easy* for the judge. I am surprised how often, in a case that involves the application of a statute, the briefs do not quote the relevant part of the statute, but merely paraphrase it. Always ask yourself what, if you were a judge, you would want the parties' briefs to contain.

The advocate who engages in the imaginative exercise that I have suggested is the key to successful appellate advocacy—that of imagining oneself the judge—will quickly see that rarely is it effective advocacy to try to convince judges that the case law *compels* them to rule in your favor. Just think: how likely is it that if the case law relating to the case at hand were totally one-sided the case (if it is a civil case—for most criminal appellants are not paying for the appeal and hence are not deterred by the unlikelihood, however great, of a successful outcome) would nevertheless have been appealed?

In a case not controlled by precedent the advocate's task is to convince the court that the position for which he is contending is the more reasonable one in light of the relevant circumstances, which include but are not exhausted by the case law, the statutory text, and the other conventional materials of legal decision making. Normally the most effective way of arguing such a case is to identify the purpose behind the relevant legal principle and show how it would be furthered by a decision in your favor.

Be sure to "front" adverse legal or factual materials that your opponent can be expected to emphasize in his response brief (if he is the appellee) or reply brief (if he is the appellant), so that the judge who formed a favorable impression when reading your brief does not feel when he turns to your opponent's brief that you were pulling the wool over his eyes.

The advocate would be well-advised to conduct background online research—to explore Google, *Wikipedia*, Google Earth, and the other riches of the Web for information that will help him help us the judges acquire a realistic understanding of his case—just as "real" people do, and just as judges and their law clerks (and jurors—though forbidden) increasingly are doing (see next chapter). It should be obvious to you, if you can imagine yourself as an appellate judge, that much that goes into a judicial decision was never a part of any evidentiary record. The judicial mind is not a *tabula rasa*. It is informed, enriched, by the judge's experiences, impressions, temperament, and outside reading, which increasingly is the reading of online materials. The Web is as great a resource for lawyers as for judges—and underutilized by both.

Wherever possible, use pictures, props (for example, trademarked items in a trademark case), maps, diagrams, and other visual aids in your brief (not at argument—presenting material on poster boards displayed to the judges invariably is a flop because the material is illegible at its distance from the judges). *Seeing* a case makes it come alive to judges.

Lawyers' lack of a visual sense, which I remarked in Chapter 5, is a striking professional deformity. I do not understand it. Information can often be presented much more effectively in pictorial than in verbal form. It is a deformity that the law schools should be addressing.

More advice for the appellate advocate: avoid jargon—business jargon, industry jargon, computerese and other technical jargon (including economic jargon), and legal jargon. Avoid like the plague legal clichés, especially "plain meaning" (pervasively intoned and typically, though futilely, argued by both sides in the same case!).

At the oral argument of a case under the Telecommunications Act of

1996, I said to one of the lawyers that my law clerks and I had read the briefs and having done so had no idea what the case was about, and would he please explain it to us in words of one syllable. He was momentarily taken aback because judges don't usually talk like that, but he was an excellent lawyer and proceeded to explain the case lucidly, without the technical jargon or communications-law jargon that had made the briefs unreadable, and the judges were duly grateful.[29] The lawyers in the case doubtless do most of their advocacy before the Federal Communications Commission, and had failed in their briefs to recognize that the judges of the Seventh Circuit, which gets very few telecommunications cases (unlike the District of Columbia Circuit), do not have the same familiarity with either modern telecommunications technology or federal telecommunications legislation as the FCC does.

In a similar vein, we were moved to write in a complex ERISA case:

Hideous complexities lurk in the briefs in this appeal. Many appellate lawyers write briefs and make oral arguments that assume that judges are knowledgeable about every field of law, however specialized. The assumption is incorrect. Federal judges are generalists. Individual judges often have specialized knowledge of a few fields of law, most commonly criminal law and sentencing, civil and criminal procedure, and federal jurisdiction, because these fields generate issues that frequently recur, but sometimes of other fields as well depending on the judge's career before he became a judge or on special interests developed by him since. But the appellate advocate must not count on appellate judges' being intimate with his particular legal nook—with its special jargon, its analytical intricacies, its commercial setting, its mysteries. It's difficult for specialists to write other than in jargon, and when they don't realize the difficulty this poses for generalist judges neither do they realize the need to write differently . . .

29. The appeal was decided in *Illinois Bell Telephone Co. v. Box*, 548 F.3d 607 (7th Cir. 2008).

All this was terribly opaque to us because the parties had failed to provide context . . . We have had to fall back on a remark by Justice Holmes: "I long have said there is no such thing as a hard case. I am frightened weekly but always when you walk up to the lion and lay hold the hide comes off and the same old donkey of a question of law is underneath."[30] We have applied ourselves to tugging the hide off this lion in search of the donkey underneath. We think we have found the donkey.[31]

My final bit of advice on appellate brief writing is to go light on district court citations, remembering that they're not precedents. (If they were, law would often differ systematically between districts in the same circuit.) In general, district court decisions should be cited only when there is an issue involving district court practice, such as the meaning or application of a rule of the district court, or when there are no appellate decisions on point and either a district court opinion is highly persuasive or there is substantial and one-sided district court authority.

I close with a few bits of advice concerning oral argument.

Be sure to know and abide by the rules for oral argument of the court you're arguing before.

If you're the appellant's lawyer, *always* save time to rebut, whether or not you decide to use it. Otherwise you give your opponent a free shot at the judges. (This is if the presiding judge is a stickler, who will not allow rebuttal if the appellant's lawyer used up his allotted time in his opening argument. I am not a stickler; I always allow the appellant an opportunity

30. *Holmes–Pollock Letters: The Correspondence of Mr. Justice Holmes and Sir Frederick Pollock, 1874–1932,* vol. 1, p. 156 (Mark De Wolfe Howe ed. 1941) (letter to Pollock of Dec. 11, 1909).

31. *Chicago Truck Drivers, Helpers & Warehouse Workers Union (Independent) Pension Fund v. CPC Logistics, Inc.,* 698 F.3d 346, 350, 352–353 (7th Cir. 2012) (emphasis in original). Holmes may have been echoing Aesop's Fable No. 188 ("The Ass in a Lion's Skin"): "An Ass, having put on the lion's skin, amused himself by terrifying all the foolish animals. At last coming upon a Fox, he tried to frighten him also, but the Fox no sooner heard the sound of his voice than he exclaimed, 'I might possibly have been frightened myself, if I had not heard your bray.'"

for rebuttal.) He may take liberties with the facts or the law, knowing that you cannot respond. The judges may detect these exaggerations—or not. If they detect them after the post-argument conference at which they make their tentative decision, it may be too late for you, because the ostensibly tentative vote that the judges take at the conference has momentum. So you shouldn't think that you can rebut your opponent effectively after the argument by submitting a letter rebuttal to the court. You are permitted to do that but it may be too late if the judges decided the case to their satisfaction at the conference.

Rehearse your oral argument before you write your brief—and rehearse it in front a panel that includes lawyers who are not experts in the field to which the case belongs, because the judges will, with rare exceptions, not be experts either.

In case the panel should ask no questions or seem poorly prepared, be prepared with a few simple, commonsensical points. Simplicity is the key, given how often the judges will know *much* less about the case than the lawyers arguing it.

A related point: do not beat the judges over the head with statutory language and precedent, because judges find it difficult in the oral setting to follow arguments that are based on highly specific language or facts. And (this applies also to your brief) do not exaggerate the cogency of reasoning by analogy by trying to persuade the judges to base their decision on a case from another field of law. The value of analogous cases lies in the reasoning or policies that the opinions disclose that may bear on your case, and it is the reasoning and policies that you should emphasize.

If rather than being silent the panel is noisy and interrupts you constantly, extend the answer to an important question in a way that makes a smooth transition to a point that you need to make.

Avoid irritating the judges. If the judge asks a question that can be answered yes or no, answer it yes or no and if necessary explain your answer. If the judge asks a hypothetical question, don't respond that "that's not this case." He knows that.

Display confidence by not using up all your allotted time unless you have something really important to say that will fill it up—especially if the argument is in the morning and lunch time is approaching. For don't forget what Alexander Pope said in *The Rape of the Lock:*

> Meanwhile, declining from the noon of day,
> The sun obliquely shoots his burning ray;
> The hungry judges soon the sentence sign,
> And wretches hang that jury-men may dine.

Better briefing and argument, based on a realistic assessment of the limitations of judicial understanding in an age of galloping complexity, would make an inestimable contribution to the quality of the judiciary.

APPENDIX

UNITED STATES V. MORRIS,
977 F.2D 617 (D.C. CIR. 1992)

Appellant Robert Morris was convicted of possession of cocaine with intent to sell, in violation of 21 U.S.C. § 841(a)(1) and § 841(b)(1)(B)(iii), and for using or carrying a firearm during and in relation to a drug trafficking offense, in violation of 18 U.S.C. § 924(c)(1). He appeals both convictions on the ground that the evidence was insufficient to support either charge. We reject both challenges and affirm the judgment below.

I. BACKGROUND

On December 11, 1990, officers of the Metropolitan Police Department executed a search warrant on a one-bedroom apartment at 2525 14th Street, N.E., in the District of Columbia. Upon entering the apartment, the officers found appellant seated on a small couch in the living room; they detained him while they searched the apartment. The search produced two ziplock bags containing a total of 15.7 grams of crack cocaine divided among one hundred smaller ziplock bags, $500 in cash, empty ziplock bags, razor blades, and three loaded and operable pistols. Two of the guns were under the cushions of the couch on which appellant sat; the third was in a nightstand in the bedroom. The cocaine and the cash were in an air duct vent in the ceiling of the bedroom. In the drawer of a dresser in the bedroom, the officers found two birthday cards; appellant's name was on the envelope of one, and the other was for a "son," signed "Mr. and Mrs. B. G. Morris" and dated November 30, 1990. No address was on either. In a hallway closet, the officers found a laundry ticket dated December 3, 1990, and bearing the name "E. Morris." There were no identifiable fingerprints on any of these items. The officers arrested appellant, who was indicted on two counts: possession with intent to distribute in excess of five grams of cocaine base and using or carrying a firearm in relation to the possession offense.

At trial, two officers testified that at the time of the search, Morris said that he had been living in the apartment for three or four weeks. The government also offered expert testimony that the quantity and the packaging of the drugs, together with the drug paraphernalia and the weapons, indicated that the apartment was a drug distribution center, where cocaine was repackaged for street sale.

At the close of the government's case, appellant moved for acquittal on the ground that the evidence showed only that he was a casual visitor to the apartment and not a participant in the drug operation. The court denied the motion. Morris then testified, denying that he had ever lived in the apartment or ever said that he lived there. He testified instead that he was visiting four friends who lived there and had been there only a few minutes when the police arrived. He said that he was not himself engaged in any drug trafficking or aware of the presence of the drugs in the apartment. He had left the cards there during a prior visit on his birthday.

At the close of all the evidence, appellant renewed his motion for acquittal, which the court again denied. The jury convicted appellant of both charges, and he was sentenced to 130 months.

II. DISCUSSION

A. Standard of Review

In this appeal, appellant challenges the sufficiency of the evidence to support each conviction. In such challenges, this court must defer to the jury's determination and affirm the conviction if "'any rational trier of fact could have found the essential elements of the crime beyond a reasonable doubt.'" *United States v. Long,* 905 F.2d 1572, 1577 (D.C.Cir.) (quoting *Jackson v. Virginia,* 443 U.S. 307, 309, 99 S.Ct. 2781, 2783, 61 L.Ed.2d 560 (1979)), cert. denied, 498 U.S. 948, 111 S.Ct. 365, 112 L.Ed.2d 328 (1990). In our review, we must "view the evidence in the light most favorable to the government, allowing the government the benefit of all reasonable inferences that may be drawn from the evidence, and permitting the jury to determine the weight and credibility of the evidence." *United States v. Sutton,* 801 F.2d 1346, 1358 (D.C.Cir.1986).

B. Possession of the Drugs

Appellant's first challenge is to the sufficiency of the evidence to sustain his conviction for possession of cocaine with intent to distribute. Possession, of course, can be either actual or constructive. Constructive possession requires evidence supporting the conclusion that the defendant had the ability to exercise knowing "dominion and control" over the items in question. *United States v. Hernandez,* 780 F.2d 113, 116 (D.C.Cir.1986). Mere proximity to the item at the time of seizure is not enough; but proximity coupled with "evidence of some other factor—including connection with a gun, proof of motive, a gesture implying control, evasive conduct, or a statement indicating involvement in an enterprise" is enough to sustain a guilty verdict. *United States v. Gibbs,* 904 F.2d 52, 56 (D.C.Cir.1990).

A jury is entitled to infer that a person exercises constructive possession over items found in his home. *United States v. Jenkins,* 928 F.2d 1175, 1179 (D.C.Cir.1991). Thus, if there was sufficient evidence from which a juror could infer that Morris lived in the apartment where he was arrested, the jury could infer that he constructively possessed the drugs. The jury had the following evidence that Morris lived in the apartment: First, two officers testified that Morris said he lived there. Although Morris himself testified to the contrary, the jurors were permitted to credit the testimony of the officers. *Jenkins,* 928 F.2d at 1178. Moreover, Morris himself may have given their testimony extra credibility by his own contradictory information about where he did live at the time of the arrest. Second, Morris admitted that the two birthday cards found in the bedroom were his. That the cards were found inside the dresser drawer in another part of the house, rather than, say, left on a coffee table beside the defendant, strengthened the inference that Morris occupied the apartment on more than a drop-in basis. In *United States v. Williams*, 952 F.2d 418 (D.C.Cir.1991), cert. denied, --- U.S. ----, 113 S.Ct. 148, 121 L.Ed.2d 99, (1992), for example, this court found it relevant that defendant's possessions were found "not in the living room where [he] was arrested, but in [the] bedroom." Id. at 420. Third, the officers found a dry cleaning ticket marked "E. Morris" in the hall closet. Morris's middle name is Eugene. Together these items of evidence support a reasonable inference that Morris lived in the apartment and, therefore, exercised constructive possession over its contents.

The inference that a person who occupies an apartment has dominion and control over its contents applies even when that person shares the premises with others, *Jenkins*, 928 F.2d at 1179, but it is particularly strong when the jury can reasonably conclude that he is the sole occupant of the premises. Appellant testified that not he but "four friends" lived in the apartment. Neither appellant nor the government claimed that he was the fifth occupant. Other than appellant's testimony, however, which the jury was permitted to disbelieve, there was no evidence that anyone other than appellant lived in the apartment, and certainly no one else was present when the arrest was made and the drugs seized. Thus, there was ample evidence from which the jury could infer that Morris lived alone in the apartment and exercised constructive possession over its contents.

There was also evidence aplenty from which a jury could infer intent to distribute. This intent can be inferred from a combination of suspicious factors. *Gibbs*, 904 F.2d at 57. The presence of the paraphernalia—razors and drug packaging materials—was evidence of such an intent, *United States v. Dunn*, 846 F.2d 761, 764 (D.C.Cir.1988) (citing *United States v. Castellanos*, 731 F.2d 979, 985 (D.C.Cir.1984)), as was the presence of the guns, *United States v. Bruce*, 939 F.2d 1053, 1056 n. 2 (D.C.Cir.1991) (citing *Dunn*, 846 F.2d at 764). Additionally, a government expert testified that the quantity and packaging of the drugs found in the apartment indicated that they were intended for street sale.

Because there was sufficient evidence both of appellant's possession of the drugs and of his intent to distribute them, we affirm his conviction for the possession offense.

C. Guns Used or Carried in Relation to the Trafficking Offense

Appellant's second challenge is to the sufficiency of the evidence to support his conviction for using or carrying a gun in relation to a drug trafficking offense. Morris was convicted under a statute that makes it a crime to "use[ ] or carr[y]" a firearm "during and in relation to any . . . drug trafficking crime. . . ." 18 U.S.C. § 924(c).

Case law from this and other circuits provides guidance in determining when someone "uses or carries" a gun in relation to a drug trafficking offense. The first principle is clear: Mere possession of a gun even by a drug trafficker does not violate the statute. As we observed in *United States v. Bruce*, 939 F.2d at 1053, when Congress wishes to criminalize the possession of a firearm, it knows how to do so. In Bruce, this court recognized the analytical difficulty in distinguishing those cases in which someone merely possesses a gun with the intent to use it in a future drug trafficking crime, such as an intended sale—which does not violate § 924(c)—from those cases in which someone actually uses the gun in relation to the trafficking crime, such as a current sale or to protect current possession in anticipation of a future sale—which does violate § 924(c). Id.

Apart from the basic requirement that "use" constitute more than simple possession, (*United States v. Long*, 905 F.2d 1572, 1577 (D.C.Cir.1990)), we have construed the term as broad enough to encompass any case in which the gun facilitated or had a role in the trafficking offense. *United States v. Harris*, 959 F.2d 246, 261–262 (D.C.Cir.1992) (using guns as medium of exchange violated the statute). Put another way, we ask whether the gun was "an integral part" of the drug trafficking operation in question. *United States v. Anderson*, 881 F.2d 1128, 1141 (D.C.Cir.1989). "Use" does not require that the defendant fire the gun or even brandish it. *United States v. Evans*, 888 F.2d 891, 896 (D.C.Cir.1989) (citing *United States v. Matra*, 841 F.2d 837, 841–843 (9th Cir.1988); *United States v. Mason*, 658 F.2d 1263, 1270–1271 (9th Cir.1981); *United States v. Moore*, 580 F.2d 360,

362 (9th Cir.), cert. denied, 439 U.S. 970, 99 S.Ct. 463, 58 L.Ed.2d 430 (1978)), cert. denied sub nom. *Curren v. United States,* 494 U.S. 1019, 110 S.Ct. 1325, 108 L.Ed.2d 500 (1990).

This court has identified a number of factors to aid in determining whether guns found at the scene of a drug trafficking offense were in fact "used" in relation to that offense. We discuss only some of them here, recognizing that courts have identified and will identify others. First, the defendant's possession of the gun is an important factor. Generally speaking, it would be difficult to "use" a gun without exercising dominion and control over it. Possession, of course, encompasses joint, as well as constructive possession. *United States v. Gibbs,* 904 F.2d 52, 57 (D.C.Cir.1990). Second, the court considers the accessibility of the gun to the defendant. A gun kept close at hand is more likely being used for protection than a gun packed away in a hard-to-reach spot. Cf. *United States v. Jefferson,* 974 F.2d 201, 207 (D.C.Cir.1992) (gun placed outside remained sufficiently accessible to support inference that it was "used" for purposes of 924(c)).

The proximity of the gun to the drugs is a third factor which, however, may cut either way, depending upon the particular facts. In Bruce, for example, the gun and the drugs were both found in the pocket of a raincoat hanging in a closet. We concluded that the gun appeared to be intended for use only at the time of a future distribution. Id. at 1055. In other cases, particularly those involving a drug distribution center, the gun's proximity to the drugs or to other indicia of a trafficking operation may support the inference that the gun was an integral part of the operation. See, e.g., *Anderson,* 881 F.2d at 1141; see also Jefferson, supra, 974 F.2d at 207 (where defendant had admitted to past use of gun, its proximity to drugs supported inference that it was used to protect drugs); *United States v. Williams,* 952 F.2d 418, 421 (D.C.Cir.1991) (in premises used for drug distribution, proximity of guns to drugs and drug paraphernalia supports conviction under 924(c)). See also *United States v. Hadfield,* 918 F.2d 987, 988 (1st Cir.1990) (location of operable firearm "in close proximity to a room or rooms in which drug distribution, processing, or storage occurs" supports inference of its use in connection with the predicate offense), cert. denied,

--- U.S. ----, 111 S.Ct. 2062, 114 L.Ed.2d 466 (1991). The permissible inferences that can be drawn from the proximity of the gun to the drugs, in the final analysis, depend on the facts of each case.

A fourth factor is whether the gun is loaded. See *Anderson*, 881 F.2d at 1141; *Dunn*, 846 F.2d at 764. Although the brandishing or display of even an unloaded gun can have a powerful deterrent effect and therefore play a role in protecting drugs and drug proceeds, the fact that a gun is loaded strengthens the inference that it is in actual use. Fifth, the number and type of guns may also be relevant to the question of their "use." *Jefferson*, supra, 974 F.2d at 207; *Williams*, 952 F.2d at 421. As to the type, we have found some relevant distinctions between an ornamental, but operative, belt-buckle derringer, which we deemed an unlikely arm to protect a crack house, *Bruce*, 939 F.2d at 1055, and a sawed-off shotgun, which we recognized as a "formidable firearm" for the same purpose. *Jefferson*, supra, 974 F.2d at 208. As to the number, we have found some significance in the existence of an "arsenal" of weapons, see *Williams*, 952 F.2d at 421, while recognizing that the use of a single gun can violate the statute. See *Jefferson*, supra, 974 F.2d at 207. In general, the presence of several guns throughout the premises strengthens the inference that they are intended to protect the stash.

The conclusion that the gun was actually used in relation to the trafficking offense can also be buttressed by an expert identifying the indicia of a drug trafficking operation—including, but not limited to, the quantity, composition and packaging of the drugs, the presence of drug paraphernalia, weapons, and large amounts of cash, the location of the premises in an area known for such activity, and the well-nigh universal use of guns to protect such operations. See *United States v. Williams*, 952 F.2d 418, 421 (D.C.Cir.1991); *United States v. Jenkins*, 928 F.2d 1175, 1179 (D.C.Cir.1991); *United States v. Anderson*, 881 F.2d 1128, 1141 (D.C.Cir.1989); *United States v. Dunn*, 846 F.2d 761, 764 (D.C.Cir.1988). Finally, we have considered relevant the defendant's recent use of the gun in relation to drug trafficking. *Jefferson*, supra, 974 F.2d at 207; *United States v. Laing*, 889 F.2d 281, 286 (D.C.Cir.1986), cert. denied, 494 U.S. 1008, 110 S.Ct. 1306, 108 L.Ed.2d 482 (1990); *Evans*, 888 F.2d at 895, 896.

In determining specifically whether a gun was used to protect the stash of drugs intended for distribution, as opposed to their actual distribution, some cases have focused on the open display of the gun as a deterrent to poachers. See, e.g., *United States v. Williams,* 923 F.2d 1397 (10th Cir.1990), cert. denied, --- U.S. ----, 111 S.Ct. 2033, 114 L.Ed.2d 118 (1991). This is not to say, however, that a gun that is within reach, though out of sight, does not also strongly suggest its intended use for protection of the drugs. See, e.g., *United States v. Meggett,* 875 F.2d 24, 29 (2d Cir.1989) ("Possession of a gun, even if it is concealed, constitutes use if such possession is an integral part of the predicate offense and facilitates the commission of that offense."), cert. denied sub nom. *Bradley v. United States,* 493 U.S. 858, 110 S.Ct. 166, 107 L.Ed.2d 123 (1989); *United States v. Stewart,* 779 F.2d 538, 540 (9th Cir.1985) (guns "embolden[ ] an actor who ha[s] the opportunity or ability to display or discharge the weapon . . . whether or not such display or discharge in fact occur[s]"), cert. denied, 484 U.S. 867, 108 S.Ct. 192, 98 L.Ed.2d 144 (1987).

Against this backdrop, we now consider the facts of this case, in light of the factors discussed, and, of course, also in the light most favorable to the government, *United States v. Sutton,* 801 F.2d 1346, 1358 (D.C.Cir.1986). The government claimed that Morris was "using" the three guns to protect the stash of drugs. It is well established that "when guns are present in order to protect contraband they may be deemed to be used in relation to the underlying felony [possession with intent to distribute]." *Evans,* 888 F.2d at 896. From the evidence in this case, we conclude that a jury could reasonably infer that Morris was using these firearms to protect the drugs in the apartment intended for future distribution.

First, there was plentiful evidence that Morris occupied the apartment and exercised constructive possession over its contents. Second, two of the guns were readily accessible to him, both within easy reach under the cushions of the couch on which he sat. He thus easily fulfilled two of the three factors generally looked to to prove possession of a firearm in § 924(c) cases. See *Long,* 905 F.2d at 1579 (possession most commonly shown by proximity to the firearm, possessory interest in the firearm, or dominion and control over the premises on which the firearm was located). The positioning of the two guns in the couch also placed them near the door through which an intruder might be expected to enter the apartment. The third gun, which was in a nightstand drawer in the bedroom, was closer to the drugs, which were in a duct in the bedroom ceiling; the bedroom was the room in which jurors could infer that appellant slept. Jurors could thus reasonably infer that all three guns were strategically placed throughout the apartment in order to protect the drugs that appellant possessed.

All three guns were loaded and fully operable. Two were .22 caliber pistols, and one was a .38 caliber pistol. While three pistols may not an arsenal make, they are not strangers to the drug trade, see *Dunn*, 846 F.2d at 764, and together they generously support an inference that their presence was geared to protecting the drugs stored in the apartment. Finally, the government offered expert testimony that the apartment was a drug packaging and distribution center. The government's expert testified that the quantity and packaging of the drugs indicated that they were intended for street sale; that drug dealers frequently "stash" their drugs in ceiling air vents because drug-sniffing dogs won't detect them there; and that someone who was involved in this kind of operation would typically use a gun to protect himself from "stick-up boys," competing dealers, or even from his street salesmen.

Because this evidence, taken as a whole, would certainly permit a reasonable juror to infer that Morris used the guns in relation to the possession with intent to distribute offense, we affirm his conviction under § 924(c).

UNITED STATES v. MORRIS, REWRITTEN

A jury convicted the defendant of possession of cocaine with intent to sell it, and of using or carrying a firearm during and in relation to a drug offense. The judge sentenced him to 130 months in prison.

Police had a warrant to search a one-bedroom apartment. Upon entering they found the defendant sitting on a small couch in the living room. The search revealed drugs, cash, and drug paraphernalia, and also three pistols—two under the cushions of the couch and the third in a nightstand in the bedroom. The officers testified that the defendant had told them he'd been living in the apartment for three or four weeks, although at his trial he testified that he had never lived there and was just visiting friends and in fact he had been there for only a few minutes when the police arrived and had known nothing about drugs or drug trafficking in the apartment.

The defendant challenges the sufficiency of the evidence on both charges. So far as possession of the drugs in concerned, the testimony of the police that the defendant had told them he lived in the apartment was corroborated by two birthday cards found in the bedroom—for the defendant's name was on the envelope of one and the other was to a "son" and signed "Mr. and Mrs. B. G. Morris"—and by a laundry ticket in the name of "E. Morris"; "Eugene" is the defendant's middle name. And there was no indication that anyone else lived in the apartment. The jury was on sound ground in inferring that the drugs in the apartment were indeed the defendant's, while the presence of drug paraphernalia, including materials for cutting and packaging drugs, supported the further inference that he intended the drugs for distribution rather than personal consumption (or solely personal consumption). And if that wasn't enough (it was), a government expert testified that the quantity and packaging of the drugs indicated that they were intended for sale.

The gun conviction was for violating a statute that punishes "a person [who] uses or carries a firearm" "during and in relation to a . . . drug trafficking crime." 18 U.S.C. § 924(c). The term "use" is broad enough to cover any way in which a gun facilitated the trafficking offense. *United States v. Harris,* 959 F.2d 246, 261–262 (D.C.Cir. 1992). The defendant need not have fired or even brandished it. *United States v. Evans,* 888 F.2d 891, 896 (D.C.Cir. 1989); *United States v. Matra,* 841 F.2d 837, 841–843 (9th Cir.1988). Accessibility is of course important. *United States v. Jefferson,* 974 F.2d 201, 207 (D.C.Cir. 1992). If the gun is loaded, this strengthens the inference that it is being "used" by the drug trafficker in relation to drug trafficking, *United States v. Anderson,* 881 F.2d 1128, 1141 (D.C.Cir. 1989); likewise if there is more than one gun. *United States v. Williams,* 952 F.2d 418, 421 (D.C. Cir. 1991).

The government claimed that the defendant was "using" all three guns to protect his drug trafficking. Two of them were immediately accessible to him beneath the cushions of the couch on which he was found sitting, which presumably was where he spent most of his time during the day; the third was immediately accessible to him when he was in bed. All three guns were loaded and in working condition. And the government's expert testified plausibly that a drug dealer would typically possess a gun in order to protect himself from "stick-up boys," competing dealers, or even from his own street salesmen. The evidence of use during and in relation to drug trafficking was sufficient.

AFFIRMED.

FORAYS INTO THE
DISTRICT COURT

I have said that any federal appellate judge who has not been a trial judge ought to try cases occasionally in the district courts of his circuit. I have been doing that since I was first appointed. I had no trial experience, except as an expert witness, prior to becoming a judge, and I committed errors, occasionally reversible ones, in my early trials. But I don't think I did major harm and I learned a lot that was and is valuable to me as a court of appeals judge and that enables me to tender suggestions regarding the trial process in the federal courts.

But though trials are the exciting part of being a federal district judge, they are no longer the main activity of such judges. The number of trials, especially civil trials, in the federal judicial system has been declining for many years. District judges now spend more time ruling on dispositive pretrial motions, mainly motions to dismiss and summary judgment motions, and on sentencing than they do on trials. They also spend a great deal of time on other pretrial motions, on posttrial motions such as motions to reconsider, on deciding appeals from the bankruptcy courts, and from the Social Security Administration in disability cases, on monitoring ongoing litigation, as by conducting periodic status hearings, on managing pretrial discovery, and on assisting settlement—though district judges often delegate the latter two activities to magistrate judges. Many rulings by district judges are oral but many are written—so many that it is unrealistic to expect district judges to write their own orders and opinions; delegation of opinion writing to law clerks (and sometimes to externs or interns) is not an option but a necessity.

The heavier workload of district judges than of court of appeals judges is another reason besides the one I gave in the preceding chapter for not giving precedential effect to district court opinions. Still another is that district court opinions are far more likely than court of appeals opinions to be reviewed and reversed by a higher court and so are less dependable evidence of what the law is. And a third reason is that district judges sit by themselves and so do not benefit from colleagues' insights.

Because district court opinions are unlikely to figure largely as sources of law, speed in decision making deserves even more emphasis at the district court level than at the appellate level. Better for the judge to rule quickly than to stew over issues that if novel or important he won't have the last word on in any event. But as I noted in Chapter 4, many judges do not give adequate weight to the private and social costs of justice delayed.[1] And of those who do, many lack management skills adequate to handling a heavy caseload with dispatch.

Management of litigation at the district court level would not be an issue if the lawyers had an incentive to expedite litigation, but generally they do not. Stretching out litigation enables a lawyer to take on more cases, which makes it less likely that at the conclusion of one case he will find himself with no new case to work on (and bill for) for some time ("all dressed up with no place to go"). And lawyers generally want to maximize

---

1. For a dramatic example, see *Wheeler v. Wexford Health Sources, Inc.*, 689 F.3d 680 (7th Cir. 2012).

the amount of pretrial discovery because it's labor intensive and therefore lucrative; most of the work is done by junior lawyers and paralegals, and in billing the client the law firm reprices their time. Protracted discovery and eventual settlement are often a more attractive combination to the lawyers than brief discovery and a trial (usually brief) to judgment. There are more hours to bill (and hourly billing is still the dominant mode of billing in civil cases, especially by defendants), and there is less risk; trials involve more variance in outcome than settlements. Especially in large commercial cases, a settlement can be represented by both teams of lawyers to the general counsels of the client corporations as a success, and likewise by each general counsel to his CEO. Explaining a loss at trial to a client is much harder; losing impels a search for mistakes and a desire to blame.

The judge who is alert to trial lawyers' perverse incentives can counter them by placing tight deadlines on discovery and on other stages of a litigation, such as the filing of motions for summary judgment. And he can limit the length of trials by limiting the number of exhibits the lawyers are allowed to submit, the number of witnesses the lawyers can call, and the number of hours that each side can consume in examination and cross-examination of witnesses. Tight limits on the length of trials are essential—especially jury trials. The rule of thumb in many federal judicial districts is that if at all possible a jury trial should not exceed two weeks. Prospective jurors are told the likely length of a trial, and those for whom jury duty for the expected length of the trial would constitute a hardship are usually excused (or excuse themselves, in effect, by giving answers to questions at voir dire that they know will cause either the judge, or the lawyer for one side or the other, to excuse them). Prospective jurors who have responsible jobs are unlikely to be able to take a leave of absence on short notice for more than a couple of weeks, yet one would like to see such persons well represented on juries.

Expert Witnesses and Trial by Jury: An Anecdotal Introduction

All the trials I've conducted have been civil trials, mostly jury trials, and in recent years mostly trials in patent cases, which are especially challenging. I have conducted pretrial proceedings, sometimes extensive, in some of the cases assigned to me and settlement negotiations in others; other cases have settled without my participation in those negotiations. But my most memorable cases have been those that went to trial. Trials are exciting, dramatic; they have unpredictable twists and turns, and cross-examination that sometimes rises to the height of a Rumpole. I will offer a few anecdotes, vivid in my mind though they concern incidents decades ago.

One of my early trials was a jury trial for election fraud that I conducted in the federal district court in Hammond, Indiana. The plaintiff was the former city judge of Gary, Indiana, who had lost his bid for reelection. His name was Grimes and the winner's name was Craddock, and Grimes charged Craddock with having persuaded a blind unemployed carpenter also named Grimes to run for another office (that of city clerk) on the ballot on which Judge Grimes and Craddock were competing for the city judgeship. The pseudo-Grimes, as I thought of him—though his name was indeed Grimes—had registered at the last minute (doubtless the timing was chosen by the Craddock team to forestall a possible countermove by Judge Grimes) as a candidate for city clerk. He had not campaigned. He truthfully reported his campaign expenditures as having been zero. Nevertheless he received several thousand votes—enough to tip the election to Craddock, assuming that a substantial number of those votes were cast in error by voters who thought they were voting to reelect Judge Grimes. Since the pseudo-Grimes, not having campaigned, had been invisible in the campaign, it would not have been surprising if many voters had voted for the first "Grimes" they saw on the ballot—and the pseudo-Grimes happened to be the first—not noticing that further along in the ballot there was a second Grimes, the one they wanted to vote for as judge.

Judge Grimes's lawyer called as one of his witnesses an attractive young woman and asked her whom she had intended to vote for as city judge, and why, and she answered "Judge Grimes" because, as she explained, he had given a talk at her high school. It was the first election in which she'd been eligible to vote. The lawyer showed her the ballot as it appeared in the voting booth and asked her to point out whom she had voted for as judge. She pointed to the name of the pseudo-Grimes. The lawyer asked her to look more closely: was that the Grimes running for judge—or a person of the same name running for another office? She looked, said "Oh my God," burst into tears (was that an act, I wondered?), and was helped weeping from the stand, only to be followed to the witness stand by another deceived voter, this one an older woman who was (or was she pretending to be?) crippled and was carried into the witness box in the arms of an attendant.

To counter these arresting theatrical displays, the Craddock forces (I suspect) contrived their own bit of drama. When their Grimes took the stand—led there by his lawyer because of his blindness—in an effort to persuade the jury that he had been a bona fide candidate for city clerk, and began testifying, he mumbled inaudibly. I asked him to move his head closer to the microphone in the witness box so that he could be heard. He thrust his head sharply forward, hitting the microphone with it with a sound like a thunderclap. I felt bad because I attributed the accident to my being insensitive to his blindness. But later in the trial, during a break, my law clerks saw him walking about in the lobby outside the courtroom, without his dark glasses and cane and with no indication of impaired vision.

One of the lawyers (I forget for which side), short and stout, was fearsome in cross-examination. He would start a question standing next to the far end of the jury box and thus at a distance from the witness box, toward which he would stride rapidly, looking like a charging rhinoceros and ending up leaning into the box, frightening the witness. I told him he must not touch or lean into the box, so from then on he stopped his charge just short of his prey.

The most effective cross-examination at the trial, however, and it provided me with real insight into the trial process, was the cross-examination by Craddock's lawyer of Judge Grimes's expert witness. A thoroughly reputable professor of political science at Indiana University at Bloomington, the witness testified on the basis of statistical studies of elections that it was entirely possible that enough voters had voted for the pseudo-Grimes intending to vote for Judge Grimes to swing the election to Craddock, given how close the election had been. Ordinarily an expert witness is deposed before trial, but Craddock's lawyer had skipped that step. If the professor had written an expert report, as is usually required, I am sure the lawyer hadn't bothered to read it. For his questions had nothing to do with the substance of the professor's expert opinion.

I don't recall the exact wording, but here's an approximation: "Are you familiar with Broadway in Gary?" "No." "Would you say that Broadway was the main street of Gary?" "I don't know." A few more questions concerning the geography of Gary, none of which the expert witness could answer, culminated in the question: "Have you ever been in Gary?" "No, but"—by this time the witness was squirming, and he tried to explain that it was irrelevant to his opinion about the likelihood and probable consequences of erroneous votes for the pseudo-Grimes whether he'd ever been in Gary—a visit to Gary would have told him nothing bearing on the matter. But the lawyer cut him off, saying he had no further questions. The jurors were snickering. I am convinced they were persuaded that someone who hadn't been in Gary couldn't offer a worthwhile opinion about the election. I don't recall whether Judge Grimes's lawyer tried to rehabilitate the witness on redirect examination, but I imagine that if he did, it was too late; the cross-examination, though devoid of substance, had demolished him. Nevertheless the jury's verdict was for Judge Grimes. He was an effective witness and there was the dramatic supporting testimony of the young woman who burst into tears and the dramatic appearance of the crippled woman. But the expert added nothing.

There is an important lesson here, concerning expert witnesses and the adversary system more broadly, to which I'll return shortly.

Some years after the trial that I've just described I presided at a jury trial that pitted a large electrical utility, charging breach of contract, against a supplier of nuclear fuel. The plaintiff sought substantial damages; the defendant contended that even if there was a breach of contract the damages were zero. The plaintiff's cross-examination of the defendant's damages expert (an accountant) went as follows (again the words are not exact, as I am "testifying" from memory). "I will write down on this easel the various damages estimates that have been presented. Do you recall what the plaintiff's estimate was?" "No." "If I told you $60 million, would that jog your memory?" The witness hesitated but eventually replied "Yes, that sounds right." The lawyer then wrote very slowly on the easel "$60 million." Then he asked: "Do you recall the document we presented which indicated that the defendant itself thought the alleged breach might have cost the plaintiff $50 million?" There was the same hesitancy but eventual acknowledgment by the expert witness followed by the lawyer's slowly inscribing the number under the previous estimate. This exchange was repeated once or twice more. Finally the lawyer said to the expert: "And now, Dr. Peterson, remind the jury what *your* estimate of the plaintiff's damages is." By this time, although the cross-examination had been devoid of substance, Peterson was visibly flustered—a common reaction to being asked a series of questions that can be answered only "yes," or "no," which makes the witness feel that he's being led by the nose. So before answering, Peterson tried to explain that he had analyzed the damages issue carefully and his conclusion was well substantiated and—but the lawyer cut him off and asked him what number he should write on the easel. And Peterson, reluctantly, embarrassedly, acknowledged that it should be zero. To which the lawyer responded: "Zero, Dr. Peterson, a great big egg? Let's go back over the estimates. The plaintiff's estimate was, right?, $60 million. The defendant's own estimate was, right?, $50 million." And so on. And then: "But your estimate, Dr. Peterson, is zero?" The witness had passed from being uncomfortable to being upset, and showed it, as he insisted that that was indeed the upshot of his analysis. The lawyer, after slowly inscribing "Dr. Peterson: $0" on the easel under the multimillion-dollar damages estimates, responded gently: "Now Dr. Peterson, don't be upset; we have a long history in this country of the lonely genius." End of cross-examination. The jurors were chuckling, Dr. Peterson was defeated, and the jury awarded the plaintiff damages, though not as much as it had sought.

Party-Appointed and Court-Appointed Expert Witnesses

In both cases that I've just discussed, the cross-examination was content-less yet seemed, so far as I could judge, effective in discrediting the expert witness in the eyes of the jury. I infer from these and other experiences that I've had in trials that jurors are prepared to dislike expert witnesses, other than a medical expert witness, whom they will respect because they deal with physicians in their personal life,[2] as distinct from economists, forensic accountants, computer scientists, automotive engineers, and statisticians. Jurors' suspicions of expert witnesses seem to go beyond the rational distrust that jury-eligible citizens have been found to have of experts who frequently appear in court and are highly paid.[3] Yet because of limitations on what a lay witness is permitted to testify to, an expert witness often is indispensable to one side or the other, and probably to both sides. When there are expert witnesses on opposite sides, who therefore clash, often they cancel each other out in the eyes of the jurors. The jurors know that the expert witnesses have been hired by the parties and assume they say whatever the parties want them to say.

The role of the expert witness is an issue important to this book because of the emphasis I place on complexity as a daunting challenge to the federal judiciary. The judge and the jurors may be unable to understand a complex case without the aid of experts. If jurors are skeptical of experts, and if in most cases experts can be found to testify plausibly on both sides of the case wherever the truth may lie, the judge and jurors may be none the wiser after listening to them.

A lawyer is not allowed to pay a lay witness to testify; the potential for corruption is obvious. But he may pay an expert witness—and the potential for corruption is obvious.[4]

A gatekeeper role has therefore been assigned to the judge: he cannot

2. And thus jurors tend to lean in favor of defendants in medical malpractice suits, see Philip G. Peters, Jr., "Doctors & Juries," 105 *Michigan Law Review* 1453 (2007), because they are reluctant to conclude that a physician or other provider of medical services was negligent.

3. Joel Cooper and Isaac M. Neuhaus, "The Hired Gun Effect: Assessing the Effect of Pay, Frequency of Testifying, and Credentials on the Perception of Expert Testimony," 24 *Law and Human Behavior* 149 (2000). See also Aaron Krivitzky, "Presenting Your Expert as a Teacher," *Wisconsin Law Journal: Legal News,* Oct. 19, 2009, http://wislawjournal.com/2009/10/19/presenting-your-expert-as-a-teacher/ (visited May 21, 2012).

4. See, for example, Michael J. Mandel, "Going for the Gold: Economists as Expert Witnesses," *Journal of Economic Perspectives,* Spring 1999, p. 113.

permit an expert witness to testify without first determining (in what is called a "*Daubert* hearing") that the testimony the expert intends to give is responsible.[5] As a practical matter this means that the expert must be shown to be knowledgeable in the relevant technical field, and in forming the expert opinion to which he wants to testify to have used the same analytical methods that he uses in his ordinary, which is to say nonlitigation, work.[6] The problem with the judge's playing this gatekeeper role is that it is difficult for a judge (or anyone else) to determine the adequacy of the prospective expert witness's methodology without knowing something about the expert's field.[7] The temptation is to let the expert testify, and rely on cross-examination to flag his deficiencies.

My court encountered this problem in a breach of contract case in which the plaintiff's expert witness on damages—a forensic accountant who had conducted a regression analysis that purported to quantify the plaintiff's damages—was challenged by the defendant (FedEx). A *Daubert* hearing ensued, on the basis of which the district judge allowed the expert to testify. FedEx lost in the district court and appealed, and we reversed. Regarding the *Daubert* hearing and its outcome we remarked:

> There were, as we're about to see, grave questions concerning the reliability of Morriss's [the expert witness] application of regression

5. See National Research Council of the National Academies, *Strengthening Forensic Science in the United States: A Path Forward*, ch. 3 (2009).

6. See, for example, Richard A. Posner, *Frontiers of Legal Theory* 403 and n. 38 (2001), and references cited there. But sometimes an expert witness doesn't do any nonlitigation work; he is a full-time professional witness.

7. See *ATA Airlines, Inc. v. Federal Express Corp.*, 665 F.3d 882, 889, 896 (7th Cir. 2011). For representative academic literature critical of expert witnesses, see Samuel R. Gross, "Expert Evidence," 1991 *Wisconsin Law Review* 1113 (1991); L. Timothy Perrin, "Expert Witness Testimony: Back to the Future," 29 *University of Richmond Law Review* 1389 (1995); Justin P. Murphy, "Expert Witnesses at Trial: Where Are the Ethics?" 14 *Georgetown Journal of Legal Ethics* 217 (2001). A variety of possible approaches, focused on one contentious area of law, are canvassed in Rebecca Haw, "Adversarial Economics in Antitrust Litigation: Losing Academic Consensus in the Battle of the Experts," 106 *Northwestern University Law Review* 1261 (2012).

analysis to the facts. Yet in deciding that the analysis was admissible, all the district judge said was that FedEx's objections "that there is no objective test performed, and that [Morriss] used a subjective test, and [gave] no explanation why he didn't consider objective criteria," presented issues to be explored on cross-examination at trial, and that "regression analysis is accepted, so this is not 'junk science.' [Morriss] appears to have applied it. Although defendants disagree, he has applied it and come up with a result, which apparently is acceptable in some areas under some models. Simple regression analysis is an accepted model."

This cursory, and none too clear, response to FedEx's objections to Morriss's regression analysis did not discharge the duty of a district judge to evaluate in advance of trial a challenge to the admissibility of an expert's proposed testimony. The evaluation of such a challenge may not be easy; the "principles and methods" used by expert witnesses will often be difficult for a judge to understand. But difficult is not impossible. The judge can require the lawyer who wants to offer the expert's testimony to explain to the judge in plain English what the basis and logic of the proposed testimony are, and the judge can likewise require the opposing counsel to explain his objections in plain English.[8]

A further problem with expert witnesses is that for many of them litigation *is* their ordinary, even their only, work. Their technical skills may be minimal, their real skill being theatrical—the ability to charm or dazzle a jury.

The *Daubert* hearing and cross-examination do not exhaust the possible solutions to the problem of the unreliable expert witness. An additional possibility would be for every professional association (for economists the American Economic Association, for doctors the American Medical Association, for engineers the Institute of Electrical and Electronic Engineers, etc.) to maintain a roster of testimonial appearances of its members, including an abstract or transcript of the member's testimony and any criti-

8. *ATA Airlines, Inc. v. Federal Express Corp.*, 665 F.3d at 889.

cisms of that testimony by the judge, the lawyers, or other expert witnesses. Another solution would be to require lawyers who use an expert witness to disclose the names of all the experts they approached as possible expert witnesses; this would alert the judge to witness shopping.[9] And finally the best solution—one I've long advocated[10] but only recently implemented in my own ventures in trial judging—is for the judge to appoint expert witnesses himself.[11] That is authorized by Rule 706 of the Federal Rules of Evidence but rarely done.[12]

Until recently, because I wanted to try cases rather than shepherd them through the lengthy pretrial stage, I had taken assignments in the district court only on the eve of trial. Most litigation is settled before trial, and the closer one gets to trial the more likely the case is to be tried—though I have had the experience of cases being settled the day on which, or the weekend before, trial was scheduled to begin. I have now begun taking cases much earlier, realizing belatedly that the pretrial stage of litigation not only is vital but is often managed inefficiently. So now I have enough lead time to be able to appoint expert witnesses in my district court cases.

The district judge can make his own choice of an expert witness, with

---

9. See Richard A Posner, "The Law and Economics of the Economic Expert Witness," *Journal of Economic Perspectives,* Spring 1999, pp. 91, 96, 98.

10. See id. at 96, 98; Posner, *Frontiers of Legal Theory,* at 405–407.

11. See, for example, Joe S. Cecil and Thomas E. Willging, *Court-Appointed Experts: Defining the Role of Experts Appointed under Federal Rule of Evidence 706* (Federal Judicial Center 1993); J. Gregory Sidak, "Court-Appointed Neutral Economic Experts" (Criterion Economics, L.L.C., Feb. 18, 2013, unpublished); Jennifer L. Mnookin, "Expert Evidence, Partisanship, and Epistemic Competence," 73 *Brooklyn Law Review* 1010, 1020–1028 (2008); Lee A. Hollaar, "The Use of Neutral Experts," 4 *Expert Evidence Report* 660 (2004); Laural L. Hooper, Joe S. Cecil, and Thomas E. Willging, "Neutral Science Panels: Two Examples of Panels of Court-Appointed Experts in the Breast Implants Product Liability Litigation" (Federal Judicial Center 2001); Lisa C. Wood, "Court-Appointed Independent Experts: A Litigator's Critique," 21 *Antitrust* 91 (2007); Samuel R. Gross, "Expert Evidence," 1991 *Wisconsin Law Review* 1113, 1187–1208 (1991). The Cecil and Willging book is the fullest discussion of court-appointed experts that I've found, and contains valuable statistics and reports of judges' views and practices, but is somewhat dated.

12. Gross, "Expert Evidence," at 1190–1191.

the assistance if he wants of the American Association for the Advancement of Science, which has a program for finding and vetting prospective expert witnesses.[13] An alternative that I've also used is to ask the parties to tell their experts to put their heads together and nominate one or more neutral experts for me to consider appointing. The parties' agreeing on the neutral expert will usually preclude any subsequent charge by one side or the other that the expert is biased.

Lawyers resist a judge's appointing an expert[14] even if both sides are satisfied that the expert is neutral and competent and can communicate with a jury, as academics (and not only academics) usually can. For the lawyers aren't interested in whether the judge or jury understands their case; they're interested in winning, and so they hire experts (and pay them very well) whom they think a judge or jury will find persuasive.

I don't mean that if the judge doesn't understand the expert's field, anything goes. There are certain inherent safeguards. One, which I suspect however is overrated, is that since most expert witnesses, unlike most lay witnesses, are repeat players, they have a financial interest in avoiding damaging cross-examination and severe criticism by judges—both are forms of criticism that could destroy their usefulness as experts in future cases. But it is also the repeat player who has an incentive to please his client so that he'll be rehired, and in many cases the opposing lawyer and the judge aren't capable of detecting even seriously misleading expert testimony. Second, an expert witness who has a record of academic publication will be subject to damaging cross-examination should he contradict his academic work—but many successful expert witnesses are not academics; often as I said they are engaged full-time in litigation-related work.

Lawyers want to control their cases, and not only in order to be able to conduct pretrial discovery to their heart's content. They particularly don't

13. See American Association for the Advancement of Science, "Court Appointed Scientific Experts," www.aaas.org/spp/case/experience.htm (visited Jan. 21, 2013).

14. Gross, "Expert Evidence," at 1197–1201; Wood, "Court-Appointed Independent Experts"; Karen Butler Reisinger, Note, "Court-Appointed Expert Panels: A Comparison of Two Models," 32 *Indiana Law Review* 225, 237 (1998).

want the judge to call the court-appointed witnesses before the parties' experts testify and to tell the jury, as he is permitted to do, that the experts appointed by him, and paid their fee half by one side and half by the other, are beholden to neither side. Lawyers and many judges see in the appointment of neutral experts a threat to the adversary system. And they are right! It is in the "inquisitorial" type of adjudicative system that prevails in the nations of Continental Europe, in Japan, and in most other countries outside the Anglo-American sphere, that judges conduct investigations, call witnesses, ask questions of witnesses, disdain most evidence that isn't documentary, are appointed and promoted strictly on merit and not by politicians, do not use juries in civil cases, and for all these reasons reduce the trial lawyers to little more than kibitzers.

Whatever the merits of such a system, it's not about to be adopted in the United States, though pockets already exist here, for example in proceedings before administrative law judges in social security disability proceedings, which are not adversary.

The negative connotation of "inquisitorial" is only one barrier toward significant movement away from our adversary system; more important is that an inquisitorial system greatly increases the ratio of judges to trial lawyers[15] because it casts the judge as player rather than as umpire—in fact as the main player in the legal drama. In an adversarial legal system, in contrast, "a large measure of judicial passivity is structurally inevitable."[16] Forcing a wholesale conversion of trial lawyers into judges—into modestly paid government employees—would be institutionally daunting and politically unthinkable in our system. Furthermore, an inquisitorial system requires a higher-quality judiciary than an adversary system does because of the judge's larger role in an inquisitorial system relative to the lawyers' role; this rules out judicial appointment by politicians. But the greater variance in the background, training, and legal skills and smarts in our lateral-entry adversary judiciary is a source of strength as well as of weakness.

15. Richard A. Posner, *Law and Legal Theory in England and America* 28 (1996) (tab. 1.1). Japan is an exception, however.

16. Gross, "Expert Evidence," at 1203.

Inquisitorial judges are criticized for being excessively insulated from worldly experience, excessively bureaucratic, legalistic, and regimented.[17]

The appointment of neutral experts by a federal judge, especially if he is able to get the party experts to agree on nominations for court-appointed experts, makes only limited inroads into the adversary system. It is a partial but promising solution to the problem of technical complexity that is gnawing at the federal courts. (It is partial for the additional reason that there are technical fields, such as the economics of competition and monopoly, that are polarized, and in which therefore there may be no neutral experts.) But it also means more work for judges.[18] That, in conjunction with the fact that many judges are former trial lawyers strongly committed to the adversary system and not always alert to its deficiencies, may explain why federal judges resort as infrequently as they do to Rule 706.[19]

It means more work for judges not only because finding, interviewing, and appointing neutral experts takes time but also because court-appointed experts have no lawyer to shepherd and protect them. The judge must play that role unless, as in a recent case, he finds a lawyer willing to represent the court-appointed experts pro bono.[20] But that is likely to encumber the process unduly. And the jury is apt to be confused to learn that the court's own expert witnesses, though they are neither parties to the lawsuit nor representatives of parties, somehow need a lawyer, who presumably will conduct a direct examination of them as well as objecting during cross-examination to misleading or otherwise improper questions by the parties' lawyers. I prefer to dispense with a lawyer for the neutrals, and in lieu of direct examination have them narrate their testimony, with perhaps an oc-

17. Gerhard O. W. Mueller and Frè Le Poole Griffiths, "Judicial Fitness: A Comparative Study: Part Two," 52 *Judicature* 238, 239–40 (1969); Carlo Guarnieri, "Appointment and Careers of Judges in Continental Europe: the Rise of Judicial Self-Government," 24 *Legal Studies* 169 (2004).

18. Gross, "Expert Evidence," at 1203–1204.

19. For evidence that respect for the adversary system deters some judges from appointing expert witnesses, see Cecil and Willging, *Court-Appointed Experts,* at 20–21.

20. Request and Notice regarding Dr. James Kearl, Filing 787, in *Oracle America, Inc. v. Google, Inc.,* 798 F. Supp. 2d 1111 (N.D.Cal. 2011).

casional question by me to keep them on track or clarify a point for the jury. But court-appointed experts who have no lawyer need the judge's protection lest the parties' lawyers, wanting to control the case—through aggressive questioning of the neutral experts at deposition or trial (recall the examples of cross-examination of expert witnesses at my trials)—groundlessly undermine those experts' credibility with the jury. My solution has been to preside at the deposition of the court-appointed expert myself, but it is somewhat time-consuming.

The Jury

I need to say more about the jury. Some judges attribute almost supernatural insight to juries, believing them to be competent to render accurate verdicts in even the most difficult cases. These are generally the same judges who swear by the adversary system and defend the judicial status quo more generally, as I do not. There is an immense social-scientific literature on the jury, a literature that I suspect few judges, whether federal or state, have delved into. In what follows I draw on some of this literature[21] as well as on my own, albeit rather limited, experience conducting civil jury trials.

21. See, for example, Dennis J. Devine, *Jury Decision Making: The State of the Science* (2012); Neil Vidmar and Valerie P. Hans, *American Juries: The Verdict* (2007); Cass R. Sunstein et al., *Punitive Damages: How Juries Decide* (2002); Valerie P. Hans, *Business on Trial: The Civil Jury and Corporate Responsibility* (2000); Matthew A. Reiber and Jill D. Weinberg, "The Complexity of Complexity: An Empirical Study of Juror Competence in Civil Cases," 78 *University of Cincinnati Law Review* 929 (2010); Theodore Eisenberg et al., "Judge-Jury Agreement in Criminal Cases: A Partial Replication of Kalven and Zeisel's *The American Jury*," 2 *Journal of Empirical Legal Studies* 171 (2005); Dennis J. Devine et al., "Jury Decision Making: 45 Years of Empirical Research on Deliberating Groups," 7 *Psychology, Public Policy, and Law* 622 (2001); Shari Seidman Diamond and Jonathan D. Casper, "Blindfolding the Jury to Verdict Consequences: Damages, Experts, and the Civil Jury," 26 *Law and Society Review* 513 (1992); Peter David Blanck, "What Empirical Research Tells Us: Studying Judges' and Juries' Behavior," 40 *American University Law Review* 775 (1991). Many of these studies build on the first major empirical study of the American jury: Harry Kalven, Jr. and Hans Zeisel, *The American Jury* (1956).

I do think that jurors are conscientious. Courtrooms are cleverly designed to awe prospective jurors; a judge and the lawyers can impress on most of them the importance to the parties and the system of conscientious discharge of the juror's role as a judicial officer *pro tempore;* and prospective jurors who are apt to prove irresponsible in the discharge of their duty as jurors are usually struck at the jury-selection stage by one of the parties, or by the judge. Moreover, although jury service is formally compulsory, a prospective juror who very much does not want to serve will either think up a plausible excuse or will answer "no" to the question whether he can consider the issues impartially; and he will be let off. Or he may reply to the jury summons with a plausible excuse for not being able to serve. Indeed he may simply ignore the jury summons. That can usually be done with impunity because follow-up is rare. The absence of follow-up makes practical sense, though: people who ignore jury summonses, which is illegal to do, are unlikely to be responsible jurors.

In only one of my trials have I encountered jury misconduct. The plaintiff was a one-man company, and its principal (whom I'll pretend for simplicity was the plaintiff), charged the defendant with, in effect, having stolen a formula for a high-protein, low-calcium milk product that the plaintiff claimed to have invented. The defendant denied that the plaintiff, a former trader in currency futures who had no background in dairy products, had invented it. In an effort to bolster his claim to have been the inventor, the plaintiff testified on direct examination that "from the commodity days, trading and everything else, I knew about proteins, and casein was a protein. It's found in milk."

This testimony was given early in the trial, and shortly after it was given the courtroom deputy informed me that one of the jurors wanted to speak to me in private. I cleared the courtroom of everyone but the reporter and court personnel and questioned the juror. He was himself a trader of financial futures, and he told me that he had a serious problem with the plaintiff's credibility but didn't know whether he had to keep it to himself or whether he could share his concern with the other jurors. He said that financial futures and commodity futures are completely different animals and that the plaintiff had tried to blur the difference in order to bolster his claim to have sufficient agricultural expertise to have invented a process for making a milk product. I told him that a juror is free to base an opinion of the truthfulness of a witness's testimony on the juror's professional experience, and to share that opinion with the other jurors—but only at the end of the case, when the jurors retire to deliberate. I reminded him, as I had instructed the jury (and I repeated the instruction every time the jury left the courtroom for a recess or at the end of the day), that he could not discuss the case with the other jurors until it came time to deliberate. (This is the rule; whether it's a good rule I discuss later in this chapter.) I also suggested that he reserve judgment about the plaintiff's testimony because the trial had just begun and he would be hearing from other witnesses and might be skeptical about their testimony too.

Trial resumed and that afternoon there was another incident, involving the same juror. After a sidebar, and with the jury having taken a recess, the plaintiff, who had been sitting in the witness box during the sidebar, said he had overheard this juror, whom I'll call *A,* and the juror sitting on his immediate right (*B*), discussing the case and calling it "bullshit." Again I interviewed juror *A,* this time in open court. He admitted having spoken with *B* during the sidebar but said that all he'd said was that the lawyers should resolve their dispute by arm wrestling, apparently an allusion to the television program *Boston Legal.* In the light of his emphatic denial of the plaintiff's account, I decided to let the juror remain on the jury.

The third and critical incident occurred the next day. The plaintiff had been recalled to the stand and was being cross-examined by the defendant's lawyer, who at one point asked the plaintiff whether milk had been traded on the Board of Trade when he was a trader there, and when he said "no" the lawyer followed up by asking (saying, really): "So, there's no way you're familiar with milk prices based on your experience as a commodities trader. Is there?" The plaintiff replied, "No, that's incorrect, counsel." The lawyer then changed the subject. But during this exchange, recalling juror *A*'s preoccupation with the plaintiff's lack of experience trading agricultural commodities, I glanced over at the jury and saw juror *B,* still sitting on *A*'s immediate right, swivel toward *A* and smirk. I didn't notice *A*'s reaction, but my law clerks, who corroborated my observation, told me they'd seen *A* nod emphatically in response to *B*. Apparently no one else in the courtroom observed the incident.

I immediately inferred that *A* had told *B* that he didn't believe that the plaintiff could have learned about agricultural commodities at his time at the Board of Trade. Such a discussion would have been a serious breach of propriety, less because these two jurors had disobeyed my instruction that the jurors were not to discuss the case until they retired to deliberate than because juror *A* had caused the bee in his bonnet about the plaintiff's credibility to buzz about inside the head of another juror (maybe more than one other juror)—had in all likelihood enlisted at least that juror in a campaign to brand the plaintiff a liar. I did not think it possible in these circumstances for the plaintiff to get a fair trial from this jury, and so I declared a mistrial and discharged the jury, though without giving a reason. The trial was almost over when I decided to grant a mistrial, and I let it finish before doing so, and offered to decide the case as if it had been a bench trial. The lawyers agreed, and I decided it in favor of the defendant.[22]

My impression that with the occasional exception (illustrated by the milk case) jurors are conscientious is supported by reputable studies.[23] I also think that juries are competent to decide cases that involve activities with which they are familiar, such as driving, or slipping and falling, especially when the key witnesses come from the same approximate social class as the jurors; it's easier to "read" a person from one's own class. ("Reading" a witness can be an especially serious problem in regard to foreign-born witnesses from countries in which behavior that Americans think of as devious, such as not looking a person in the eyes when he is talking to

22. *Dominion Nutrition, Inc. v. Cesca,* 467 F. Supp. 2d 870 (N.D. Ill. 2006).

23. See Vidmar and Hans, *American Juries,* for confirmation based on extensive research, their own and others'. In general their book is highly favorable to the American jury system, and while it acknowledges that juries have difficulty understanding scientific and other complex cases, particularly when statistics are involved, see *id.,* ch. 8, it points out that judges often have similar difficulty. The book deals primarily with state rather than federal courts, and the average quality of federal judges is higher than that of state judges. The average quality of federal juries may also be higher, however, in part because federal juror lists are based on voting rolls, and voters tend to be better educated and more public-spirited than nonvoters.

you, is actually a mark of respect.) But in my experience jurors have great difficulty with issues that exceed the limits of their education and experience, such as commercial cases (other than the simplest) and cases involving technical subject matter or statistical or other technical evidence, as distinct from eyewitness testimony—which, as I noted in Chapter 3, we are belatedly learning is very often unreliable. It is true that many judges say they agree with "their" juries' verdicts most of the time, but experienced trial judges often don't pay much attention to the evidence presented at a jury trial other than to determine its admissibility. Also they would feel they weren't doing a very good job if they found themselves often disagreeing with "their" juries' verdicts—they would feel they hadn't been guiding the juries well. Moreover, a witness's subtle, often unconscious, communicative behavior ("microbehavior") of which the judge may not even be aware, such as failing to maintain eye contact with jurors or witnesses, may influence a jury's verdict.[24]

Also, judges generally adhere to the traditions of the judicial profession even when those traditions are unsound. An example is the "limiting" instruction: telling the jury to give no weight to an inadmissible bit of evidence that has snuck into the trial, yet without explaining to the jury *why* it should give no weight to what is likely to strike the jurors as especially significant evidence. The ineffectuality of limiting instructions is well known.[25] Yet still they're given, and rationalized with judicial falsehoods, such as that "our theory of trial relies upon the ability of a jury to follow instructions."[26]

Cutting the other way is the fact that judges often know more of the facts of the case than the jury does, because the judge may have ruled certain evidence inadmissible—which means he read or heard it and the jurors did not. If jurors knew everything the judge knew, disagreements between judges and jurors regarding the correct outcome of a case would be rarer.

Anyway trial judges are stuck with the jury system and don't like to admit to themselves that it's a highly imperfect system—time-consuming,

24. This is a theme of Blanck's article, "What Empirical Research Tells Us."
25. See studies cited in Posner, *Frontiers of Legal Theory*, at 384–385.
26. *Opper v. United States*, 348 U.S. 84, 95 (1954).

expensive (in disrupting the jurors' normal lives), and, in many cases, unreliable in comparison to a bench trial by a competent judge (an important qualification, obviously). The social science literature confirms what trial lawyers certainly understand, that jurors bring a variety of personal biases to their evaluation of a case.[27] Though so do judges.

Jury Trials in Patent Cases

Jurors have particular difficulty understanding complex cases, and as I have insisted throughout this book the complexity of the activities that give rise to federal litigation is increasing, notably though not only in the patent field, where a plaintiff who is seeking damages is entitled by the broadly worded Seventh Amendment to a jury trial if he wants one. And usually he does.[28] The reason appears to be that as a variety of studies have found, juries are more sympathetic than judges to patentees,[29] the usual plaintiffs in patent damages suits, charging infringement. Jurors tend to think that if the patent is valid, the defendant should not have attempted to make something similar. "Inventing around," though a legitimate response to a valid patent (as is implicit in the requirement that patents be published—a requirement aimed, in part at least, at providing information for other inven-

27. Devine et al., "Jury Decision Making," at 699–712, provides an exemplary summary of the many flaws in the jury system, and the many possibilities, beyond the few that I discuss, for significant improvement.

28. From 1983 to 1999, the proportion of patent cases tried by juries rose substantially. Kimberly A. Moore, "Judges, Juries and Patent Cases—An Empirical Peek inside the Black Box," 99 *Michigan Law Review* 365, 384 (2000) (tab. 1).

29. For example, Greg Upchurch, "LegalMetric Nationwide Patent Litigation Statistics," *LegalMetric*, slides 7, 24 (2009), concludes that from 1991 to 2009 patentees who survived summary judgment won 66 percent of jury trials but only 46 percent of bench trials. Yan Leychkis, "Of Fire Ants and Claim Construction: An Empirical Study of the Meteoric Rise of the Eastern District of Texas as a Preeminent Forum for Patent Litigation," 9 *Yale Journal of Law and Technology* 193, 210 (2007), finds that patentees won 90 percent of all jury trials in the Eastern District of Texas between 1998 and 2006 and that during this period the district unsurprisingly became one of the most popular districts in which to file a patent case.

tors to use[30]), strikes many jurors as copying, and therefore infringing. Of course if the patent is invalid—a standard defense in suits for infringement—the plaintiff loses. But the defendant has the burden of proving invalidity by clear and convincing evidence, and that is a heavier burden of proof than the patentee's burden of proving infringement, which requires just a preponderance of the evidence (that is, a showing that it is more likely than not that the defendant infringed).

The court-appointed expert in a patent case can be the life preserver for the jury to cling to, and such an appointment should therefore be a routine feature of patent cases, but is not. Another pressing need is for jury instructions that eschew both the jargon of patent law and the jargon of the technical field to which the patented invention belongs, and this will usually require that the judge himself or his law clerks write the instructions rather than, as is typically the practice, picking and choosing among the instructions proposed by the parties. Even the Seventh Circuit's lucid and carefully drafted pattern jury instructions are too long, complex, and ambitious when they address that archetypal technical field of law—patent law. They seek to educate the jury in the jargon of patent law, when what the judge should be doing is requiring the lawyers and the witnesses to use ordinary language, and using ordinary language in his jury instructions, in place of patent jargon like "means plus function," "prosecution history" (which has nothing to do with what laypersons understand by the word "prosecution"), patent "limitation" (ditto), and "prior art" (which usually is simply an "earlier invention"—and, when it is, that's the right term to use with a jury).

I reprint at the end of this chapter a set of instructions I prepared for a patent jury trial that never took place, because the case settled on the Friday before the Monday that the trial was to begin. The case, *Chamberlain Group, Inc. v. Lear Corp.* (No. 05 CV 3449 on the docket of the Northern District of Illinois), charged infringement of a patent on an encryption device for garage-door openers, to prevent unauthorized persons from open-

---

30. See Lisa Larrimore Ouellette, "Do Patents Disclose Useful Information?" 25 *Harvard Journal of Law and Technology* 545 (2012). Her answer is yes.

ing the door to one's garage. A transmitter, usually fastened to the driver's visor, sends an electrical signal to a receiver in the garage door, and the signal is encrypted and then decoded by the receiver; only the decoded form of the signal will be recognized by the receiver and so open the door. The jury instructions were, as the reader will see, brief, pretty simple, and relatively free of both legal and technical jargon. Yet in retrospect (they were drafted in March 2011) not as clear as they could have been. I include both the introductory instructions, which would have been given right after the jury was selected and before the actual trial began, and the final instructions, which would have been given at the end of the trial, just before the jury began its deliberations.

Quite apart from neutral experts and lucid instructions, judges can do more than they typically do to try to enhance jurors' understanding, for example by instructing technical witnesses and the lawyers to discuss probability in terms of frequencies (for example, 1 in 100 persons exposed to some contaminant develop asthma) rather than statistical probabilities (a person exposed to some contaminant has a 1 percent chance of developing asthma), because frequencies are more intuitive for most people.[31]

What may save patent adjudication from total futility is a promising experiment by the administrative arm of the federal judiciary—seeking volunteers among district judges to undergo training in patent law and having completed it to handle the bulk of the federal patent cases in their districts.[32] The invitation to specialized training in the most difficult class of federal litigation has been accepted by many of the ablest district judges. They are rising to the challenge of complexity. But their role may remain limited largely to ruling on dispositive motions and managing rather than deciding the trial—a jury will still decide the often very technical issues of infringement and validity in any case in which the relief sought is damages

31. See, for example, Gerd Gigerenzer and Ulrich Hoffrage, "How to Improve Bayesian Reasoning without Instruction: Frequency Formats," 102 *Psychological Review* 684 (1995).

32. "District Courts Selected for Patent Pilot Program," *United States Courts: News Item,* June 7, 2011. www.uscourts.gov/news/newsview/11-06-07/District_Courts_Selected_for_Patent_Pilot_Program.aspx (visited Jan. 21, 2013).

and a party demands a jury.[33] Still, this experiment with a form of judicial specialization alternative to specialized courts (largely a flop in the American legal culture, as I noted in Chapter 3) is promising.[34]

Internet Research by Jurors

Another problem that arises from the complexity of many of the cases that are being tried in federal district courts these days—though more from the proliferation of social media and other online resources—is concern that some jurors are conducting their own online research, as by asking for advice about the case from Facebook "friends" or Googling a party's name, such as the name of the defendant in a criminal trial.[35] They may even "friend" a party to the case. In doing such things they are acting contrary

33. While insisting that courts cannot get around the Seventh Amendment's applicability to jury trials, Lisa S. Meyer, Note, "Taking the 'Complexity' out of Complex Litigation: Preserving the Constitutional Right to a Civil Jury Trial," 28 *Valparaiso University Law Review* 337, 341 (1993), suggests that it might be permissible to require that the jurors in difficult patent cases be technically qualified. This is an attractive suggestion, although implementation would be difficult because persons having the necessary qualifications might either be conflicted out of the case or too busy to take the time off from their job to serve on a jury.

34. For empirical evidence that district judges with more experience in patent cases make fewer errors, see Jay P. Kesan and Gwendolyn G. Ball, "Judicial Experience and the Efficiency and Accuracy of Patent Adjudication: An Empirical Analysis of the Case for a Specialized Patent Trial Court," 24 *Harvard Journal of Law and Technology* 393 (2011).

35. See, for example, Amy J. St. Eve and Michael A. Zuckerman, "Ensuring an Impartial Jury in the Age of Social Media," 11 *Duke Law and Technology Review* 1 (2012); Marcy Zora, Note, "The Real Social Network: How Jurors' Use of Social Media and Smart Phones Affects a Defendant's Sixth Amendment Rights," 2012 *University of Illinois Law Review* 577. Jerry Crimmins, in "New Jury Instructions Look at Social Media," *Chicago Daily Law Bulletin*, Aug. 28, 2012, p. 1, reports that 29 percent of federal judges confiscate jurors' cell phones during jury deliberations. For a recent case in which a new trial was ordered because a juror had conducted Internet research on an issue in the case and the trial judge had failed to investigate the possible effect on the verdict, see *McGee v. City of Chicago*, 2012 WL 4801527 (Ill. App. Oct. 9, 2012).

to the judge's emphatic instructions that they are not to discuss the case even with each other until the trial ends and they go to the jury room to deliberate, and that they must discuss it with no one else, either, until they have rendered their verdict and been discharged, or do their own research on the case. Many jurors find it difficult to understand why such restraints should be placed on them—especially why they shouldn't be able to discuss the case with each other before the end of the trial[36]—and judges are remiss in failing to explain the reason for imposing such restraints. Juror resistance to what they are told has been documented.[37] Judges exaggerate jurors' docility.

"Comprehension [by jurors] declines as factual complexity increases."[38] In complex cases, therefore, which often are poorly explained to jurors by judge, lawyers, and witnesses alike, the impulse to conduct online research is natural. It is not enough simply to tell jurors not to do it; that is treating them like children. They must be given a reason (as my instructions in the *Chamberlain* case failed to do, however). The obvious reason is that they may misunderstand what they find online, or may chance on a biased source without realizing it, or become mired in confusion because of the diversity of the views they encounter, or stumble upon evidence ex-

36. Arizona allows jurors in trials in its courts to discuss the case with each other while they are in the jury room during recesses and also before the case is called in the morning. Transcripts of their discussions suggest that this is a sensible reform; it makes their deliberations fuller and more natural. See Vidmar and Hans, *American Juries*, at 400. On the subject of borrowing from the practices of a different judicial system, I note that juries are found in many legal systems besides the American, and the variance across countries in the rules and procedures governing selection, deliberation, and other dimensions of trial by jury are dizzying. For a comprehensive recent discussion, see Jon Elster, *Securities against Misrule: Juries, Assemblies, Elections*, ch. 2 (2013). But borrowing from the legal systems of foreign countries is a tricky business because of cultural and institutional differences, and I do not discuss possibilities for such borrowing in this book. The federal judiciary's borrowing from a state court system is much less problematic.

37. Tonja Jacobi, "The Law and Economics of the Exclusionary Rule," 87 *Notre Dame Law Review* 585, 621–627 (2011).

38. Reiber and Weinberg, "The Complexity of Complexity," at 963.

cluded from a trial for reasons of sound policy that the jurors are unlikely to be aware of, such as evidence that in a negligence case the defendant, after the accident to the plaintiff, took measures to eliminate the dangerous condition that had caused the accident. Such evidence is excluded from federal trials by Rule 408 of the Federal Rules of Evidence, on the theory that admitting it at a trial of the defendant's negligence would make him reluctant to repair the dangerous condition until the litigation was concluded.

Other Issues

Telling jurors why they can't do their own research is not enough. More is needed to make them feel full participants in the adjudicative process. So the judge should tell them they can ask questions during the trial, directed in the first instance to the judge so that he can decide whether a juror's question is proper and if so who should be asked to try to answer it (and if not why not). And he should explain to them that asking a question in court is a better way of eliciting relevant information than searching online. I have permitted jurors to ask questions in my trials, with no untoward consequences; they ask very few questions, but the questions they do ask are generally helpful. I have always allowed jurors to take notes—when I began as a judge, that was rarely done, though even in the mock trial in *Alice's Adventures in Wonderland* the animal jurors are given slates and pencils with which to take notes during the trial. Taking notes enables jurors to become more actively engaged with the evidence being presented, more attentive, and also more critical.

Other promising improvements in the conduct of jury trials include instructing the jury (that is, explaining to them the law that they are to apply to determine the winner of the case) at the beginning as well as end of the trial (and maybe also at particular junctures during the trial), having the expert witnesses for the opposing parties testify in pairs back to back, and allowing lawyers to make interim statements to the jury before their closing arguments. I don't know whether a federal judge is authorized to allow the interim deliberations permitted by Arizona courts.[39]

39. See note 36 above; also Posner, *Frontiers of Legal Theory*, at 358–359.

The proposed reforms have in common the aim of making jurors more active, better-informed participants in the decision-making process. It's a mistake for judges to condescend to jurors by giving them counterintuitive orders without an explanation: "Don't ask why, just do what I tell you." The goal in managing a jury trial and the pretrial proceedings in a jury case is to make not only the evidence and the law to be applied to the facts intelligible, but to make the structure of the trial and the reasons for its peculiarities (as they would appear to most laypersons) transparent.

A great deal of fact finding is done by judges rather than by jurors, and not only in bench trials, where the judge is the trier of fact. There is concern that the judges aren't always up to the job of finding facts and applying legal rules to them, even when the case is not complex. Cognitive psychologists have found that even educated, intellectually sophisticated people are prone to cognitive errors, such as anchoring, hindsight bias, and excessive reliance on intuition. These are problems at all levels of the judiciary, but the focus of concern has been on trial judges because they make most factual determinations and the appellate judges tend to defer to those determinations.

But no one seems to know what can be done about such problems. I illustrate with an article that begins by positing two contrasting models of judging—formalism and realism—the latter defined incorrectly as "follow[ing] an intuitive process to reach conclusions which they only later rationalize with deliberative reasoning." The authors say that neither model "has proved satisfactory."[40] So formalism is deliberation and realism is intuition, and the authors want judges to become more deliberative because they rely too heavily on intuition and make the mistakes to which intuitive judging is prone.

But the authors have no good ideas (I don't either) about how to make judges more deliberative. They suggest appointing more judges, so that judges would have more time to think about each case. But would they use

40. Chris Guthrie, Jeffrey J. Rachlinksi, and Andrew J. Wistrich, "Blinking on the Bench: How Judges Decide cases," 93 *Cornell Law Review* 1, 2 (2007).

the extra time for deliberation? And if they did, wouldn't that increase delay? I agree with the authors that it is better for judges to rule on objections to the admissibility of evidence before trial than during trial—it gives them more time to think and if necessary research the issue—but not that they should "delay ruling . . . until the issues arise during the trial, and even then after a recess in which the judge has had some time to study the papers and deliberate."[41] Those recesses will slow up the trial terribly! In bench trials, moreover, evidentiary issues tend to be inconsequential. The judge sees the evidence even if he decides to exclude it, and if it is probative it is likely to influence his decision even if it isn't supposed to.

The authors also suggest that judges should write opinions more often, because a written opinion is likely to be a more reflective product than an oral ruling. But most trial judges are too busy to write opinions; they delegate writing to the law clerks even more than appellate judges do. And opinions written by law clerks, I pointed out in Chapter 8, are likely to be briefs in support of the judge's decision, a decision he arrived at without writing anything and that he simply told the law clerk whom he'd assigned to write the opinion.

The authors suggest training and peer review designed to make judges more self-critical, more aware of the cognitive quirks to which we are all subject. Maybe that would have some value. But they surprise me by going on to commend multifactor tests of liability—four- and five- and even seven- and eight-factor tests—as a way of encouraging judges to "proceed methodically, thereby ensuring that they touch all of the deliberative bases . . . A system that forces judges to weigh each of the factors expressly also might help reduce judges' reliance on intuition."[42] On the contrary, since usually no weights are assigned to the factors, what besides intuition can a judge use in applying a multifactor test?

I mentioned delay at the trial court level; the broader problem is inefficient case management. One is struck not only by the often excruciating

41. Id. at 36.
42. Id. at 40–41.

delays in getting a case to trial or judgment but also by the inordinate length of many trials. I attribute that to judges' inability or unwillingness to prune witness and exhibit lists, to compress jury instructions, to set tight deadlines, and to resolve issues of admissibility of testimony and of documents to the extent possible before trial, so that jurors aren't forced to mark time during interminable sidebars at which the lawyers and the judge wrangle over issues of admissibility of evidence.

Undue protraction both of pretrial and of trial proceedings reflects not only poor case management but also the deficiencies of the American legal culture. A drawn-out process with lots of wasted time is often what judges are used to from their careers as trial lawyers, before they became judges, and from the example set for them by older district judges. It is also what lawyers expect and often, as I explained earlier, desire—and deference to their expectations and desires suits the umpireal conception of the judicial role that so many judges internalize.

Another serious problem is the failure of judges to converge on sentencing. There are harsh sentencers (concentrated in the former states of the Confederacy[43] but found elsewhere as well) and lenient sentencers; sentencers who are very hard on drug offenders but soft on white-collar criminals; sentencers who have the reverse propensity; sentencers who emphasize deterrence and others who emphasize retribution or incapacitation. There is also evidence of racial and sexual bias in federal sentencing.[44] The absence of convergence bespeaks a failure of the judiciary, the Sentencing Commission, and the probation service of the Department of Justice to make adequate efforts to formulate, and to educate the judges in, a coherent, evidence-based theory of criminal punishment.[45] But I grant that the

---

43. See Lee Epstein, William M. Landes, and Richard A. Posner, *The Behavior of Federal Judges: A Theoretical and Empirical Study of Rational Choice* 251 (2013) (tab. 5.19).

44. See Todd Sorensen, Supriya Sarnikar, and Ronald L. Oaxaca, "Race and Gender Differences under Federal Sentencing Guidelines," 102 *American Economic Review, Papers and Proceedings Issue* 256 (May 2012).

45. See generally Mary Kreiner Ramirez, "Into the Twilight Zone: Informing Judicial Discretion in Federal Sentencing," 57 *Drake Law Review* 591 (2009).

soft variables in sentencing, which I discussed in Chapter 3, will continue to retard efforts to achieve reasonable sentencing uniformity across judges.

APPENDIX

JURY INSTRUCTIONS IN *CHAMBERLAIN V. LEAR*

INTRODUCTORY INSTRUCTIONS

1.1

This is a case involving two patents, called '544 and '123. They are patents on technology for preventing other people from opening your garage door—in other words, a technology, which happens to be mathematical in character, for encryption. It is like a password, but more complicated. It will be explained at the trial.

I'm going to give you some preliminary instructions to help orient you to the case. I'll give you more detailed instructions later, when the trial is over and you are about to consider what your verdict will be.

Patents are issued by the U.S. Patent and Trademark Office, a federal agency. They are intended to encourage innovation by giving an inventor the right to exclude others from making, using, selling, or offering to sell his patented invention, without his permission, for a period of years. If someone violates that exclusive right—in other words, infringes the patent—the owner of the patent can sue the alleged violator (the infringer) in a federal district court. Even if the defendant did infringe the patent, the patent owner will lose the case if the defendant proves that the patent was invalid, that is, that the Patent and Trademark Office made a mistake in issuing it. Both infringement and validity are issues in this lawsuit, as I'll explain.

The parties to the lawsuit are Chamberlain, Johnson Controls (which the parties call "JCI"), and Lear Corporation. Chamberlain and JCI are the plaintiffs and Lear is the defendant. Chamberlain owns the patents and JCI has an exclusive license (right) to make products based on them. (For most purposes, you won't have to distinguish between Chamberlain and JCI; you can just think of them as "the plaintiffs.") Lear has created a product that is capable of operating the plaintiffs' garage door openers. That is not improper as long as Lear's product doesn't infringe the plaintiff's patents. Chamberlain and JCI contend that Lear has infringed the patents by making, using, selling, or offering to sell the inventions covered by the patents without the plaintiffs' permission. Lear denies that it infringes the patents and also contends that the patents are invalid, in which event infringing them would not be a violation of the plaintiffs' legal rights.

Lear's product is called "Car2U," but for simplicity's sake I will refer to it just as "Lear's product." You may hear about some earlier versions of the product that Lear never introduced. These preproduction versions are not accused of infringing the plaintiffs' patents, but the plaintiffs argue that they are evidence of willfulness.

1.2

The invention protected by a patent is described in the section of the patent labeled "patent claims," which are set forth in separately numbered paragraphs at the end of the patent. When a product (in this case the defendant's product) is accused of infringing a patent, the patent claims must be compared to the product.

To be entitled to patent protection, an invention must be new, useful, and nonobvious. A patent is not new if the invention was already known, or, in patent lingo, was part of the "prior art." I will give you further instructions about what counts as prior art at the end of the case.

1.3

The jury's job is to determine the facts relating to the legal issues. I will tell you what the law is and you'll apply the law to the facts to determine which side wins. Nothing I say during the trial is intended to indicate what I think the facts are or your verdict should be. You're the decision makers; I'm the traffic cop. Although this is a civil case rather than a criminal case, it is very important to the parties. They and I expect you to make a careful, thoughtful, conscientious decision, bearing in mind the importance of the case to the parties. The parties are business firms rather than individuals, but they have legal rights just as individuals do and are entitled to the same consideration that you would give a case between individuals.

1.4

For the plaintiffs to prove infringement of the two patents at issue in this case, they must persuade you that their position is more likely true than false. You don't have to be certain, in order to find infringement, but you have to be convinced that they have a stronger case than the defendant. Concretely, the plaintiffs must prove that every element in each claim contained in the patents is found in the defendant's product, whether as an exact duplicate of the element or as being equivalent to it in the sense that a person of ordinary skill in the relevant technology would have considered the differences between them to be insubstantial. (A person of "ordinary skill" in the technological field to which the patented invention belongs means a person who has the education and experience necessary for a competent understanding of the technology described in the patent; he doesn't have to be a genius.) Any difference is insubstantial if, for each element of the patented claims, a feature of the defendant's product performs substantially the same function and works in substantially the same way to achieve substantially the same result. One factor you may consider in making that determination is whether a person of ordinary skill (as defined above) would have regarded a part of Lear's product to be interchangeable with the element of the claim.

1.5

The plaintiffs contend not only that the defendant infringed their two patents, but that it did so willfully. To prove this, they must prove by "clear and convincing evidence" that it was highly likely that the defendant's product infringed and that the defendant either knew that it was highly likely or should have known.

"Clear and convincing" evidence means evidence that convinces you that it is highly probable that the particular proposition is true. You must decide whether there was simple infringement, under the lower standard of proof that I mentioned earlier, and if you find there was, you should go on to decide whether the infringement was willful.

1.6

The defendant contends that all of the claims that the plaintiffs contend are infringed are invalid. Patents are issued by the U.S. Patent and Trademark Office, so the law presumes they're valid. But a court can invalidate a patent or a particular claim in a patent. To prevail on its claim of invalidity, the defendant must prove invalidity by clear and convincing evidence.

1.7

A patent claim is invalid if the invention claimed is obvious. An invention is obvious if a person who had ordinary (though not necessarily extraordinary) skill in the technology relevant to the invention and who knew all the prior art existing at the time of the invention would have come up with the invention at that time, or in other words would have viewed the invention as obvious.

1.8

The evidence you'll be hearing or reading consists of testimony of witnesses, documents admitted into evidence as exhibits, and any facts that the lawyers agree to or that I may instruct you to accept as being true. The exhibits are in binders, one for each side, which you will be given momentarily.

The parties may present the testimony of a witness by reading from a deposition transcript or by playing a videotape of the witness's deposition testimony. A deposition is the sworn testimony of a witness taken before trial and is entitled to the same consideration as if the witness had appeared in court.

Certain things are not evidence and must not be considered by you:

Statements, arguments, and questions by lawyers.

Objections to questions or exhibits. Lawyers are entitled to object when evidence being offered is inadmissible. If the objection is sustained, ignore the question or exhibit. If the objection is overruled, treat the answer or exhibit like any other.

Testimony that I have excluded or told you to disregard.

Anything you may see or hear outside the courtroom. You're to decide the case solely on the basis of the evidence presented in the courtroom.

Certain exhibits that are called "demonstrative exhibits," such as models, diagrams, graphs, and sketches, may be shown to you but they are not themselves evidence; they're just to help you understand the case better.

In deciding whether any fact has been proved, you should consider all the evidence relating to the question regardless of which side introduced it. You should also decide how much of a witness's testimony to accept or reject.

1.9

A few words about your conduct as jurors.

You are not to discuss the case among yourselves until at the end of the case you go to the jury room to deliberate and to decide on your verdict.

You're not to talk to anyone (including members of your family, and friends) or make any public or online comments about this case until the trial has ended and you have been discharged as jurors.

You're not to read or listen to anything bearing on this case in any way, including news stories, radio or television reports, or the internet. You're not to do any research online or conduct any other type of investigation of the case, the lawyers, the witnesses, or the companies that are the parties. If anyone tries to talk to you about the case, bring that to my attention promptly.

Don't form an opinion until all the evidence is in.

You've been given pads on which to make notes if you want, but leave the pads in the jury room at the end of each day, until you begin your deliberations with the other jurors, and don't be unduly influenced by the notes of other jurors, because they may not be accurate.

If you want to ask a question of a witness, raise your hand and I'll ask you to ask me the question first, so that I can make sure that it's in a form that's proper for the witness to answer.

1.10

The trial will now begin. Each side will make an opening statement. That is not evidence, but just a sketch of what the party intends to prove. Next each side will question its witnesses, and the lawyers for the other side will cross-examine them, to try to bring out errors in their testimony. After all the witnesses have testified, the lawyers will present closing arguments. I will then give you final instructions, setting forth the law in somewhat greater detail than in these preliminary instructions, and you'll then go to the jury room with a copy of the instructions, your notes, and your evidence binders, to deliberate on your verdict.

FINAL INSTRUCTIONS

2.1

Members of the jury, you've seen and heard all the evidence and arguments of the lawyers. Now it's your turn. You'll decide, on the basis of the evidence you've heard and read, what the facts are that relate to how the case should be decided, and you'll apply the law that I explain to you in these instructions to the facts. You must follow my legal instructions even if you disagree with them, because they state the law, and you must apply the law, just like a judge.

Perform these duties fairly and impartially.

Nothing I say now, and nothing I said during the trial, are meant to indicate what I think the facts are or your verdict should be.

2.2

The evidence consists of the testimony of the witnesses, the exhibits admitted in evidence, and stipulations, which are agreements between both sides that certain facts are true. You should give the same consideration to testimony presented to you by video or by reading from deposition transcripts as you would if the witnesses had come to court and testified live.

2.3

These things are not evidence:

Testimony or exhibits that I ordered stricken.

Anything you saw or heard outside this courtroom.

Questions to witnesses, and objections to questions by lawyers.

The lawyers' opening statements and closing arguments

Any notes you took during the trial; they are just to help you remember things.

2.4

In determining whether any fact has been proved, you should consider all of the evidence relating to the question regardless of which side introduced it.

2.5

You must decide whether the testimony of each of the witnesses is truthful and accurate, in part, in whole, or not at all, and how much weight, if any, to give the testimony in resolving a factual issue. You shouldn't just count noses: the fact that one side presents more witnesses, testimony, or other evidence on an issue than the other side doesn't mean that the first side is right.

2.6

You have heard some opinions from witnesses who are called "expert witnesses" because they have specialized knowledge. You should weigh this testimony in the same way that you weigh the testimony of any other witness. You are not required to accept an expert's opinion, but you must give an expert's testimony the weight you think it deserves, considering the reasons the witness gave for the opinion, the witness's qualifications, and the other evidence, including other expert evidence, in the case.

2.7

The issues you have to decide are (1) whether the plaintiffs have proved by a preponderance of the evidence that Lear infringed claims 1, 2, and 4 of the '544 patent and claim 1 of the '123 patent and (2) whether Lear has proved by clear and convincing evidence that claims 1, 2, and 4 of the '544 patent and claim 1 of the '123 patent are obvious and therefore invalid.

A few terms in the patents don't have their everyday meaning, but instead a special meaning, as follows: "binary code" means a binary number and "binary signal" means an electrical transmission of a binary number; "trinary code" means a trinary number and "trinary signal" means an electrical transmission of a trinary number. Remember that binary numbers are quantities represented in the base-2 system, and trinary numbers are quantities represented in the base-3 system. You heard about these systems, and their relevance to the case, when you saw the video tutorial and heard testimony, during the trial, but I want to give you a brief refresher course, with examples that you can go over in your deliberations.

A binary number is a number in base 2; a trinary number in base 3. A base is just a number used as a building block for expressing numerical quantities. Most of our counting is in base 10. Base 10 denotes the base number 10. A number can be expressed as a sum of base numbers. Here is how to express 1,254 as a sum of numbers based on 10:

$$1,000 = 1 \times 10^3 \text{ (a cube)}$$
$$200 = 2 \times 10^2 \text{ (a square)}$$
$$50 = 5 \times 10^1 \text{ (just plain 10)}$$
$$4 = 4 \times 10^0 \text{ (any number to the power of 0 equals 1)}$$

——

Hence 1,254

Other bases can be used to express the quantity 1,254. This results in the same quantity being expressed by a different series of numbers.

So for base 2:
$$1,024 = 1 \times 2^{10}$$
$$0 = 0 \times 2^9$$
$$0 = 0 \times 2^8$$
$$128 = 1 \times 2^7$$
$$64 = 1 \times 2^6$$
$$32 = 1 \times 2^5$$
$$0 = 0 \times 2^4$$
$$0 = 0 \times 2^3$$
$$4 = 1 \times 2^2$$

$$2 = 1 \times 2^1$$
$$0 = 0 \times 2^0$$

$$1{,}254 = 10011100110$$

And now for base 3:

$$729 = 1 \times 3^6$$
$$486 = 2 \times 3^5$$
$$0 = 0 \times 3^4$$
$$27 = 1 \times 3^3$$
$$9 = 1 \times 3^2$$
$$3 = 1 \times 3^1$$
$$0 = 0 \times 3^0$$

$$1{,}254 = 1201110$$

Notice therefore that these are three different ways—three different sets of numbers—for expressing the *identical* quantity, and you must know what base system is being used in order to know what quantity is being expressed.

Base 10	Base 2	Base 3
1,254	10011100110	1201110

The reason that encryption devices for the garage-door openers use base-2 or base-3 systems rather than the more familiar, everyday base-10 is that base 2 uses only two digits (numbers)—0 and 1—and base 3 uses only three digits—0, 1, and 2—whereas the base-10 system uses ten digits (0, 1, 2, 3, 4, 5, 6, 7, 8, 9). It is easier for the transmitter in the garage-door opener to signal the receiver in the garage door with just two or three separate digits than with ten; for example, with only two digits, the transmitter could transmit a series of long (1) and short (2) electrical signals.

2.8

A product infringes a patent if every element in a claim is found in Lear's product. (Remember that the preproduction versions of Lear's product are not alleged to infringe the plaintiffs' patents; their only relevance is as possible evidence of willfulness.)

The claims in dispute are claims 1, 2, and 4 of the '544 patent and claim 1 of the '123 patent.

To find infringement of claim 1 of the '544 patent, you must find that Lear's product contains: a "binary code generator responsive to the enabling apparatus for generating a variable binary code, said variable code being different for each enabling by the enabling device," and also a "trinary code generator for generating a three-valued or trinary code responsive to the variable binary code."

The other elements in claim 1 are not in dispute, so you don't have to worry about them.

Claims 2 and 4 of the '544 patent:

Lear's product can't infringe claims 2 and 4 in the '544 patent if it doesn't infringe claim 1. If, therefore, you find that Lear's product does not infringe claim 1, you shouldn't consider claims 2 and 4.

To find infringement of claim 2 of the '544 patent, you must find that Lear's product infringes claim 1 and also that it contains: an "apparatus for receiving said variable binary signal and producing a mirrored binary signal, said mirrored binary signal being supplied to said trinary code generator for generating the trinary signal from the variable binary signal."

To find infringement of claim 4 of the '544 patent, you must find that Lear's product infringes claims 1 and 3 and that it also contains "a trinary interleaved fixed and rolling code signal."

Claim 1 of the '123 patent:

To find infringement of claim 1 of the '123 patent, you must find that Lear's product contains "a source of a sequence of binary codes, successive binary codes in the sequence being different from predetermined preceding codes in the sequence" and also a "trinary code generator for converting said sequence of binary codes to a sequence of trinary codes."

2.9

You don't have to be absolutely certain in order to find infringement, but you have to be convinced that the plaintiffs have a stronger case for infringement than Lear has for noninfringement. The plaintiffs must prove that every element in the claim that you are considering is found in Lear's product. This can be proved in either of two ways. An element of a claim is found in Lear's product if the element in its product is exactly the same as it is in the claim in the plaintiffs' patent, or alternatively if the element in Lear's product is equivalent to an element in the claim.

So what exactly is "equivalence"? An element in the product that is alleged to infringe the plaintiffs' patent is equivalent to an element in the patent if the differences between the two would be thought insubstantial by a person of "ordinary skill" in the field of knowledge relating to the invention. (A person of "ordinary skill" in the technological field to which the patented invention belongs just means a person who has the education and experience necessary for a competent understanding of the technology described in the patent; he doesn't have to be a genius.) To determine whether the differences are insubstantial or substantial, you should consider whether the element in question performs substantially the same function, in substantially the same way, to achieve substantially the same result, as an element of the claim. If so, the elements are equivalent.

The fact that Lear has its own patent does not give it a right to infringe someone else's patent. The government's decision to issue Lear the patent is relevant, though not conclusive, evidence that the Lear patent is not the equivalent of a previously patented invention, such as the inventions covered by the plaintiffs' patents. But Lear's patent is irrelevant to the issue of equivalence unless you find that Lear actually practices its patented invention.

2.10

The plaintiffs contend not only that Lear infringed their two patents, but that it did so willfully. You are to consider willful infringement only if you have found that Lear infringed. To prove willfulness, the plaintiffs must prove by "clear and convincing evidence" both that it was highly likely that Lear's product infringed and that Lear either knew that it was highly likely or should have known that.

"Clear and convincing" evidence is evidence that makes it highly probable that a particular proposition is true. You must decide whether there was simple infringement, under the lower standard of proof that I mentioned earlier ("preponderance of the evidence"—that is, more likely than not, even if just a little more likely than not), and if you find there was, you should go on to decide whether the infringement was willful.

2.11

Even if you find that there was infringement, that isn't the end of the case. Lear contends that claims 1, 2, and 4 of the '544 patent and claim 1 of the '123 patent are invalid because they were obvious before the patents were issued. If Lear proves this contention, it wins the case even if it infringed the plaintiffs' patents. But to prove obviousness and hence invalidity, Lear must prove by clear and convincing evidence that a person of ordinary skill as defined earlier, and who knew all the "prior art" existing when the invention was made, would have invented the patented product at that time, or in other words would have viewed the invention as obvious. "Prior art" means all the information that is publicly known, used by others, or available on the date of the invention to a person of ordinary skill. For example, other patents, inventions, products, articles, books, and scientific literature are all prior art. To evaluate obviousness, you should assume that the person of ordinary skill knows all the "prior art" existing when the invention was made. You should then determine what he would have thought obvious. You must not use hindsight; that is, you must not consider what is known now, including what could be learned from the plaintiffs' patents.

In making your decision regarding obviousness, you should consider the scope and content of the prior art and also any differences between the prior art and the invention in the patent claim. These factors (scope and content of the prior art and any differences between the prior art and the invention in the patent claim) are the primary factors that you should consider in deciding the question of obviousness, but you should also consider the following secondary factors, which may indicate that the plaintiffs' invention was not obvious: whether other inventors failed in attempting to make the invention in the patent claim; or copied the invention; or praised it; or sought or obtained a license to the patent from the patent holder. None of these factors has to be present for you to conclude that the plaintiffs' invention was not obvious. And it is for you to decide how much weight to give each factor that you find is present. But remember that these are secondary factors, and you must not give them as much weight as the primary factors listed above.

Two more points: (1) Because most inventions are built on prior knowledge, the fact that each element of a claim is found in prior art is not enough, by itself, to prove obviousness. (2) In determining whether Lear has proved obviousness, you may combine multiple items of prior art, if a person of ordinary skill would have thought it obvious to combine them.

2.12

When you go to the jury room for your deliberations, first select a presiding juror to be the foreperson. He or she will preside over your deliberations and will be your representative here in court.

Forms of verdict have been prepared for you. Take them to the jury room, and when you have reached unanimous agreement on the verdict, your presiding juror will fill in and date the appropriate form, and all of you will sign it.

2.13

The verdict must represent the considered judgment of each juror and must be unanimous, whether the verdict is in favor of the plaintiffs or the defendant, or for the plaintiffs on some issues and the defendant on others. You should make every reasonable effort to reach a unanimous verdict and in doing so you should consult with one another, express your own views, and listen to the opinions of your fellow jurors. Discuss your differences with an open mind. Do not hesitate to reexamine your own views, and to change your opinion if you come to believe it is wrong. But you should not surrender your honest beliefs about the weight or effect of evidence solely because of the opinions of other jurors or for the purpose of returning a unanimous verdict.

2.14

If it becomes necessary during your deliberations to communicate with me, you may send a note by a court security officer, signed by your foreperson or by one or more members of the jury. No member of the jury should ever attempt to communicate with me by any other means. If you have trouble reaching a unanimous verdict, you're not to tell me or anyone else which side is favored by more jurors.

❦ 10 ❧

WHAT CAN BE DONE,
MODESTLY?

As a general matter, lawyers and science don't mix.

Peter Lee

The United States is not about to discard the adversary system or the appointment of federal judges by politicians. I have no interest in proposing Utopian solutions to the problem of increasing complexity that confronts and baffles the federal judiciary. But there are some feasible incremental measures that would contribute to solving the problem, though how much they would contribute is another question. Some of these measures I've discussed in earlier chapters, such as a greater dose of legal realism in the appellate process and a greater use of court-appointed expert witnesses. Others are the subject of this chapter.

Staffing

I begin with some suggestions relating to the staffing of the federal courts. One suggestion is that the public and private bodies involved in the appointment of federal judges or the screening of judicial aspirants deem the possession of some modest technical competence, or at least interest, to be a plus factor in deciding whether to appoint or report favorably on the aspirant. It's ridiculous in this day and age for a would-be federal judge to have to confess to having a "math block." Anyone intelligent enough to be a competent federal judge is capable of understanding a good deal of math and science (including technical versions of social sciences such as economics and sociology), though of course not enough to contribute to the advance of knowledge in these fields.

The obstacle is the appointment of federal judges by politicians, who are unlikely to be technically sophisticated themselves and who in any event are buffeted by interest groups, lobbyists, and donors—and how many politicians, interest groups, lobbyists, or donors are interested in the competence of judges to cope with technological or otherwise complex issues? So I verge on the Utopian in suggesting that greater weight be given to the technical sophistication of candidates for federal judgeships.

A more realistic possibility for reform concerns the selection of law clerks, because they are appointed by the judges. Judging, especially by federal judges, for whom there is no mandatory retirement age, is the archetypal geriatric profession. Most sitting judges and Justices encountered math and science in high school and college in an era far less technologically complex than today (and think what tomorrow may bring). When hiring law clerks educated in the modern era of rapid technological change, judges, if they would overcome their own generational handicap, should be looking to hire every year one or two applicants who have a good background in some technical field that bears on law. That has become my practice in recent years. It doesn't matter critically which technical field the clerk is proficient in; a person proficient in one such field will usually find it easy to grasp and explain to his or her judge the essential features of another so far as it relates to cases before the judge. My court is beginning to experiment with hiring for its staff attorney office (recall that staff attorneys are law clerks hired by the court rather than by individual judges) some young lawyers who have solid technical backgrounds and who can therefore be resources for the judges to draw on if their own law clerks lack the requisite background. In addition the American Association for the Advancement of Science is seeking funding for a "judicial fellow" program that would provide scientifically trained advisers to federal courts, at no cost to the judiciary.[1] That's a great idea.

Initial Judicial Training

A major implication of the challenge of growing complexity, and the emphasis of this chapter, is that federal judges at all levels need more training,[2] both initial and continuing.

Federal judges receive little of either—and especially little initial train-

---

1. The program would be modeled on the AAAS's existing programs of providing scientific advisers to Congress and the executive branch. See "AAAS Science & Technology Policy Fellowships," http://fellowships.aaas.org/ (visited Aug. 30, 2012).

2. For a useful survey of judicial training the world over, see Paul M. Li, "How Our Judicial Schools Compare to the Rest of the World," 34 *Judges' Journal* 17 (1995). A comprehensive survey of the science training programs for American judges, both state and federal, that were offered between 1992 and 2000 can be found in Mara L. Merlino et al., "Science Education Programs for the State and Federal Judiciary at Year 2001" (Grant Sawyer Center for Justice Studies, University of Nevada, May 2001), www.unr.edu/justicestudies/JudicialSciencePrograms.pdf (visited May 29, 2012). A notable example of an ambitious current program of education in science for judges, which is financed mainly by the Department of Justice, is ASTAR (Advanced Science & Technology Adjudication Resource Center), www.astarcourts.net/index. html (visited May 29, 2012), discussed in Thomas J. Moyer and Stephen P. Anway, "Biotechnology and the Bar: A Response to the Growing Divide between Science and the Legal Environment," 22 *Berkeley Technology Law Journal* 671, 726–730 (2007). ASTAR offers standardized training to judges around the nation to handle the increasing volume of complex cases on court dockets.

The vast majority of judges are state rather than federal, and there are a large number of training programs (of course not limited to science) for state judges. See Catharine M. White and Maureen E. Conner, "Issues and Trends in Judicial Branch Education: 2005" (Judicial Education Reference Information and Technical Transfer Project, 2005), http://jeritt.msu.edu/documents/IssuesandTrends_PDF.pdf (visited May 19, 2012). I do not discuss those programs.

ing. As the education director of the Federal Judicial Center (the research and training arm of the federal judiciary[3]) explains,

> New district judges attend a five day orientation program within their first few months on the bench (Phase I) and another five day program (Phase II) later in their first year on the bench. The Phase I Orientation is held in a city located near a federal prison; the Phase II Orientation is held at the Center in Washington. New district judges are also invited to attend a separate two-day hands-on training program (taught by district judge faculty) on how to use technology to manage their case loads and work more efficiently. New circuit judges who have not previously been on the federal bench are invited to attend the Phase I Orientation for new district judges, and all new circuit judges are invited to attend a two-day orientation program later in their first year on the bench. All of these orientation programs place considerable emphasis on case and chambers management, as well as judicial ethics and demeanor and the role of the judge—in an effort to bridge the largest gap in most new judges' knowledge and skills, that is, the gap between being a lawyer and being a judge.[4]

Owing to a perennial shortage of district judges, attributable in part to the glacial pace of the nomination and confirmation processes, judges cannot spare much time for being trained, while the Federal Judicial Center has never had adequate resources for training and has seen its budget cut in recent years and anticipates further cuts. So one day you're a lawyer and the next day you're a judge and it's natural to think that not much has changed—you were a player, now you're the referee, but it's the same

3. See "The Federal Judicial Center: Education and Research for the U.S. Federal Courts," www.fjc.gov/public/pdf.nsf/lookup/FJCEdRes.pdf/$file/FJCEdRes.pdf (visited May 29, 2012).

4. Email of May 29, 2012, from Bruce M. Clarke. For a brief summary of other continuing education programs for federal judges, some sponsored by the Federal Judicial Center, see Mary Krein Ramirez, "Into the Twilight Zone: Informing Judicial Discretion in Federal Sentencing," 57 *Drake Law Review* 591, 617–621 (2009).

game. Not quite. A good judge is impartial, of course, but he's a product manager rather than just a referee, trying to produce a good product (good decisions) with inputs from lawyers and staff. And that requires, besides the impartiality of a referee, an aggressive approach at both the trial and appellate levels.

The limited character of judges' initial training contributes both to the passivity displayed by many judges and to their frequent lack of good management skills. Poor management is a major factor in the frequent long delays between the oral argument of an appeal and the issuance of the opinion deciding the appeal, and at the district court level in long delays in bringing litigation to conclusion.

Our managerial deficiencies are exacerbated by the fact that chief district judges and chief circuit judges are appointed on the basis solely of seniority. No management experience or aptitude is required—just being the senior judge in active service when the chief judge's job becomes vacant. On balance this musical-chairs system of appointment may well be a good thing because it eliminates politicking and reduces rivalry among the judges. But random appointment of managers obviously has a downside. It is fortunate that each court of appeals has a "circuit executive"—a career judicial civil servant who assists the chief judge and provides continuity across successive chiefs. But that can be only a partial solution to the problem of chief judges who lack managerial aptitude. The other judges, moreover, need some managerial skills to manage their own staffs competently, small as those staffs are.

The Federal Judicial Center should be given the resources it needs to enable it to do more than it can do at present to provide management training to federal judges and to improve their understanding of the technological and other complexities that bear on their work. (The need to enlarge the Center's role is a theme of this chapter.) The Center has published some excellent material on scientific evidence[5] and on court-appointed experts (which I cited in the last chapter, while noting that the Center's ambitious

5. See, in particular, Federal Judicial Center and National Research Council of the National Academies, *Reference Manual on Scientific Evidence* (3d ed. 2011).

study on experts is by now rather dated). But the body of relevant technical material is vast and the Center's resources, as I have said, are severely limited. For example, although there is a rich social scientific literature on the jury, of the seventeen papers and books and videos about the jury that the Center has issued in the last forty-two years I find only one, by Michael Saks, that uses the social science of small-group decision making to study juries. The Center would render a great service to judges by searching the academic literature continuously for technical material directly relevant to the work of federal judges (for example, studies of cognitive quirks in fact finding) and providing intelligible summaries of the best and most accessible (comprehensible, compact, practical) such material to the judges.

It would be good too if the Center had resources to train those district judges who, as I mentioned in the last chapter, have volunteered to try more than a random allotment of patent cases.

Law schools also have a role to play in judicial education. Before becoming a federal court of appeals judge at the end of 1981, I had been a full-time law professor for thirteen years, so it is natural for me to want to consider how the law schools might contribute to the alleviation of the problems that have preoccupied me in the preceding chapters.

Continuing Judicial Education

I do not favor judicial continuing education, whether by law schools or by the Federal Judicial Center, that takes the form of giving judges short courses in specific technical areas, such as economics or statistical analysis.[6]

6. See, for example, Mason Judicial Education Program 2012 Fall Programs, www.masonlec.org/wp-content/uploads/2012/05/2012-programs_webfull-1.pdf (visited July 8, 2012). Programs range from three-day symposia on civil justice and on business law and a four-day symposium on antitrust law and economics to two one-week economics institutes designed to give "a solid grounding in economics, finance and statistics" plus (second week) "in-depth coverage of advanced topics such as accounting, finance, environmental economics, scientific methodology, entrepreneurship, and the financial crises and its [sic] aftermath." As described, the program may be trying to cover too much in too short a time.

Middle-aged and elderly people don't learn technical fields in two-week courses, let alone in two- or three-day ones. What judges need and can realistically be taught in small bites is, for example, not how modern statistical analysis can be used to generate probative evidence but how it can be screened for accuracy and explained to a jury. Judges need instruction not *in* statistics, or *in* medical technology, etc., but in *how* statistics and in *how* medical technology, etc., can properly be used in a litigation. That's knowledge that they need in order to be able to shape and decide cases sensibly and that they should be able to absorb in training sessions.

If the shortage of federal judges could be overcome (as should be possible—there are plenty of qualified candidates for a judiciary of fewer than a thousand judges in a legal profession that has a million members), the judiciary could borrow a leaf from the military and alternate judicial work with substantial training interludes—interludes not of two days or two weeks but of six months. But at present that's a pipe dream.

There is no dearth of competent reference works on the use of scientific insights and methods in law.[7] The problem is the willingness and ability of judges to make the often considerable effort required to understand them. Most of the reference works are not very reader-friendly[8] if the reader is a judge rather than a specialist lawyer. Because the federal judiciary is not specialized (with some exceptions, of which the most pertinent to this book is the U.S. Court of Appeals for the Federal Circuit), judges' encounters with technical issues are scattered across a vast array of techni-

7. Besides the Federal Judicial Center and National Research Council of the National Academies' very long and comprehensive *Reference Manual on Scientific Evidence,* there is a massive multivolume work on scientific evidence for lawyers and judges: David L. Faigman et al., *Modern Scientific Evidence: The Law and Science of Expert Testimony* (2011).

8. A notable exception, however, is *Statistical Science in the Courtroom* (Joseph L. Gastwirth ed. 2000). There are doubtless others but I have not tried to take a census of science reference works for lawyers. My recently coauthored book with Lee Epstein and William M. Landes, *The Behavior of Federal Judges: A Theoretical and Empirical Study of Rational Choice* (2013), endeavors, beginning in its Technical Introduction, id. at 17, to present statistical analysis in a way intelligible to judges and lawyers who have no background in the subject.

cal fields. A judge can devote only a limited amount of time to learning a particular technical field because of the breadth of the federal docket; and with infrequent application of newly acquired knowledge of a particular field he will quickly lose it. The technical education that the judge needs is education in dealing with cases involving technical issues that he can't realistically be expected to be knowledgeable about.

The problem of technical training is less acute in the case of judges of specialized courts. Such courts are a rarity in the federal system, but administrative agencies that engage in adjudication,[9] such as the Social Security Administration, provide a close parallel. And, sure enough, the Social Security Administration provides a degree of technical training of its administrative law judges that has no parallel in the Article III courts. Newly hired administrative law judges are required to participate in a training program conducted in three phases.[10] Phase one consists of on-the-job and video-on-demand training, with many of the videos geared toward medical information. But despite the mandatory character of this as of the other phases of the training, some administrative law judges have reported that they didn't participate in this phase, and some who did failed to complete it because they didn't know about the videos.

Phase two involves four weeks of classroom instruction at the National Training Center for the Office of Disability Adjudication and Review. The instruction covers social security statutes, regulations, and hearing procedures but also medical terminology, and there is a series of ninety-minute lectures on various medical conditions. All incoming administrative law judges receive the same classroom training regardless of prior experience, leading some with no relevant prior experience to feel lost and others, who do have such experience (roughly a half), to question whether they were learning anything new.

9. Thirty federal administrative agencies employ administrative law judges. See David E. Lewis and Jennifer L. Selin, *Sourcebook of United States Executive Agencies* 130–131 (2012) (tab. 19).

10. See Office of the Inspector General, "Audit Report: Training of New Administrative Law Judges at the Office of Disability Adjudication and Review" 2 (2011), http://oig.ssa.gov/sites/default/files/audit/full/pdf/A-12-11-11126.pdf (visited Dec. 23, 2012). My discussion of the training program is based on this report.

The third phase is a "mentoring program" that is supposed to last for about six months. The mentors, experienced administrative law judges, provide the neophytes with guidance on how to meet their expected quota of five hundred to seven hundred decisions per year.

The problematics of technical training of generalist judges are illustrated by an experimental project of the Federal Judicial Center to create (I quote from the abstract of an article introducing just one phase of the project) "prototype materials for a software product designed to teach statistics to judges with legal examples."[11] The project was overly ambitious. It presented (again I'm quoting from the abstract) "Fisher's exact, chi-squared, and bivariate and multivariate logistic regression analyses" along with "odds ratios, expected values, and *p*-values." It would have taken months to teach a judge enough to grasp the statistical concepts underlying the article well enough to understand its statistical analysis. Judges can't spare those months from their job given the judge shortage I've mentioned, but even if they could, unless somehow their docket were crowded with cases in which parties presented statistical analyses they would forget before their next such case what they had learned. The rudiments of modern statistical analysis can be presented more simply than the article attempts,[12] and rudiments are all that can realistically be imparted to most judges in the way of technical knowledge. The Federal Judicial Center has wisely abandoned the "software prototypes" project.

The Widening Gap between Academia and the Judiciary

The United States is unusual in the porousness of the membranes that separate the different branches of the legal profession. The judiciary both federal and state is a lateral-entry institution rather than a conventional civil service; and unlike the British lateral-entry judiciary (which however is

11. Robert Timothy Reagan, "Federal Judicial Center Statistical Examples Software Prototype: Age Discrimination Example," 42 *Jurimetrics* 281 (2002), with comments by eleven experts on statistical analysis and the use of such analysis in law. Id. at 297–372.

12. As in the Technical Introduction in Epstein et al., *The Behavior of Federal Judges.*

loosening up and becoming more like ours), in which the judges are drawn from a narrow, homogeneous slice of the legal profession—namely, senior barristers—American judges are drawn from all branches of the profession, including the academic. Among appellate judges who came to the bench from academia are Oliver Wendell Holmes (although he had joined the Harvard Law School faculty only months before being appointed to the Supreme Judicial Court of Massachusetts, he had been doing academic writing for many years), Harlan Fiske Stone, William O. Douglas, Felix Frankfurter, Wiley Rutledge, Antonin Scalia, Ruth Bader Ginsburg, Stephen Breyer, and Elena Kagan (U.S. Supreme Court); Calvert Magruder, Charles Clark, Joseph Sneed, Harry Edwards, Robert Bork, Ralph Winter, Frank Easterbrook, Stephen Williams, J. Harvie Wilkinson III, John Noonan, Douglas Ginsburg, S. Jay Plager, Kenneth Ripple, Guido Calabresi, Michael McConnell, William Fletcher, and Diane Wood (U.S. courts of appeals); and Roger Traynor, Hans Linde, Benjamin Kaplan, Robert Braucher, Ellen Peters, Charles Fried, and Goodwin Liu (state supreme courts). All these are appellate judges, but a number of distinguished federal district judges have been appointed from the academy as well, such as Jack Weinstein, Robert Keeton, and Louis Pollak. And these lists, which I've compiled without research, are not exhaustive.

One might think that with such a tradition of academics becoming judges, the gap between the academy and the judiciary would be small— and narrowing, because the trend in the federal courts of appeals and the Supreme Court has been toward increasing recruitment from academia; four Justices are former full-time law professors (Scalia, Ginsburg, Breyer, and Kagan), which is unprecedented. Actually the gap is widening. The reason is increased specialization. Suppose there are two adjacent fields, neither highly specialized. It would be easy enough to be conversant with both—even proficient in both—and draw from both no matter which of the two fields one happened to be in. And that was once the case with academic law and judging. I mentioned that Holmes had done academic writing for many years before joining a law faculty. (His most important academic work—*The Common Law* (1881)—preceded his academic appointment.) He continued to do important academic writing after becoming a judge (notably the famous article "The Path of the Law"[13]). Brandeis, never a professor, wrote one of the all-time most important law review articles when he was in practice ("The Right of Privacy,"[14] nominally co-authored with Samuel Warren—but Brandeis wrote it all). Cardozo, also never an academic (in fact he left law school after two years, without graduating), wrote *The Nature of the Judicial Process* (1921)—a much-celebrated book, of academic quality—and other books and articles as well. Learned Hand, and, above all other federal court of appeals judges Henry Friendly, neither of whom had ever taught, wrote influential books and articles.[15] This tradition of influential scholarship by judges who had not been law professors has waned.

Not only did judges who had not been academics once write influential legal scholarship, but leading law professors produced down-to-earth scholarship—books and articles, legal treatises, restatements of the law and model codes, that influenced American common law, and books and articles that shaped an understanding of the overall judicial process. In the last category I place the challenges to legal formalism mounted by the legal realists (though largely echoing Holmes and Cardozo), by the legal-process school of Hart and Sacks, and by economic analysis of law, although a later academic effort, by the critical legal studies movement, to influence judicial decision making fizzled.

Law professors continue to write about the judicial process, of course, and in fact the volume of academic writings on law has grown more or less in proportion to the increase in the amount and complexity of American law and in the size of the profession. But with the exception of economic analysis of law, the current academic literature—at least the literature that emanates from the elite law schools—has less influence on judges than the older literature had on the judges of its era.

13. O. W. Holmes, "The Path of the Law," 10 *Harvard Law Review* 457 (1897).

14. Samuel D. Warren and Louis D. Brandeis, "The Right to Privacy," 4 *Harvard Law Review* 193 (1890).

15. See, for example, Learned Hand, *The Bill of Rights* (1958); Henry J. Friendly, *Benchmarks* (1967); Friendly, *Federal Jurisdiction: A General View* (1973).

It may help the reader to see this if I divide legal scholarship into five types. The first is traditional doctrinal scholarship, typified by the treatises and the restatements. They continue to be produced in quantity by law professors. But this form of legal scholarship has tended to migrate to the less prestigious law schools. It no longer engages the interest of many academics at the elite schools, as it once did, even though those schools produce a high fraction of federal judges and an even higher fraction of their law clerks.[16] The turning away from the production of such scholarship is also a turning away from the teaching of legal doctrine. Though it still dominates legal teaching, the tendency in elite law schools is to subordinate emphasis on doctrine to emphasis on economic, philosophical, and other nondoctrinal perspectives on law, including perspectives supplied by jurisprudence and by constitutional theory. This tendency is found, though to a lesser extent, in law schools generally, not just the elite ones.

The second type of legal scholarship consists of the nondoctrinal scholarship that draws on the social sciences. Only economic analysis of law has obtained a secure footing in legal practice and in judging, yet though applicable and applied to many fields of law much of the current scholarship is remote from the practical interests that engage judges and practitioners.

The third type of legal scholarship I'll call "legal theory." It deals with abstract issues involving the nature of law and justice, and the role of judges particularly in interpreting the Constitution. One might think of it as jurisprudence crossed with politics. It engages the attention of many very able academics. Yet though it addresses issues that are important to judges, especially appellate judges and above all Supreme Court Justices, it has little impact on the judicial process. This is partly because the literature is too abstract, borrowing heavily from philosophy and social theory, and partly because both it *and* adjudication at the highest levels are strongly political and judges are unlikely to take their political cues from professors.

16. Some 80 percent of Supreme Court law clerks in the 2000 through 2010 terms were graduates of the eight top-ranked law schools. Computed from Brian Leiter, Law School Supreme Court Clerkship Placement, www.leiterrankings.com/new/2010_SCClerkshipPlacement.shtml (visited Jan. 12, 2013).

Think back to the books by Amar and by Scalia and Garner on interpretation. Amar is a professor; Scalia and Garner are not professors though Scalia once was. I wager that very few judges will read Amar's book, and that very few academics will take the Scalia-Garner book seriously. Amar's book will strike judges as unprofessional, while the Scalia-Garner book will strike academics as unprofessional.

The fourth type of legal scholarship is empirical: the collection and analysis of data about the legal system and about activities (crimes, prosecution, accidents, innovation, politics, etc.) that give rise to legal disputes. This type of legal scholarship is the least developed, least accessible, and least prestigious and rewarded field of legal scholarship that relates to the modern federal judiciary, though potentially the most important.

Last is the scholarship published in law and technology journals. There are a number of such journals—in fact thirty-seven in English—though only four are heavily cited: *Michigan Telecommunications and Technology Law Review, Harvard Journal of Law and Technology, Santa Clara Computer and High Technology Law Journal,* and *Berkeley Technology Law Journal.* I have dipped into them and discovered that they focus very heavily on patent law, to a lesser extent on copyright law, but only to a small extent on other fields of what might be called law and technology. They are addressed to specialists, they are valuable resources for research, but they are not congenial reading matter to any but a very small number of judges, as they more often assume knowledge of the relevant technology than try to explain it. I wonder how many judges or law clerks are familiar with any of these journals.

Rather desperately needed, to repeat an earlier suggestion, is an impartial body—again the Federal Judicial Center is the obvious candidate—that would screen for difficulty the voluminous book and journal literature on the sciences and technologies relevant to law and advise judges on a current basis of those works that judges would find brief, pertinent, and accessible.

Inaccessibility by judges is a serious problem with respect not only to purely technical materials but also to the interdisciplinary legal scholarship—found for example in the law and technology and law and economics journals—that ought to be informing judicial practices. The rebarbative qualities of this scholarship are the result of increased specialization. If there is one law professor, he has to know something about all fields of law; and American judges, especially federal judges (because the diversity of citizenship and habeas corpus jurisdictions bring a great deal of state law before federal judges) are approximately in that position. If there are four thousand law professors, there can be (at a guess) an average of one hundred to two hundred professors in each field. At that point, with scholars crowding into every field, each field becomes divided into subfields, placing generalists at a double disadvantage: they do not have time to keep up with so much scholarly writing, and specialists develop a specialized vocabulary (much as family members communicate with each other in a cryptic private language) that creates a barrier to understanding by non-specialists. And as subfields expand, the scholars in each one find they have audience enough among their fellow specialists and so feel no need to try to reach a wider audience, an effort that would require them to retool their vocabulary.

"Jargon" has a bad name but used nonpejoratively all it means is the adaptation of ordinary language to communication within a group having special interests most efficiently discussed within that in-group in a special, a tailored, vocabulary. But American judges, being mostly generalists rather than specialists, are outsiders to the jargon of law's subfields.

The trend toward ever greater specialization in legal scholarship affects the selection of persons into a career in academic law in a way that drives a further wedge between the academy and the judiciary. It used to be that most law professors, even the most distinguished, did not have advanced degrees in law (just the LL.B., now called the J.D. to make it sound more impressive) and only became academics after several—and sometimes a good many—years of practicing law. In these respects they were much like judges. They came from the same pool and identified with judges and other legal practitioners (as opposed to academics in other fields); all this facilitated intercommunication. Although they usually became academics at a much younger age than lawyers become judges, they would often continue to be involved in legal practice as consultants or part-time practitioners and their scholarship would be oriented toward service to bench and bar. Nowadays the legal academy is increasingly peopled by refugees from fields such as economics and philosophy that are at once more competitive and less well remunerated than legal teaching. These refugees have the tastes and background that augur a productive career in specialized, interdisciplinary legal research, and often a Ph.D. They constitute a very different pool from the one from which judges are drawn. Identifying with the academy rather than with the legal profession, unlike earlier generations of law professors (you even see this in how they dress), they have a much greater interest in acquiring specialized knowledge in nonlegal degree programs, and place much greater emphasis on writing for publication in scholarly journals. Quantity of scholarly publication has become a major criterion of success in academic law and a condition of advancement— as used *not* to be the case in law. Legal academics have diminishing interest in service to the practical side of the profession, as Judge Harry Edwards of the U.S. Court of Appeals for the District of Columbia Circuit—a former academic—has complained.[17] (The separation reaches its apogee in Amar; the runners-up may be the "civil recourse" theorists whom I discuss in the conclusion of this book.) Very few federal judges have been appointed from such fields.

At the same time that legal scholarship has become more specialized, the judiciary has become more professionalized, and this has driven the two branches of the legal profession still further apart. By judicial professionalization I mean mainly increases in the size and quality of judicial staff and the rise of electronic research, developments that have enabled judges to rely less for research and direction on the academy. A traditional form of legal scholarship—the legal treatise—was valuable in part because it aggregated the cases relating to a particular field of law. Now law clerks (or for that matter the judge himself), using electronic research tools, can find all the cases pertinent to an issue without consulting a treatise.

17. See, for example, Harry T. Edwards, "A New Vision for the Legal Profession," 72 *New York University Law Review* 567 (1997); Edwards, "Reflections (On Law Review, Legal Education, Law Practice, and My Alma Mater)," 100 *Michigan Law Review* 1999 (2002).

Judges are unlikely to be persuaded to adopt law professors' conceptions of the judicial role. This is not only because they don't think that the modern law professor understands that role, but also because the conceptions are contested and politicized. Academics like to tell the judges that they should be more restrained or more freewheeling, more deferential to other branches of government or less so; to cling to the "original meaning" of the Constitution or adopt the concept of a "living," evolving Constitution; to be left activist or right activist, Brennan activist or Scalia activist. The judges have their own strongly held views on such matters. They do not want their job description to be written by law professors. They may find it helpful in deciding an antitrust case to learn the economic motivation and consequences of an economic practice, but they find it unhelpful to be told that they should conform their judicial decisions to this or that concept of judicial legitimacy.

The Role of the Law Schools in Continuing Judicial Education

All this is by way of background, but essential background because it suggests the limitations of legal academia in helping judges deal with the growing complexity of the activities that modern law regulates. Legal education launches law students on a legal career, but since very few students become judges, and none right out of law school, the curriculum is not oriented toward educating students to become judges. It imparts skills that judges need, but no more than any lawyer needs. I therefore want to consider the role of law schools in providing *continuing* education for judges, specifically federal judges since they are the subject of this book.

New York University School of Law has a program of continuing judicial education.[18] It emphasizes both substantive and administrative aspects of the judge's job (including editing law clerks' drafts, assumed realistically to be the major form of composition by judges nowadays). Duke

18. The program is organized by the Dwight D. Opperman Institute of Judicial Administration, www.law.nyu.edu/centers/judicial/index.htm (visited May 15, 2012).

has such a program also.[19] Some law schools offer judges instruction in particular fields, such as economic analysis of law.[20] Most continuing judicial education, however, is conducted by nonacademic institutions, such as the Federal Judicial Center and the American Association for the Advancement of Science.[21] And the focus is on district judges, for whom the nuts and bolts of the job are much more numerous than the nuts and bolts of appellate judging.

One problem with continuing judicial education programs is that many judges have not heard of them. The Federal Judicial Center has been remiss in communicating to federal judges information about programs, its own and others',[22] from which the judges might benefit. But in fairness to

19. See Duke Law Center for Judicial Studies, Continuing Judicial Education (Spring 2012), www.law.duke.edu/judicialstudies/continuing (visited June 13, 2012).

20. See for example, the Economics Institute for Judges, a component of George Mason University law school's Mason Judicial Education Program, www.masonlec .org/program/judicial-education-program/ (visited May 15, 2012), one aspect of which I mentioned in note 6 above. See also the Economics Institute for Judges, a component of Northwestern law school's Judicial Education Program, www.law.north western.edu/jep/economics/ (visited May 15, 2012).

21. See, for example, American Association for the Advancement of Science, "Judicial Seminars on Emerging Issues in Neuroscience," http://srhrl.aaas.org/projects/ law_science/judicialseminars/index.shtml (visited Aug. 26, 2012). For lists of all judicial education programs attended in recent years by federal and state judges, including national, regional, and local programs sponsored by courts, judicial councils, bar associations, law schools, or other organizations, see Federal Judicial Center, "List of All Programs By Topic," www.fjc.gov/fsje/home.nsf (visited May 15, 2012). See also The Judicial Education Reference, Information and Technical Transfer Project, http://jeritt.msu.edu/default.asp (also visited May 15, 2012); Catharine M. White and Maureen E. Conner, "Issues and Trends in Judicial Branch Education: 2005" (Judicial Education Reference Information and Technical Transfer Project, 2005), http://jeritt.msu.edu/documents/IssuesandTrends_PDF.pdf (visited May 19, 2012).

22. Such as seminars on neuroscience for federal, state, and administrative law judges, sponsored by the American Association for the Advancement of Science. See "Programs: Judicial Seminars on Emerging Issues in Neuroscience," http://srhrl .aaas.org/projects/law_science/judicialseminars/index.shtml (visited Aug. 30, 2012).

the Center, budget cuts have impeded its ability not only to create but to promote programs, as well as to screen reference works, a service that I suggested earlier most judges need in order to be able to deal competently with technical issues in our cases.

Continuing judicial education needs, like initial judicial education, to focus on helping judges cope with complexity, which is different from trying to turn them into part-time scientists, physicians, statisticians, and engineers. Judges need to be taught how to manage encounters with statistical analysis in litigation, including appeals. They need instruction in screening prospective expert witnesses and in appointing and directing neutral experts; instruction in the cognitive abilities and psychological characteristics of judges, jurors, and witnesses; and instruction in the probative value (and psychological impact on judges and jurors) of evidence both technical and otherwise ("otherwise" including for example eyewitness testimony). They need instruction in avoiding fallacies in reasoning; in the selection and management of law clerks and other judicial staff to assure that the judge has adequate help in dealing with technical issues; and in the culture rather than the details of scientific inquiry and proof and in the differences between lay intuition and the testing of hypotheses by empirical methodology applied to data. They need instruction in Bayes's theorem and other methods of rational decision making. And in all these areas they (or many of them, at any rate) need instruction geared to the limitations of the aging judge—for many federal judges serve into their seventies and eighties and occasionally beyond, and elderly judges are likely to find today's rapid pace of technological advance particularly difficult to keep up with.

What is needed in continuing judicial education in short is a change in emphasis from legal doctrine, formal legal procedure, and discrete areas of social science (such as economics and political science) to meeting the challenge that complexity poses to reliable decision making by federal judges at all levels. The need can't be met by the Federal Judicial Center alone; the active involvement of universities is required. The universities have tremendous resources and are churning out a good deal of interdisciplinary legal scholarship that relates to the judiciary's needs. But it is not clear what interest law schools (let alone any other parts of a university) have in providing the kind of training that judges need in order to be able to deal with complexity.

I have been discussing continuing judicial education, but judicial education needs to start in law school. I said that law school should not try to train judges, because so few law students will ever become judges, and those few long after graduating. But in our adversary legal system, what judges need to know lawyers need to know because they play so large a role in trial and appellate litigation. Many college students choose to go to law school because they have (or think they have) a "math block"[23] (others, however, because they are more interested in human interactions than in interactions between molecules or lines of software code). No longer will they be able to escape technology in their legal practice—and I don't mean just the technology of computer-assisted legal research. Law schools should require students who lack a technical background (some of course will have such a background, because of their college studies) to take a course in accounting and a course in statistics; a course that places a field or fields of law in its (or their) technological context;[24] and at least one course, elsewhere in the university, of a purely scientific or technical character, such as applied math, statistics, economics (at the level at which it employs calculus and statistical analysis), physics, physiology, biochemistry, organic chemistry, some branch of engineering, or environmental or computer science, pitched at whatever level of sophistication the student's previous education enables him to attain.[25] If room needs to be made in the curriculum by cutting or shortening other courses, there is a good place to

23. "Law students as a group, seem peculiarly averse to math and science." David L. Faigman et al., *Modern Scientific Evidence: Standards, Statistics, and Research Methods* v (2008 student ed.).

24. An exemplary casebook for such a course is *Genetics: Ethics, Law and Policy* (3d ed., Lori B. Andrews, Maxwell J. Mehlman, and Mark A. Rothstein eds. 2010).

25. Merlino et al., "Science Education Programs," report that as of 2000 only twenty-seven of the 172 accredited U.S. law schools offered a science course. I have not been able to discover the current number. For discussion of the science courses that are offered, and the characteristics of law schools that offer them, see Mara Merlino et al., "Science in the Law School Curriculum: A Snapshot of the Legal Education Landscape," 58 *Journal of Legal Education* 190 (2008).

start: it is called constitutional law. Dominated as it is by the most political court in the land, constitutional law occupies far too large a role in legal education.

A promising recent development is the creation at the University of Pennsylvania Law School of a center (the Detkin Intellectual Property and Technology Legal Clinic[26]) to bridge the law school and the university's technology-related departments such as engineering, medicine, and business, including "financial engineering."

I don't think that the choice of the scientific or technical field for the law student or the judge to study is critical. As I've said before, a person comfortable in one such field will usually be comfortable (though not as comfortable) dealing with legal issues arising from technical problems in other fields. I have found this to be the case with my law clerks who've had a technical background.

MOOCs to the Rescue?

The most promising solution to the problems I've been discussing may lie with the MOOCs.[27] An acronym for "massive open online courses," the

26. www.law.upenn.edu/clinic/intellectualproperty/ (visited Nov. 14, 2012). The Detkin Clinic is complemented by a research center—the Center for Technology, Innovation and Competition, also in the University of Pennsylvania Law School. See www.law.upenn.edu/institutes/ctic/ (visited Dec. 16, 2012).

27. See, for example, Salman Khan, *The One World School House: Education Reimagined* (2012); Tamar Lewin, "College of Future Could Be Come One, Come All," *New York Times*, Nov. 20, 2012, p. A1; Laura Pappano, "The Year of the MOOC," *New York Times*, Nov. 4, 2012, p. ED26; Nick Anderson, "Elite Education for the Masses," *Washington Post*, Nov. 3, 2012, www.washingtonpost.com/local/education/elite-education-for-the-masses/2012/11/03/c2ac8144-121b-11e2-ba83-a7a396e6b2a7_story.html (visited March 27, 2013); Will Oremus, "Online Higher-Education Startup Coursera Is Taking Over the World," *Slate*, Sept. 19, 2012, www.slate.com/blogs/future_tense/2012/09/19/online_education_coursera_adds_17_universities_aims_to_take_over_world.html (visited March 13, 2013); "Class Central: A Complete List of Free Online Courses Offered by Stanford, Coursera, MIT and Harvard led edX (MITx + Harvardx + BerkeleyX), and Udacity," www.class-central.com/; "Massive Open Online Course," *Wikipedia*, http://en.wikipedia.org/wiki/Massive_open_online_course (visited March 27, 2013).

word denotes an important—quite possibly a revolutionary—development in education and one potentially applicable to judicial education. MOOCs are online lecture courses, free of charge, open to anyone in the world who has a laptop and an Internet connection. They are offered by entities with strange names, such as Coursera, Codeacademy, edX, Khan Academy, and Udacity. The offerors are mainly university consortia or university-affiliated, and the universities involved include such elite ones as Stanford, Berkeley, Harvard, Columbia, and Michigan.

Online education is not new. There have been adult-education online courses for some time, such as those offered by The Teaching Company; there are even online college degree programs offered mainly by for-profit colleges. What is new is the scale and potential of free online education offered by, or in conjunction with, the nation's leading universities.

Like conventional college courses, MOOCs are sequenced by difficulty, enabling the student to progress from beginner to advanced. The course offerings cover not only a very broad range of technical subjects such as math, statistics, computer science, the natural sciences, and engineering, but increasingly include courses in the social sciences and the humanities. MOOCs are not offered for credit; they do not count toward an undergraduate or graduate degree; they are (at present) for people who want to obtain not a credential but skills or knowledge, whether for enjoyment or to put to some practical use. Anyone anywhere in the world can enroll; some individual MOOCs are attracting tens, even hundreds, of thousands of students (though most don't complete the courses). There can be frequent quizzes embedded in each online course and sometimes there are midcourse or end-of-course exams as well. The exams are graded by peer groups (other students enrolled in the course—in one program a student's exam is graded by five other students and the grade on the exam is the average of the grades given by the five graders). Some students form online study groups, or in-person groups with students who live nearby.

The format is superior to the conventional lecture. The average quality of the lecturers is very high since there is no limit on the number of students "attending" the lectures and so no reason why any student should be stuck with a mediocre lecturer. A first-rate lecturer can communicate more effectively than a textbook (and of course the student can supplement the lecture with a textbook). Because the lectures are prerecorded, the student can scroll back, or fast forward, at will—in short can go at his own speed, which one cannot do in a live lecture. The lecture can be watched at any time convenient to the student, and one doesn't have to travel anywhere to attend; these are features that should endear MOOCs to judges, as should the fact that most MOOCs deal with technical subjects, including math, statistics, and computer science, that should be of particular interest to modern federal judges.

But given the novelty of the MOOCs (few are more than two years old), the variety of the courses offered and of the offerors, and differences in quality and in level of difficulty, the judges need help in picking courses. How many judges have even heard of MOOCs? I hadn't until November 2, 2012. This is still another area in which the Federal Judicial Center is failing to provide the guidance that federal judges need if they are to overcome the challenge of complexity. Support of MOOCs by the Center would benefit not only the judiciary but also the providers of MOOCs, who can't continue indefinitely providing MOOCs free of charge.[28]

28. On the issue of financing MOOCs, see Tamar Lewin, "Students Rush to Web Classes, But Profits May Be Much Later," *New York Times,* Jan. 7, 2013, p. A1.

CONCLUSION

Realism, the Path Forward

Federal judges are falling behind. The problem is not caseload; it is case content. Judges aren't coping well with the increased complexity, mainly but not only scientific and technological, of modern society. In Chapter 3 I quoted Daniel Arbess's remark that we live "in a world of increasingly complex, fragmented, and ubiquitous information." The "we" includes judges. But we judges are not inhabiting this new world comfortably. Rather than try to understand the world outside our books and traditions, we (most of us anyway) burrow deeper into a complex world of our own making, as if to validate Coke's claim that law is a species of "*artificial* reason."[1] Legal formalism is tightening its grip on the judiciary at a time when legal realism has never been more needful. We are complexifying the judi-

---

1. Prohibitions del Roy, 12 Co. Rep. 63, 65, 77 Eng. Rep. 1342, 1343 (1608).

cial process when we should be simplifying it, and neglecting the unavoidable complexities pressing in on us from outside the legal culture when we should be embracing and overcoming them.

The causes of this perverse judicial behavior are various. One is expansion of judicial staff, in part a response to increased, and increasingly complex, caseload and in part a self-generated bureaucratic phenomenon ("managerialism"). A consequence of that expansion, and of the increasingly hierarchical structure of law firms and other legal agencies (prosecutors' offices, for example)—which turns senior lawyers, eligible for judicial appointment, from legal writers and legal analysts into supervisors—is an increasing delegation of judicial opinion writing to law clerks. This has had the untoward results discussed in earlier chapters. The obvious results —opinions that are unclear, uncandid, jargon-laden, inauthentic—are less significant than the insidious effect on the ability of the legal system to cope with the growing complexity of the subject matter of federal litigation.

Much of that complexity—which I have termed external complexity to distinguish it from the complexity that seems to grow naturally within institutions, reaching its apogee in the 511-page *Bluebook* guide to legal citations—is technological in origin. The extraordinarily rapid advances in computer technology are the obvious example but not the only one: medical technology has grown in complexity at a rapid rate, and likewise what is aptly termed "financial engineering," not to mention environmental technology and the increasingly refined psychology of management, marketing, and other business activities. That is on the substantive side, and on the procedural side statistical analysis along with scientific methods of forensic analysis, such as DNA testing (in which statistics plays a role as well, in determining the validity of particular DNA matches presented as evidence in criminal cases), are used increasingly to generate evidence for use in litigation.

Judges resist engagement with the scientific world. Assisted by their law clerks, who imbibe formalistic legal analysis in law school, judges seek to finesse science with semantics when interpretation is needed and with delegation when fact finding is needed. So jurors are asked to resolve technical issues that would stump judges, who are relieved to be able to hand off issues they don't understand to hapless laypersons. And so textual originalism is promoted as a way of deciding cases without considering the consequences of decisions, though interpretive ambiguities permeate legal texts and cannot be resolved by resort to dictionaries and grammar books and judges' lame efforts to play historian. We have seen Justice Scalia, the arch textualist, endorsing sundry "canons of construction" that empower judges to resolve interpretive issues on nontextual grounds. The judiciary needs better tools for deciding cases. It needs a return to legal realism, but this time realism with depth, realism grounded in modern analytical and empirical methods, realism that goes beyond the hunch.

One reason the legal realism of the 1920s and 1930s was widely disparaged was that it seemed to involve the substitution of personal beliefs and emotions—at best of common sense (which often is untrustworthy)—for the legal "science" represented by formalism, with its claims to objectivity and impersonality. Those claims were and are wildly overstated—intuition, personal beliefs, and like sources of subjectivity play a large role in judicial decisions, even when a decision comes wrapped in a rhetorical cloak of objectivity. But that is no reason to be complacent about realism. Realism, to be realistic in this day and age, has to be grounded, to a considerably greater extent than at present, in scientific theory and empirical understanding.

It is strange that formalism should have made a comeback in a culture increasingly dominated by technology. It's as if judges had decided that the only escape from becoming technocrats was to become eighteenth-century men of letters. I don't think escape was the principal motive, however. Conservative judges, reacting to the Warren Court (and to a lesser extent the Burger Court), found formalism to be an effective disguise for conservative activism. (Liberals, as we saw in the discussion of Akhil Amar's book, are now, in a retrograde movement, donning the same disguise.)[2] And the increased role of staff in judicial opinion writing has encouraged formalist drafting.

2. See also Jack M. Balkin, *Living Originalism* (2011).

In Chapter 8 I quoted one of Holmes's great sayings: "I long have said there is no such thing as a hard case. I am frightened weekly but always when you walk up to the lion and lay hold the hide comes off and the same old donkey of a question of law is underneath." This is funny, but it's also profound (it's Holmes, after all). A lion is a magnificent but dangerous animal. It belongs in a zoo or, preferably, in its natural habitat (alas too crowded with people). A donkey is a service animal. It has patience and charm but lacks magnificence—as does, or should, law, which is not an art or a science, but a service. All that legal realism ought to mean—all that it means to me—is making law serviceable by bringing it closer, in point of intelligibility and practical utility, to the people it's supposed to serve, which is the population as a whole. It ought to be possible to decide most cases in a way that can be explained in ordinary language and justified as consistent with the expectations of normal people. This requires judges to understand what is really going on in the cases they hear, which increasingly is bound up with technology. In this endeavor they will be hindered, not helped, by the canons of statutory construction, by invisible and unwritten constitutions, by the *Bluebook*, by ghostwriter law clerks, by legal jargon, by multifactor tests, by multiple standards of appellate review, by prolixity, by quotation out of context.

Law attracts some very bright people. But it is not profound. It is one of the simplest professional fields. You see this in the delegation of opinion writing to law clerks, externs, and interns. I disapprove of such delegation at the appellate level (at the trial level it is unavoidable because of caseload), yet the opinions these neophytes turn out are on the whole quite polished professional products. Many a second-year law student, serving as a judge's intern or extern, has written a very good published opinion for a federal or state appellate judge. It's as if second-year medical students performed brain surgeries or heart transplants. It's because legal analysis doesn't really cut very deep that young judges are rare. The young are analytically sharper than the old but lack experience. In an analytically weak field, experience may be essential to successful problem solving.

The opinions of the great judges are rarely works of subtle analysis. An opinion by Holmes or a Hand or a Jackson doesn't read like a law review article. A great judge is not a great professor *manqué* even if he is a former professor. Holmes's book *The Common Law* is an academic work of great distinction but his judicial opinions are not academic—yet they are wonderful. Some readers may think it puzzling, in light of the "scientistic" approach that I may seem to be urging on judges, that I have placed such emphasis, especially but not only in Chapter 8, on judges' writing well. There is no inconsistency. For I'm not trying to turn judges into scientists communicating in symbols and jargon. I'm urging greater judicial recognition of the ever-increasing complexity of the factual underpinnings of modern federal litigation. That makes good judicial writing more rather than less important, because judges have to learn to write about complexity in ways that they and their audience, primarily other judges and practicing lawyers, can understand. Law must come to terms with modernity but will remain a humanity, and should.

Judge Leval gave an interesting talk recently in which he asked why Judge Henry Friendly, quite possibly the all-around analytically most proficient appellate judge in American history, has, a mere quarter century after his death, "slid into obscurity," as Leval puts it.[3] Learned Hand died a half century ago and his opinions are still read (not all of them of course—he wrote almost 1,500).

One reason Leval gives for forgetfulness of Friendly is that "Friendly was not a flashy judge; not a headline grabber; not one to look for the quotable one liner. He shunned rhetorical flourishes" and had a "powerful inclination toward moderation."[4] In a review of Friendly's biography, Professor Vermeule, addressing the same issue, remarks in a somewhat similar vein that "seen in its best light, Friendly's contribution was not to enrich the theory of the law but to provide a living model of lawyerly craft and good judgment . . . The reputations of judges such as Friendly generally have a shorter half-life than the reputations of judges who offer fertile the-

3. Pierre N. Leval, "Remarks on Henry Friendly on the Award of the Henry Friendly Medal to Justice Sandra Day O'Connor," 15 *Green Bag* (second series) 257, 260 (2012). Neglect of Friendly may change as a result of a superb biography of him: David M. Dorsen, *Henry Friendly, Greatest Judge of His Era* (2012).

4. Leval, "Remarks on Henry Friendly," at 261.

oretical ideas that can be distilled into formulas, theorems, and pithy aphorisms."[5]

Vermeule's assessment underrates Friendly (and may overrate judges in general as sources of "fertile theoretical ideas," unless "theory" is defined very broadly). Many of Friendly's ideas, expressed either in his opinions or in his very influential nonjudicial writings, were adopted by the Supreme Court, which having done so got the credit for them. But what is true is that his opinions, unlike both his nonjudicial writings and his letters,[6] are not exceptionally well written. They tend to be longer than they need to be and to be crammed with too much detail. The sentences are long and the overall impression is one of heaviness—sprightly they are not. They are not badly written but rhetorically, stylistically, they don't compare with the opinions of the other great judges.

In a short book on Cardozo, I put at the head of the list of factors that explained his great success as a judge and his continuing lofty reputation "rhetorical skill," but denied that this was "a prelude to declaring Cardozo's reputation unearned or exaggerated . . . It would be if Cardozo had been a law professor rather than a judge. But it is a mistake to suppose that the best judge is the judge who most resembles the best law professor."[7] After explaining that the conditions of a judicial career do not conduce to academic creativity I said that what we can expect in a very good judge, and "find in abundance in Cardozo's opinions, are (1) a vivid, even dramatic, bodying forth of the judge's concerns, (2) a lucid presentation of arresting particulars—fodder for academic analysis, (3) a sense of the relatedness of these particulars to larger themes, (4) a point of view that transcends the litigants' parochial concerns. . . , (5) a power of clear and forceful statement, and (6) a high degree of sensitivity to the expectations of one's audi-

5. Adrian Vermeule, "Local Wisdom" [Review of Dorsen, *Henry Friendly*], in *The Book: An Online Review at the New Republic*, March 22, 2012, www.tnr.com/book/review/henry-friendly-supreme-court-david-dorsen (visited Nov. 7, 2012).

6. See William Domnarski, ed., "The Correspondence of Henry Friendly and Richard A. Posner 1982–86," 51 *American Journal of Legal History* 395 (2011). Skip my part of the correspondence.

7. Richard A. Posner, *Cardozo: A Study in Reputation* 133 (1990).

ence." And I added: "Anyone conversant with literature will recognize these as virtues commonly associated with works of imaginative literature."[8] Cardozo was not as brilliant as Friendly, but he had the virtues I've just described in greater abundance.

The complexity of modern American law, both internal and external, makes the Cardozan virtues (possessed in even greater abundance by Holmes, and abundant also in Robert Jackson and Learned Hand and intermittently in Felix Frankfurter) more rather than less important today. And I don't think it's an accident that most of the best judicial writers have been realists rather than formalists; formalism trades in obscurantism.

But what of the education of federal judges? There is much talk these days about a crisis in American education. There is, if not a crisis in, then warranted deep disappointment with, judicial education, both initial and continuing. As I keep saying, you are a lawyer one day and a federal judge the next—literally. And maybe a few months later you receive a few days of training and then you're on your own again. With the rise of complexity, both technological and institutional, both external and internal (the two types interacting, magnifying the overall problem), the educational needs of federal judges have grown. Too little is being done to meet those needs, leaving the federal judge pretty much on his or her own and thereby amplifying the judicial tendency to retreat to formalism, conceived of as a method of deciding cases without empirical understanding.

Lawyers aren't helping. I don't understand their inability to see their cases from the judges' perspective. If they could do that they might realize that they are not giving the judges what they need—the full context of the case, both factual and legal, making no unrealistic assumptions about the extent of judicial preparation and depth of judicial understanding of novel cases. Lawyers who can imagine themselves as judges would understand the importance of visual aids, the importance of scene setting, the necessity of radical simplification, and the acute judicial need for patient explanation of the mysteries of modern technology, an ever more salient element of modern litigation.

8. Id. at 133–134.

I wish the Federal Judicial Center could do more to improve the management skills of judges. And I wish the law schools would step up to the plate, both by educating law students in all facets of modern legal realism and by creating scholarship that would help judges to cope with complexity. The schools are taking some steps in this direction, but not enough. Akhil Amar's book on constitutional law that I discussed in Chapter 7 is an example of a contrary trend—a trend toward scholarship ever more remote from the culture of legal practice and judicial decision making. The counter countertrend is the textual originalism of Scalia and Garner, but it is another dead end. Both approaches take the judiciary farther from its rendezvous with reality.

Academic law used to be of the legal profession though in the university. This has changed. From a faculty perspective a law school is now the university department of law. Academic lawyers write for each other rather than for judges and lawyers. They do not try to be useful or even intelligible to the practical profession—not all academic lawyers, of course, but many of the most prominent ones, whose true interests may lie in other fields, such as philosophy or economics. From the perspective of the judicial profession the change in the character of academic law (a change particularly pronounced at the most prestigious law schools) is an ominous trend. Here is an illustration, with which I'll end the book.

Tort law is an important common law field, and dealing as it does with injuries caused by careless conduct and defective products, and pervaded as it is by issues of causality and remedy, it needs to be brought abreast of the best contemporary understanding of science, economics, and statistics. Yet at this writing the hottest area in tort scholarship (or maybe I should say the only hot area) is antimodern, antirealist. It goes by the name "civil recourse theory."

The realist approach to tort law is epitomized by Judge Learned Hand's famous negligence formula, $B < PL$, which declares negligent and therefore culpable the failure to take a precaution against causing an accidental injury if the cost of precaution is lower than the cost of the accident to the victim discounted by the probability that such an accident would have occurred even in the absence of the precaution.[9] By thus making economically wasteful activity more costly to the actor, liability based on the Hand formula is expected to deter such activity.

Civil resource theory, which occupies the opposite end of the spectrum of tort theories from Hand's, is the brainchild of law professors John Goldberg and Benjamin Zipursky and has been expounded by them in a series of law review articles.[10] Professor Zipursky has explained that "the core idea of civil recourse theory is that tort law is about empowering people who have been wrongly injured to obtain some sort of redress from the injurers . . . Tort law functions best as a means of reinforcing social norms."[11] The original legal realists argued that modern tort law was about shifting the costs of accidents to producers (as in products liability law) and insurers (and hence to insurance pools—spreading the risk of accidents widely). Economic analysts of law argue that tort law is about minimizing the sum of accident and accident-avoidance costs (but also about

9. *B* is the burden (cost) of precautions that would avert the accident, *P* the probability the accident will occur if the precautions aren't taken, and *L* the loss to the victim if the accident occurs. *United States v. Carroll Towing Co.*, 159 F.2d 169, 173 (2d Cir. 1947). The "Hand Formula" is restated in formal economic terms in Richard A. Posner, *Economic Analysis of Law* 214 n. 2 (8th ed. 2011). On the economic approach to tort law generally, see William M. Landes and Richard A. Posner, *The Economic Structure of Tort Law* (1987).

10. Listed in Christopher J. Robinette, "Why Civil Recourse Theory Is Incomplete," 78 *Tennessee Law Review* 431, 432 n. 3 (2011). The place to start is with Goldberg and Zipursky's article "Torts as Wrongs," 88 *Texas Law Review* 917 (2010). Other articles by them (separately or together) are cited in Table 3 below. And soon there will be a book by them explaining their approach at greater length: *Recognizing Responsibilities* (Harvard University Press, forthcoming 2013). They respond to criticisms of their theory (including an earlier version of my criticisms) in their article "Civil Recourse Defended: A Reply to Posner, Calabresi, Rustad, Chamallas, and Robinette," 88 *Indiana Law Journal* (forthcoming spring 2013).

11. The first sentence, which is Zipursky's, is quoted in Larry Reibstein, "Rethinking Tort Law: Professor Benjamin Zipursky's Civil Recourse Theory Moves to a Leading Position in American Tort Theory," *Fordham Lawyer*, Spring 2012, pp. 12, 14. The second sentence is Reibstein's characterization of Zipursky's approach.

deterring intentional and reckless loss-inflicting acts). Modern corrective-justice analysts argue that it is about implementing a moral duty to redress an imbalance created by an injury. Civil recourse theorists argue that tort law is about implementing a more complex set of moral notions—a set that includes limitations on redress for injuries (limitations on punitive damages, for example).

One tends to think of moralists as normative rather than positive analysts, yet Goldberg and Zipursky argue that civil resource theory describes the existing tort system better than any other positive theory. This is mistaken, as shown in two recent articles.[12] I will add my two cents' worth by noting, as one example of erroneous analysis, Goldberg and Zipursky's use of an opinion of mine[13] to argue that the principles governing awards of punitive damages cannot be explained by utilitarian concerns such as deterrence.[14] They say that my opinion "suggest[s] that punitive damages are awarded to induce plaintiffs with modest compensatory claims to sue, and to encourage litigants to uncover hidden wrongs, thereby promoting the private prosecution of conduct that would otherwise go unsanctioned," and that "on this theory, one should never see an award of punitive dam-

---

12. Robinette's article, "Why Civil Recourse Theory Is Incomplete," and Michael L. Rustad, "Torts as Public Wrongs," 38 *Pepperdine Law Review* 433 (2011). Another article highly critical of civil-recourse theory is Jane Stapleton, "Evaluating Goldberg and Zipursky's Civil Recourse Theory," 75 *Fordham Law Review* 1529 (2006). Strangely, though, at the start of an analysis that concludes that Goldberg and Zipurksy's "project was unnecessary and has resulted in a civil recourse theory that is overblown in its claims, awkward and inconvenient in application, and internally incoherent," id. at 1562, Stapleton says that "the civil recourse model of tort law is definitely an improvement on efficiency and corrective justice models" because "it seeks to address and accept tort law as it exists" and "does not fall into the trap of depending on the assertion of some 'goal' of tort law such as 'compensation' or 'deterrence' or 'loss-spreading.' These may be the effects of the imposition of tort liability, but none could be the goal of tort; otherwise, no injured plaintiff suing an insured wrongdoer would ever lose!" Id. at 1538. I don't know what she could mean by these statements (which she doesn't explain) or how they connect to her analysis.

13. *Mathias v. Accor Economy Lodging, Inc.*, 347 F.3d 672 (7th Cir. 2003).

14. Goldberg and Zipursky, "Torts as Wrongs," at 961.

ages in cases of tortious conduct causing substantial harms, nor should courts permit punitive damages in cases of open and obvious misconduct. The law allows punitive awards in both kinds of cases."[15]

The decision in question, *Mathias v. Accor Economy Lodging*, upheld an award of $186,000 in punitive damages to each of two guests of a motel who had been bitten by bedbugs. Under the applicable law, that of Illinois, an award of punitive damages was permissible because the jury had found that the failure of the hotel to warn the plaintiffs of its infestation was not simply negligent, but "willful and wanton." The jury awarded each plaintiff only $5,000 in compensatory damages, however, and this raised the question whether the punitive damages awards were excessive in light of their very high ratio to the compensatory damages awards.

Here is what the opinion says at the page cited by Goldberg and Zipursky:[16]

> One function of punitive-damages awards is to relieve the pressures on an overloaded system of criminal justice by providing a civil alternative to criminal prosecution of minor crimes. An example is deliberately spitting in a person's face, a criminal assault but because minor readily deterrable by the levying of what amounts to a civil fine through a suit for damages for the tort of battery. Compensatory damages would not do the trick in such a case, and this for three reasons: because they are difficult to determine in the case of acts that inflict largely dignitary harms; because in the spitting case they would be too slight to give the victim an incentive to sue, and he might decide instead to respond with violence—and an age-old purpose of the law of torts is to provide a substitute for violent retaliation against wrongful injury—and because to limit the plaintiff to compensatory damages would enable the defendant to commit the offensive act with impunity provided that he was willing to pay, and again there

---

15. Id. at 961 n. 220.

16. *Mathias v. Accor Economy Lodging, Inc.*, 347 F.3d at 677, some citations omitted. To make the discussion on that page intelligible, however, I have begun the quotation shortly before the end of the preceding page.

would be a danger that his act would incite a breach of the peace by his victim.

When punitive damages are sought for billion-dollar oil spills and other huge economic injuries, the considerations that we have just canvassed fade. As the [Supreme] Court emphasized in [*State Farm Mutual Automobile Ins. Co. v. Campbell*, 538 U.S. 408 (2003)], the fact that the plaintiffs in that case had been awarded very substantial compensatory damages—$1 million for a dispute over insurance coverage—greatly reduced the need for giving them a huge award of punitive damages ($145 million) as well in order to provide an effective remedy. Our case is closer to the spitting case. The defendant's behavior was outrageous but the compensable harm done was slight and at the same time difficult to quantify because a large element of it was emotional. And the defendant may well have profited from its misconduct because by concealing the infestation it was able to keep renting rooms. Refunds were frequent but may have cost less than the cost of closing the hotel for a thorough fumigation. The hotel's attempt to pass off the bedbugs as ticks, which some guests might ignorantly have thought less unhealthful, may have postponed the instituting of litigation to rectify the hotel's misconduct. The award of punitive damages in this case thus serves the additional purpose of limiting the defendant's ability to profit from its fraud by escaping detection and (private) prosecution. If a tortfeasor is "caught" only half the time he commits torts, then when he is caught he should be punished twice as heavily in order to make up for the times he gets away.

Finally, if the total stakes in the case were capped at $50,000 ($2 \cdot [\$5,000 + \$20,000]$), the plaintiffs might well have had difficulty financing this lawsuit. It is here that the defendant's aggregate net worth of $1.6 billion becomes relevant. A defendant's wealth is not a sufficient basis for awarding punitive damages. That would be discriminatory and would violate the rule of law, as we explained earlier, by making punishment depend on status rather than conduct. Where wealth in the sense of resources enters is in enabling the defendant to mount an extremely aggressive defense against suits such as this and by doing so to make litigating against it very costly, which in turn may make it difficult for the plaintiffs to find a lawyer willing to handle their case, involving as it does only modest stakes, for the usual 33–40 percent contingent fee.

In other words, the defendant is investing in developing a reputation intended to deter plaintiffs. It is difficult otherwise to explain the great stubbornness with which it has defended this case, making a host of frivolous evidentiary arguments despite the very modest stakes even when the punitive damages awarded by the jury are included.

Contrary to Goldberg and Zipursky's summary, the opinion does not say or imply that punitive damages are awarded *only* in order to induce suits to enforce modest claims or to encourage plaintiffs "to uncover hidden wrongs" and therefore that punitive damages should never be awarded in cases of tortious conduct that cause substantial harm or of "open and obvious misconduct." The summary is not only inaccurate, but internally inconsistent. If it were true that awards of punitive damages had only two possible aims, that of inducing suits to enforce modest claims and that of encouraging plaintiffs to uncover hidden wrongs, then such awards would be proper in cases of substantial harm caused by hidden wrongs, and in cases of modest claims even if they were based on open and obvious misconduct. Punitive damages can be excessive, as the Supreme Court had held in *Campbell* and other cases. But the main point in the *Mathias* opinion is that the smaller the award of compensatory damages, the higher the ratio of punitive to compensatory damages needs to be in order have a deterrent effect. For example, if the compensatory damages for the bedbug bites had been only $100, even a 145 to 1 ratio of punitive to compensatory damages (the ratio in the *Campbell* case) would have been insufficient to motivate the plaintiffs to sue or the defendant to take a less casual attitude toward infestation, because the punitive-damages award would have been only $14,500.

But supposing that the civil recourse theorists are right in thinking that tort law is dedicated to providing "some sort of redress" for people injured by "wrongful" conduct, where do we go to find out what is a "wrong"? Without an answer to that question, the theory collapses into tautology: tort law provides redress for wrongful injury; injury is wrongful if tort law provides redress for it.

All that the civil recourse theorists insist upon, moreover, is "some sort" of redress. They realize that tort law does not provide complete remedies for a number of losses inflicted by wrongful acts, and they are fine with this, explaining these remedial limitations in instrumental terms, as an economist would do. If, then, as they assume, everyone knows right from wrong (I'll question this assumption in a moment), what is there to civil recourse theory except instrumental limitations on tort remedies for wrongs, limitations already well studied?

A great deal of tort law is about those limitations: think of contributory and comparative negligence, assumption of risk, causation and foreseeability, the economic loss rule, contribution and indemnity, res ipsa loquitur, punitive damages, limitations on duties to avoid injuries to trespassers and licensees, general damages, the choice between negligence and strict liability, the distinction between independent-contractor liability and respondeat superior, sovereign immunity, official immunity, contractual waivers of liability, loss of a chance (latent or probabilistic injury), mass torts, and constitutional limitations on defamation and on the tort right of privacy. Tort remedies are an issue about which economic analysis of law has had a lot to say, and I find nothing in civil recourse theory to challenge what it has said. Since all that the theory requires is "some sort of redress" for wrongful injury, the implication is that all the traditional limitations are in principle acceptable; whether particular limitations are acceptable in practice is a pragmatic issue outside the scope of the theory.

It's not enough to say that we all know a wrong when we see one and so we don't have to get analytical about it. That won't do even apart from the fact that such a throwing up of hands leaves the civil recourse theorist with nothing interesting to say. Often there is no agreement about what is wrongful conduct, conduct that law ought to redress. Is it wrongful to defame a person by accident? (Maybe you innocently and indeed nonnegligently mixed him up with someone else.) Or to defame a dead person? Is it wrongful for a pharmaceutical manager to fail to disclose on the label of a drug that it can cause serious injury to one out of a million users? Or for a doctor to disclaim liability for an injury caused by his negligence? Or for a railroad to fail to install flashing signals at all rail crossings, and instead to rely in the less busy crossings on just cross-buck signs? These are analyzable issues, rather than issues that can be shrugged off by saying that "everyone in our society, in our culture, knows that . . ." I don't think civil recourse theory can have much impact if it doesn't address such questions. So I'll address them.

To begin with, much can be referred to conditions of survival in what scientists refer to as the "ancestral environment," the environment of primitive man in which human beings evolved to approximately their current biological state. It is easy to see that early man would not have thrived without a lively sense of "rights," not in a modern sense but in the sense of being quick to resist aggressions threatening survival. One is put in mind of Holmes's aphorism that even a dog knows the difference between being kicked and tripped over; we respond more quickly and emphatically to what we perceive as deliberate invasions of our property and bodily integrity and reputation than to accidental ones. That is instinctual but in a primitive culture it is often difficult to distinguish between the instinctual and the instrumental, and so we find strict liability a more pervasive standard of liability in such cultures than in modern law,[17] though the result is a degree of overdeterrence. Only in a much more advanced stage of human social development is it recognized that some injuries are unavoidable, or if not strictly unavoidable then unavoidable at a cost less than the risk-adjusted cost of the injury. Instinct gives way to cost-benefit analysis, and more broadly to instrumental or pragmatic considerations designed to make tort law along with other social responses to injury a sensible regulatory and compensatory regime, as well as a means for deflecting vengeful acts—which play a critical regulatory role in deterring aggression in pre-legal cultures—into socially less costly systems of redress.

17. See Richard A. Posner, *The Economics of Justice* 199–203 (1981).

So some principles of tort law rest on primitive, though not irrational, reactions to invasions of rights—the torts of assault and of battery are examples—and others on sophisticated notions of optimal social ordering, which give rise to new rights and to elaborate systems of remedy and procedure. The list of rights and wrongs evolves, and lawyers and economists and psychologists and sociologists can identify and evaluate the new rights and wrongs that emerge in the evolutionary process. Civil recourse theory has played no role in this process.

Goldberg and Zipursky began expounding civil recourse theory in articles published in 1998. In the fourteen years since, these and their subsequent articles have been cited in only twenty-one judicial opinions.[18] Of the twenty-one, seven are by Judge Jack Weinstein, the well-known federal district judge, for whom Goldberg clerked. Seven is also the number of the articles that cite Goldberg and/or Zipursky on points related to civil recourse theory.

In books on constitutional theory (not only by Amar), in articles on civil recourse theory, in a variety of other domains of modern legal scholarship, we encounter a hermetic legal scholarship that cannot help lawyers and judges to master the complexity of modernity as it impinges on the law. Meanwhile judicial training, both initial and continuing, lags. Judges struggle on one front to manage growing staff, on another to cope with the growing complexity of the activities that give rise to the cases they must decide, and on a third to integrate the two fronts. Many still think they can finesse the need for an empirical understanding of an increasingly complex world by embracing some version of formalist analysis. But that will not work. The path forward is the path of realism.

---

18. The twenty-one opinions are cited and summarized in my article "Instrumental and Noninstrumental Theories of Tort Law," 88 *Indiana Law Journal* (forthcoming spring 2013). The count of those citations is complete through January 8, 2013.

ACKNOWLEDGMENTS

INDEX

ACKNOWLEDGMENTS

Parts of this book draw on previously published work of mine, though with much revision. Chapter 3 draws on "The Bluebook Blues" [review of *The Bluebook: A Uniform System of Citation* (19th ed. 2010)], 120 *Yale Law Journal* 852 (2011), and Chapters 4, 5, and 8 on "Judicial Opinions and Appellate Advocacy in Federal Courts: One Judge's Views," 51 *Duquesne Law Review* 3 (2013). Chapter 6 draws on "The Rise and Fall of Judicial Self-Restraint," 100 *California Law Review* 519 (2012), and Chapter 7 on "In Defense of Looseness: The Supreme Court and Gun Control," *New Republic*, Aug. 27, 2008, p. 32; "The Spirit Killeth, But the Letter Giveth Life" [review of Antonin Scalia and Bryan A. Garner, *Reading the Law: The Interpretation of Legal Texts* (2012)], *New Republic*, Sept. 13, 2012, p. 18; and "A Lawyer's Dozen" [review of Akhil Reed Amar, *America's Unwritten Constitution: The Precedents and Principles We Live By* (2012)], *New Repub-*

lic, Nov. 8, 2012, p. 36. Chapter 8 draws on "Convincing a Federal Court of Appeals," *Litigation*, Winter 1999, p. 3, and the Conclusion on "Instrumental and Noninstrumental Theories of Tort Law," 88 *Indiana Law Journal* 469 (2013).

I gave a talk based on Chapter 3 at Columbia Law School's Colloquium on Courts and the Legal Process on October 17, 2012; I thank the discussants, Erin Murphy and Jed Rakoff, and other participants, for comments. On the same day I gave the Marshall Lecture to Columbia's chapter of the Federalist Society. I based my talk on Chapter 7 and I thank the audience for its comments.

I thank Lauren Barnett, Rachel Block, Sam Boyd, Sean Cooksey, Adina Goldstein, Michael Kenstowicz, Emily Rush, Adam Solomon, and Michael Zhu for their research assistance; and DePaul Law Review and Alan Devlin for permission to reprint the substantial passage from the article Alan Devlin, "Systemic Bias in Patent Law," 61 *DePaul Law Review* 57, 77–80 (2011), that I quote in Chapter 3, text at footnote 55. I thank Joseph Cecil and Bruce Clarke, both of the Federal Judicial Center, and Mark Frankel of the American Association for the Advancement of Science, for advice and materials relating to my discussion of judicial education in Chapter 10. I also thank Sarah Herman for research relating to that discussion; Dennis Hutchinson for comments on Chapter 2; Abbe Gluck, David Strauss, and Jeremy Tor for comments on Chapter 7; Raaj Sah for discussion of judicial management issues; Michael Aronson, Charlene Posner, Mark Savignac, and two anonymous readers for the Harvard University Press for comments on the entire manuscript; and William Domnarski both for his comments on an early draft of the manuscript and for encouraging me to put my thoughts about the contemporary federal judiciary into book form.

INDEX